DATE DUE

To Reason Why

The Debate about the Causes of U.S. Involvement in the Vietnam War

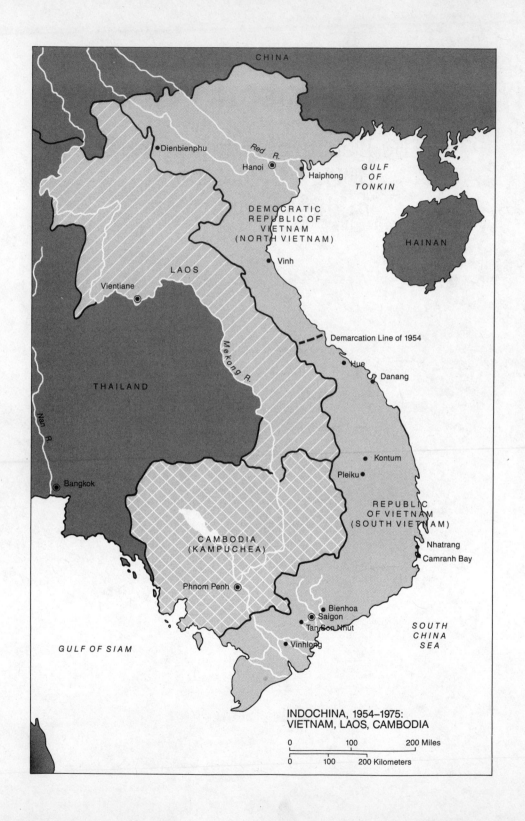

INDOCHINA, 1954–1975:
VIETNAM, LAOS, CAMBODIA

To Reason Why

The Debate about the Causes of U.S. Involvement in the Vietnam War

Jeffrey P. Kimball
Miami University

Temple University Press
Philadelphia

TO REASON WHY
The Debate about the Causes of
U.S. Involvement in the Vietnam War

Temple University Press, Philadelphia 19122

ISBN 0-87722-709-8

This book was set in Palatino by the College Composition Unit
in cooperation with Monotype Composition Company.
The editors were Christopher J. Rogers and Jennifer Sutherland;
the production supervisor was Laura Lamorte.
The cover was designed by Rafael Hernandez.
R. R. Donnelley & Sons Company was printer and binder.

Cover photograph by Andrew Rakoczy ©/Black Star

Library of Congress Cataloging-in-Publication Data

To reason why: the debate about the causes of U.S. involvement in the
  Vietnam War/[edited by] Jeffrey P. Kimball.
      p.   cm.
    ISBN 0-87722-709-8
    1. Vietnamese Conflict, (dates)—United States.   2. United
States—Foreign relations—Indochina.   3. Indochina–Foreign
relations–United States.   I. Kimball, Jeffrey P.
DS558.T6   1990
959.704'3373—dc20   89-12158

About
the Editor

Jeffrey P. Kimball received an M.A. from Queen's University, Kingston, and a Ph.D. from Louisiana State University. He is Director of Graduate Studies and an Associate Professor at Miami University in Oxford, Ohio, where he teaches courses on the Vietnam War, U.S. foreign policy, and peace history. He has published articles in *Armed Forces and Society, The History Teacher, Military Affairs, The Old Northwest,* and *Peace and Change*. He has contributed to the *Encyclopedia of Southern History* and *Great Events in American History* and is associate editor of the journal *Diplomatic History*. He is a member of the executive committee of the Council on Peace Research in History. In December/January 1987/88 he traveled to Vietnam with the U.S.–Indochina Reconciliation Project Educators' Delegation No. 4.

For Leslie, Daryl, and Linda M.

Someone had blundered.
Theirs not to make reply,
Theirs not to reason why,
Theirs but to do and die.

—Alfred, Lord Tennyson, *The Charge of the Light Brigade*

DIRECTOR PETER DAVIS: Why did they need us there?
FORMER PRESIDENTIAL ADVISER WALT W. ROSTOW:... Are you really asking me this goddamn silly question?

—*Hearts and Minds*

I will be quiet and talk with you,
And reason why you are wrong.

—Robert Browning, *James Lee's Wife*

Contents

PART SEVEN
WAYS OF LIVING: CULTURAL MISUNDERSTANDING
AND CONFLICT

CHRONOLOGICAL CHART OF READINGS

This chart marks the period or periods of American involvement in the Vietnam War covered in whole or part by each reading.

Reading

Period	1	2	3	4	5	6	7	8	9	10	11	12	13	14	15	16	17	18	19	20	21	22	23	24	25	26	27	28	29	30	31	32	33	34	35	36	37	38
1945–1950	X									X			X							X												X	X	X		X	X	
1950–1954		X								X	X		X	X	X	X				X	X											X	X	X		X	X	
1954–1961			X							X			X		X	X	X			X	X											X	X	X	X	X	X	X
1961–1964				X	X					X			X		X	X	X		X	X	X	X	X			X		X				X	X	X	X	X		
1964–1969						X	X	X		X		X	X		X	X	X	X	X	X	X		X	X	X	X	X	X	X	X		X	X	X	X	X		
1969–1975									X				X			X			X						X										X	X		X

Preface

More than a decade after its end, the Vietnam war refuses to lie quiet in its historical grave.

—Jonathan Schell, *The Real War*

This book is about the past and continuing debate over the causes of United States involvement in the Vietnam War. It brings together readings that best exemplify the widely varying answers that historians, political scientists, social scientists, policymakers, journalists, and novelists have given to the essential question of American involvement: why did the U.S. intervene diplomatically and militarily in Vietnam between 1945 and 1975? The documents, essays, and excerpts included were in many cases written by people who played key parts in shaping the debate. In order to provide a sense of both the history of the war and the evolution of ideas explaining it, I have chosen readings covering different chronological periods of American involvement and written both during and after the war. I have also made every effort to represent points of view fairly, but inevitably the anthology reflects this editor's vision of American involvement in Vietnam.

The literature on all aspects of the American role in the Vietnam War is large, rich, and growing. It has already become an integral part of the grand body of American nonfiction and fiction writing. When I began to work on this volume, however, I could not find a book that systematically described the past and continuing debate about the causes of American involvement. Nor was there an anthology of representative readings on the subject, which curious readers might use to sample the range of opinions. Postwar compilations of writings on the conflict had attempted through documents and essays to tell the story of the war in several of its facets, but none dealt directly or fully with the debate about the war's causes. This gap was particularly unfortunate, because the question of why the United States intervened in Vietnam was in many respects the most basic one about the conflict. It was also the question that most vexed many Americans at the time their country was deepening its involvement, especially those young men who went off to fight but did not really understand why. Today's students, having been born during the war, grew up with the political tumult, family conversations, and television images of the Vietnam era, so that many regard these events as significant to themselves and earnestly want to understand them. As one anonymous professor observed: "My students have expressed the...feelings that they never understood the war, but that it troubles them and that it is related in some way to what we and our society have become today.... It is as if they are curious about some mysterious family scandal that was important to their lives but which nobody would ever explain to them."*

To Reason Why helps students, teachers, and general readers make sense of the multiple explanations about the causes of U.S. involvement in the Vietnam War in several ways. First, it calls attention to the fact and importance of the intense controversy about this issue. Second, it organizes the conflicting theories under seven comprehensible major themes: (1) the U.S. government's public explanation; (2) the causal role of abstract ideas and states of mind; (3) the quagmire and stalemate-machine theories about the process of involvement; (4) the role of the President; (5) the role of the President's advisers and national security managers; (6) the role of political and economic systems, pressures, and aims; and (7) American misunderstanding of Vietnamese culture. These categories reflect the actual clash of ideas and are consistent with approaches used by scholars of international relations; on the other hand, they avoid the risk of confusing non-professional readers with the esoteric, sometimes sterile terms employed by historiographers, terms such as "realist," "revisionist," and "postrevisionist." The readings illustrate all seven major themes as well as their minor variations. Third, an introduction defines the meaning of the phrase "U.S. 'involvement' in the Vietnam War" and provides an analytical overview of the seven explanatory themes; headnotes to the individual readings then place them in their chronological and conceptual contexts. Fourth, for the convenience of those preferring a chronological rather than a thematic approach, a "Chronological Chart of Readings" identifies the periods or phases of U.S. involvement covered by the readings. Finally, a glossary of abbreviations and a map of Indochina are provided for reference.

Readers of *To Reason Why* can sample the literature of the causal debate; gain an understanding of its structure, texture, and variety; become acquainted with the idioms of Vietnam War discourse; follow the evolution of U.S. involvement; and be encouraged to ponder the reasons for disagreement. Teachers of history, political science, American studies, and Southeast Asian studies courses can use the text in at least three ways: (1) they can build a whole unit around it about the explanations of U.S. involvement in Vietnam; (2) they can assign readings on periods of the war as they proceed chronologically through the war's history; or (3) they can select readings on the basis of topical content, assigning selections randomly to suit their courses.

Many friends and colleagues helped make this book possible. Historians Alan Brinkley of the City University of New York, George C. Herring of the University of Kentucky, Michael O'Brien of Miami University, Daniel J. Singal of Hobart and William Smith Colleges, and Sandra C. Taylor of the University of Utah read drafts of the manuscript at different stages and made valuable suggestions for improvement. Daniel Singal was particularly helpful with recommendations about organi-

---

*Quoted in *The Project of the Vietnam Generation Report* 1 (December 1985): 3.

zation and selections for readings. A research grant and a research leave from Miami University provided the opportunity to develop the concept of the book. A National Security Faculty Award from the Mershon Center of Ohio State University facilitated the writing of the introduction. Fellow academics and educators I accompanied on a trip to Vietnam in December/January 1987/1988 enlarged my understanding of the war and the country. Among these stalwart and cheerful travelers, Philip Brown of the University of North Carolina at Charlotte, Harry Haines of Trinity University, David Hunt of the William Joiner Center of the University of Massachusetts at Boston, Larry Rottmann of Southwest Missouri State University, and Mary Ann Tétreault of Old Dominion University made suggestions for the book. Years of conversation about history and the Vietnam War with Steve Anders of the U.S. Quartermaster School at Fort Lee, Jack Pesda of Camden Community College, and the late Charles DeBenedetti of the University of Toledo have found their way into the book. Miami University History Department colleagues as well as my students have indulged my interest in the historiography of the causes of the war and contributed ideas. Allan M. Winkler, chair of the History Department, was especially supportive of the project. Miami University librarians Christine Africa, Karen Clift, Susan Eacker, Karin Ford, Rebecca A. Morgenson, Richard H. Quay, and Cathy Seitz were generous with their bibliographical assistance. Daryl, Leslie, and Linda Musmeci Kimball were patient, encouraging, and constructively critical. My thanks also goes to those who gave permission for reproducing their thoughts on American involvement.

A few words about words are in order. In the introduction and the headnotes I have used Americanized spellings for Vietnamese names; for example, Vietnam, Hanoi, and Dienbienphu for Viêt Nam, Hà Nôi, and Diên Biên Phu. In addition, and without any political meaning intended, I have sometimes subscribed to the American convention of writing North Vietnam for the Democratic Republic of Vietnam, South Vietnam for the Republic of Vietnam, Vietcong for the People's Liberation Armed Force and its political arm, the National Liberation Front, and North Vietnamese Army for the People's Army of Vietnam. In the readings themselves, the original names and spellings have all been retained.

Jeffrey P. Kimball

To Reason Why

The Debate about the Causes
of U.S. Involvement
in the Vietnam War

INTRODUCTION

An Argument without End

History is indeed an argument without end.
—Pieter Geyl, *Napoleon: For and Against*, 1949

THE NAMES OF THE VIETNAM WAR

There is no universally agreed-upon beginning-date or name for the war the United States fought in Vietnam. In part this is because American diplomatic and military intervention was gradual, escalating in size and intensity over a long period of time. In part it is because Congress never declared war. Some would say that we cannot even speak of U.S. intervention *in* the Vietnam War because there would have been no war had it not been for American "involvement."

What is clear is that the origins of this involvement date back to at least 1945, though there is disagreement among knowledgeable commentators about whether it was inevitable that the United States would end up fighting a war once it got involved in Vietnam. Some observers say that there were a number of decision points between 1945 and the end of the fighting in 1975 when the U.S. government could have turned away from war. For example, it could have refused to support the French in the 1940s and 1950s, or deescalated its diplomatic and advisory role in South Vietnam from the 1950s on, or withdrawn its own forces from the fighting in the mid-1960s—or at least before 1973, when it actually withdrew. The most important of these decision points came in 1945, 1950, 1954, 1961, 1964–65, and 1969. Other experts suggest that direct U.S. involvement in war was inevitable, given the assumptions held and commitments made by American officials in the 1945–54 period. Whichever position is correct, there is little doubt that the course of history in Vietnam would have been very different had the United States not intervened in Indochina between 1945 and 1975.

In 1945 the U.S. government ignored Vietnam's pleas for American recognition of its independence and acquiesced in France's return to Vietnam. For the Vietnamese and the French, the real, shooting war began in December 1946, when

1

Names for the Wars in Vietnam, 1946–1975

1946–54	First Indochina War (international term)
	French-Vietminh War (U.S. Army term)
	Indochina War (*la guerre d'Indochine,* France's term)
	Anti-French War of Resistance (Vietminh term)
1959–75	Second Indochina War (international term)
	War of Liberation (National Liberation Front—"Vietcong"—term)
1965–73	Anti-U.S. War of Resistance for National Salvation (Vietnamese term for U.S.-dominated phase of the war)
	American War (Vietnamese term)
	Vietnam War (U.S. term)

the Vietnam Independence League, or Vietminh, resorted to armed resistance against France's effort to reassert its control. In early 1950 President Harry S. Truman's administration began to play an active role in Vietnam by recognizing the French-created client governments of Vietnam, Laos, and Cambodia and providing direct military and economic aid to the French in their war against the Vietminh. But victory for the French was not to be. In July 1954 the Geneva Conference on Indochina concluded international agreements on a cease-fire, the temporary partitioning of Vietnam, the withdrawal of French forces, and national unification elections to be held in 1956.

The U.S. Army referred to the 1946 to 1954 struggle between the French and Vietminh as the "French-Vietminh War"; the French called it "la guerre d'Indochine"; and the Vietminh named it the "War of Resistance." Internationally, this conflict is more commonly known as the "First Indochina War." Its American-dominated sequel, which scholars usually date from 1959 to 1975, is referred to as the "Second Indochina War."

The seeds of the Second Indochina War were planted in July 1954, when Ngo Dinh Diem, supported by President Dwight D. Eisenhower's government, became premier of the Republic of (South) Vietnam. In response to Diem's refusal to participate in national unification elections, his unpopular land policies, and his repressive campaign against former Vietminh and other political challengers, Diem's opponents began a limited guerrilla war in January 1959. On July 8 of that year, the first American military advisers died of hostile fire at the town of Bienhoa, twenty miles northeast of Saigon; their names now begin the somber list of inscriptions on the Vietnam War Memorial in Washington, D.C. By late December 1960, the armed opposition to Diem was fighting under the banner of the National Liberation Front, which Diem dubbed the Vietcong, or Vietnamese Communists. Called the "War of Liberation" by opponents of the Saigon government, the fighting after 1959 saw an escalation in U.S. economic and military assistance to Diem and, after Diem's assassination at the hands of his own generals on 1 November 1963, to his successors. On 22 November, in an unrelated incident, President John F. Kennedy was also assassinated. American assistance to the Saigon army during

Kennedy's three years in office and Lyndon B. Johnson's first year as President included a dramatic increase in the number of military advisers, from about 900 under Eisenhower in December 1960 to over 23,000 under Johnson in December 1964.

The U.S. Veterans Administration marks the beginning of the Vietnam War as 5 August 1964, the day American warplanes attacked the Democratic Republic of (North) Vietnam in reprisal for allegedly unprovoked PT-boat attacks on the U.S. destroyers *Maddox* and *C Turner Joy* off the North Vietnamese coast in the Gulf of Tonkin. Two days later, at the request of President Johnson, Congress passed Public Law 88-408, popularly known as the "Tonkin Gulf Resolution," authorizing the President to "take all necessary measures to repel any armed attack against the forces of the United States and to prevent further aggression." In February and March 1965 Johnson began to "Americanize" the war through accelerated aerial bombardment of North and South Vietnam and massive ground combat intervention south of the temporary demarcation line dividing the two Vietnams. By April 1969 American troop strength in South Vietnam had peaked at about 545,000.

After April the recently elected administration of President Richard M. Nixon began to re-"Vietnamize" the fighting by slowly withdrawing American ground troops while increasing monetary, matériel, and training support for Saigon's forces. But at the same time as it was reducing American troop strength, the Nixon administration escalated the weight and extent of the U.S. air bombardment of Indochina and expanded the ground war into Cambodia and Laos. Nearly four years later, on 27 January 1973, after a bloody military stalemate and long negotiations, the United States and the Democratic Republic of Vietnam signed the Paris Agreement on Ending the War and Restoring Peace in Vietnam. On 29 March 1973 the last American troops left the country, officially ending the U.S. military role. But it was not until 30 April 1975 that all American aid and advice to South Vietnam was terminated, when the Saigon government surrendered to North Vietnamese and Vietcong forces and fighting between Vietnamese ceased.

In addition to the earlier term "War of Liberation," Vietnamese opponents of the United States called the phase of the fighting from 1965 to 1973 the "American War" and the "Anti-U.S. War of Resistance for National Salvation." In the United States, Americans referred to it as the "Vietnam War," the "Vietnamese War," or simply "Vietnam." Perhaps because Congress did not declare war, some government agencies, like the Library of Congress, still call it the "Vietnamese *Conflict*."

THE DEBATE ABOUT THE CAUSES OF U.S. INVOLVEMENT

After the war and into the 1980s and 1990s, as Americans continued to argue about their involvement in Vietnam and the lessons it had for the future course of U.S. foreign policy, they drew on the theories and ideas of the debates of the 1960s and early 1970s. Some of these theories appeared in new forms. Scholarly accounts in particular reflected the perspectives of hindsight, the dispassion of time elapsed, and the information revealed in recently uncovered documents and manuscripts. But these later theories contained the kernel of earlier ones. Like aging wines, the postwar arguments were mellower and subtler than the original fermenting juices, but their vintage was the season of war. And even though the dedication of the Vietnam War Memorial in 1982 inspired healing and the observance of the tenth anniversary of the war's end in 1985 encouraged reconciliation, it is not likely that the argument over involvement will end soon.[1]

According to conventional wisdom, the wartime argument among Americans about U.S. involvement in Vietnam was between two groups: "hawks" and "doves." Hawks believed the war was one against Communist aggression, supported the decision to intervene militarily, and wanted to "win." Doves opposed the war, which they regarded as a civil war, and wanted to extricate the United States from Vietnam.

The reality of the debate, however, was more complicated. Some hawks favored the use of more military power and were consequently critical of the government's management of the war effort. Although some of these were willing to persist in fighting into the indefinite future, others wanted either to win or to get out. Doves were also a varied group. Some opposed military intervention but agreed with the professed interventionist purpose of stopping Communist aggression; others opposed intervention, doubted the purpose, and thought the methods used were immoral and senseless. Outspoken antiwar-activist doves were split into three main factions: liberals, who viewed the war as a mistake; leftists, who regarded corporate imperialism as the cause; and pacifists, who identified militarism as the problem.[2]

Many other concerned Americans rejected either label. Some antiwar activists, for example, were uncomfortable with the label of dove, believing it applied only to fence-sitting, "moderate" liberals and conservatives, who may have had reservations about involvement but still accepted most of the assumptions of the cold war and the national security state. On the other hand, some of these moderates, like Republican Senator George Aiken, disliked the tag because they asso-

[1] Readers who want to follow the scholarly, historiographical debate can begin with the following sources: Peter Braestrup, "Vietnam as History," *The Wilson Quarterly* 2 (Spring 1978): 178–87; Richard Dean Burns and Milton Leitenberg, *The Wars in Vietnam, Cambodia, and Laos, 1945–1982: A Bibliographic Guide* (Santa Barbara: ABC-Clio, 1984); Fox Butterfield, "The New Vietnam Scholarship," *New York Times Magazine*, 13 Feb. 1983; Robert A. Divine, "Vietnam Reconsidered," *Diplomatic History* 12 (Winter 1988): 79–93; Joe P. Dunn, "In Search of Lessons: The Development of a Vietnam Historiography," *Parameters: Journal of the U.S. Army War College* 9 (December 1979): 28–40; Edward K. Eckert, "The Vietnam War: A Selective Bibliography," *Choice* 21 (September 1986): 51–71; George C. Herring, "United States, Southeast Asia, and the Indochina Wars since 1941," in *Guide to American Foreign Relations since 1700*, ed. Richard Dean Burns (Santa Barbara: ABC-Clio, 1983), 883–85; Herring, "America and Vietnam: The Debate Continues," *American Historical Review* 92 (April 1987): 350–62; Walter LaFeber, "The Last War, the Next War, and the New Revisionists," *Democracy* 1 (January 1981): 93–103; Richard A. Melanson, *Writing History and Making Policy: The Cold War, Vietnam, and Revisionism* (Lanham, Md.: University Press of America, 1983); John Schlight, ed., *Second Indochina War Symposium: Papers and Commentary* (Washington, D.C.: Center of Military History, 1984).

[2] Charles DeBenedetti, *The Peace Reform in American History* (Bloomington: Indiana University Press, 1980), 171–73.

ciated it with the vociferous antiwar activists who were criticizing them. Aiken coined the term "owls" to distance himself from both hawks and doves and to identify his position with reason and wisdom.[3] Journalist David Halberstam, who in the early 1960s "thought the war was worth winning but...doubted the effectiveness of the fight against the enemy and sensed the seed of failure in our own efforts," declared that he was neither a hawk nor a dove.[4] The arch-conservative, hawkish *National Review* magazine, however, derisively described the moderates in 1965 as "sparrows."[5] Supporters of President Johnson, meanwhile, portrayed him in 1966 as a beleaguered leader caught in the middle between noisily screeching hawks and cooing doves.[6] Later, President Nixon appealed for help to the "silent majority"—the majority of American citizens who he claimed had simply been silent in their support of the war effort.

Although commonly used to characterize the continuing debate about why the United States became involved in the Vietnam War, these simplistic, politically charged labels should be put aside. They never were and are certainly no longer satisfactory in helping us understand the complexity of ideas and theories put forward about the causes of U.S. intervention. Professional historians and political scientists have tried to substitute terms like "revisionist," "postrevisionist," "realist," and "rationalist" in order to describe the various so-called schools of thought, but while helpful in some respects, these labels remain obscure to most students and the public. Perhaps a better approach to the debate would be to focus more attention on the theories themselves than on the political or historiographical schools of thought. There are many theories on the causes of the involvement that deserve study, and they can be divided into seven categories to simplify the challenge of understanding them:

• Public explanations by the U.S. government
• The causal role of abstract ideas, ideals, strategic concepts, and states of mind
• The process of involvement, namely the quagmire theory and the stalemate-machine theory
• The role of the head of state, the President
• The role of national security managers and bureaucrats
• Political and economic systems, pressures, and aims
• American cultural differences with and misunderstanding of the Vietnamese

Writers, speakers, and publicists who have attempted to explain American involvement in Vietnam have often employed more than one theory from more than one of these categories, but usually they stress one theory over the others. While some theories are contradictory, several are complementary. The official theory stands alone, because it is the one to be tested and interpreted by the rest.

[3] William Safire, *Safire's Political Dictionary* (New York: Random House, 1978), 179.
[4] David Halberstam, "Return to Vietnam," *Harper's Magazine* 235 (December 1967): 47–57.
[5] James Burnham, *National Review*, 18 May 1965, 412.
[6] Jim Dobbins, "Sometimes ah feel ah'm in no-man's land!" cartoon, *Boston Traveler*, 25 Aug. 1966, in Cartoon Collection, folder 22, Lyndon B. Johnson Library.

The Official View:
The U.S. Government's Public Explanation

The containment doctrine, the government's public explanation of involvement in Vietnam, has been used by liberal and conservative wartime administrations, postwar conservative administrations, and policymaking publicists and memoirists since the late 1940s.[7] In its extreme form, it begins with the postulate that communism is malevolent. The connecting links between its evil nature and the threat it posed in Vietnam to the interests of the United States are explained by the Munich analogy, the red-fascism equation, the aggression thesis, the argument of Red China as an instrument of aggression, the contention of Vietnam as proxy, the domino effect, and the credibility claim.[8]

On the basis of their interpretation of British and French appeasement of Hitler in the 1930s, especially at the Munich Conference in 1938, post–World War II American policymakers believed that the democratic West had invited Nazi Germany's later aggressions. Appeasement at Munich and elsewhere, it was thought, had demonstrated that free nations could not compromise with aggressors, for if aggression by an inveterate aggressor were not nipped in the bud, the aggressor would be encouraged to commit further aggressions, and a larger war would have to be fought down the road, or other aggressors would be encouraged to act. Applied to the postwar world, the Munich metaphor blended nicely with the equating of Adolf Hitler to Joseph Stalin and Mao Ze-dong and of right-wing fascism with left-wing communism. Soviet and Chinese communism became "red fascism," which was said to threaten peaceful, free-world states in the same aggressive way that Nazism had.[9] Although to most Americans the Soviet Union is and has been the locus of communism, the U.S. government increasingly argued that "Red China" was the instrument and sometimes even the source of Communist aggression in Asia after Mao's victory over Jiang Jie-shī (Chiang Kai-shek) in 1949. Vietnamese Communists in turn were but proxies for Chinese—or Soviet—aggression.

Even though Vietnam may not have been vitally important to the national interest in and of itself, U.S. governments argued, it was nonetheless necessary to prevent a Communist takeover there because of the mechanical, geopolitical dy-

---

[7] The Cold War and the containment doctrine have spawned a vast literature. Begin with Richard Dean Burns, ed., *Guide to American Foreign Relations since 1700* (Santa Barbara: ABC-Clio, 1983); Thomas H. Etzold and John Lewis Gaddis, eds., *Containment: Documents on American Policy and Strategy, 1945–1950* (New York: Columbia University Press, 1978); John Lewis Gaddis, *Strategies of Containment: A Critical Appraisal of Postwar American National Security Policy* (Oxford: Oxford University Press, 1982); Walter LaFeber, *America, Russia, and the Cold War: 1945–1984*, 5th ed. (New York: Alfred A. Knopf, 1985).

[8] In *Prisoners of the Past? The Munich Syndrome and Makers of American Foreign Policy in the Cold War Era* (Lund, Sweden: CWK Gleerup, 1982), Göran Rystad defines the Munich syndrome as a composite of the Munich analogy, the aggression thesis, and the domino theory.

[9] Les K. Adler and Thomas G. Paterson, "Red Fascism: The Merger of Nazi Germany and Soviet Russia in the American Image of Totalitarianism," *American Historical Review* 75 (April 1970): 1046–64.

namic of "falling dominoes."[10] If Vietnam fell into the Soviet or Chinese Communist orbit, then neighboring Laos and Cambodia would too; all of Southeast Asia might fall; America would lose the strategic Strait of Malacca; communism would spread westward through India toward Turkey and eastward through Japan to the Philippines. Communist aggression, whether in Vietnam or elsewhere, therefore had to be contained and even rolled back. Evil must be rooted out in every obscure corner of the globe, or else it would ensnare the United States too, overturning national security, liberty, and free enterprise. Developments in Vietnam were not appreciated in their indigenous context, because Vietnam was seen as but a pawn in a global, geopolitical, economic, strategic, great-power struggle.

In the long course of U.S. involvement, different administrations emphasized different theories as policymakers and circumstances changed. The Truman administration stressed the Munich syndrome and the machinations of the international Communist conspiracy. The Eisenhower administration refined the domino thesis and linked it with the struggle for political freedom and economic liberty. The Kennedy administration reiterated previous themes but expressed particular concern with the dual threat of Chinese aggression and wars of national liberation. The Johnson and Nixon administrations also perpetuated previous arguments, but Johnson frequently underscored U.S. credibility and commitments to defend South Vietnam, while Nixon warned of Communist bloodbaths should the United States precipitously withdraw. After the war, the administration of Ronald W. Reagan revived the argument that the United States had sent troops to Vietnam in order to stop outside aggression and defend a friend.[11]

Occasionally, wartime policymakers put forward other claims to strengthen their case. In the pre–Geneva Accords period, they argued that the United States must be involved in Vietnam because it had an obligation to an ally, France, which, after 1949, was fighting the good fight against Communist aggression in Indochina. In the post-1954 period, they argued that America not only had to help an ally, or friend—the anti-Communist government of South Vietnam—but that the United States was committed to upholding an inviolable treaty obligation, the Southeast Asia Treaty Organization (SEATO). In the late 1950s and early 1960s, the U.S. government argued that involvement in Vietnam was necessary to build a new nation of South Vietnam and make it a freer and better place to live for the Vietnamese. By the mid-1960s, advisers like Defense Secretary Robert McNamara were por-

---

[10] William Safire claims that Joseph Alsop invented the phrase: *Safire's Political Dictionary* (New York: Random House, 1978), 179. But the concept is older than the phrase. In 1947 Sen. Arthur Vandenberg talked about a "chain reaction" of aggression unless Congress voted for aid to Greece and Turkey; *Congressional Record*, 80th Cong., 1st sess., 1947, Vol. 93, pt. 3, p. 3772–73. In the same year over the same issue Dean Acheson said: "Like apples in a barrel infected by one rotten one, the corruption of Greece would infect Iran and all to the east"—as well as Africa and Europe: *Present at the Creation: My Years in the State Department* (New York: W. W. Norton, 1969), 219.

[11] Ronald W. Reagan, *Public Papers of the Presidents of the United States: Ronald Reagan, 1982*, Book 1 (Washington, D.C.: GPO, 1983), 184–85.

traying South Vietnam as a "test case" for the Communist strategy of revolutionary, guerrilla war, a test that the United States must meet and win.[12]

The official explanation is at once the easiest and the most difficult one to discuss. It is easy because it is the best-known theory, and one that applies not only to Vietnam but to other cold war events and issues. It is difficult because it is impossible to know whether policymakers really believed in it themselves or whether it was rhetoric designed to persuade the public that intervention in Vietnam was necessary, just as Senator Arthur H. Vandenberg once advised President Truman to "scare the hell out of the country" in order to gain their support for cold war policies. If it was all lies or mostly lies, were there deeper, even secret, motives and goals? Or did schizophrenic, doublespeaking, doublethinking Orwellian policymakers believe their own rhetoric but simultaneously harbor a partially secret agenda, which the official, public argument contradicted and thus wittingly or unwittingly hid? In one very real sense, the other theories of U.S. involvement in Vietnam are attempts to solve this riddle.[13]

States of Mind:
Abstract Ideas, Ideals, Strategic Concepts

One of the most common explanations of the underlying cause of U.S. involvement takes policymakers at their word. It holds that during the early years of the cold war

[12] The U.S. government's public argument can be traced in presidential statements and State Department white papers; e.g., *Aggression from the North: The Record of North Vietnam's Campaign to Conquer South Vietnam* (Washington, D.C., [February] 1965). Its secret argument can be partially followed in the Pentagon Papers: *The Senator Gravel Edition, The Pentagon Papers: The Defense Department History of United States Decisionmaking on Vietnam*, vols. 1–5 (Boston: Beacon Press, 1971); and *The Pentagon Papers as Published by The New York Times* (New York: Bantam Books, 1971). There are several studies of government rhetoric. One of the best is F. M. Kail, *What Washington Said: Administration Rhetoric and the Vietnam War, 1949–1969* (New York: Harper & Row, 1973). His study, he said, revealed "the correlation between the emergence and development of an official argument and the progressive increases in the U.S. military role," and it produced evidence that officials and speechwriters designed public statements to persuade the public to support government policy. William L. Griffen and John Marciano, in *Lessons of the Vietnam War: A Critical Examination of School Texts and an Interpretive Comparative History Utilizing the Pentagon Papers and Other Documents* (Totowa, N.J.: Rowman & Allanheld, 1979), maintain that many school texts uncritically accepted the official explanation. The 1964 to 1973 issues of the conservative *National Review* and the John Birch Society's *American Opinion* provide a good sampling of right-wing, nongovernmental expressions of containment-doctrine assumptions.

[13] Documents in the Pentagon Papers contradict official public statements. Daniel Ellsberg commented on the problem of fathoming the motives of the policymakers in *Papers on the War* (New York: Simon and Schuster, 1972), 75: "Presidential decisions, estimates, plans, and studies...remain opaque as to the motives of the major policy-makers and their decisions. This is not only because the President and White House staff—who leave only a closely guarded and insubstantial trail of documents—necessarily figure in a shadowy, inferential way in these accounts based primarily on documents. Nor is it mainly because of lacunae in the documentation.... It is because the documents available, even the frankest, do not reveal motives; nor do they provide an adequate basis for inferring the motives, attitudes, or perspectives even of the bureaucrats whose names appear most often or who signed them or who may even have written them." See also pp. 76–80.

the containment doctrine became a psychologically obsessive, ideological dogma in the minds of the Presidents, national security managers, cabinet members, and others who made government policy. Captives of the containment mind-set—with its supporting notions of the Munich analogy, aggression thesis, and domino effect—and construing revolution and civil war in Vietnam as external Communist aggression, U.S. policymakers led the country into the longest war in its history. The mind-set argument is at least as old as the war itself and can be found, for example, in the internal narrative histories that accompanied the documents in the Pentagon Papers, which were collected between 1967 and 1969. Scholars continue to regard it as an important explanation of American involvement.

Some analysts are implicitly or explicitly critical of policymakers' cold war mind-set, suggesting that it was inappropriate to the situation in Vietnam, blinding them to the realities of the struggle.[14] Other analysts more or less share the policymakers' values and assumptions and believe the application of the containment policy in Vietnam to have been appropriate and well-intentioned.[15] But to both sets of analysts, an important cause of intervention in Vietnam was a cold war vision of events and issues.

Because decision makers in fact defended their policies in the terminology of containment, the argument that a containment state of mind caused U.S. involvement in Vietnam possesses great plausibility. Be that as it may, the theory's primary weakness seems to be that it does not usually or clearly explain how the containment state of mind came about. To be sure, it has been suggested that the policy of containment was rooted in American history and culture—in the lessons of World War II, the events of the cold war, 1950's McCarthyism, and even in manifest destiny, the Puritan heritage, the liberal heritage, the conservative heritage, or the anti-Communist strains in American society.[16] But this interpretation itself falls short of explaining the social basis of these historical and cultural phenomena. For example, who are the groups most likely to hold containment ideas and why? And what is the social basis for anticommunism? Moreover, the mind-set theory does not fully explain how the doctrine was pursued for thirty years and more in the face of contemporary evidence to the contrary and much contemporary criticism. To say that policymakers were ignorant, or captives of a conformist mind-set, or victims of doctrinal closed-mindedness, or blind participants in their culture does not explain why the "best and the brightest" of the political and managerial elite were ignorant victims of a flawed doctrine or unwitting participants in a culture of anticommunism, whose own roots are seldom adequately explained by the containment mind-set theorists.

Other commentators who emphasize the role of ideas point to the zealous, crusading, missionary idealism inherent in U.S. foreign policy as a cause of U.S.

[14] Loren Baritz, *Backfire: A History of How American Culture Led Us into Vietnam and Made Us Fight the Way We Did* (New York: William Morrow, 1985), Parts I and II; George C. Herring, *America's Longest War: The United States and Vietnam, 1950–1975*, 2d ed. (New York: Alfred A. Knopf, 1986); *The Pentagon Papers: Senator Gravel Edition*, Vol. 1:81–88.

[15] Norman Podhoretz, *Why We Were in Vietnam* (New York: Simon and Schuster, 1982).

[16] See, e.g., Stanley Karnow, *Vietnam: A History* (1983; rpt. New York: Penguin Books, 1984), 11–15.

involvement in Vietnam. It is an old theory in American foreign policy studies, which was used during the war to explain involvement in Vietnam and continues to be applied after the war. Although in some respects it complements the mind-set thesis, the idealistic mission–redeemer nation interpretation is different in its emphasis on the active, crusading zeal of the foreign policy mission, as opposed to the reactive quality of the containment doctrine.

In its conservative form, idealistic American foreign policy has sought to root out communism and leftism abroad as though they represented demonism itself. In its liberal form, the American mission is idealistic, millennial, and universalist, rejecting spheres of influence and balances of power. Stretching back to the intention of the Puritans to establish a "city on a hill," Americans, it is argued, have seen it as their mission to re-create the world in the image of the United States. In one version of the thesis, U.S. policymakers desired not to impose U.S. imperialism on Vietnam, or simply to contain the Soviet Union or China, but hoped to give the Vietnamese, or at least the South Vietnamese, a better, freer way of life—an alternative to right-wing dictatorship on the one hand and Communist dictatorship on the other.[17]

To some interpreters, the idealistic mission was reasonable and practical as well as high-minded and well-intentioned. But to "realist" critics of U.S. policy, idealistic missionary goals were impractical, unrealistic, and naive. Some realists say that even though America's vital interests were not at stake in Vietnam, idealists nonetheless committed the country to the pursuit of ends in Vietnam beyond American means.[18]

Some other nonrealist critics question the claim that U.S. purposes were ever truly idealistic, well-meaning, and generous, and contend that American behavior evidenced an arrogance stemming from great power. The concept of arrogance includes the assumption that the United States had a right to bring its idealism to Vietnam and decide the fate of another country; the hubris of U.S. policymakers; their faith in U.S. omnipotence, or the certainty that the United States could not be defeated, especially by a "fourth-rate peasant country," as Henry Kissinger referred to North Vietnam; the belief that the United States could succeed where the Chinese, Japanese, and French had failed; and the conviction that the reputation of the United States could not tolerate a defeat in any case.[19]

Another set of theories stressing the role of ideas in causing U.S. involvement examines U.S. strategic doctrine. Some suggest, for example, that the Eisenhower

---

[17] Frances FitzGerald, "The American Millennium," *The New Yorker*, 11 Nov. 1985, 88–113; J. William Fulbright, *The Arrogance of Power* (New York: Vintage Books, 1966), 11–19; David Halberstam, *The Making of a Quagmire* (New York: Random House, 1965), 320; Michael H. Hunt, *Ideology and U.S. Foreign Policy* (New Haven: Yale University Press, 1987), Chap. 5.

[18] Hans J. Morgenthau, *Vietnam and the United States* (Washington, D.C.: Public Affairs Press, 1965); Norman A. Graebner, *America as a World Power: A Realist Appraisal from Wilson to Reagan* (Wilmington, Del.: Scholarly Resources, 1984), Chap. 9.

[19] Henry Steele Commager, "The Defeat of America," *New York Review of Books*, 5 Oct. 1972, 7–12; Halberstam, *The Best and the Brightest* (New York: Random House, 1972); Herring, "The Legacy of the First Indochina War," in Schlight, ed., *Second Indochina War*, 24–25; Fulbright, *Arrogance of Power*; Richard Hofstadter, "Uncle Sam Has Cried 'Uncle' Before," *New York Times Magazine*, 19 May 1968, 30; Arnold R. Isaacs, *Without Honor: Defeat in Vietnam and Cambodia* (New York: Vintage Books, 1984); Neil Sheehan, *A Bright Shining Lie: John Paul Vann and America in Vietnam* (New York: Random House, 1988).

administration's reliance on covert aid and operations contributed to U.S. involvement, locking the U.S. government into a commitment trap. The Kennedy administration's infatuation with special forces, counterinsurgency, and flexible response—ideas originating during the Eisenhower administration—deepened the commitment. The Johnson administration's pursuit of flexible response, graduated escalation, and capital-intensive warfare both caused and prolonged an already enlarged war. Some argue that the U.S. combat strategy of attrition—as opposed to possible alternatives, such as counterinsurgency—had much to do with the vast increases in U.S. troop strength and the prolongation of the war. In the Nixon administration, a belief in the efficacy of massive bombing not only escalated but extended the war.[20] Thus, by defining how the Vietnam crisis could be managed militarily, strategic doctrine helped cause escalating involvement.

The Process of Involvement: Stumbling into the Quagmire or Knowingly Accepting Stalemate?

Theorists have explained U.S. involvement in one of two basic ways: they find the cause either in the motivations and beliefs of U.S. government leaders or in the processes by which escalation took place. The first approach examines why there was escalation, and the other examines how escalation was managed.

Perhaps the best known "how explanation" is the quagmire theory, which is also known by other names: slippery slope, inadvertence, investment trap, commitment trap, riding the tiger's back, downward spiral, and tar baby. It is usually a subtext of other theories and is the explanation that most immediately comes to mind when one looks at the step-by-step deepening of U.S. involvement. Suggesting scenes of rice paddies and the Mekong Delta, the quagmire argument evokes the image of a person who walks into a morass and incrementally becomes mired in muck, hindering or preventing him or her from reaching the destination.[21]

As old as the First Indochina War, the quagmire theory became familiar to Americans through the writings of David Halberstam and Arthur Schlesinger, Jr.,

---

[20] Larry E. Cable, *Conflict of Myths: The Development of American Counterinsurgency and the Vietnam War* (New York: New York University Press, 1986); Committee of Concerned Asian Scholars, *The Indochina Story: A Fully Documented Account* (New York: Pantheon Books, 1970), Chap. 5, 230–31; Jerald Combs, "The Path to Vietnam: Kennedy, Johnson, and Flexible Response," Chap. 18 of *The History of American Foreign Policy* (New York: Alfred A. Knopf, 1986); James A. Donovan, *Militarism, U.S.A.* (New York: Charles Scribner's Sons, 1970), 18–26; Gaddis, *Strategies of Containment*, Chaps. 7 and 8; Guenter Lewy, *America in Vietnam* (New York: Oxford University Press, 1978), Chap. 2; Institute of the History of the Communist Party of Vietnam, *History of the Communist Party of Vietnam* (Hanoi: Foreign Languages Publishing House, 1986), 167–69; Jonathan Schell, *The Time of Illusion* (New York: Vintage Books, 1975); Russell F. Weigley, *The American Way of War: A History of United States Military Strategy and Policy* (New York: Macmillan, 1973), Chap. 18.

[21] Ellsberg opens his chapter, "The Quagmire Myth and the Stalemate Machine," *Papers on the War*, 42, with a descriptive quotation from Victor Hugo's *Les Misérables* to illustrate the quagmire metaphor. Better than quagmire perhaps, slippery slope, investment-commitment trap, and riding the tiger's back convey the sense of escalatory inevitability; that is, once having made the first move, what followed was inevitable. The tar baby metaphor suggests the idea of an angry, stupid, helpless giant being drawn into an inextricable mess by friend and foe alike.

in the 1960s. To Halberstam, a reporter who arrived in Saigon in late 1962, the quagmire was a frustrating military and diplomatic dilemma. While he thought the United States should be fighting in Vietnam, he believed that American overreliance on military rather than political solutions was doomed to failure; but to withdraw precipitously from Vietnam—before our South Vietnamese clients could continue the fight on their own—would undermine American honor and credibility.[22] To Schlesinger, a respected historian and adviser to Kennedy, the quagmire metaphor described the one-step-at-a-time process by which the United States inadvertently became entrapped in the military and diplomatic swamp of Vietnam.[23]

One of the corollary notions of the quagmire metaphor is that every escalatory step of the United States was taken with the hope or expectation that it would result in progress toward the desired goal. But instead of leading to its victorious end, each step led to other predicaments—as well as greater commitments of pride, prestige, money, troops, bombs, and lives—producing even more investments and additional cycles of optimism and despair. Thus, for example, Truman's commitment to France led to Eisenhower's hopeful support of Ngo Dinh Diem, which in turn led to ever-growing commitments of political verbiage, money, advisers, and prestige—all steering Kennedy into even greater entrapment in the Vietnamese quagmire. Turning a blind eye to the coup against and assassination of Diem, the Kennedy and then the Johnson administrations found themselves mired even more deeply in the muck of Vietnamese politics in the months following. Finally, by 1975, after other optimistic steps had been taken to win the war by the Johnson and Nixon administrations, winning proved to be an illusion—perhaps a self-delusion—and anticipated victory became bitter defeat.

For the most part the quagmire theory is compatible with every other explanation but two: the official theory and a rival how-it-happened explanation of U.S. involvement, the stalemate machine theory, which is sometimes subtitled "the system worked." Challenging the quagmire theory mainly on the ideas of inadvertent decision making and hoped-for victory, the stalemate argument maintains that policymakers *advertently* took escalatory steps, not because they promised victory but in order to prevent a defeat; that is, in this sense, to achieve a stalemate. Successive administrations believed that the political, social, and economic costs of winning in Vietnam were too high. On the other hand, they also believed they could not risk the political and international consequences of losing a country to communism. Convinced they could not afford either to win or to lose, they deliberately tried to avoid defeat until either the Vietnamese or the American people tired of the

---

[22] Halberstam, *Making of a Quagmire*. Halberstam's early views on the war had been influenced in the 1960s by Lieutenant Colonel John Paul Vann, a U.S. military adviser in Vietnam. See, ibid., Chap. 10, and Sheehan, *A Bright Shining Lie*, 317ff. In a later book, *The Best and the Brightest* (1972), Halberstam argued that policymakers were deprived of the information necessary to make reasoned judgments, partly because they did not want that information.

[23] Arthur M. Schlesinger, Jr., *The Bitter Heritage: Vietnam and American Democracy, 1941–1966* (Boston:Houghton Mifflin, 1967), Chaps. 1 and 2. See Schlesinger's "Eyeless in Indochina," *New York Review of Books*, 21 Oct. 1971, 23–32, for a clarification of his position following criticisms by Daniel Ellsberg and Leslie Gelb.

war. They chose short-term, stop-gap measures and occasionally aimed for negotiated settlements. Americans did indeed tire of the war, and accordingly, some
stalemate theorists have argued that the managerial system worked; that is, the
Presidents and their advisers stalemated the war until the American people were
ready—after 1968 or certainly after 1970—to accept peace and defeat, so long as the
President and his advisers could make it seem a "peace with honor."

The stalemate thesis is primarily the brainchild of two former advisers to the
government during the Vietnam years, Daniel Ellsberg and Leslie H. Gelb, whose
articles on the subject first appeared in the early 1970s. (With Richard Betts, Gelb
elaborated on the idea in 1979.)[24] Their arguments vary in both minor and major ways.
To Ellsberg, the decision-making system worked for the United States only to the
extent that it "cheaply" prevented a Communist victory, that is, with relatively few
combat troops engaged and minimal political damage to Presidents up to 1965. He
maintains that there were key turning points of U.S. government decision making, at
which times deescalation rather than escalation was possible. Gelb casts doubt on this
model, positing instead a kind of big bang theory, whereby the Truman and Eisenhower
administrations made original commitments that "set the course of escalation" for
succeeding administrations.[25] Ellsberg speaks of alternating periods of optimism and
pessimism and emphasizes the pressures of domestic politics, while Gelb stresses pessimism and mentions other influences on decision making—presidential caution, bureaucratic influences, and international considerations. Denying that American intervention was inadvertent, Ellsberg points out that U.S. policymakers deliberately made
Vietnam into a quagmire of death for the Vietnamese. Gelb puts less emphasis on
methods used. Ellsberg accuses the government of lying about involvement, and he
sees this tragic war as the product of U.S. counterrevolutionary policies that would be
difficult to change. Gelb sees policymakers as prisoners of the paradoxes of the political
and international system; in the future, such mistakes can be avoided by changing
political attitudes—if the President tones down anti-Communist rhetoric, for example.

One of the problems with the sophisticated stalemate machine thesis is its
subtlety. While the thesis professes to refute the quagmire argument, the differences between the two are very fine. Presidents and national security managers may
have been pessimistic about victory in the beginning or at some point later on, and
they may have come to realize that, all things considered, they could at best hope
to achieve a deadlock. Attempting to stalemate the conflict in the short term, they
nevertheless raised the stakes and mired themselves more deeply in a seemingly
endless war, from which withdrawal proved excruciatingly difficult. If the government was secretly pessimistic about the likelihood of success, officials projected
optimism in public; as a result, many Americans were convinced of the necessity
and possibility of victory, while others grew increasingly frustrated with the tar

---

[24] Ellsberg, "The Stalemate Machine"; Gelb, "Vietnam: The System Worked," *Foreign Policy* 7 (Summer
1971): 140–67; Gelb, "The Essential Domino: American Politics and Vietnam," *Foreign Affairs* 50 (April
1972): 459–75; Leslie Gelb, with Richard Betts, *The Irony of Vietnam: The System Worked* (Washington,
D.C.: Brookings Institution, 1979). Cf. Lewy, *America in Vietnam*, 418–26.

[25] Gelb and Betts, *The Irony of Vietnam*, 25.

baby of Vietnam.[26] It is also true that some bureaucracies—the military, for example—tended to be more optimistic (and thus unwitting victims of the quagmire syndrome), while others—the civilian intelligence agencies, for example—tended to be more pessimistic (and thus cogs in the stalemate machine).[27] Accordingly, different moods of pessimism and optimism settled on Washington decision makers from one year to another and from one office building to the next. Quagmire and stalemate mentalities operated at different levels at different times, as well as simultaneously.

Most of all, some critics argue that the stalemate machine thesis falls short because, maintaining that minimal methods were used and victory was not sought, it ignores the history of U.S. policy and strategy. The U.S. government sought victory through the French over the Vietminh before 1954 and a permanently partitioned Vietnam with an anti-Communist southern half from 1954 to the very end. These are facts that some would argue account for U.S. involvement itself. If U.S. policymakers thought that these objectives were limited and defensive, a large number of Vietnamese who wanted independence, national unity, and revolution regarded them as total and offensive. The final irony is that the stalemate argument provided an opening after the war to those hawks who claimed that civilian national security managers did not play the game to win and who blamed these civilians and others for the defeat of U.S. policy and strategy—a conclusion quite contrary to the wishes of stalemate machine theorists.[28]

The Buck Stops Here:
The President as Primary Cause

A more traditional approach to the explanation of American foreign policy focuses on the central role of the President as chief executive, politician, and maker of foreign and military policy—and as the person who appoints his advisers and is ultimately responsible for their decisions. Beginning in the Johnson years and continuing through the Nixon years, critics of involvement in the political arena more often than not saw the war as "Johnson's war" and "Nixon's war." Supporters of the war in turn rallied behind their Presidents.[29] These were unsurprising responses in a nation that gives its Presidents so much influence over foreign policy and where

[26] Some polls suggest that the quagmire syndrome was very real for the public; i.e., once committed in Vietnam, the public tended to want to accept the domino theory, the need to support the fighting men, etc. In *War, Presidents and Public Opinion* (New York: John Wiley, 1973), 49, John E. Mueller cites a February 1968 poll in which the questions asked reflected the arguments of the U.S. government, giving support to the point that what we know of public opinion is often filtered through others' lenses. Most of the questions seem to have contributed to a quagmire mentality: "If we do not continue, the Communists will take over Vietnam and then move on to other parts of the world. . . . We must support our fighting men. . . ." And so on.

[27] Schlesinger, *Bitter Heritage*, Chaps. 1 and 2; James Clay Thompson, *Rolling Thunder: Understanding Policy and Program Failure* (Chapel Hill: University of North Carolina Press, 1980), 49–70.

[28] Jeffrey P. Kimball, "The Stab-in-the-Back Legend and the Vietnam War," *Armed Forces and Society* 14 (Spring 1988): 433–58, and "Lessons of the Vietnam War: The Myth of the Liberals' Last, Limited War," *Indochina Newsletter*, no. 55 (Jan.–Feb. 1989): 1–8.

[29] Mueller, *Public Opinion*, Chap. 9.

presidential politics dominates all politics. At the core of theories about presidential causation is a focus upon the role of the Presidents in leading the United States up the staircase of escalation into the Vietnam War. Johnson's handling of the Gulf of Tonkin "incident" in August 1964 is widely regarded as one of the best examples of unilateral presidential decision making and manipulation of congressional and public opinion. In this case, Johnson used the Gulf of Tonkin Resolution to legitimate his waging an undeclared war.[30]

Given the importance of centralized, presidential decision making, Presidents' personalities take on great importance and come under special scrutiny in scholarly accounts: Franklin D. Roosevelt's vagueness about his post–World War II trusteeship policy toward Indochina;[31] Truman's foreign policy ignorance, deep-seated anticommunism, and containment dogmatism;[32] Eisenhower's concern with the threat of communism to world capitalism;[33] Kennedy's vigorous, crusading, suavely heroic anticommunism;[34] Johnson's insecurity, dominating personality, and complexity;[35] and Nixon's paranoia, deviousness, secretiveness, disdain of bureaucracy, and love of brute force[36]—to name just a few apropos character traits of Presidents.

Looking beyond personality, some analysts examine the relative powers of the institutions of the presidency and Congress. Contending that twentieth-century hot and cold wars had caused the presidency to grow in power to the point where it was no longer checked and balanced by the Congress, the courts, the states, or the citizenry, they speak of the emergence of an "imperial presidency."[37] Wielding

---

[30] Anthony Austin, *The President's War* (Philadelphia: J. B. Lippincott, 1971).

[31] Thomas D. Boettcher, *Vietnam: The Valor and the Sorrow* (Boston: Little, Brown, 1985), Chap. 2.

[32] Truman's personality is discussed mainly in connection with the origins of the cold war. See, e.g., David Horowitz, *The Free World Colossus: A Critique of American Foreign Policy in the Cold War*, rev. ed. (New York: Hill and Wang, 1971); Thomas G. Paterson, *American Foreign Policy: A History* (Lexington, Mass.: D. C. Heath, 1988), 437–39. Boettcher, *Vietnam*, Chap. 4, and Herring, *Longest War*, Chap. 1, touch on this theme in relation to Vietnam.

[33] Blanche Wiesen Cook, *The Declassified Eisenhower: A Divided Legacy* (Garden City, N.Y.: Doubleday, 1981).

[34] Stephen Ambrose, *Rise to Globalism: American Foreign Policy since 1938*, 3d ed. (New York: Penguin Books, 1983), Chap. 10; David Burner, *John F. Kennedy and a New Generation* (Glenview, Ill.: Scott, Foresman/Little, Brown, 1988); Richard J. Walton, *Cold War and Counter-Revolution: The Foreign Policy of John F. Kennedy* (Baltimore: Penguin Books, 1972).

[35] Paul K. Conkin, *Big Daddy from the Pedernales: Lyndon Baines Johnson* (Boston: Mass.: G. K. Hall, 1986), 262–66; Doris Kearns, *Lyndon Johnson and the American Dream* (New York: Harper & Row, 1976), pp. 265–85.

[36] Baritz, *Backfire*, 178–222; Herring, *Longest War*, 221–23; Karnow, *Vietnam*, 577–612.

[37] Anthony D'Amato, "The American Constitution and the Air War," *The Air War in Indochina*, rev. ed., eds. Raphael Littauer and Norman Uphoff (Boston: Beacon Press, 1971), 113–23; Leon Friedman and Burt Neuborne, introduction by Senator George S. McGovern, *Unquestioning Obedience to the President: The ACLU Case against the Illegal War in Vietnam* (New York: W. W. Norton, 1972); Barbara Garson, *MacBird!* (New York: Grove Press, 1967); Schell, *Time of Illusion*, 338; Arthur M. Schlesinger, Jr., *The Imperial Presidency* (Boston: Houghton Mifflin, 1973); Harvey G. Zeidenstein, "The Vietnam War and the Reassertion of Congressional Power," in *The President's War Powers: From the Federalists to Reagan*, ed. Demetrios Caraley, with a special introduction by Jacob K. Javits (New York: Academy of Political Science, 1984), 163–79.

power as though they were Roman emperors,[38] Vietnam-era Presidents waged an undeclared war in Indochina, deceived the people, manipulated Congress, dominated advisers, rode roughshod over the Constitution, presumed to represent the whole nation in their person, and overextended American resources.

The Advisers:
Managers and Bureaucrats

While conceding the importance of presidential power, other interpreters point out that it was presidential advisers, cabinet members, and national security managers— along with the institutions and bureaucracies they represented—who shaped and even made foreign and military policies. Among the most prominent of these men were Dean Acheson, John Foster Dulles, Robert S. McNamara, McGeorge Bundy, Walt W. Rostow, Dean Rusk, Maxwell D. Taylor, and Henry A. Kissinger. The national security bureaucracies and institutions included the Presidents' personal staffs and ad hoc advisory committees, the State Department, the Defense Department, the Joint Chiefs of Staff, the Military Assistance Command Vietnam, the Commander in Chief Pacific, the Central Intelligence Agency (CIA), the National Security Agency, the Defense Intelligence Agency, the Bureau of Intelligence and Research, and the ambassador to Vietnam.

Explanations of the role of national security managers are numerous, overlapping, intricate, and sometimes conflicting. But taken as a whole, some of the essential points of the theory are these: Governments are not single individuals but are composed of many people and organizations with different outlooks and interests. Presidents make decisions on the basis of information and advice given them by the individuals and institutions they rely on to manage the government. Presidents' decisions are strongly influenced by the recommendations made, the options presented, the personalities of the presenters, and the power of the bureaucracies represented. Managers also compete with one another for presidential favor—and personal power—and tend to pursue the interests of their own agencies and bureaucracies, which, in turn, vie with others for institutional influence. Bureaucratic policy implementation in the end alters in content and intent the original policy.[39]

The complex, dynamic interplay of these elements within the bureaucratic structure attracts certain personality types and elicits certain kinds of individual and group behavior. Thus theorists typically say that national security managers possess a drive for power, feel the need to assert and prove their machismo, view crises as

---

[38] Larry Berman discusses the "Caligula syndrome" in *Planning a Tragedy: The Americanization of the War in Vietnam* (New York: W. W. Norton, 1982), which deals with the issue of whether President Johnson intimidated and dominated his advisers. In *Time of Torment* (New York: Random House, 1967), 62–68. I. F. Stone compares LBJ to Louis XIV.

[39] Morton H. Halperin, with the assistance of Priscilla Clap and Arnold Kanter, *Bureaucratic Politics and Foreign Policy* (Washington, D.C.: Brookings Institution, 1974); Graham T. Allison, *Essence of Decision: Explaining the Cuban Missile Crisis* (Boston: Little, Brown, 1971); Wallace Thies, *When Governments Collide: Coercion and Diplomacy in the Vietnam Conflict, 1964–1968* (Berkeley: University of California Press, 1982).

tests of toughness and will, disdain the softhearted, have proclivities for the use of military force, are tempted to mislead and deceive superiors, tend toward wishful thinking, are preoccupied with public relations, and practice groupthink. Also, they are arrogant, lack informed judgment about certain aspects of foreign and military affairs, put excessive emphasis on can-do, pragmatic, short-term problem solving, and are amoral actors in the sphere of international affairs.[40]

Concerning involvement in Vietnam, James C. Thomson, a midlevel manager himself, argued in 1968 that national security bureaucrats lacked expertise on Southeast Asia, were confused about the nature of the war, sought technocratic solutions to political problems, entertained excessive optimism, avoided dissent lest they lose their effectiveness within the government, and fell prey to executive fatigue and miscalculation. Richard Barnet, who with Thomson was an important early exponent of the theory of bureaucratic management, maintained in 1968 and 1972 that national security advisers adhered to an interventionist "operational code" of behavior rooted in their social background and the structure of the bureaucracy. Rarely if ever questioning the underlying assumptions of U.S. policy, they instead argued among themselves over the most effective means of accomplishing their policy goals—however flawed or immoral. Internal dissenters, like George Ball, who took positions deemed beyond the pale were ostracized or "domesticated," and therefore real alternatives to escalation were passed over.[41] Postwar analyses further argued that any meaningful differences between tough-minded managers tended to be compromised in the interest of superficial consensus and bureaucratic self-interest. The results varied, ranging from indecision to prolonged escalation, but in general policymakers lost their ability to recognize reality.[42] The controversial 1982 Columbia Broadcasting System television program on the role of General Westmoreland in the war claimed that he and other managers misled their superiors, constructing policy and strategy alternatives that led to both escalation and failure.[43]

The argument that bureaucratic dynamics explains U.S. involvement in the Vietnam War is valuable for its description of the structure and process of decision making and the personalities of policy managers. But it does not entirely explain why managers and bureaucrats make and pursue particular policies and not others—beyond those reasons having to do with bureaucratic dynamics.[44]

One special group of national security advisers was the military, which included special adviser Maxwell Taylor; Commander of Military Assistance Command Vietnam, William Westmoreland; the members of the Joint Chiefs of Staff; Commander in Chief Pacific Ulysses S. Grant Sharp; counterinsurgency expert

---

[40] Fredric Branfman, "Beyond the Pentagon Papers: The Pathology of Power," *Gravel Edition, The Pentagon Papers*, 5:294–313.

[41] James C. Thomson, Jr., "How Could Vietnam Happen? An Autopsy," *Atlantic Monthly* 221 (April 1968): 47–53; Richard J. Barnet, *Roots of War* (New York: Atheneum, 1972), Part I. Essays on these subjects by Thomson and Barnet appeared earlier in *No More Vietnams? The War and the Future of American Foreign Policy*, ed. Richard M. Pfeffer (New York: Harper & Row, 1968).

[42] Thies, *When Governments Collide*; Thompson, *Rolling Thunder*.

[43] "The Uncounted Enemy: A Vietnamese Deception," CBS, 23 Jan. 1982.

[44] Barnet, in *Roots of War*, does try, however, to explain the underlying social and historical causes of bureaucratic behavior.

Edward Lansdale; members of the Defense Intelligence Agency; and others. Some theorists have argued that these military professionals exerted greater influence over U.S. policy than the supposedly more cautious advisers of the State Department and the CIA, since they leaned in the direction of military escalation.

This theme takes on a much broader cast in the hands of other analysts, who identify militarism in general as a major cause of U.S. involvement. Exemplifying the militarization of America were those civilian individuals and groups who supported high military spending and interventionist foreign policies: presidential adviser Walt W. Rostow, Francis Cardinal Spellman, the McDonnell-Douglas aircraft corporation, the leadership of the AFL-CIO, and right-wing publishers and members of Congress, for example. Some theorists point to the influence of a structural phenomenon, the military-industrial-governmental complex—a term popularized by President Eisenhower and otherwise known as the national security state or the warfare state. To these analysts, the military-industrial-governmental complex refers to those individuals, groups, institutions, and classes who have vested material and psychological interests in the maintenance of high levels of weaponry and the use of military force in support of imperial, interventionist policies.[45]

Pressures and Aims:
Politics and Economics

To a greater or lesser degree, most analysts of American foreign policy give some consideration to politics and economics as causes of U.S. intervention in Vietnam. Policymakers operate in the context of political and economic systems and structures. Their thoughts and behavior reflect their political and economic milieu and, at the simplest level, they feel the pressures of domestic politics and pursue national economic aims. Theories about presidential culpability and the stalemate machine, for example, depend heavily on assumptions about domestic politics, assumptions that make up a whole explanation in themselves.

The domestic politics theory is an old but continuing approach to historical and political analysis and has many versions. In general, though, it roots policymaking in party, congressional, presidential, electioneering, ethnic, and special-interest-group politics. More specifically, its different versions link domestic politics to several strains in American culture and foreign policy tradition: namely, anti-

---

[45] Donovan, *Militarism, U.S.A.*; John Kenneth Galbraith, *How to Control the Military* (New York: New American Library, 1969); Fulbright, *The Pentagon Propaganda Machine* (New York: Vintage Books, 1971); Sidney Lens, *The Military-Industrial Complex* (Philadelphia and Kansas City: Pilgrim Press and the National Catholic Reporter, 1970); Marc Pilisuk and Thomas Hayden, "Is There a Military Industrial Complex Which Prevents Peace? Consensus and Countervailing Power in Pluralistic Systems," *Journal of Social Issues* 21 (July 1965): 67–117; *Report from Iron Mountain on the Possibility and Desirability of Peace*, with introductory material by Leonard C. Lewin (New York: Dell, 1967); "The War Game" (collected at the SDS literature table at the University of Kansas student union, Lawrence, Kan., 21 June 1969), and "U.S. Involvement in Vietnam Is Not an Accident" (collected from the Radical Student Union at the University of California at Berkeley on 11 Dec. 1969) in *Mutiny Does Not Happen Lightly: The Literature of the American Resistance*, ed. G. Louis Heath (Metuchen, N.J.: Scarecrow Press, 1976), 464–72.

communism, red-baiting, the desire for peace, isolationism, and containment. Thus, for example, Democratic Presidents intervened and escalated in Vietnam for fear of right-wing, Republican, McCarthyite criticism, in addition to their own belief in containment. Republican Presidents intervened and escalated for fear of losing a country to communism and because of their own containment convictions. Both wanted to uphold perceived U.S. responsibilities abroad while maintaining public support for the costs of those responsibilities. Neither Democratic nor Republican Presidents wanted to be the "first to lose a war." But both Democratic and Republican administrations were constrained in their ability to escalate by the "contradictory" attitudes of the American people; that is, the people wanted to win wars and to stop communism but were opposed to sending U.S. troops abroad. One respected account suggests that in 1964 President Johnson had as much reason to be concerned with congressional opposition to escalation as with pressure to escalate.[46] Another recent study argues that Johnson tried to steer a middle course between dovish and hawkish advisers, while his concern for the survival of the Great Society influenced his war strategy, having the effect of protracting the war.[47]

The domestic politics theory has great appeal, as well as much evidence to support it. It is undeniable that domestic politics, however defined, shapes foreign policy. But the theory does not explain the causes of the politics of anticommunism or the social and ideological origins of the anti-Communist right wing. Such an analysis might reveal that there are not only historical and ideological sources of anticommunism but socioeconomic ones as well. The domestic politics argument, moreover, does not come to grips with the fact that Presidents and national security managers themselves have contributed as much if not more than anyone else to stirring up anti-Communist emotions in the American people in order to persuade them to support their particular domestic and global policies.

Most economic explanations of U.S. involvement in the Vietnam War can be put under the umbrella of what may be called the theory of U.S. neocolonialism. Although its critics tend to oversimplify this approach by portraying it as simple-minded economic determinism, it is in fact a complex and varied collection of explanations. Some proponents of the theory, like Gabriel Kolko, have argued both in terms of narrow- and broad-minded economic determinism. In one study, Kolko emphasized the importance of the U.S. desire to protect its sources of raw materials in Indochina.[48] But elsewhere he traced the social roots of U.S. foreign policy to the American capitalist system and stressed the broad American "commitment to create an integrated, essentially capitalist world framework out of the chaos of World War Two and the remnants of the colonial systems."[49] William A. Williams and his

---

[46] William Conrad Gibbons, *The U.S. Government and the Vietnam War: Executive and Legislative Roles and Relationships*, Part II (Washington, D.C.: GPO, 1984), 394–97.

[47] Berman, *Planning a Tragedy*.

[48] Gabriel Kolko, *The Roots of American Foreign Policy: An Analysis of Power and Purpose* (Boston: Beacon Press, 1969).

[49] Kolko, *Anatomy of a War: Vietnam, the United States, and the Modern Historical Experience* (New York: Pantheon, 1985), 73; Joyce and Gabriel Kolko, *The Limits of Power: The World and United States Foreign Policy, 1945–1954* (New York: Harper & Row, 1972).

students have spoken of a broad socioeconomic determinism rooted not only in the American class system but also in ideological traditions of expansionism. The result for America and the world has been since at least the turn of the century a policy that has largely rejected old-style imperialism—that is, late-nineteenth-century colonialism—in favor of "indirect imperialism." This neocolonialism adds up to a policy of opening doors abroad to investments, raw materials, and markets that benefit corporate America and produce economic, political, and cultural hegemony.[50] Some theorists argue that the internal dynamics of capitalism inevitably lead to policies of imperialism and intervention, while others say that these policies were only the product of a faulty perception of necessity and that there were in reality other choices.

In general, the theory of American neocolonialism maintains that U.S. intervention was not the result of the economic importance of Vietnam itself to the United States—for it was not that important—but came about because American leaders believed the Vietnamese revolution, as a leftist, nationalistic revolution, posed a threat to the global capitalist system they had brought into being after World War II. Policymakers thought it necessary to defeat the Vietnamese revolution in order to demonstrate their will and ability to put down leftist threats. Their real fear was not of military danger to the United States or to Asia but of allowing the dangerous precedent of a successful revolution that took Vietnam out of the orbit of American influence, thereby inspiring other revolutionaries.

In postwar Vietnam, the neocolonial theory is commonplace—just as it was during the war. Even though some Vietnamese express visceral bewilderment about the reasons for America's military intervention,[51] the predominant official and academic explanation emphasizes neocolonial motives, as well as some other factors, including imperial Presidents, domestic politics, and militarism.[52]

---

[50] William Appleman Williams, Thomas McCormick, Lloyd Gardner, and Walter LaFeber, *America in Vietnam: A Documentary History* (New York: Anchor Press, 1985). See also Noam Chomsky, *At War with Asia: Essays on Indochina* (New York: Vintage Books, 1970); Noam Chomsky, *The Political Economy of Human Rights*, 2 vols. (Boston: South End Press, 1979); Lloyd C. Gardner, *Approaching Vietnam: From World War II through Dienbienphu, 1941–1954* (New York: W. W. Norton, 1988); Felix Greene, *The Enemy: What Every American Should Know about Imperialism* (New York: Vintage Books, 1970); Archimedes L. A. Patti, *Why Vietnam? Prelude to America's Albatross* (Berkeley: University of California Press, 1980); Andrew J. Rotter, *The Path to Vietnam: Origins of the American Commitment to Southeast Asia* (Ithaca: Cornell University Press, 1987); and Paul M. Sweezy, Leo Huberman, and Harry Magdoff, *Vietnam: The Endless War* (New York: Monthly Review Press, 1970).

[51] Do Xuan Oanh, Director, Viet-My Society, Hanoi, interview by J. P. Kimball and Educators' Delegation No. 4, 3 Jan. 1988, tape recording and notes.

[52] General Vo Nguyen Giap, "The Liberation War in South Vietnam: Its Essential Characteristics," in *South Vietnam, 1954–1965: Articles and Documents, Vietnamese Studies*, no. 8 (Hanoi: N.p. 1966), 5–11; Nguyen Khanh Toan, "Victory over Fascism: A Decisive Turning Point in the Transition from Capitalism to Socialism," *Viet Nam Social Sciences* 2, 4 (1985): 1–14; Nguyen Khac Vien, "A Short History of U.S. Neo-colonialism," *Glimpses of U.S. Neo-colonialism*, Vol. I: *Neo-colonialism and Global Strategy*, ed. Nguyen Khac Vien, *Vietnamese Studies*, no. 26 (Hanoi: Foreign Languages Publishing House, 1970); Nguyen Khac Vien, *Contemporary Vietnam: 1858–1980* (Hanoi: Foreign Languages Publishing House, 1981); Nguyen Can, Deputy Director of North American Department, Vietnam Foreign Ministry, Hanoi, interview by J. P. Kimball and Educators' Delegation No. 4, 2 Jan. 1988, tape recording and notes.

The central analytical problem of the theory is that of describing the links between the corporate elite and the policymaking elite.[53] Some critics have also insisted that the theory takes too little notice of the self-perpetuating role of ideas in the making of foreign policy and places too much emphasis on the social and economic basis of ideas.[54]

Ways of Living:
Cultural Misunderstanding and Conflict

Another complex set of theories comes under the heading of culture, "one of the two or three most complicated words in the English language," according to Raymond Williams.[55] In general, those writers who self-consciously employ a cultural analysis understand culture to mean the interrelated system of ideas, values, language, politics, institutions, social relationships, economy, and technology that defines a people's way of life, enabling them to exploit and make sense of their environment and give order to their society.[56]

But in the hands of different authors, the cultural approach moves along different paths. Each places emphasis on some elements of culture more than on others. In *Backfire*, for example, Loren Baritz implicitly defines culture as the combined product of ideas, myths, politics, bureaucracy, and technology (but not apparently of economics). To explain American involvement in Vietnam, he emphasized Americans' nationalistic, missionary idealism, their anti-Communist, cold war politics, and their ethnocentric misunderstanding and ignorance of Vietnamese culture, language, and history. He also unearthed the roots of U.S. intervention in an American culture of strategic fads, weapons and warrior cults, technocracy, belief in omnipotence, bureaucratic ignorance, and egotistical pride and frustration. In the hands of Frances FitzGerald in her classic 1972 study, *Fire in the Lake*, the theme of ethnocentricity became an overarching one of cultural clash between the individualistic, capitalist Western culture of the United States and the communal, Confucian-Buddhist culture of Vietnam, which was in the throes of an indigenous social and political revolution when the United States intervened.[57] In *Ideology and Foreign Policy* Michael H. Hunt treated American ideology as the prime manifestation of American culture. A culture-bound, color-conscious, paternalistic, cru-

---

[53] Sympathetic with the theory of neocolonialism, Ellsberg writes, however: "If these studies...seem far from satisfactory, perhaps the main reason is that they tend to neglect the roles both of the bureaucracy and...of the U.S. domestic political system, including the special role of the President." *Papers on the War*, p. 11. Also sympathetic, but wanting to find links between the economic and governing elites, Paul Joseph, in *Cracks in the Empire: State Politics in the Vietnam War* (Boston: South End Press, 1981), analyzes U.S. intervention in Vietnam on the basis of capitalist "policy currents" in government.

[54] Hunt, *Ideology and U.S. Foreign Policy*, Chap. 1.

[55] Raymond Williams, *Keywords: A Vocabulary of Culture and Society* (New York: Oxford University Press, 1976), 76.

[56] See Daniel J. Singal's definition in *The War Within: From Victorian to Modernist Thought in the South, 1919–1945* (Chapel Hill: University of North Carolina Press, 1982), p. 6.

[57] FitzGerald, *Fire in the Lake: The Vietnamese and the Americans in Vietnam* (New York: Vintage Books, 1972); Kearns, *Lyndon Johnson*, 265–66.

sading, technological world view led America to fight a "frightfully expensive and destructive...war in a small and distant country where no tangible interests were at stake and where the central justifications for American involvement were...ultimately based on faith."[58] John Hellman examined cultural ideas as expressed in literary and popular myths. The American myths of the reforming mission, the frontier hero, and the errand in the wilderness—among others, he writes—played themselves out in Americans' sojourns in Vietnam.[59] To Rufus Brooks, a character in John M. Del Vecchio's novel of combat, *The 13th Valley*, the cause of war was simple and fundamental: its source was the Western language tradition, which analyzes phenomena by breaking them down into dichotomous, polarized components, skewing our perceptions and rhetoric toward images and words of confrontation and conflict.[60]

With so many competing theories of American intervention in Vietnam, it seems doubtful that a consensus will emerge soon. The pattern of disagreement in the evolution of Vietnam War debate appears reasonably clear, however. It resembles one identified by Thomas Pressly many years ago in connection with the American Civil War. Pressly suggested that the theoretical disagreements between historians and others in the years and decades after that war merely repeated arguments that had first appeared during the war.[61] This also seems to be the case for the Vietnam conflict. It is striking that each one of the theories discussed above surfaced sometime in the period from 1945 to 1975 and has been repeated since in more or less elaborate form and subdued tones by historians, political scientists, journalists, policymakers, and other members of the intelligentsia. Some theories are better than others in the sense of possessing sounder logic and better evidence. Still, as long as there are adherents to a theory, it lives. Most academics would probably maintain that the official argument is on the whole false and not worthy of serious consideration. Yet others continue to use it to explain why the U.S. government intervened in Vietnam and should intervene in other "Vietnams."

There are several reasons for the continuing disagreement. To begin with, the task of understanding human motivation and reconstructing complex past events is inherently difficult—a difficulty compounded by the incompleteness of the documentary record. Further, those who try to explain history are captives of their own ideology and theoretical perspective, leading them to pose questions, perceive events, and define historical meaning differently.[62] These varying ideological and theoretical perspectives reflect deep-rooted social, political, and intellectual currents in

[58] Hunt, *Ideology and U.S. Foreign Policy*, 173–74.

[59] John Hellman, *American Myth and the Legacy of Vietnam* (New York: Columbia University Press, 1986).

[60] John M. Del Vecchio, *The 13th Valley* (New York: Bantam Books, 1982), 556–65.

[61] Thomas J. Pressly, *Americans Interpret Their Civil War* (New York: Free Press, 1962).

[62] Kimball, "The Influence of Ideology on Interpretive Disagreement: A Report on a Survey of Diplomatic, Military, and Peace Historians on the Causes of 20th Century U.S. Wars, *The History Teacher* 17 (May 1984): 355–85.

American culture, and the alleged neutrality of hindsight rarely succeeds in replacing subjectivity. In addition, different generations have dissimilar memories of the "Vietnam experience." Even members of the "Vietnam generation," who came of age during the tumultuous war era, experienced diverse realities of the war and now as then hold conflicting opinions about it.[63] Helping to keep the pot boiling are the policymakers and political parties who use history to plan and justify competing foreign policies. In the postwar era some policymakers defend American involvement in Vietnam, blame its failure on the doves, and uphold the practicality and necessity of third-world interventions. Aligned against them are other officials who question America's involvement in Vietnam, blame its failure on the difficulty of fighting a popular revolution in a faraway jungle, and advocate caution in future interventions.

Even though the enormity of the task of understanding the debate and searching for truth has led some to despair of trying, and a few have expressed fear of drawing the wrong lessons,[64] it is still important for scholars, students, and the citizenry—using logic, evidence, and a knowledge of the arguments—to continue to reason why the United States intervened in Indochina. While there will probably never be agreement on fundamental issues of perspective and ideology, it is worth noting that many of the theories are not mutually exclusive. Perhaps one day it will be possible to combine some of these ideas into an eclectic synthesis. But if the writing of history is in fact an argument without end, so be it. To know how and why Americans and others disagree on crucial issues of international history is almost as important as knowing that history. And knowing the theories, dissecting them, and holding them up to scrutiny may allow us to understand better, if not fully explain, the facts we know now and those we will discover in the future.

[63] Center for the Study of the Vietnam Generation, *Enduring Legacies: Expressions from the Hearts and Minds of the Vietnam Generation* (Washington, D.C.: Center for the New Leadership, 1987).

[64] Samuel P. Huntington, comments in *No More Vietnams?* ed. Pfeffer, 1–2.

PART ONE

The Official View
The U.S. Government's Public Explanation

If Indochina went Communist, Red pressure would increase on Malaya, Thailand, and Indonesia and other Asian nations. The main target of the Communists in Indochina, as it was in Korea, is Japan. Conquest of areas so vital to Japan's economy would reduce Japan to an economic satellite of the Soviet Union.

—Vice President Richard M. Nixon, 1954

Vietnam represents the cornerstone of the Free World in Southeast Asia, the keystone to the arch, the finger in the dike. Burma, Thailand, India, Japan, the Philippines and obviously Laos and Cambodia are among those whose security would be threatened if the red tide of Communism overflowed into Vietnam.

—Senator John F. Kennedy, 1956

We will keep our commitments from South Vietnam to West Berlin.

—President Lyndon B. Johnson, 1963

1

THE MUNICH ANALOGY AND THE INTERNATIONAL COMMUNIST CONSPIRACY

HARRY S. TRUMAN

Many speak for the government, but Presidents speak with the loudest voices. On 11 April 1951, President Truman addressed the nation "to talk...plainly...about what we are doing in Korea and about our policy in the Far East." It was eleven months after the United States began direct grants of military and economic aid to the French in Indochina (May 1950), ten months after the outbreak of the Korean War (June 1950), and the same day on which Truman relieved General Douglas MacArthur of his command in Korea. Truman hoped to reaffirm the necessity of American military commitments in Asia, while rebuking MacArthur for having publicly challenged U.S. policy through his advocacy of drastic offensive measures against China. He portrayed communism as monolithic and aggressive, located the source of aggression in the Soviet Union and China, linked events in Korea, Indochina, and elsewhere, appealed to World War II analogies, and associated the United States with the fight for freedom and the cause of peace. Having built a case for containment, he nevertheless warned of the dangers of general war if military strikes were launched against China.

...The Communists in the Kremlin are engaged in a monstrous conspiracy to stamp out freedom all over the world. If they were to succeed, the United States would be numbered among their principal victims. It must be clear to everyone that the United States cannot—and will not—sit idly by and await foreign conquest. The only question is: What is the best time to meet the threat and how is the best way to meet it?

The best time to meet the threat is in the beginning. It is easier to put out a fire in the beginning when it is small than after it has become a roaring blaze. And

Harry S. Truman, "Radio Report to the American People on Korea and on U.S. Policy in the Far East, 11 Apr. 1951," No. 78, *Public Papers of the Presidents of the United States: Harry S. Truman, 1951* (Washington, D.C.: GPO, 1965), 223–25.

the best way to meet the threat of aggression is for the peace-loving nations to act together. If they don't act together, they are likely to be picked off, one by one.

If they had followed the right policies in the 1930's—if the free countries had acted together to crush the aggression of the dictators, and if they had acted in the beginning when the aggression was small—there probably would have been no World War II.

If history has taught us anything, it is that aggression anywhere in the world is a threat to the peace everywhere in the world. When that aggression is supported by the cruel and selfish rulers of a powerful nation who are bent on conquest, it becomes a clear and present danger to the security and independence of every free nation.

This is a lesson that most people in this country have learned thoroughly. This is the basic reason why we joined in creating the United Nations. And, since the end of World War II, we have been putting that lesson into practice—we have been working with other free nations to check the aggressive designs of the Soviet Union before they can result in a third world war.

That is what we did in Greece, when that nation was threatened by the aggression of international communism.

The attack against Greece could have led to general war. But this country came to the aid of Greece. The United Nations supported Greek resistance. With our help, the determination and efforts of the Greek people defeated the attack on the spot.

Another big Communist threat to peace was the Berlin blockade. That too could have led to war. But again it was settled because free men would not back down in an emergency.

The aggression against Korea is the boldest and most dangerous move the Communists have yet made.

The attack on Korea was part of a greater plan for conquering all of Asia.

I would like to read to you from a secret intelligence report which came to us after the attack on Korea. It is a report of a speech a Communist army officer in North Korea gave to a group of spies and saboteurs last May, 1 month before South Korea was invaded. The report shows in great detail how this invasion was part of a carefully prepared plot. Here, in part, is what the Communist officer, who had been trained in Moscow, told his men: "Our forces," he said, "are scheduled to attack South Korean forces about the middle of June. The coming attack on South Korea marks the first step toward the liberation of Asia."

Notice that he used the word "liberation." This is Communist doubletalk meaning "conquest."

I have another secret intelligence report here. This one tells what another Communist officer in the Far East told his men several months before the invasion of Korea. Here is what he said: "In order to successfully undertake the long-awaited world revolution, we must first unify Asia. . . . Java, Indochina, Malaya, India, Tibet, Thailand, Philippines, and Japan are our ultimate targets. . . . The United States is the only obstacle on our road for the liberation of all the countries in southeast Asia. In other words, we must unify the people of Asia and crush the United States." Again, "liberation" in "commie" language means conquest.

That is what the Communist leaders are telling their people, and that is what they have been trying to do.

They want to control all Asia from the Kremlin.

This plan of conquest is in flat contradiction to what we believe. We believe that Korea belongs to the Koreans, we believe that India belongs to the Indians, we believe that all the nations of Asia should be free to work out their affairs in their own way. This is the basis of peace in the Far East, and it is the basis of peace everywhere else.

The whole Communist imperialism is back of the attack on peace in the Far East. It was the Soviet Union that trained and equipped the North Koreans for aggression. The Chinese Communists massed 44 well-trained and well-equipped divisions on the Korean frontier. These were the troops they threw into battle when the North Korean Communists were beaten.

The question we have had to face is whether the Communist plan of conquest can be stopped without a general war. Our Government and other countries associated with us in the United Nations believe that the best chance of stopping it without a general war is to meet the attack in Korea and defeat it there.

That is what we have been doing. It is a difficult and bitter task.

But so far it has been successful.

So far, we have prevented world war III.

So far, by fighting a limited war in Korea, we have prevented aggression from succeeding, and bringing on a general war. And the ability of the whole free world to resist Communist aggression has been greatly improved.

We have taught the enemy a lesson. He has found that aggression is not cheap or easy. Moreover, men all over the world who want to remain free have been given new courage and new hope. They know now that the champions of freedom can stand up and fight, and that they will stand up and fight.

Our resolute stand in Korea is helping the forces of freedom now fighting in Indochina and other countries in that part of the world. It has already slowed down the timetable of conquest.

In Korea itself there are signs that the enemy is building up his ground forces for a new mass offensive. We also know that there have been large increases in the enemy's available air forces.

If a new attack comes, I feel confident it will be turned back. The United Nations fighting forces are tough and able and well equipped. They are fighting for a just cause. They are proving to all the world that the principle of collective security will work. We are proud of all these forces for the magnificent job they have done against heavy odds. We pray that their efforts may succeed, for upon their success may hinge the peace of the world.

The Communist side must now choose its course of action. The Communist rulers may press the attack against us. They may take further action which will spread the conflict. They have that choice, and with it the awful responsibility for what may follow. The Communists also have the choice of a peaceful settlement which could lead to a general relaxation of the tensions in the Far East. The decision is theirs, because the forces of the United Nations will strive to limit the conflict if possible.

We do not want to see the conflict in Korea extended. We are trying to prevent a world war—not to start one. And the best way to do that is to make it plain that we and the other free countries will continue to resist the attack.

But you may ask why can't we take other steps to punish the aggressor. Why don't we bomb Manchuria and China itself? Why don't we assist the Chinese Nationalist troops to land on the mainland of China?

If we were to do these things we would be running a very grave risk of starting a general war. If that were to happen, we would have brought about the exact situation we are trying to prevent.

If we were to do these things, we would become entangled in a vast conflict on the continent of Asia and our task would become immeasurably more difficult all over the world.

What would suit the ambitions of the Kremlin better than for our military forces to be committed to a full-scale war with Red China?...

2

FALLING DOMINOES

DWIGHT D. EISENHOWER

In a press conference on 7 April 1954, at a time when the battle of Dienbienphu was raging and a month before the Geneva Conference on Indochina was to begin, President Eisenhower defined the importance of Vietnam in terms of freedom, raw materials, and the domino theory.

Dwight D. Eisenhower, "The President's News Conference of April 7, 1954," No. 73, *Public Papers of the Presidents of the United States: Dwight D. Eisenhower, 1954* (Washington, D.C.: GPO, 1960), 382–83.

Q: Robert Richards, Copley Press: Mr. President, would you mind commenting on the strategic importance of Indochina to the free world? I think there has been, across the country, some lack of understanding of just what it means to us.

THE PRESIDENT: You have, of course, both the specific and the general when you talk about such things.

First of all, you have the specific value of a locality in its production of materials that the world needs.

Then you have the possibility that many human beings pass under a dictatorship that is inimical to the free world.

Finally, you have broader considerations that might follow what you would call the "falling domino" principle. You have a row of dominoes set up, you knock over the first one, and what will happen to the last one is the certainty that it will go over very quickly. So you could have a beginning of a disintegration that would have the most profound influences.

Now, with respect to the first one, two of the items from this particular area that the world uses are tin and tungsten. They are very important. There are others, of course, the rubber plantations and so on.

Then with respect to more people passing under this domination, Asia, after all, has already lost some 450 million of its peoples to the Communist dictatorship, and we simply can't afford greater losses.

But when we come to the possible sequence of events, the loss of Indochina, of Burma, of Thailand, of the Peninsula, and Indonesia following, now you begin to talk about areas that not only multiply the disadvantages that you would suffer through loss of materials, sources of materials, but now you are talking really about millions and millions and millions of people.

Finally, the geographical position achieved thereby does many things. It turns the so-called island defensive chain of Japan, Formosa, of the Philippines and to the southward; it moves in to threaten Australia and New Zealand.

It takes away, in its economic aspects, that region that Japan must have as a trading area or Japan, in turn, will have only one place in the world to go—that is, toward the Communist areas in order to live.

So, the possible consequences of the loss are just incalculable to the free world....

3

CAPITALIST VS. COMMUNIST ECONOMIC GROWTH

DWIGHT D. EISENHOWER

*Beginning in 1955, the United States pursued a policy on building" in South
Vietnam through direct and extensive economic aid to President Ngo Dinh Diem's
embattled government. By May 1960 there would also be 327 U.S. military personnel in
South Vietnam; by December 1960, 900. In April 1959, while defending the Pentagon
budget and programs of U.S. economic and military assistance to foreign governments,
Eisenhower again talked about military security, freedom, the domino principle, and
economic factors. This time, however, his economic reasoning was not as crudely expressed
as it had been five years earlier when he had spoken of the importance of Indochina's
raw materials. Eisenhower now put the economic question in terms of a world struggle
between different models for growth in developing countries, contrasting methods of
international capitalist investment with those of internal socialist investment. Linking the
former with freedom, he portrayed the latter negatively.*

...We must study, think, and decide on the governmental program that we term
"Mutual Security."

The true need and value of this program will be recognized by our people only
if they can answer this question: "Why should America, at heavy and immediate
sacrifice to herself, assist many other nations, particularly the less developed ones,
in achieving greater moral, economic, and military strength?"

What are the facts?

The first and most important fact is the implacable and frequently expressed
purpose of imperialistic communism to promote world revolution, destroy freedom, and communize the world.

Dwight D. Eisenhower, "Address at the Gettysburg College Convocation: The Importance of Understanding, April 4, 1959," No. 71, *Public Papers of the Presidents of the United States: Dwight D. Eisenhower,
1959* (Washington, D.C.: GPO, 1960), 310–13.

Its methods are all-inclusive, ranging through the use of propaganda, political subversion, economic penetration, and the use or the threat of force.

The second fact is that our country is today spending an aggregate of about 47 billion dollars annually for the single purpose of preserving the nation's position and security in the world. This includes the costs of the Defense Department, the production of nuclear weapons, and mutual security. All three are mutually supporting and are blended into one program for our safety. The size of this cost conveys something of the entire program's importance—to the world and, indeed, to each of us.

And when I think of this importance to us, think of it in this one material figure, this cost annually for every single man, woman, and child of the entire nation is about 275 dollars a year.

The next fact we note is that since the Communist target is the world, every nation is comprehended in their campaign for domination. The weak and the most exposed stand in the most immediate danger.

Another fact, that we ignore to our peril, is that if aggression or subversion against the weaker of the free nations should achieve successive victories, communism would step-by-step overcome once free areas. The danger, even to the strongest, would become increasingly menacing.

Clearly, the self-interest of each free nation impels it to resist the loss to imperialistic communism of the freedom and independence of any other nation.

Freedom is truly indivisible.

To apply some of these truths to a particular case, let us consider, briefly, the country of Viet-Nam, and the importance to us of the security and progress of that country.

It is located, as you know, in the southeastern corner of Asia, exactly halfway round the world from Gettysburg College.

Viet-Nam is a country divided into two parts—like Korea and Germany. The southern half, with its twelve million people, is free, but poor. It is an underdeveloped country—its economy is weak—average individual income being less than $200 a year. The northern half has been turned over to communism. A line of demarcation running along the 17th parallel separates the two. To the north of this line stand several Communist divisions. These facts pose to South Viet-Nam two great tasks: self-defense and economic growth.

Understandably, the people of Viet-Nam want to make their country a thriving, self-sufficient member of the family of nations. This means economic expansion.

For Viet-Nam's economic growth, the acquisition of capital is vitally necessary. Now, the nation could create the capital needed for growth by stealing from the already meager rice bowls of its people and regimenting them into work battalions. This enslavement is the commune system—adopted by the new overlords of Red China. It would mean, of course, the loss of freedom within the country without any hostile outside action whatsoever.

Another way for Viet-Nam to get the necessary capital is through private investments from the outside, and through governmental loans and, where necessary, grants from other and more fortunately situated nations.

In either of these ways the economic problem of Viet-Nam could be solved. But only the second way can preserve freedom.

And there is still the other of Viet-Nam's great problems—how to support the military forces it needs without crushing its economy.

Because of the proximity of large Communist military formations in the North, Free Viet-Nam must maintain substantial numbers of men under arms. Moreover, while the government has shown real progress in cleaning out Communist guerillas, those remaining continue to be a disruptive influence in the nation's life.

Unassisted, Viet-Nam cannot at this time produce and support the military formations essential to it, or, equally important, the morale—the hope, the confidence, the pride—necessary to meet the dual threat of aggression from without and subversion within its borders.

Still another fact! Strategically, South Viet-Nam's capture by the Communists would bring their power several hundred miles into a hitherto free region. The remaining countries in Southeast Asia would be menaced by a great flanking movement. The freedom of twelve million people would be lost immediately, and that of 150 million others in adjacent lands would be seriously endangered. The loss of South Viet-Nam would set in motion a crumbling process that could, as it progressed, have grave consequences for us and for freedom.

Viet-Nam must have a reasonable degree of safety now—both for her people and for her property. Because of these facts, military as well as economic help is currently needed in Viet-Nam.

We reach the inescapable conclusion that our own national interests demand some help from us in sustaining in Viet-Nam the morale, the economic progress, and the military strength necessary to its continued existence in freedom.

Viet-Nam is just one example. One-third of the world's people face a similar challenge. All through Africa and Southern Asia people struggle to preserve liberty and improve their standards of living, to maintain their dignity as humans. It is imperative that they succeed.

But some uninformed Americans believe that we should turn our backs on these people, our friends. Our costs and taxes are very real, while the difficulties of other peoples often seem remote from us.

But the costs of continuous neglect of these problems would be far more than we must now bear—indeed more than we could afford. The added costs would be paid not only in vastly increased outlays of money, but in larger drafts of our youth into the Military Establishment, and in terms of increased danger to our own security and prosperity.

No matter what areas of Federal spending must be curtailed—and some should—our safety comes first. Since that safety is necessarily based upon a sound and thriving economy, its protection must equally engage our earnest attention.

4

WARS OF NATIONAL LIBERATION

JOHN F. KENNEDY

*On 20 December 1960 southern insurgents established the National Front for the
Liberation of South Vietnam, better known as the National Liberation Front, or
NLF. In January 1961 Nikita Khrushchev declared that the Soviet Union would
support movements of national liberation. Engaged in negotiations over the fighting in
neighboring Laos, President Kennedy was nonetheless determined to continue the
struggle in Vietnam. He told the General Assembly of the United Nations in
September 1961 that wars of national liberation were really wars of aggression,
which the United States opposed in the name of peace and freedom. In later years,
after Kennedy's death, other Presidents and their advisers would emphasize the threat
of third-world guerrilla wars of liberation as well. They would claim that American
intervention in South Vietnam was a critical test case of whether this new technique
of Communist aggression would succeed.*

...[A]s President of the United States, I consider it my duty to report to this Assembly on two threats to the peace which are not on your crowded agenda, but
which causes us, and most of you, the deepest concern.

The first threat on which I wish to report is widely misunderstood: the smol-
dering coals of war in Southeast Asia. South Viet-Nam is already under attack—
sometimes by a single assassin, sometimes by a band of guerrillas, recently by full
battalions. The peaceful borders of Burma, Cambodia, and India have been repeatedly violated. And the peaceful people of Laos are in danger of losing the independence they gained not so long ago.

No one can call these "wars of liberation." For these are free countries living
under their own governments. Nor are these aggressions any less real because men
are knifed in their homes and not shot in the fields of battle.

John F. Kennedy, "Address in New York City Before the General Assembly of the United Nations,
September 25, 1961," No. 387, *Public Papers of the Presidents of the United States: John F. Kennedy, 1961*
(Washington, D.C.: GPO, 1962), 624.

The very simple question confronting the world community is whether measures can be devised to protect the small and the weak from such tactics. For if they are successful in Laos and South Viet-Nam, the gates will be opened wide.

The United States seeks for itself no base, no territory, no special position in this area of any kind. We support a truly neutral and independent Laos, its people free from outside interference, living at peace with themselves and with their neighbors, assured that their territory will not be used for attacks on others, and under a government comparable (as Mr. Khrushchev and I agreed at Vienna) to Cambodia and Burma.

But now the negotiations over Laos are reaching a crucial stage. The cease-fire is at best precarious. The rainy season is coming to an end. Laotian territory is being used to infiltrate South Viet-Nam. The world community must recognize—and all those who are involved—that this potent threat to Laotian peace and freedom is indivisible from all other threats to their own....

5

CHINESE DOMINOES

JOHN F. KENNEDY

In September 1963, when anchormen Chet Huntley and David Brinkley interviewed Kennedy for NBC television news, there were 16,000 U.S. military "advisers" in South Vietnam, Buddhists and students in Saigon had been demonstrating against the government since May, and Diem's Army of the Republic of Vietnam had lost battles and territory to the Vietcong, or People's Liberation Armed Forces, the army of the NLF. Some in Congress were also questioning the validity of the domino theory.

John F. Kennedy, "Transcript of Broadcast on NBC's 'Huntley-Brinkley Report,' September 9, 1963," No. 349, *Public Papers of the Presidents of the United States: John F. Kennedy, 1963* (Washington, D.C.: GPO, 1964), 658–59.

Expressing belief in the idea, Kennedy talked about the threat of China, not the Soviet Union.

MR. HUNTLEY: Mr. President, in respect to our difficulties in South Viet-Nam, could it be that our Government tends occasionally to get locked into a policy or an attitude and then finds it difficult to alter or shift that policy?

THE PRESIDENT: Yes, that is true. I think in the case of South Viet-Nam we have been dealing with a government which is in control, has been in control for 10 years. In addition, we have felt for the last 2 years that the struggle against the Communists was going better. Since June, however, the difficulties with the Buddhists, we have been concerned about a deterioration, particularly in the Saigon area, which hasn't been felt greatly in the outlying areas but may spread. So we are faced with the problem of wanting to protect the area against the Communists. On the other hand, we have to deal with the government there. That produces a kind of ambivalence in our efforts which exposes us to some criticism. We are using our influence to persuade the government there to take those steps which will win back support. That takes some time and we must be patient, we must persist.

MR. HUNTLEY: Are we likely to reduce our aid to South Viet-Nam now?

THE PRESIDENT: I don't think we think that would be helpful at this time. If you reduce your aid, it is possible you could have some effect upon the government structure there. On the other hand, you might have a situation which could bring about a collapse. Strongly in our mind is what happened in the case of China at the end of World War II, where China was lost, a weak government became increasingly unable to control events. We don't want that.

MR. BRINKLEY: Mr. President, have you had any reason to doubt this so-called "domino theory," that if South Viet-Nam falls, the rest of southeast Asia will go behind it?

THE PRESIDENT: No, I believe it. I believe it. I think that the struggle is close enough. China is so large, looms so high just beyond the frontiers, that if South Viet-Nam went, it would not only give them an improved geographic position for a guerrilla assault on Malaya, but would also give the impression that the wave of the future in southeast Asia was China and the Communists. So I believe it.

6

COMMITMENT AND CREDIBILITY

LYNDON B. JOHNSON

Fearing that South Vietnam was near collapse, President Johnson had authorized the sustained bombing of North Vietnam in February 1965 and sent the first official U.S. combat troops to the south in March. In April and May, faced with mounting international and domestic criticism of military escalation, the administration launched a peace offensive consisting of speeches and a temporary bombing halt. Speaking at Johns Hopkins University on 7 April 1965, Johnson proposed an economic development plan for Indochina to be funded by the United States. But the United States was unprepared to begin concrete negotiations. The proposal was designed more to outmaneuver domestic opposition than to establish a basis for negotiation, because it treated North and South Vietnam as separate nations and rejected the key concern of the other side: Vietnam's unification. Johnson's speech was also noteworthy because of the reasons he gave for American involvement in his opening remarks. While restating themes advocated by previous Presidents, Johnson stressed the role of North Vietnam as aggressor, the importance of upholding the American commitment to South Vietnam, and the necessity of maintaining the credibility of America's promises.

...I have come here to review once again with my own people the views of the American Government.

Tonight Americans and Asians are dying for a world where each people may choose its own path to change.

This is the principle for which our ancestors fought in the valleys of Pennsylvania. It is the principle for which our sons fight tonight in the jungles of Viet-Nam.

Viet-Nam is far away from this quiet campus. We have no territory there, nor do we seek any. The war is dirty and brutal and difficult. And some 400 young men,

Lyndon B. Johnson, "Address at Johns Hopkins University: 'Peace Without Conquest,' April 7, 1965," No. 172, *Public Papers of the Presidents of the United States: Lyndon B. Johnson, 1965*, Book 1 (Washington, D.C.: GPO, 1966), 394–96.

born into an America that is bursting with opportunity and promise, have ended their lives on Viet-Nam's steaming soil.

Why must we take this painful road?

Why must this Nation hazard its ease, and its interest, and its power for the sake of a people so far away?

We fight because we must fight if we are to live in a world where every country can shape its own destiny. And only in such a world will our own freedom be finally secure.

This kind of world will never be built by bombs or bullets. Yet the infirmities of man are such that force must often precede reason, and the waste of war, the works of peace.

We wish that this were not so. But we must deal with the world as it is, if it is ever to be as we wish.

THE NATURE OF THE CONFLICT

The world as it is in Asia is not a serene or peaceful place.

The first reality is that North Viet-Nam has attacked the independent nation of South Viet-Nam. Its object is total conquest.

Of course, some of the people of South Viet-Nam are participating in attack on their own government. But trained men and supplies, orders and arms, flow in a constant stream from north to south.

This support is the heartbeat of the war.

And it is a war of unparalleled brutality. Simple farmers are the targets of assassination and kidnapping. Women and children are strangled in the night because their men are loyal to their government. And helpless villages are ravaged by sneak attacks. Large-scale raids are conducted on towns, and terror strikes in the heart of cities.

The confused nature of this conflict cannot mask the fact that it is the new face of an old enemy.

Over this war—and all Asia—is another reality: the deepening shadow of Communist China. The rulers in Hanoi are urged on by Peking. This is a regime which has destroyed freedom in Tibet, which has attacked India, and has been condemned by the United Nations for aggression in Korea. It is a nation which is helping the forces of violence in almost every continent. The contest in Viet-Nam is part of a wider pattern of aggressive purposes.

WHY ARE WE IN VIET-NAM?

Why are these realities our concern? Why are we in South Viet-Nam?

We are there because we have a promise to keep. Since 1954 every American President has offered support to the people of South Viet-Nam. We have helped to build, and we have helped to defend. Thus, over many years, we have made a national pledge to help South Viet-Nam defend its independence.

And I intend to keep that promise.

To dishonor that pledge, to abandon this small and brave nation to its enemies, and to the terror that must follow, would be an unforgivable wrong.

We are also there to strengthen world order. Around the globe, from Berlin to Thailand, are people whose well-being rests, in part, on the belief that they can count on us if they are attacked. To leave Viet-Nam to its fate would shake the confidence of all these people in the value of an American commitment and in the value of America's word. The result would be increased unrest and instability, and even wider war.

We are also there because there are great stakes in the balance. Let no one think for a moment that retreat from Viet-Nam would bring an end to conflict. The battle would be renewed in one country and then another. The central lesson of our time is that the appetite of aggression is never satisfied. To withdraw from one battlefield means only to prepare for the next. We must say in southeast Asia—as we did in Europe—in the words of the Bible: "Hitherto shalt thou come, but no further."

There are those who say that all our effort there will be futile—that China's power is such that it is bound to dominate all southeast Asia. But there is no end to that argument until all of the nations of Asia are swallowed up.

There are those who wonder why we have a responsibility there. Well, we have it there for the same reason that we have a responsibility for the defense of Europe. World War II was fought in both Europe and Asia, and when it ended we found ourselves with continued responsibility for the defense of freedom.

OUR OBJECTIVE IN VIET-NAM

Our objective is the independence of South Viet-Nam, and its freedom from attack. We want nothing for ourselves—only that the people of South Viet-Nam be allowed to guide their own country in their own way.

We will do everything necessary to reach that objective. And we will do only what is absolutely necessary.

In recent months attacks on South Viet-Nam were stepped up. Thus, it became necessary for us to increase our response and to make attacks by air. This is not a change of purpose. It is a change in what we believe that purpose requires.

We do this in order to slow down aggression.

We do this to increase the confidence of the brave people of South Viet-Nam who have bravely borne this brutal battle for so many years with so many casualties.

And we do this to convince the leaders of North Viet-Nam—and all who seek to share their conquest—of a very simple fact:

We will not be defeated.

We will not grow tired.

We will not withdraw, either openly or under the cloak of a meaningless agreement.

We know that air attacks alone will not accomplish all of these purposes. But it is our best and prayerful judgment that they are a necessary part of the surest road to peace.

We hope that peace will come swiftly. But that is in the hands of others besides ourselves. And we must be prepared for a long continued conflict. It will require patience as well as bravery, the will to endure as well as the will to resist.

I wish it were possible to convince others with words of what we now find it necessary to say with guns and planes: Armed hostility is futile. Our resources are equal to any challenge. Because we fight for values and we fight for principles, rather than territory or colonies, our patience and our determination are unending.

Once this is clear, then it should also be clear that the only path for reasonable men is the path of peaceful settlement.

Such peace demands an independent South Viet-Nam—securely guaranteed and able to shape its own relationships to all others—free from outside interference—tied to no alliance—a military base for no other country.

These are the essentials of any final settlement.

We will never be second in the search for such a peaceful settlement in Viet-Nam.

There may be many ways to this kind of peace: in discussion or negotiation with the governments concerned; in large groups or in small ones; in the reaffirmation of old agreements or their strengthening with new ones.

We have stated this position over and over again, fifty times and more, to friend and foe alike. And we remain ready, with this purpose, for unconditional discussions.

And until that bright and necessary day of peace we will try to keep conflict from spreading. We have no desire to see thousands die in battle—Asians or Americans. We have no desire to devastate that which the people of North Viet-Nam have built with toil and sacrifice. We will use our power with restraint and with all the wisdom that we can command.

But we will use it.

This war, like most wars, is filled with terrible irony. For what do the people of North Viet-Nam want? They want what their neighbors also desire: food for their hunger; health for their bodies; a chance to learn; progress for their country; and an end to the bondage of material misery. And they would find all these things far more readily in peaceful association with others than in the endless course of battle....

7

STILL FIGHTING AGAINST THE MUNICH ANALOGY

LYNDON B. JOHNSON

In July 1965, with U.S. troop strength in Vietnam at almost 60,000, the Johnson administration decided to step up the bombing of the north and to send 100,000 additional American troops to the south during the remainder of the year, with promises of more if needed. The troops would be employed in a new strategy of large-scale maneuvers and sustained combat. By the end of the year, American military personnel in Vietnam would number over 184,000. The President misled Congress and the public about his intentions and the size of the buildup planned for the future, but at a news conference on July 28, he tried to explain why American youth must die in a remote, distant land. He spoke of freedom, security, previous presidential commitments, and the lessons of appeasing Hitler before World War II.

WHY WE ARE IN VIET-NAM

My fellow Americans:

Not long ago I received a letter from a woman in the Midwest. She wrote:

Dear Mr. President:

In my humble way I am writing to you about the crisis in Viet-Nam. I have a son who is now in Viet-Nam. My husband served in World War II. Our country was at war, but now, this time, it is just something that I don't understand. Why?

Well, I have tried to answer that question dozens of times and more in practically every State in this Union. I have discussed it fully in Baltimore in April, in

Lyndon B. Johnson, "The President's News Conference of July 28, 1965," No. 388, *Public Papers of the Presidents of the United States: Lyndon B. Johnson, 1965*, Book 1 (Washington, D.C.: GPO, 1966), 794–95.

Washington in May, in San Francisco in June. Let me again, now, discuss it here in the East Room of the White House.

Why must young Americans, born into a land exultant with hope and with golden promise, toil and suffer and sometimes die in such a remote and distant place?

The answer, like the war itself, is not an easy one, but it echoes clearly from the painful lessons of half a century. Three times in my lifetime, in two World Wars and in Korea, Americans have gone to far lands to fight for freedom. We have learned at a terrible and a brutal cost that retreat does not bring safety and weakness does not bring peace.

It is this lesson that has brought us to Viet-Nam. This is a different kind of war. There are no marching armies or solemn declarations. Some citizens of South Viet-Nam at times, with understandable grievances, have joined in the attack on their own government.

But we must not let this mask the central fact that this is really war. It is guided by North Viet-Nam and it is spurred by Communist China. Its goal is to conquer the South, to defeat American power, and to extend the Asiatic dominion of communism.

There are great stakes in the balance.

Most of the non-Communist nations of Asia cannot, by themselves and alone, resist the growing might and the grasping ambition of Asian communism.

Our power, therefore, is a very vital shield. If we are driven from the field in Viet-Nam, then no nation can ever again have the same confidence in American promise, or in American protection.

In each land the forces of independence would be considerably weakened, and an Asia so threatened by Communist domination would certainly imperil the security of the United States itself.

We did not choose to be the guardians at the gate, but there is no one else.

Nor would surrender in Viet-Nam bring peace, because we learned from Hitler at Munich that success only feeds the appetite of aggression. The battle would be renewed in one country and then another country, bringing with it perhaps even larger and crueler conflict, as we have learned from the lessons of history.

Moreover, we are in Viet-Nam to fulfill one of the most solemn pledges of the American Nation. Three Presidents—President Eisenhower, President Kennedy, and your present President—over 11 years have committed themselves and have promised to help defend this small and valiant nation.

Strengthened by that promise, the people of South Viet-Nam have fought for many long years. Thousands of them have died. Thousands more have been crippled and scarred by war. We just cannot now dishonor our word, or abandon our commitment, or leave those who believed us and who trusted us to the terror and repression and murder that would follow.

This then, my fellow Americans, is why we are in Viet-Nam.

8

NIGHTMARES OF CRUCIFIXION

LYNDON B. JOHNSON

Explaining in his 1971 memoir The Vantage Point *why he had not withdrawn from Vietnam, former President Lyndon Johnson wrote:*

> If we ran out on Southeast Asia, I could see trouble ahead in every part of
> the globe....I knew our people well enough to realize that if we walked
> away from Vietnam and let Southeast Asia fall, there would follow a divisive
> and destructive debate within our country....A divisive debate over "who
> lost Vietnam" would be, in my judgment, even more destructive to our
> national life than the argument over China had been. It would inevitably
> increase isolationist pressures from the right and from the left and cause a
> pulling back from our commitments....*

When talking about the same issue in a 1970 interview, Johnson's language was more descriptive. He confided to Doris Kearns, a 1967 White House Fellow and a future Johnson biographer and Harvard political science professor, that in 1965 he had had recurring nightmares about being "crucified" on the cross of Vietnam.†

Pages 251–253 from *Lyndon Johnson and the American Dream* by Doris Kearns. Copyright © 1976 by Doris Kearns. Reprinted by permission of Harper & Row, Publishers, Inc.

*Lyndon Baines Johnson, *The Vantage Point: Perspectives of the Presidency, 1963–1969* (New York: Holt, Rinehart and Winston, 1971), 148, 151–52.

†Kearns was moved to ask rhetorically: "Did Johnson believe all this? Yes...some of the time. Was it true? Some of it; and the rest was not simply pure illusion. For even Johnson's most grotesque exaggerations were always constructed on some fragment of reality, so that they could never be totally disproven by factual evidence or unanswerable logic alone, only by rejecting his judgment for one more reasonable, more consonant with the known facts.... Johnson's description of the nature of the challenge in Vietnam was, of course, a product of his unique personal qualities. But it is important to remember that many others shared this view, although they would not have expressed it with such color or hyperbole. And they, like Johnson, derived their convictions from historical experience." Doris Kearns, *Lyndon Johnson and the American Dream* (New York: Harper & Row, 1976), p. 253.

I knew from the start that I was bound to be crucified either way I moved. If I left the woman I really loved—the Great Society—in order to get involved with that bitch of a war on the other side of the world, then I would lose everything at home. All my programs. All my hopes to feed the hungry and shelter the homeless. All my dreams to provide education and medical care to the browns and the blacks and the lame and the poor. But if I left that war and let the Communists take over South Vietnam, then I would be seen as a coward and my nation would be seen as an appeaser and we would both find it impossible to accomplish anything for anybody anywhere on the entire globe.

Oh, I could see it coming all right. History provided too many cases where the sound of the bugle put an immediate end to the hopes and dreams of the best reformers: the Spanish-American War drowned the populist spirit; World War I ended Woodrow Wilson's New Freedom; World War II brought the New Deal to a close. Once the war began, then all those conservatives in the Congress would use it as a weapon against the Great Society. You see, they'd never wanted to help the poor or the Negroes in the first place. But they were having a hard time figuring out how to make their opposition sound noble in a time of great prosperity. But the war. Oh, they'd use it to say they were against my programs, not because they were against the poor—why, they were as generous and as charitable as the best of Americans—but because the war had to come first. First, we had to beat those Godless Communists and then we could worry about the homeless Americans. And the generals. Oh, they'd love the war, too. It's hard to be a military hero without a war. Heroes need battles and bombs and bullets in order to be heroic. That's why I am suspicious of the military. They're always so narrow in their appraisal of everything. They see everything in military terms. Oh, I could see it coming. And I didn't like the smell of it. I didn't like anything about it, but I think the situation in South Vietnam bothered me most. They never seemed able to get themselves together down there. Always fighting with one another. Bad. Bad.

Yet everything I knew about history told me that if I got out of Vietnam and let Ho Chi Minh run through the streets of Saigon, then I'd be doing exactly what Chamberlain did in World War II. I'd be giving a big fat reward to aggression. And I knew that if we let Communist aggression succeed in taking over South Vietnam, there would follow in this country an endless national debate—a mean and destructive debate—that would shatter my Presidency, kill my administration, and damage our democracy. I knew that Harry Truman and Dean Acheson had lost their effectiveness from the day that the Communists took over in China. I believed that the loss of China had played a large role in the rise of Joe McCarthy. And I knew that all these problems, taken together, were chickenshit compared with what might happen if we lost Vietnam.

For this time there would be Robert Kennedy out in front leading the fight against me, telling everyone that I had betrayed John Kennedy's commitment to South Vietnam. That I had let a democracy fall into the hands of the Communists. That I was a coward. An unmanly man. A man without a spine. Oh, I could see it coming all right. Every night when I fell asleep I would see myself tied to the ground in the middle of a long, open space. In the distance, I could hear the voices of thousands of people. They were all shouting at me and running toward me:

"Coward! Traitor! Weakling!" They kept coming closer. They began throwing stones. At exactly that moment I would generally wake up...terribly shaken. But there was more. You see, I was as sure as any man could be that once we showed how weak we were, Moscow and Peking would move in a flash to exploit our weakness. They might move independently or they might move together. But move they would—whether through nuclear blackmail, through subversion, with regular armed forces or in some other manner. As nearly as anyone can be certain of anything, I knew they couldn't resist the opportunity to expand their control over the vacuum of power we would leave behind us. And so would begin World War III. So you see, I was bound to be crucified either way I moved.

9

TALKING TO THE DOMINOES

RICHARD M. NIXON

Elected in part on the promise that he would end the long and bloody Vietnam War, President Nixon still pursued the policy goal of previous Presidents, to bring about an independent, non-Communist South Vietnam. But he altered American strategy. To quell domestic opposition to the war, he began the phased withdrawal of American troops in 1969. To fight the war effectively in spite of American troop withdrawal, he turned to "Vietnamization"—the intensified buildup of South Vietnamese forces—and he accelerated "pacification"—programs of civic action and assassination. In addition, he struck out at enemy sanctuaries in Cambodia with B-52 bombing strikes. On 30 April 1970, he sent U.S. troops into Cambodia and on 3 May resumed the bombing of North Vietnam. These actions sparked widespread criticism and massive*

Richard Nixon, "A Conversation with the President about Foreign Policy, July 1, 1970," *Public Papers of the Presidents of the United States: Richard Nixon, 1970* (Washington, D.C.: GPO, 1971), 546–49.
*In his postwar book, *No More Vietnams* (New York: Arbor House, 1985), 104–7, Nixon wrote: "When Johnson administration officials briefed me about Vietnam before I took office, they presented no plan

demonstrations and stalled the negotiations with the North Vietnamese in Paris.
Defending his Vietnam strategy before a panel of prominent television journalists on
1 July 1970, Nixon came full circle to the themes he had used in the 1950s as Vice
President under Eisenhower and which other Presidents had also used: the domino
principle, the need to defend freedom, the risk of bloodbaths, and the indivisibility of
peace and freedom. Then, as had previous Presidents—and as he would over a decade
later—Nixon argued that his military steps were aimed at ending the war and
winning the peace.

MR. [HOWARD K.] SMITH: Mr. President, one of the things that happened in the
Senate last week was the rescinding of the Gulf of Tonkin resolution by the
Senate. Mr. Katzenbach,[1] in the previous administration, told the Foreign Relations Committee that resolution was tantamount to a congressional declaration
of war. If it is rescinded, what legal justification do you have for continuing to
fight a war that is undeclared in Vietnam?

THE PRESIDENT: First, Mr. Smith, as you know, this war, while it was undeclared,
was here when I became President of the United States. I do not say that critically. I am simply stating the fact that there were 549,000 Americans in Vietnam
under attack when I became President.

The President of the United States has the constitutional right—not only the
right, but the responsibility—to use his powers to protect American forces when
they are engaged in military actions, and under these circumstances, starting at the
time that I became President, I have that power and I am exercising that power.

MR. SMITH: Sir, I am not recommending this, but if you don't have a legal authority to wage a war, then presumably you could move troops out. It would be
possible to agree with the North Vietnamese. They would be delighted to have
us surrender. So that you could—

What justification do you have for keeping troops there other than protecting
the troops that are there fighting?

THE PRESIDENT: A very significant justification. It isn't just a case of seeing that
the Americans are moved out in an orderly way. If that were the case, we could
move them out more quickly, but it is a case of moving American forces out in
a way that we can at the same time win a just peace.

Now, by winning a just peace, what I mean is not victory over North Vietnam—
we are not asking for that—but it is simply the right of the people of South
Vietnam to determine their own future without having us impose our will upon
them, or the North Vietnamese, or anybody else outside impose their will upon
them.

When we look at that limited objective, I am sure some would say, "Well, is
that really worth it? Is that worth the efforts of all these Americans fighting in
Vietnam, the lives that have been lost?"

---

for how we should end the war. . . . In the first months of my administration, we put together a five-point
strategy to win the war—or more precisely, to end the war and win the peace." He claimed that the plan
included Vietnamization, pacification, diplomatic isolation of North Vietnam, negotiations coupled with
"irresistible military pressure," and gradual withdrawal of American combat troops.

[1] Nicholas deB. Katzenbach, Under Secretary of State from 1966 to 1968.

I suppose it could be said that simply saving 17 million people in South Vietnam from a Communist takeover isn't worth the efforts of the United States. But let's go further. If the United States, after all of this effort, if we were to withdraw immediately, as many Americans would want us to do—and it would be very easy for me to do it and simply blame it on the previous administration—but if we were to do that, I would probably survive through my term, but it would have, in my view, a catastrophic effect on this country and the cause of peace in the years ahead.

Now I know there are those who say the domino theory is obsolete. They haven't talked to the dominoes. They should talk to the Thais, to the Malaysians, to the Singaporans, to the Indonesians, to the Filipinos, to the Japanese, and the rest. And if the United States leaves Vietnam in a way that we are humiliated or defeated, not simply speaking in what is called jingoistic terms, but in very practical terms, this will be immensely discouraging to the 300 million people from Japan clear around to Thailand in free Asia; and even more important it will be ominously encouraging to the leaders of Communist China and the Soviet Union who are supporting the North Vietnamese. It will encourage them in their expansionist policies in other areas.

The world will be much safer in which to live.

MR. SMITH: I happen to be one of those who agrees with what you are saying, but do you have a legal justification to follow that policy once the Tonkin Gulf Resolution is dead?

THE PRESIDENT: Yes, sir, Mr. Smith, the legal justification is the one that I have given, and that is the right of the President of the United States under the Constitution to protect the lives of American men. That is the legal justification. You may recall, of course, that we went through this same debate at the time of Korea. Korea was also an undeclared war, and then, of course, we justified it on the basis of a U.N. action. I believe we have a legal justification and I intend to use it.

MR. [ERIC] SEVAREID: Mr. President, you have said that self-determination in South Vietnam is really our aim, and all we can ask for. The Vice President says a non-Communist future for Indochina, or Southeast Asia. His statement seems to enlarge the ultimate American aim considerably. Have we misunderstood you or has he or what is the aim?

THE PRESIDENT: Mr. Sevareid, when the Vice President refers to a non-Communist Southeast Asia that would mean of course, a non-Communist South Vietnam, Laos, Cambodia, Thailand, Malaysia, Singapore, and Indonesia. That is the area we usually think of as Southeast Asia.

This is certainly something that I think most Americans and most of those in free Asia and most of those in the free world would think would be a desirable goal.

Let me put it another way: I do not think it would be in the interest of the United States and those who want peace in the Pacific if that part of the world should become Communist, because then the peace of the world, the peace in the Pacific, would be in my opinion very greatly jeopardized if the Communists were to go through that area.

However, referring now specifically to what we are doing in Vietnam, our aim there is a very limited one, and it is to provide for the South Vietnamese the right of self-determination. I believe that when they exercise that right they will choose a non-Communist government. But we are indicating—and incidentally, despite what everybody says about the present government in South Vietnam, its inadequacies and the rest, we have to give them credit for the fact that they also have indicated that they will accept the result of an election, what the people choose.

Let us note the fact that the North Vietnamese are in power not as a result of an election, and have refused to indicate that they will accept the result of an election in South Vietnam, which would seem to me to be a pretty good bargaining point on our side.

MR. [JOHN] CHANCELLOR: Mr. President, I am a little confused at this point because you seem in vivid terms to be describing South Vietnam as the first of the string of dominoes that could topple in that part of the world and turn it into a Communist part of the world, in simple terms.

Are you saying that we cannot survive, we cannot allow a regime or a government in South Vietnam to be constructed that would, say, lean toward the Communist bloc? What about a sort of Yugoslavia? Is there any possibility of that kind of settlement?

THE PRESIDENT: Mr. Chancellor, it depends upon the people of South Vietnam. If the people of South Vietnam after they see what the Vietcong, the Communist Vietcong, have done to the villages they have occupied, the 40,000 people that they have murdered, village chiefs and others, the atrocities of Hue—if the people of South Vietnam, of which 850,000 of them are Catholic refugees from North Vietnam, after a blood bath there when the North Vietnamese took over in North Vietnam—if the people of South Vietnam under those circumstances should choose to move in the direction of a Communist government, that, of course, is their right. I do not think it will happen. But I do emphasize that the American position and the position also of the present Government of South Vietnam, it seems to me, is especially strong, because we are confident enough that we say to the enemy, "All right, we'll put our case to the people and we'll accept the result." If it happens to be what you describe, a Yugoslav type of government or a mixed government, we will accept it.

MR. CHANCELLOR: What I am getting at, sir, is, if you say on the one hand that Vietnam—South Vietnam is the first of the row of dominoes which we cannot allow to topple, then can you say equally, at the same time, that we will accept the judgment of the people of South Vietnam if they choose a Communist government?

THE PRESIDENT: The point that you make, Mr. Chancellor, is one that we in the free world face every place in the world, and it is really what distinguishes us from the Communist world.

Again, I know that what is called cold war rhetoric isn't fashionable these days, and I am not engaging in it because I am quite practical, and we must be quite practical, about the world in which we live with all the dangers that we have in the Mideast and other areas that I am sure we will be discussing later in this program.

But let us understand that we in the free world have to live or die by the proposition that the people have a right to choose.

Let it also be noted that in no country in the world today in which the Communists are in power have they come to power as a result of the people choosing them—not in North Vietnam, not in North Korea, not in China, not in Russia, and not in any one of the countries of Eastern Europe, and not in Cuba. In every case, communism has come to power by other than a free election, so I think we are in a pretty safe position on this particular point.

I think you are therefore putting, and I don't say this critically, what is really a hypothetical question. It could happen. But if it does happen that way we must assume the consequences, and if the people of South Vietnam should choose a Communist government, then we will have to accept the consequences of what would happen as far as the domino theory in the other areas.

MR. CHANCELLOR: In other words, live with it?

THE PRESIDENT: We would have to live with it, and I would also suggest this: When we talk about the dominoes, I am not saying that automatically if South Vietnam should go the others topple one by one. I am only saying that in talking to every one of the Asian leaders, and I have talked to all of them. I have talked to Lee Kuan Yew—all of you know him from Singapore of course—and to the Tunku[2] from Malaysia, the little countries, and to Suharto from Indonesia, and of course to Thanom and Thanat Khoman, the two major leaders in Thailand—I have talked to all of these leaders and every one of them to a man recognizes, and Sato of Japan recognizes, and of course the Koreans recognize that if the Communists succeed, not as a result of a free election—they are not thinking of that—but if they succeed as a result of exporting aggression and supporting it in toppling the government, then the message to them is, "Watch out, we might be next."

That's what is real. So, if they come in as a result of a free election, and I don't think that is going to happen, the domino effect would not be as great....

[2] A Malaysian title meaning Prince or My Lord; Tunku Abdul Rahman Putra Al-Haj was Prime Minister.

PART TWO

States of Mind
Abstract Ideas, Ideals, and Strategic Concepts

All over Asia we have found that the basic American ethic is revered and honored and imitated when possible. We must, while helping Asia toward self-sufficiency, show by example that America is still the America of freedom and hope and knowledge and law. If we succeed, we cannot lose the struggle.
—William J. Lederer and Eugene Burdick, *The Ugly American,* 1958

War is always attractive to young men who know nothing about it, but we had also been seduced into uniform by Kennedy's challenge to "ask what you can do for your country" and by the missionary idealism he had awakened in us.
—Philip Caputo, *A Rumor of War,* 1977

In the field of counter-insurgency as nowhere else, Kennedy found full scope for his imagination and drive.... Through counter-insurgency, the West would win the battle for the Third World.
—Stephen E. Ambrose, *Rise to Globalism,* 1972

This was a moment of the supremacy of abstract principles.
—Arthur M. Schlesinger, Jr., *A Thousand Days,* 1965

10

IMAGES OF THE PAST

GÖRAN RYSTAD

According to Swedish historian Göran Rystad, the domino principle of the post–World War II period was only one part of a set of assumptions that he called the "Munich syndrome" or "Munich paradigm," which also included the Munich appeasement analogy and the theory of totalitarian aggression. In a 1982 study exploring the relationship between interpreting history and making foreign policy, Rystad maintained that American policymakers unthinkingly applied the lessons they drew from the history of events leading up to World War II to the crises they faced during the cold war, including Vietnam. The most powerful image they had was that of the Western democracies' appeasement of Hitler at Munich in 1938, which symbolized to them the encouragement of aggression and the coming of global conflict.

PRE-EXISTING IMAGES, PERCEPTUAL PREDISPOSITIONS, AND FOREIGN POLICY MAKING

...A study of American foreign policy making in the post-war era convincingly reveals that the historian has to open this Chinese box: In order to understand and explain actions and decisions by foreign policy makers at any given time, it is also necessary to establish and elucidate their images of the past....

There will always be a discrepancy between image and reality as a result of impediments and limits to the flow of information.[1] More important, however, is the discrepancy resulting from the distortion of reality by perceptual predispositions, especially those originating from pre-existing images of the past.[2]

Reprinted from Göran Rystad, *Prisoners of the Past? The Munich Syndrome and Makers of American Foreign Policy in the Cold War Era* (Lund, Sweden: CWK Gleerup, 1982), 14–15, 17, 18, 31–33, 39–41, 44–53, 63–67, by permission of the author.

[1] Robert Jervis, *Perception and Misperception in International Politics* (Princeton, 1976), p. 143ff.

[2] Pointing to the remoteness of what penetrates our cognition from the operational environment Joseph Frankel suggests that instead of using the expression "knowledge" it may be more appropriate to speak

Once assumptions are formed and stabilized, they decide what perceptual predispositions a person will have in a given situation. They screen out what seems to be irrelevant or what apparently contradicts his pre-existing images, his assumptions about the actors and problems involved, fitting incoming information to pre-existing beliefs....

...Confirming evidence, on the other hand, is noted and accepted quickly....

...Images of the past cause powerful perceptual predispositions, influencing the policy-makers' perceptions of contemporary problems and thus their choice of policies and actions....

THE MUNICH PARADIGM AND THE AGGRESSION THEORY

The basic assumptions of what might be called the Munich paradigm...were established by the experiences of the 1930s, conditioned by the Second World War, and applied to post-war realities. Two key concepts were *aggression* and *appeasement*. The following assertions are characteristic and illustrative:

1. "Few things are more certain than that during the 1930s peace-loving nations, had they not been hamstrung by isolationist forces in and out of governments, could have armed adequately in time, and by joint representation could have demanded a showdown with the aggressors, Germany, Italy, and Japan, and averted the recent World War. In the same way they could have prevented its predecessor."... "What happened in the thirties in China, Ethiopia, Austria, Czechoslovakia, and Poland—all far removed from us geographically—was a cumulative series of steps that led unerringly to our involvement in the Second World War." (*Cordell Hull*)[3]

"...timidity breeds conflict, and courage often prevents it.... History teaches with unmistakable emphasis that appeasement but begets new and bloodier war." (*Douglas MacArthur*)[4]

2. "If the Kaiser had known for sure that Great Britain and the United States would come into World War I, he would not have permitted the war to break out. If Hitler had had the same certainty he would not have started World War II." (*John Foster Dulles*)[5]

---

of "the image." Joseph Frankel, *The Making of Foreign Policy. An Analysis of Decision Making* (Oxford University Press, 1967), p. 103. Cf Kenneth Boulding, *The Image* (1956), p. 5 f. In this study the term "image" is used as meaning an individual's "perceptions of an object, fact, or condition, his evaluation of that object, fact or condition in terms of goodness or badness, friendliness or hostility, or value, and the meaning ascribed to, or deduced from that object, fact, or condition," as defined by K. J. Holsti, *International Politics: A Framework for Analysis* (Englewood Cliffs, New Jersey, 1965), p. 159.

[3] Cordell Hull, *Memoirs, II* (New York, 1948), p. 1734ff.

[4] Douglas MacArthur, *Reminiscences* (New York, 1964), p. 404.

[5] Henry P. Van Dusen (ed), *The Spiritual Legacy of John Foster Dulles. Selections from His Articles and Addresses* (Philadelphia, 1958), p. 127 f.

"Our best hope of peace lies in our ability to make absolutely plain to aggressors that aggression cannot succeed." (*Dean Acheson*)[6]

3. "Unhappily, the Kellog-Briand Pact did not stop World War II by a single day...[but] tempted the aggressions of Hitler, Mussolini, and the Japanese war lords. We should learn from that experience that it is not possible to abolish war by slogans or strokes of a pen." (*John Foster Dulles*)[7]

"Strong nations which want peace cannot buy it by shoving bits of weaker nations into the jaws of ambitious despots. That only makes them more rapacious." (*John Foster Dulles*)[8]

"Twice in one generation the United States has had the opportunity to lead countries of the world to peace. After World War I we shirked our responsibilities. World War II taught us a lesson." (*Harry S. Truman*)[9]

"I believe there are wars we should not have had to fight if we had been properly prepared in time, if we had shown the aggressors what might we were equipped to wield." (*Joseph Grew*)[10]

4. Soviet communism is "as incompatible with democracy as was Nazism or Fascism." (*James V. Forrestal*)[11]

"...the Russians, like the Japanese, are essentially Oriental in their thinking, and...it seems doubtful that we should endeavor to buy their understanding and sympathy. We tried it once with Hitler. There are no returns on appeasement." (*James V. Forrestal*)[12]

"...the record shows that despotism, whatever its form, has a remorseless compulsion for aggression.... Today another power, wearing the false mask of freedom for the people, seeks to spin its web over all Western Europe." (*James V. Forrestal*)[13]

"There are aggressive forces in the world coming from the Soviet Union which are just as destructive in their effect on the world and our own way of life as Hitler was, and I think are a greater menace than Hitler was." (*Averell Harriman*)[14]

[6] Address, September 2, 1950. *State Department Bulletin*, XX. Also in McGeorge Bundy (ed), *The Pattern of Responsibility* (Boston, 1952), p. 26.

[7] Van Dusen, p. 187.

[8] *Ibid.*, p. 25. Cf also John Foster Dulles, *War and Peace* (1950), p. x.

[9] Address, September 27, 1948. Quotation from Louis W. Koenig, *The Truman Administration* (1956), p. 270.

[10] Statement during *Hearing on Universal Military Training*, 1945. Joseph C. Grew, *Turbulent Era: A Diplomatic Record of Forty Years*, ed. by Walter Johnson (London, 1953), p. 1452. Cf also, for example, Dean Acheson, *Power and Diplomacy* (Harvard University Press, 1958), p. 35.

[11] Quoted from Ernest R. May, *"Lessons" of the Past: The Use and Misuse of History in American Foreign Policy* (London, 1973), p. 21.

[12] Walter Millis (ed), *The Forrestal Diaries: The Inner History of the Cold War* (New York, 1951), p. 95 f.

[13] *Ibid.*, p. 400.

[14] *State Department Bulletin*, XVIII, March 7, 1948; cf Robert A. Divine, *Foreign Policy and U.S. Presidential Elections* (New York, 1974), p. 179, and Rudolf L. Trenefels (ed), *Eisenhower Speaks. Dwight D. Eisenhower in His Memoirs and Speeches* (New York, 1948), p. 153 f; p. 251. Also Averell Harriman, *Peace with Russia?* (London, 1960), p. 3.

"Even more than was the case with Hitler, it is the evident and expressed intention of the Russian government to dominate the world." (*Ralf Flanders*)[15]

"...there is something of a 'parallel' in remembering what occurred prior to a similar cleavage between democracy and nazism, when we surely learned that we cannot escape trouble by trying to run away from it and when 'appeasement' proved to be a fatal investment." (*Arthur H. Vandenberg*)[16]

"...as 'a war to end wars' the war will have been futile, for the result will be merely the transfer of totalitarian dictatorship and power from Germany and Japan to Soviet Russia, which will constitute in future as grave a danger to us as did the Axis." (*Joseph Grew*)[17]

"...the principle of morality and considerations for our own security will never permit us to acquiesce in a peace dictated by aggressors and sponsored by appeasers." (*Franklin D. Roosevelt*)[18]

The content of these statements may be summarized: the failure of the democracies in the 1930s to stand up to the aggressive totalitarian states brought on the Second World War. Totalitarian states are inherently aggressive.[19] Attempts to appease only increase their appetite. After the war Germany, Nazism and Hitler had been replaced as a threat to peace and to the security of the democracies by the Soviet Union, Communism and Stalin. The danger was identical and the lessons must be applied.

These assumptions about problem realities, the intentions of the actors, attainable goals, and the effectiveness of means determined the perceptions, interpretations and evaluations of issues and events and decided responses and policies. The policy of containment was to a considerable extent based on these assumptions. Early apparent successes—Iran, Greece, Turkey—served to reinforce them and the perceptual predispositions stemming from them, as did events such as the coup in Prague and the Berlin blockade. At the same time, the Communist victory in China was seen as an extremely serious and dangerous setback for "the Free World."...

[15] Ralph Flanders, *The American Century* (Cambridge, Mass., 1950), p. 57. Cf Sumner Welles, *We Need Not Fail* (Boston, 1948), p. XII.

[16] Arthur H. Vandenberg, Jr. (ed), *The Private Papers of Senator Vandenberg* (Boston, 1952), p. 342.

[17] Joseph C. Grew, *Turbulent Era: A Diplomatic Record of Forty Years*, ed. Walter Johnson (London, 1953), p. 1445.

[18] *"The Four Freedoms Speech."* For a discussion of the U.S. Aggression Theory, cf Lars-Göran Stenelo, *Foreign Policy Predictions* (Lund, 1980), p. 159ff.

[19] Charles E. Bohlen has elaborated on what he sees as the dynamics behind the Soviet—or Communist—aggressiveness. To a Communist frontier applied what Friedrich Engels said about a military frontier, namely that the difficulty is that "anything that is 100 kilometers further out is preferable." The Communist system means a closed society, and any common frontier with a country where there is freedom represents the point of danger for the Communists. Thus there is a natural tendency for them to move that line of confrontation further away. Charles E. Bohlen, *The Transformation of American Foreign Policy* (London, 1969), p. 117f. James E. Byrnes, on the other hand, emphasized that "...expansionism...is rooted in Russian history. Only the personalities and the tactics have changed." Byrnes, *Speaking Frankly* (1947), p. 282f.

THE DOMINO THEORY AND THE CONFLICT IN SOUTHEAST ASIA

The Domino Theory belongs, together with the Munich analogy, to the Munich Syndrome. In both cases we find the basic assumption of the inherent and uncompromising aggressiveness of the enemy and of the mortal danger of retreat. To appease and to compromise would only lead to increased aggression. F. M. Kail has argued that the domino principle was "a dramatic way of demonstrating that an apparently peripheral contest could, strategically, be of pivotal significance."[20] However, those implications were more easily clarified by using the Munich analogy. The Domino Theory presents a special case in that it applies to aggression in the form of expansion over borders into adjacent countries, an almost mechanical effect, a chain reaction of sorts. The more general Munich analogy is not limited to a local area or to bordering countries. Successful aggression in one part of the world might very well result in an attack on another continent. For example, in his speech to Congress in April 1954, a few days after Eisenhower's first launching of the Domino Theory, General MacArthur used the more general formula, where the linkage to the anti-appeasement rhetoric is immediately recognizable:

> The Communist threat is a global one. Its successful advance in one sector threatens the destruction of every other sector. You cannot appease or otherwise surrender to communism in Asia without simultaneously undermining our efforts to halt its advance in Europe.[21]

John Foster Dulles, Eisenhower's Secretary of State, pointed out the necessity "to prevent the loss in northern Vietnam from leading to the extension of Communism throughout Southeast Asia and Southwest Pacific."[22]

A typical elaboration on the theory was presented by John F. Kennedy...on June 1, 1956. The young senator argued that Vietnam represented "the cornerstone of the Free World in Southeast Asia, the keystone to the arch, the finger in the dike...." If "the Red tide of Communism" flooded Vietnam, the next countries in line would be "Burma, Thailand, India, Japan, the Philippines, and obviously Laos and Cambodia."[23]

Seven years later Kennedy repeated the metaphor, this time, however, in a discussion of the role of the United States: "We are still the keystone in the arch of freedom...."[24]

The concept—if not necessarily the same metaphor—was repeated and varied innumerable times, by Eisenhower himself, by John Foster Dulles, Thomas Dewey, Chester Bowles, Dean Acheson, and many, many others. Sometimes the specter of economic blackmail was added to that of military aggression. Typical of this special

---

[20] F. M. Kail, *What Washington Said: Administration Rhetoric and the Vietnam War, 1949–1969* (New York, 1973), p. 88.

[21] Douglas MacArthur, Speech to Congress, April 4, 1954, *Reminiscences* (London, 1964), p. 400.

[22] John Foster Dulles, Statement before the Council on Foreign Relations, August 2, 1954.

[23] Cf May, p. 87ff.

[24] Lyndon B. Johnson, *The Vantage Point: Perspectives of the Presidency* (New York, 1971), p. 42.

version was Chester Bowles' assertion on one occasion that, once in possession of
Southeast Asia, Communist China would control some six million tons of surplus
rice annually and then be in a position to "blackmail those Asian countries which
are now dependent upon rice from those areas for their people—Indonesia, Japan,
Ceylon, and to a certain extent India herself."[25] Similar ideas were expressed by,
among others, Thomas Dewey,[26] John Foster Dulles[27] and Richard Nixon. The
Domino Theory was to play an important role in bringing about the Vietnam war....

THE VIETNAM WAR

The experiences of the 1930s, conditioned by the Second World War and reinforced
by subsequent events, had established an assumptive world dominated by a few
general propositions which decided American responses to new events and developments. They might be formulated as follows:

1. The world is bipolar, divided into the Free World and a monolithic Communist
   totalitarian bloc.
2. Communist regimes are inherently aggressive and Communist leaders conspire
   to conquer, subjugate and dominate the Free World.
3. Local conflicts do not exist. They are testing grounds where the Communists are
   probing for soft spots, battles in the world wide contention of a Cold War.
4. Appeasement and compromise are not only ineffective but disastrous and
   suicidal.

These are basic propositions, and all of the policy actors did not subscribe to
them entirely or in exactly this form. However, they represent the key elements of
the Munich Syndrome, and they have—in my opinion—to be taken into account
in any effort to explain the American involvement in Vietnam. Even when the conception of a bipolar world was dissolving or, at least, was being seriously questioned
by an increasing number of people, the old images were still powerful and the set
of assumptions described in the previous chapters was resistant to change.

The existence of a mortal threat to the Free World from the Communists had
hardly been questioned during the 1950s. The statement by Christian Herter, Secretary of State, that he was convinced that "the survival of free men is being seriously threatened," was fairly typical.[28] President Eisenhower asserted that "the
truly virulent problems in international affairs spring from the persistent, continuing struggle between freedom and Communism," and he saw this struggle as part
of the conflict between "liberty and slavery."[29]

[25] Chester Bowles, *Ambassador's Report* (London, 1954), p. 247f; Thomas E. Dewey, *Journey to the Far Pacific* (London, 1949), p. 202ff.

[26] Singer, *Campaign Speeches*, p. 202ff.

[27] John Foster Dulles, *War or Peace* (New York, 1950), pp. 17; 147. Also Acheson, *Present at the Creation*, p. 407.

[28] Christian A. Herter, *Toward an Atlantic Community* (New York, 1963), p. 5.

[29] Eisenhower, *Mandate for Change*, p. 624.

This image of the Communists persisted into the early 1960s. A typical conservative and anti-Communist such as Barry Goldwater talked about the Communist plan for world conquest and declared as his most important task to "persuade the enemy that we would rather follow the world to Kingdom come than consign it to Hell under Communism."[30]

Rhetorics aside—and style—there was in essence no differences in foreign policy matters between the two Presidential candidates in 1960. In his Inaugural Address Kennedy made this often quoted declaration:

Let every nation know, whether it wishes us well or ill, that we shall pay any price, bear any burden, meet any hardship, support any friend, oppose any foe to assure the survival and the success of liberty....

We dare not tempt them with weakness. For only when our arms are sufficient, beyond all doubt can we be certain that they will never be employed.[31]

In Richard Nixon's more pedestrian Acceptance Speech at the Republican convention in Chicago half a year earlier, the Republican candidate told his audience:

...he [the next President] must leave no doubt at any time that whether it is in Berlin or in Cuba or anywhere else in the world, America will not tolerate being pushed around by anybody, any place. Because we have already paid a terrible price in lives and resources to learn that appeasement leads not to peace but to war.[32]

The style differs, but the message is basically the same.

In an address in November 1961 President Kennedy stated: "We are neither warmongers nor appeasers, neither hard nor soft. We are Americans determined to defend the frontiers of freedom by an honorable peace if peace is possible but by arms if arms are used against us."[33] Hans Morgenthau has rightly said of Kennedy that he didn't say much on foreign policy but he said it in beautiful prose. However, a statement such as the one quoted is fraught with possibilities, and open to rather far-reaching interpretations. When Lyndon Johnson and Dean Rusk placed "the frontier of freedom" in Vietnam, and when Nixon then delayed withdrawal in search of "an honorable peace" they could well argue that they did not deviate from the policy outlined by Kennedy.

Even if the Munich analogy, the Domino Principle and the Aggression Theory—all manifestations of the Munich Syndrome—dominated, there were individuals who did not subscribe to these assumptions. One of those who questioned the standard conception of a monolithic Communist bloc was Chester Bowles, Kennedy's

[30] Barry Goldwater, *Why not Victory?* (New York, 1962), pp. 24; 57ff.

[31] John F. Kennedy, Inaugural Speech, January 21, 1961. In Theodore C. Sorenson, *Kennedy* (New York, 1965), p. 245ff.

[32] Richard M. Nixon, Acceptance Speech, July 28, 1960. In Singer, *Campaign Speeches*, p. 313.

[33] James MacGregor Burns (ed), *To Heal and to Build: The Programs of Lyndon B. Johnson* (New York, 1968), p. 130.

Under Secretary of State. In July, 1961, he argued the danger of the growing American involvement in Indo China and recommended efforts "to seek a rational basis for conversations with the Russians."[34] Adlai Stevenson also warned against self-defeating rigidity. Compromise was not immoral or unreasonable, he argued, and pointed to the need for a new China policy.[35]

Influential commentators such as Hans Morgenthau, George F. Kennan, Arthur Schlesinger, Jr., and Kenneth Galbraith continued to pay tribute to the Truman Doctrine, the Marshall Plan and NATO as policies consistent with their times, adequate responses to the problems of the early postwar era. At the same time they condemned the American foreign policy in the 1960s, especially in Southeast Asia, as utterly out of date. "These policies have become obsolete," asserted Hans Morgenthau, deploring that the United States had been unable "to devise new policies capable of dealing successfully with the issues of a new period."[36] The revisionists went one step further, contending that the European containment doctrine owed its success to its being a defense against a nonthreat.[37]

The position taken by J. William Fulbright in 1966 in his famous series of lectures "The Arrogance of Power," has strong similarities with that of Morgenthau. He makes a fundamental distinction between Korea and Vietnam. The American intervention in 1950 was "justified and necessary," argued Fulbright, simultaneously fiercely criticizing the American involvement in Vietnam.[38]

That reality rapidly outstripped the perceptions of reality and was an underlying source of America's troubles with foreign policy was also a point made by Arthur M. Schlesinger, Jr. In "Remarks on United States Foreign Policy" on March 8, 1967, he maintained—just as Morgenthau and Fulbright did—that the ideas and the policies of the forties and the early fifties were admirably suited for that world and most satisfactory in achieving their objectives. They were shaped by "a world threatened by massive, unitary, centralized aggression and social fanaticism: Adolf Hitler and Nazism in the thirties and Josef Stalin and Communism in the forties and fifties."[39] It was only natural that the men who grew up at that time, with these experiences, found it hard to relinquish the ideas they had acquired then. But the world had changed drastically, and policies must change accordingly. Schlesinger,

[34] Chester Bowles, *Promises to Keep: My Years in Public Life, 1941–1969* (New York, 1971), p. 717. However, even Bowles contended that "every intelligent man knows that a world-wide conspiracy exists." Bowles, The *Conscience of a Liberal. Selected Writings and Speeches* (New York, 1962), p. 52.

[35] Adlai E. Stevenson, *Call to Greatness*, p. 100ff.

[36] Roy Bennet, "Containing Communism in Asia: Theory and Practice." In Neal D. Houghton (ed.), *Struggle against History: U.S. Foreign Policy in an Age of Revolution* (New York, 1968), p. 222ff. Cf also Henry A. Kissinger, "Central Issues of American Foreign Policy." In Kermit Gordon (ed), *Agenda for the Nation* (Washington, D.C., 1968), p. 585ff.

[37] Bennet, p. 223.

[38] J. William Fulbright, "On the Arrogance of Power," Marcus G. Raskin and Bernard B. Fall (eds), *The Viet-Nam Reader. Articles and Documents on American Foreign Policy and the Viet-Nam Crisis* (New York, 1967), p. 444ff.

[39] Cf Rystad, "In Quest of a Usable Past: Foreign Policy and the Politics of American Historiography in the 1960s," *Scandia*, 1982, p. 3.

not only a prominent and influential historian but also, as Special Assistant to President Kennedy, a man with a background of personal involvement in policy making, was more than most aware of the problems of the interaction between history and decision making.

The distinction between the Korean and the Vietnam War made by Schlesinger, Fulbright and others was rejected by many.[40] Adolf A. Berle contended that the opponents of the American intervention in Vietnam were the same group of intellectuals "with additions and subtractions for age and death," that wanted a truce with Hitler at the time of Munich, opposed the American engagement in Greece in 1947, wanted to get out of Korea and wanted hands off Cuba in 1961.[41]

Senator Dodd—not surprisingly—applied the analogy of the 1930s in order to explain the Vietnam situation: "The situation in Vietnam today bears many resemblances to the situation just before Munich.... We are again confronted by an incorrigible aggressor, fanatically committed to the destruction of the free world, whose agreements are as worthless as Hitler's," he contended.[42] The Joint Chiefs of Staff put it in less emotional terms: "...the military and political effort of Communist China in South Vietnam... is part of a major campaign to extend Communist control beyond the periphery of the Sino-Soviet bloc and overseas to both islands and continental areas in the Free World.... It is, in fact, a planned phase in the Communist timetable for world domination."[43]

Senator Dodd's rhetoric is typical of the Cold War era and he has better than most expressed the world view of the practitioners sharing the assumptions of the Munich paradigm. On May 3, 1961 Dodd addressed the Asian People's Anti-Communist League at a meeting in Manila. The title of his address was: "Southeast Asia: The Dangers of Appeasement."

> When Prime Minister Chamberlain returned from Munich, he justified the surrender of the Sudetenland to Hitler with the words "Czechoslovakia is a far away land about which we know little." The Munich psychosis did not begin with Prime Minister Chamberlain and it did not end with him.... How many historical catastrophes does it take to prove that softness and appeasement foster aggression, insecurity and war?... The period of allied retreat in Europe prior to World War II came to an end with the invasion of Poland. If the Communists push their luck too hard in Laos, Laos may well turn out to be the Poland of Asia. But even if it should turn out to be an Asian Munich, I would

---

[40] Cf, for example, Eugene Rostow, *Peace in the Balance: The Future of U.S. Foreign Policy* (New York, 1972), pp. 179ff; 190.

[41] Berle, *Navigating the Rapids*, p. 806.

[42] Thomas J. Dodd, Speech in the Senate 1965, *Congressional Record*, 89th Congress, 1st Session, p. 3350.

[43] *Pentagon Papers*, II, p. 664. In his study of American Foreign Policy officials Bernard Mennis found—not surprisingly—that political-military officers were more "hard-line" than political Foreign Service officers. Bernard Mennis, *American Foreign Policy Officials: Who They Are and What They Believe Regarding International Politics* (Ohio University Press, 1971), p. 166ff.

remind the Communist despots that Munich was the final allied con-
cession, that the very next act of Nazi aggression resulted in World War
II.[44]

Similarly Lyndon Johnson saw the contest in Vietnam as part of a wider pattern of aggressive intention and also made the point that surrender in Vietnam
would not bring peace "because we learned from Hitler at Munich that success only
feeds the appetite of the aggression. The battle would be renewed in one country
and then another country, bring with it perhaps even larger and crueler conflict, as
we have learned from the lessons of history."[45]

He repeated and varied this message again and again. Defeat in Vietnam "would
encourage and spur on those who seek to conquer all free nations within their
reach. . . . This is the clearest lesson of our time. From Munich until today we have
learned that to yield to aggression brings only greater threats."[46]

In *Vantage Point* Lyndon Johnson commented on his frequent references to the
lessons of history. No President could separate himself from his own experience and
memory and for him it was natural to recall crises of the past and how they had been
met—or not met: "Like most men and women of my generation, I felt that World
War II might have been avoided if the United States in the 1930s had not given such
an uncertain signal of its likely response to aggression in Europe and Asia."[47]

Again and again Lyndon Johnson emphatically defended his administration's
Vietnam policy with the same standard arguments. The bipolarity of the world and
the relentless, ruthless aggressiveness of the Communists are the fundamental assumptions and their consequence the necessity to resist the aggressors and the danger of appeasement.

Communists, using force and intrigue, seek to bring about a Communist
dominated world. Our convictions, our interests, our life as a nation
demand that we resolutely oppose, with all our might, that effort to
dominate the world.

The Gulf of Tonkin may be distant Asian waters, but none can be detached about what happened there. Aggression—deliberate, willful, and
systematic aggression—unmasked its face to the entire world. The world
remembers—the world must never forget—that aggression unchallenged
is aggression unleashed."[48]

Congress responded to these words with the fateful Tonkin Gulf Resolution.
Virtually identical words were used by John F. Kennedy in his Radio-TV address

[44] Thomas J. Dodd, *Freedom and Foreign Policy* (New York, 1962), p. 178ff. Cf Raskin and Fall (eds),
Viet-Nam Reader, p. 174.

[45] John Foster Dulles, *War or Peace*, p. 25. Cf also David Halberstam, *The Best and the Brightest*
(London, 1974), p. 729; and Eugene V. Rostow, *Law, Power and the Pursuit of Peace* (New York, 1968),
p. 208. Also Howard Zinn, *The Logic of Withdrawal* (Boston, 1967), p. 83ff.

[46] *Public Papers of the Presidents: Lyndon Johnson*, 1965, I, p. 449.

[47] Cf W. W. Rostow, *The Great Transition* (Leeds, 1967), p. 497.

[48] Lyndon B. Johnson, *My Hope for America* (New York, 1964), p. 66.

on October 22, 1962, during the Cuban missile crisis, a formula repeated by practically every American foreign policy maker since World War II:

> The 1930s taught us a clear lesson: aggressive conduct, if allowed to go unchecked and unchallenged, ultimately leads to war.[49]

The bottom line was repeated by Lyndon Johnson in his speech "Pattern for Peace in Southeast Asia":

> The central lesson of our time is that the appetite of the aggressor is never satisfied. To withdraw from one battlefield means only to prepare for the next.[50]

He even quoted the Bible: "We must say in Southeast Asia, as we did in Europe, in the words of the Bible: Hitherto shalt thou come, but no further."[51]

The Aggression Theory was a mainstay not only of Lyndon Johnson's beliefs. It was shared and repeated by numerous other policy makers and commentators; "What we are doing is right," said Vice President Hubert Humphrey. "We have learned that aggression unchecked is aggression unleashed."[52] And the U.S. Ambassador to the United Nations, Arthur Goldberg, asserted that the "cannibalistic appetite of the aggressor" was endless and continually growing.[53]

In Lyndon Johnson's reasoning we find the same decisive argument that is used by all practitioners within the Munich paradigm. By seeing the struggle through now the chances of a much larger war—perhaps a nuclear war—would be greatly reduced: "I would rather stand in Vietnam in our time, and by meeting this danger now, and facing up to it, thereby reduce the danger for our children and for our grandchildren."[54]

As might be expected, the parallel between the Korean and Vietnam situations was constantly referred to. One obvious reason was the fact that the Korean decision was generally accepted and supported. Another—equally important one— was that the decision makers believed the problem and situations to be more or less identical—that their perceptual predispositions made them place the two events in the same, larger context. "We sent our troops into Korea two and one half years ago because we knew that mobsters who get away with one crime are only encouraged to start another," Adlai Stevenson asserted in 1952, adding that "Korea was a crucial test in the struggle between the Free World and Communism."[55] The

---

[49] John F. Kennedy, *The Burden and the Glory* (New York, 1964), p. 89; Hans Trefousse (ed), *The Cold War: A Book of Documents* (New York, 1965).

[50] Lyndon B. Johnson, "Pattern for Peace in Southeast Asia." In David L. Larson (ed), *The Puritan Ethic in United States Foreign Policy* (New York, 1966). Also in Marvin E. Gettleman (ed), *Vietnam: History, Documents and Opinions on a Major World Crisis* (New York, 1965).

[51] Lyndon B. Johnson, *My Hope for America*, p. 66.

[52] Kail, p. 98. Also *Department of State Bulletin*, LII, April 26, 1965.

[53] Kail, p. 99f. Similarly, Undersecretary of State, Nicholas Katzenbach, expressed doubts "about the capacity of idealism and vision alone to withstand calculated aggression and force."

[54] Lyndon B. Johnson, Speech, September 29, 1967. In James MacGregor Burns, *To Heal and to Build*, p. 127.

[55] Adlai E. Stevenson, Speech, October 31, 1951. *Speeches* (1953), p. 240.

dichotomy of the Free World—Communism, their total incompatibility, the criminal aggressiveness of the Communists, the necessity of intervention and of a rejection of appeasement—all these basic assumptions of the Munich paradigm were present. Twelve years later, as U.S. Ambassador to the United Nations, Stevenson made a statement to the effect that "the point is the same in Vietnam today as it was in Greece in 1947 and in Korea in 1950."[56]

There is a common belief that the Vietnam War was unpopular from the start and that it never had a support equalling that of the Korean War. However, as shown by John E. Mueller in his study *War, Presidents and Public Opinion*, this is not correct. In general the support was similar, starting at the same level, and in both cases it declined as a logarithmic function of American casualties. Eventually the support for the war in Vietnam dropped below those levels found during the Korean War, but that did not happen until the Vietnam War had gone on considerably longer and the American casualties had far surpassed those of the earlier war.[57] But if the popular opposition to the wars was of similar size, the opposition against the Vietnam War was considerably more vocal. Mueller's explanation is that the small but increasingly influential intellectual, non-union Left supported the Korean War as an unpleasant but necessary conflict, a battle in the Cold War, but did not see the Vietnam War in the same light and did not find it worthy of support.[58]

An elaborate and comprehensive formulation of the rationale for the American intervention in Vietnam was presented by Lyndon Johnson in an address before the National Legislative Conference in San Antonio, Texas, on September 29, 1967. The key to the policy pursued by all American Presidents after the war was "our own security," and the question finally to be answered by Eisenhower, Kennedy and himself concerning Vietnam was the following: "Is the aggression a threat—not only to the immediate victim—but to the United States of America and to the peace and security of the entire world of which we in America are a very vital part?" To Lyndon Johnson the answer was unequivocally affirmative, and he quoted Eisenhower and Kennedy to illustrate that his predecessors had also shared his conviction. Interestingly enough, the emphasis is primarily on the Domino argument:

> Strategically, South Vietnam's capture by the Communists would bring their power several hundred miles into the hitherto free region. The remaining countries in Southeast Asia would be menaced by a great flanking movement. The freedom of 12 million people would be lost immediately, and that of 150 million in adjacent lands would be seriously endangered. The loss of South Vietnam would set in motion a crumbling process that could, as it progressed, have grave consequences for us and for freedom.[59]

---

[56] *Department of State Bulletin*, June 1965, p. 908.

[57] John E. Mueller, *War, Presidents and Public Opinion* (New York, 1973), p. 23ff.

[58] *Ibid.*, p. 155ff.

[59] James MacGregor Burns, *To Heal and to Build*, p. 126.

Lyndon Johnson added two quotations from Kennedy, the first one from 1962 and the second one from the following year: "Withdrawal in the case of Vietnam and in the case of Thailand might mean the collapse of the entire area," and "We are not going to withdraw from that effort. In my opinion, for us to withdraw from that effort would mean a collapse not only of South Vietnam, but Southeast Asia. So we are going to stay there."

State Department's *White Paper on Vietnam*, February 27, 1965—by Eric Goldman not unjustly characterized as "a ringing exercise in oversimplifications and questionable inferences"—contends unequivocally that the commitment of the North Vietnam Communists to conquer "a sovereign people in a neighboring state" was no less total than that of the regime in North Korea in 1950.[60] The meaning of the aggression was the same and had to be met. And Barry Goldwater, the Republican candidate for the Presidency in 1964, stated bluntly: "Yesterday it was Korea, tonight it is Vietnam. Make no bones about this. Don't try to sweep it under the rug. We are at war in Vietnam."[61]

The Munich Syndrome dominated the thinking of Dean Rusk, Secretary of State. He varied his message to some extent, but his address at a meeting of the *U.S. Council of the International Chamber of Commerce* in March 1965 is fairly typical:

> ...So what is our stake? What is our commitment in that situation? Can those of us in this room forget the lesson that we had on this issue of war and peace, when it was only 10 years from the seizure of Manchuria to Pearl Harbor: about two years from the seizure of Czechoslovakia to the outbreak of World War II in Western Europe? Don't you remember the hopes expressed in those days: that perhaps the aggressor will be satisfied by this next bite, and perhaps he will be quiet. Remember that?...We learned that, by postponing the issue, we made the result more terrible, the holocaust more dreadful. We cannot forget this experience.[62]

On another occasion he exhorted his audience: "Once again we hear expressed the views which cost the men of my generation a terrible price in World War II. We are told that Southeast Asia is too far away—but so were Manchuria and Ethiopia."[63] George W. Ball, Under Secretary of State and the number two man in the State Department, has been represented as one of the few voices in the Johnson

---

[60] Eric F. Goldman, *The Tragedy of Lyndon Johnson* (New York, 1969), p. 475. Aggression From the North: The Record of North Vietnam's Campaign to Conquer South Vietnam. *U.S. Department of State Publication 7839. Far Eastern Series 130* (Washington, D.C., February 1965). Also in Gettleman (ed), *Vietnam: History, Documents, and Opinions on a Major World Crisis.*

[61] Barry M. Goldwater, Acceptance Speech, July 17, 1964, *Campaign Speeches*, p. 341. Also Goldwater, *The Conscience of a Majority* (Englewood Cliffs, New Jersey, 1970), p. 78ff; Goldwater, *Why not Victory?* p. 22.

[62] David Larson, *The Puritan Ethic*, p. 173. *Department of State Bulletin*, LII, March 22, 1965.

[63] Dean Rusk, *The Winds of Freedom* (1963).

administration raised in opposition to the war in Vietnam.[64] However, his opposition came at a rather late stage and was hardly vociferous. In fact, there is no indication that he differed from the President and the Secretary of State in basic assumptions. He was, at any rate, prepared to present almost identical views on the war:

> We have...come to realize from experience of the past years that aggression must be dealt with where ever it occurs and no matter what mask it may wear....In the 1930s Manchuria seemed a long way away....Ethiopia seemed a long way away. The rearmament of the Rhineland was regarded as regrettable but not worth a shooting war. Yet after that came Austria, and after Austria Czechoslovakia. Then Poland. Then the Second World War. The central issue we face in South Vietnam...is whether a small state on the periphery of Communist power should be permitted to maintain its freedom. And that is an issue of vital importance to small states everywhere.[65]

George Ball might have held other views in private. However, publicly he performed as a practitioner within the Munich paradigm.

As Vice President, Hubert Humphrey had no option but to support the Vietnam policy of the Johnson administration. However, there is no indication that he himself was unaffected by the Munich Syndrome, that he questioned the basic assumptions that were the very basis of the American intervention in the Vietnam War. He had "not forgotten the lessons of the 30s, when men cried peace and failed a generation."[66]

Senator Henry Jackson (D. Wash) became known as one of the hawks in Congress concerning the Vietnam War. However, the truth is that he often expressed himself rather more cautiously and with more qualifications than many others cited above. This is the case especially after 1968 which, on the other hand, is hardly surprising, since the war—and the basic assumptions underlying it—were then increasingly under attack. The bipolar concept was losing its credibility and the world view of the practitioners within the Munich paradigm was disintegrating—or at least showed serious signs of crumbling.

"Analogies with the past may be misleading and I would not argue that this is the 30's all over again," Jackson warned, but continued:

> But looking back we think, as I am sure many of you do, that it is wise to stop aggression before the aggressor becomes strong and swollen with ambition from small successes. We think the world might have been spared enormous misfortunes if Japan had not been permitted to succeed in Manchuria, or Mussolini in Ethiopia, or Hitler in Czechoslovakia or in the Rhineland. And we think that our sacrifices in this dirty war in little Vietnam will make a dirtier and bigger war less likely.[67]

[64] George W. Ball, *Diplomacy for a Crowded World. An American Foreign Policy* (Boston, 1976).

[65] *Department of State Bulletin*, LI, 1965, p. 922. Cf May, p. 113.

[66] *International Herald Tribune*, October 25, 1967.

[67] *Report, Senate Committee on Foreign Relations*, October 15, 1968, p. 570. Henry M. Jackson (ed), *The Atlantic Alliance* (New York, Washington, London, 1968).

In a similar effort to counter the criticism that the analogy of the 1930s was inaccurate Secretary of State Dean Rusk explained:

> The clearest lesson of the 1930s and 40s is that aggression feeds on aggression. I am aware that Mao and Ho Chi Minh are not Hitler and Mussolini. But we should not forget what we have learned about the anatomy and physiology of aggression. We ought to know better than to ignore the aggressor's openly proclaimed intentions or to fall victim to the notion that he will stop if you let him have just one more bite or speak to him a little more gently.[68]

It has been argued that no issue in American politics since the Civil War had created as much dissension as Vietnam, nor had any public issue "involved greater complexities of judgment in interpreting information, in predicting the consequences of possible actions, and in balancing pragmatism and idealism, justification of official policies, wishful thinking and bandwagon psychology."[69] This may be a fairly accurate characterization of the situation during the late 1960s—or, at least, a reasonable one. However, it certainly did not fit the situation during the early years of the decade, neither public opinion nor the perceptions of the policy makers. At that time the perceptual predispositions, originating in the images of the 1930s and enforced during the Cold War, were still powerful and pervasive, and the Munich Analogy, the Domino Principle and the Aggression Theory were dominant factors when it came to interpreting and evaluating the international problems facing the United States in Formosa or Berlin, the Middle East or Vietnam.[70] ...

THE DOMINO METAPHOR AND THE MUNICH ANALOGY

What then was the function of the Domino metaphor (Theory, Principle) and the Munich Analogy? Obviously they became common rhetorical devices repeated, reiterated and restated again and again for public consumption. They had a persuasive function, and to some analysts that is all that was to it: "The analogy comes first, I would suggest, out of a need to pile up more and more reasons to persuade the public, because it is evident that the public has been in great need of persuasion," argued Howard Zinn, discussing the Vietnam War.[71] As Arthur Schlesinger, Jr. has posed the question: "Is the history invoked really the source of policies, or is it the source of arguments designed to vindicate policies adopted for antecedent reasons?"[72] Also Holsti and Rosenau have suggested, that there obviously are cases, where historical analogies are part of the rhetoric used by decision makers to justify

[68] Kail, *What Washington Said* (1973), p. 98.

[69] Leo Bogart, *Silent Politics: Polls and the Awareness of Public Opinion* (New York, 1972), p. 89f.

[70] *Ibid.*, p. 90.

[71] Howard Zinn, *The Logic of Withdrawal* (Boston, 1967), p. 82ff.

[72] Arthur M. Schlesinger, Jr., *The Bitter Heritage*, p. 90.

policies and decisions arrived at by other means.[73] However, it would be a serious mistake to conceive of these ideas as pure rhetorical ornaments or as nothing but devices for persuasion and propaganda.

In a thoughtful and stimulating study Lars-Göran Stenelo has analyzed the linkages between analogies and predictions, discussing the Munich analogy as well as the Domino Theory in terms of their function in the prediction process.[74] He argues that theory oriented predictions, by which he means for example the Domino Theory and the Aggression Theory "seem to have been perceived by the predictor as more independent of specific situation characteristics than the analogy-based predictions." He also makes a distinction between "analogy" and "precedence." Stenelo is concerned with analogies—as well as with the Domino and Aggression theories—mainly in their predictive functions but to some extent even in their persuasive functions, whereas the focus in this study is on the inferences made by policy makers when interpreting a situation, that is, on analogies etc. as a source of perceptual predispositions.

There is an obvious similarity between the American analyses in 1946–47 of the situation in the Near East and those we encounter in 1954 and the following years of the problems in Southeast Asia. It was a common belief among American decision makers that the Soviet Union had withdrawn its forces from Iran as a result of mounting American pressure. Similarly, the Russian efforts to accomplish a breakthrough in Greece and Turkey were believed to have been stifled by the Truman Doctrine and the policy of containment. This was regarded as a success and also, somehow, as a confirmation of the validity of the Domino Theory or, rather, its early equivalents.

The Domino metaphor was not the only one used in describing the nature of the perceived Soviet or Communist threat. Dean Acheson had implored the Congressional leaders to support Greece, or else: "Like apples in a barrel infected by a rotten one, the corruption of Greece would infect Iran and all to the east. It would also carry infection to Africa through the Asia Minor and Egypt, and to Europe through Italy and France, already threatened by the strongest Communist parties in the Western Europe."[75] And in a speech in the Senate in support of the Mutual Defense Assistance Bill Tom Connally argued: "We can't let our friends be picked off one by one like pigeons in a shooting gallery."[76] However, none of these metaphors were as catching as the Domino one.

When the complicated situation in Vietnam and Southeast Asia arose, the Domino Theory was applied more or less automatically. It could—with a concept used by Bruce Kuklick and borrowed from the Harvard psychologist Jerome Bruner—be said to work as a "pre-emptive metaphor."[77] The Korean War, and almost a decade of Cold War, had meant not only immense pressures from the outside but also enormous internal tensions. This had led to serious damages to the ability to learn, to receive and evaluate new information, to recognize and cope with

---

[73] Stenelo, *Foreign Policy Predictions*, p. 114.

[74] *Ibid.*, p. 197ff; 135ff.

[75] Leila Zenderland, *Recycling the Past: Popular Use of American History* (Philadelphia, 1978), p. 129ff.

[76] Tom Connally and Alfred Steinberg, *My Name is Tom Connally* (New York, 1954), p. 339.

[77] Douglas MacArthur, *Reminiscences* (New York, 1964), pp. 330; 404.

new realities. Instead there was a strong tendency to rely on assumptions based on previous experiences and its "lessons," to screen and interpret incoming information according to these perceptual predispositions, and to let a pre-emptive metaphor give meaning to the new situation.

An elaborate version of the Domino Theory was introduced in a classified statement formulated by President Eisenhower and the Secretary of State, John Foster Dulles on September 4, 1958, in order to explain the necessity of the American commitment to the defense of the offshore islands in the Formosa Straits. The loss of the islands would, according to the statement, mean a threat not only to Taiwan but also to the American position in Japan, Korea, the Philippine Islands, Thailand and Vietnam. Furthermore, it might push Indonesia, Malaya, Cambodia, Laos and Burma under Communist influence.[78]

The Domino Theory still held sway in the early 1960s. The National Security Action Memorandum of March 1964, endorsed by President Johnson, sounded like an echo of Kennedy's stated position in 1956:

> We seek an independent non-Communist South Vietnam.... Unless we can achieve this object... almost all of Southeast Asia will probably fall under Communist(s) (all of Vietnam, Laos, and Cambodia), accommodate to Communism so as to remove effective U.S. and anti-Communist influence (Burma), or fall under the domination of forces not now explicitly Communist but likely to become so (Indonesia taking over Malaya). Thailand might hold for a period without help, but would be under grave pressure. Even the Philippines would become shaky, and the threat to India on the West, Australia and New Zealand to the South, and Taiwan, Korea, and Japan to the North and East would be greatly increased.[79]

This certainly was the Domino Theory with a vengeance. In his important Tonkin Gulf message to Congress a few months later, Lyndon Johnson restated the theory in its more limited version: "The issue is the future of Southeast Asia as a whole. A threat to any nation in that region is a threat to all, and a threat to us."[80]

The Domino Principle was cited frequently at this time. Thus Ambassador Henry Cabot Lodge asserted that "the well-advertised domino theory" applied to Vietnam, and Maxwell Taylor elaborated on the same theme:

> After Communist success in South Vietnam, the remainder of Southeast Asia would very shortly thereafter go neutralist, possibly eventually Communist. Burma would be affected, India also. Indonesia would soon line up with the Communists. We could be pushed out of the Western Pacific to Honolulu. That would be the short term effect over the next few years.[81]

[78] Dwight D. Eisenhower, *White House Years*, p. 691ff. Alexander L. George and Richard Smoke, *Deterrence in American Foreign Policy* (New York, 1974), p. 385.

[79] *Pentagon Papers*, III, p. 50f.

[80] Lyndon B. Johnson, Message to Congress, August 1964, cf *Vantage Point*, p. 152.

[81] Maxwell Taylor, September 10, 1964, Kail, *What Washington Said* (1973), p. 91.

William P. Bundy emphasized the threat not only to India but to Australia and Japan in the event of the fall of South Vietnam.[82]

A sophisticated version of the Domino Principle was presented by Robert Scalopino at the Washington Teach-In in 1965: American withdrawal from Vietnam would precipitate a loss of credibility and give a green light to new "Communist-dominated National Liberation Movements" already getting under way. If America could be forced into a unilateral withdrawal from Vietnam, that strategy would work elsewhere and be tried everywhere.[83] The same formula was advanced by Tom Wicker in the *New York Times* in February 1967. Wicker argued that the Domino Theory had much truth. A Communist victory in Vietnam achieved through internal subversion assisted by a neighboring nation "would greatly encourage the use of the same technique for attempted conquest elsewhere in the world." And much later Guenter Lewy maintained that exactly this was the "real and deeper meaning" of the Domino Theory.[84]

Starting with the increasingly doubtful premise of the Domino Theory, America went down the road without stopping to check if the direction was right, the goal really in the national interest, attainable, or worth the price. Howard Trivers, a former Foreign Service officer, has aptly summarized the weakness of the Domino Theory in its application to Southeast Asia, pointing out its failure to recognize "the likelihood in view of past history that a Vietnam united under the Communists would be more apt to serve as an impediment than an aid to Chinese expansionism." The Domino Theory likewise failed to grasp the individuality of the Southeast Asian countries.

Contributing to the American Presidents' preference for continuing a risky and devastating war to cutting the losses and getting out was, as we have previously mentioned, a domestic factor: fear of the political consequences of a "loss" of Vietnam, induced by the vituperations of the early 1950s over "the loss of China."

The belief in the mortal danger of the Domino effect, combined with the fear of the conceivable domestic political consequences of being held responsible for "losing" another part of the free world to Communism, were powerful elements, vital parts of the Munich Syndrome.

Analogies and images are seen by John D. Steinbruner as structures utilized for anchoring a set of beliefs when direct evidences are weak or contradictory. Their function is to summarize and clarify complex ideas. The image of falling dominoes is regarded as such an organizing concept, providing an internal anchor "around which inference mechanisms of the mind can structure ambiguous information."[85] As we have seen, the Munich analogy as well as the Domino Theory are vital elements of the Munich syndrome, of the assumptions that for almost two decades permeated American thinking on foreign policy and determined the way in which the fundamentals of the international system were perceived.

---

[82] William P. Bundy, September 29, 1964. *Ibid.*

[83] George McT. Kahin and Robert A. Scalapino, "Excerpts from National Teach-In on Viet-Nam Policy." In Raskin/Fall, p. 289ff. Howard Zinn (1967), p. 88f.

[84] Guenter Lewy, *America in Vietnam* (New York, 1978), p. 426.

[85] John D. Steinbruner, *The Cybernetic Theory of Decision: New Dimensions of Political Analysis* (Princeton, 1974), p. 115ff.

11

UNQUESTIONED ASSUMPTIONS

THE PENTAGON PAPERS

Between June 1967 and January 1969, thirty-six professionals from government agencies and think tanks collected documents and wrote analyses for a secret history of U.S. involvement in the Vietnam War commissioned by Secretary of Defense Robert McNamara. Their study became known as the Pentagon Papers *when Daniel Ellsberg and Anthony Russo leaked it to the public in 1971. In an analysis of the period from 1950 to 1954, one of these anonymous authors described the unquestioned assumptions underpinning American decisions, the most important of which was the domino principle.*

PERCEPTIONS OF THE COMMUNIST THREAT TO SOUTHEAST ASIA AND TO BASIC U.S. INTERESTS

Three major perceptions dominated U.S. thinking and policy-making on Indochina during the years 1950–1954. The first was the growing importance of Asia in world politics. The process of devotion [*sic*] from colonial empires to independent states, it was thought, would create power vacuums and conditions of instability which would make Asia susceptible to becoming a battleground in the growing East-West cold war conflict. Second, there was an undeniable tendency to view the worldwide "communist threat" in monolithic terms. This was perhaps understandable given the relatively extensive influence then exerted by the Soviet Union over other communist nations, and the communist parties in non-communist states. Moreover, the West, and especially the U.S., was challenged by the expansionist policies openly proclaimed by leaders of virtually all the communist movements. Third, the attempt of the patently Communist Ho Chi Minh regime to evict the French from

The Pentagon Papers: The Defense Department History of United States Decisionmaking on Vietnam. The Senator Gravel Edition, vol. 1 (Boston: Beacon Press, 1971), 81–88.

Indochina was seen as part of the Southeast Asian manifestation of the communist world-wide aggressive intent. The resistance of France to Ho, therefore, was seen as a crucial stand on the line along which the West would contain communism.

A. "Domino Principle" before Korea

These three perceptions help explain the widely held assumption in official Washington that if Indochina was "lost" to communism, the remaining nations of Southeast Asia would inexorably succumb to communist infiltration and be taken over in a chain reaction. This strategic conception of the communist threat to Southeast Asia pre-dated the outbreak in June 1950 of the Korean War. It probably had its period of gestation at the time of the Nationalist withdrawal from mainland China. NSC 48/1 was the key document in framing this conception. Drawn up in June 1949, after Secretary of Defense Louis Johnson had expressed concern at the course of events in Asia and had suggested a widening of the previous country-by-country memorandum approach to a regional plan, NSC 48/1 included the statements that "the extension of communist authority in China represents a grievous political defeat for us. . . . If Southeast Asia is also swept by communism, we shall have suffered a major political rout the repercussions of which will be felt throughout the rest of the world, especially in the Middle East and in a then critically exposed Australia."

It was Russia rather than China that was seen in 1949 as being the principal source of the communist threat in Asia. Although it was conceded that in the course of time China (or Japan or India) may attempt to dominate Asia:

> now and for the foreseeable future it is the USSR which threatens to dominate Asia through the complementary instruments of communist conspiracy and diplomatic pressure supported by military strength. For the foreseeable future, therefore, our immediate objective must be to contain and where feasible to reduce the power and influence of the USSR in Asia to such a degree that the Soviet Union is not capable of threatening the security of the United States from that area and that the Soviet Union would encounter serious obstacles should it attempt to threaten the peace, national independence or stability of the Asiatic nations.

NSC 48/1 also recognized that "the colonial-nationalist conflict provides a fertile field for subversive communist movements, and it is now clear that Southeast Asia is the target for a coordinated offensive directed by the Kremlin."

At this time, the NSC believed that the United States, as a Western power in any area where the bulk of the population had long been suspicious of Western influence, should insofar as possible refrain from taking any lead in Southeast Asia. The United States should instead "encourage the peoples of India, Pakistan, the Philippines and other Asian states to take the leadership in meeting the common problems of the area," recognizing "that the non-communist governments of South Asia already constitute a bulwark against communist expansion in Asia." NSC 48/2 pointed out that particular attention should be given to the problem of Indochina where "action should be taken to bring home to the French the urgency of removing the barriers to the obtaining by Bao Dai or other non-communist nationalist leaders of the support of a substantial proportion of the Vietnamese."

B. Importance of Indochina

Indochina was of special importance because it was the only area adjacent to China which contained a large European army which was in armed conflict with "communist" forces. The Chinese Communists were believed to be furnishing the Viet Minh with substantial material assistance. Official French sources reported that there were some Chinese troops in Tonkin, as well as large numbers ready for action against the French on the Chinese side of the border. The first NSC memorandum dealing solely with Indochina (NSC 64) [Doc. 1] was adopted as policy on February 27, 1950. This paper took note of Chinese assistance to the Viet Minh and estimated that it was doubtful that the French Expeditionary forces, combined with Indochinese troops, could successfully contain Ho Chi Minh's forces should they be strengthened by either Chinese troops crossing the border, or by communist-supplied arms and material in quantity.

NSC 64—written, it should be noted, by the Truman Administration and before the outbreak of the Korean War—observed that "the threat of Communist aggression against Indochina is only one phase of anticipated communist plans to seize all of Southeast Asia." It concluded with a statement of what came to be known as the "domino principle":

It is important to United States security interests that all practicable measures be taken to prevent further communist expansion in Southeast Asia. Indochina is a key area of Southeast Asia and is under immediate threat.

The neighboring countries of Thailand and Burma could be expected to fall under Communist domination if Indochina were controlled by a Communist-dominated government. The balance of Southeast Asia would then be in grave hazard.

C. Impact of Start of Korean War

The outbreak of the Korean War, and the American decision to resist North Korean aggression, sharpened overnight our thoughts and actions with respect to Southeast Asia. The American military response symbolized in the most concrete manner possible the basic belief that holding the line in Southeast Asia was essential to American security interests. The French struggle in Indochina came far more than before to be seen as an integral part of the containment of communism in that region of the world. Accordingly, the United States intensified and enlarged its programs of aid in Indochina. Military aid shipments to Indochina acquired in 1951 the second highest priority, just behind the Korean war program.

A consequence of the Korean War, and particularly the Chinese intervention, was that China replaced the Soviet Union as the principal source of the perceived communist threat in Southeast Asia. This was made explicit in NSC 124/2 (June 1952) [Doc. 13] which stated that "the danger of an overt military attack against Southeast Asia is inherent in the existence of a hostile and aggressive Communist China."

The "domino principle" in its purest form was written into the "General Considerations" section of NSC 124/2. It linked the loss of any single state of Southeast Asia to the stability of Europe and the security of the United States:

2. Communist domination, by whatever means, of all Southeast Asia would seriously endanger in the short term, and critically endanger in the longer term, United States security interests.

    a. The loss of any of the countries of Southeast Asia to communist control as a consequence of overt or covert Chinese Communist aggression would have critical psychological, political and economic consequences. In the absence of effective and timely counteraction, the loss of any single country would probably lead to relatively swift submission to or an alignment with communism by the remaining countries of this group. Furthermore, an alignment with communism of the rest of Southeast Asia and India, and in the longer term, of the Middle East (with the probable exceptions of at least Pakistan and Turkey) would in all probability progressively follow. Such widespread alignment would endanger the stability and security of Europe.

    b. Communist control of all of Southeast Asia would render the U.S. position in the Pacific offshore island chain precarious and would seriously jeopardize fundamental U.S. security interests in the Far East.

    c. Southeast Asia, especially Malaya and Indonesia, is the principal world source of natural rubber and tin, and a producer of petroleum and other strategically important commodities. The rice exports of Burma and Thailand are critically important to Malaya, Ceylon and Hong Kong and are of considerable significance to Japan and India, all important areas of free Asia.

    d. The loss of Southeast Asia, especially of Malaya and Indonesia, could result in such economic and political pressures in Japan as to make it extremely difficult to prevent Japan's eventual accommodation to communism.

The possibility of a large-scale Chinese intervention in Indochina, similar to the Chinese intervention in Korea, came to dominate the thinking of American policy-makers after the start of the Korean War. Such an intervention would not have been surprising given the larger numbers of Chinese troops massed along the Tonkin border and the material assistance being given to the Viet Minh. The NIE of December 1950 considered direct Chinese intervention to be "impending." The following year it was estimated that after an armistice in Korea the Chinese would be capable of intervention in considerable strength, but would be inhibited from acting overtly by a number of factors, including the risk of American retaliation and the disadvantages attendant upon involvement in another protracted campaign. By early 1952, as the French position showed signs of deterioration, intelligence authorities believed that the Chinese would be content to continue aiding the Viet Minh without undertaking direct involvement (except for material aid) unless provoked into it. Thus, the intelligence community, after estimating a high risk of Chinese intervention at the start of the Korean War, gradually reduced its estimate of Indochina being broadened into a wider war as the Viet Minh showed signs of doing well enough on their own.

Nevertheless, the NSC undertook in 1952 to list a course of action for the "resolute defense" of Indochina in case of a large-scale Chinese intervention. It included the provision of air and naval forces; the interdiction of Chinese communication lines, including those in China proper; and a naval blockade of the China coast. If these "minimum courses of action" did not prove to be sufficient, the U.S. should take air and naval action "against all suitable military targets in China," when possible in conjunction with British and French forces.

In prescribing these recommended actions, the NSC focused on the less likely contingency of a Chinese intervention rather than the more likely contingency of the continued deterioration of the French position in Indochina itself. It did so despite the fact that NSC 124/2 conceded that the "primary threat" was the situation in Indochina itself (increasing subversive efforts by indigenous communist forces, increased guerrilla activity, and increased Viet Minh civil control over population and territory). Apparently, the NSC wanted to make clear that direct U.S. involvement in Indochina was to be limited to dealing with direct Chinese involvement. In the absence of this contingency, however, and to meet the existing situation in Indochina, the NSC recommended that the United States increase its level of aid to French Union forces but "without relieving the French authorities of their basic military responsibility for the defense of the Associated States."

D. Republican Administration and Far East

Two events in 1953 served to deepen the American commitment in Indochina. The first was the arrival of a Republican Administration following a long period in which the G.O.P. had persistently accused the Truman Administration of being responsible for the "loss" of China to communism. The writings and speeches of John Foster Dulles before the election left no doubt that he regarded Southeast Asia as a key region in the conflict with communist "imperialism," and that it was important to draw the line of containment north of the Rice Bowl of Asia—the Indochina peninsula. In his first State of the Union Message on February 3, 1953, President Eisenhower promised a "new, positive foreign policy." He went on to link the communist aggression in Korea and Malaya with Indochina. Dulles subsequently spoke of Korea and Indochina as two flanks, with the principal enemy—Red China—in the center. A special study mission headed by Representative Walter Judd, a recognized Republican spokesman on Asia, surveyed the Far East and reported on its view of the high stakes involved:

> The area of Indochina is immensely wealthy in rice, rubber, coal, and iron ore. Its position makes it a strategic key to the rest of Southeast Asia. If Indochina should fall, Thailand and Burma would be in extreme

danger, Malaya, Singapore and even Indonesia would become more vulnerable to the Communist power drive....Communism would then be
in an exceptional position to complete its perversion of the political and
social revolution that is spreading through Asia....The Communists
must be prevented from achieving their objectives in Indochina.

The Republican Administration clearly intended to prevent the loss of Indochina
by taking a more forthright, anti-communist stand.

E. Impact of Korean Armistice

Second, the armistice in Korea created apprehension that the Chinese Communists
would now turn their attention to Indochina. President Eisenhower warned in a
speech on April 16, 1953, that any armistice in Korea that merely released armed
forces to pursue an attack elsewhere would be a fraud. Secretary Dulles continued
this theme after the Korean armistice in a speech on September 2, 1953, on the war
in Indochina. After noting that "a single Communist aggressive front extends from
Korea on the north to Indochina in the south" he said:

Communist China has been and now is training, equipping and supplying the Communist forces in Indochina. There is the risk that, as in
Korea, Red China might send its own Army into Indochina. The Chinese
Communist regime should realize that such a second aggression could
not occur without grave consequences which might not be confined to
Indochina. I say this soberly...in the hope of preventing another aggressor miscalculation.

Underlying these warnings to China was the belief that the difference between
success or failure in avoiding a takeover of all Vietnam by Ho Chi Minh probably
depended upon the extent of Chinese assistance or direct participation. Signaling
a warning to China was probably designed to deter further Chinese involvement.
Implicit in the signals was the threat that if China came into the war, the United
States would be forced to follow suit, preferably with allies but, if necessary, alone.
Furthermore, the Eisenhower Administration implied that in keeping with its policy of massive retaliation the United States would administer a punishing nuclear
blow to China without necessarily involving its land forces in an Asian war.

F. Deepening of U.S. Commitment to Containment

In addition to the new mood in Washington created by the strategic perceptions of
a new Administration and the Korean armistice, the Viet Minh invasion of Laos in
the spring of 1953 and the deepening war weariness in France served to strengthen
those who favored a more assertive policy in Indochina. The United States rushed
supplies to Laos and Thailand in May 1953 and provided six C-119's with civilian
crews for the airlift into Laos. It increased substantially the volume and tempo of
American military assistance to French Union forces. For fiscal year 1954, $460
million in military assistance was planned. Congress only appropriated $400 mil-
lion, but following the presentation by the French of the Navarre Plan an additional

$385 million was decided upon by the NSC. No objection was raised when France asked our views in August, 1953, on the transfer of its battalion in Korea to Indochina and subsequently took this action. The Navarre Plan, by offering a format for victory which promised success without the direct involvement of American military forces, tended, because of its very attractiveness, to have the effect of enlarging our commitment to assist the French towards achieving a military solution.

In the last NSC paper approved before the Indochina situation was totally transformed by the French defeat at Dien Bien Phu and the Geneva Conference, the "successful defense of Tonkin" was said to be the "keystone of the defense of mainland Southeast Asia except possibly Malaya." NSC 5405 [Doc. 20] took some, but probably not sufficient, account of the deterioration in the French position which had occurred since NSC 124/2 was approved eighteen months earlier. It, nevertheless, repeated the domino principle in detail, including the admonition that "such is the interrelation of the countries of the area that effective counteraction would be immediately necessary to prevent the loss of any single country from leading to submission to, or an alignment with, communism by the remaining countries of Southeast Asia and Indonesia." The document also noted that:

> In the conflict in Indochina, the Communists and non-Communists worlds clearly confront one another in the field of battle: The loss of the struggle in Indochina, in addition to its impact in Southeast Asia and South Asia, would therefore have the most serious repercussions on U.S. and free world interests in Europe and elsewhere.

The subject of possible negotiations was broached in NSC 5405, following the observation that political pressures in France may impel the French Government to seek a negotiated rather than a military settlement. It was noted (before Dien Bien Phu) that if the Navarre Plan failed or appeared doomed to failure, the French might seek to negotiate simply for the best possible terms, irrespective of whether these offered any assurance of preserving a non-communist Indochina.

In this regard the NSC decided the U.S. should employ every feasible means to influence the French Government against concluding the struggle on terms "inconsistent" with the basic U.S. objectives. The French should be told that: (1) in the absence of a marked improvement in the military situation, there was no basis for negotiation on acceptable terms; (2) the U.S. would "flatly oppose any idea" of a cease-fire as a preliminary to negotiations, because such a cease-fire would result in an irretrievable deterioration of the Franco-Vietnamese military position in Indochina; (3) *a nominally non-communist coalition regime would eventually turn the country over to Ho Chi Minh with no opportunity for the replacement of the French by the United States or the United Kingdom.*[Emphasis Added]

G. Conclusion

In conclusion, two comments can be made:

> (a) With the growing perception of a Chinese threat to Indochina, and, therefore, to all of Southeast Asia, the U.S. Government tended to concentrate on the military rather than the political aspects of the French–Viet Minh

struggle. In consequence, American attention focused on (1) deterring external intervention from China, and (2) assisting the French in successfully prosecuting the war through the implementation of the Navarre Plan. The result of this was that the encouragement and support of the non-communist nationalist governments in the Associated States was almost inadvertently given lower priority. The United States was reluctant to press the French too strongly on taking measures to foster Vietnam nationalism because of its overriding interest in halting the potential sweep of communism through Southeast Asia. Moreover, it was easier to develop a policy for dealing with the external threat of intervention than to meet the internal threat of subversion, or the even more difficult process of finding and sustaining a genuine nationalist alternative to the Viet Minh.

(b) The "domino theory" and the assumptions behind it were never questioned. The homogeneity of the nations of Southeast Asia was taken as a given, as was the linkage in their ability to remain democratic, or at an acceptable minimum, non-communist, nations. Undoubtedly, in the first decade of the cold war there existed an unfortunate stereotype of a monolithic communist expansionary bloc. It was reinforced by a somewhat emotional approach on the part of many Americans to communism in China and Asia. This "syndrome" was, in part, the result of the "fall" of China, which some felt could have been averted, and a few hoped would still be reversed.

Accordingly, not sufficient cognizance was taken of the individuality of the states of Southeast Asia and the separateness of their societies. Probably there was some lack of knowledge in depth on the part of Washington policy-makers about the area. No one before World War II had expected that the United States would be called upon to take a position of leadership in these remote colonial territories of our European allies. In hindsight, these shortcomings may have led to the fallacious belief that a neutralist or communist Indochina would inevitably draw the other states of Asia into the communist bloc or into neutralism. But the "fallacy" was neither evident then, nor is it demonstrable now in retrospect....

The debate over the wisdom and manner of American intervention in Indochina was based primarily on the desirability of military involvement, not on questions concerning Indochina's value to United States security interests in the Far East. The Eisenhower Administration was in general agreement with the rationale for American interest in Indochina expressed by the Truman Administration. The United States Government first came to full grips with the question of intervention in late 1953–early 1954 as the fall of Indochina seemed to become imminent....

12

AVOIDING HUMILIATION AND PRESERVING THE PILLAR OF PEACE

THE PENTAGON PAPERS

Volume 4 of the Senator Gravel edition of the Pentagon Papers *describes the July 1965 debate among President Johnson's advisers about the pace of U.S. escalation. The author of the section on the air war against North Vietnam points out that their fear of humiliation along with fears about the perceived reliability of the U.S. commitment in Vietnam were "much on the minds" of the advisers. According to Secretary of State Dean Rusk, the integrity of the U.S. commitment was "the principal pillar of peace throughout the world."*

The full U.S. entry into the Vietnam War in the spring of 1965—with the launching of air strikes against NVN, the release of U.S. jet aircraft for close support of ARVN troops in SVN, and the deployment to SVN of major U.S. ground forces for combat—did not bring an immediate turnabout in the security situation in SVN. The VC/NVA may have been surprised and stunned at first by the U.S. actions, but by the summer of 1965 they had again seized the initiative they held in late 1964 and early 1965 and were again mounting large-scale attacks, hurting ARVN forces badly. In mid-July Assistant Secretary McNaughton described the situation in ominous terms:

> The situation is worse than a year ago (when it was worse than a year before that)....A hard VC push is on....The US air strikes against the North and US combat-troop deployments have erased any South Vietnamese fears that the US will forsake them; but the government is able to provide security to fewer and fewer people in less and less territory, fewer roads and railroads are usable, the economy is deteriorat-

The Pentagon Papers: The Defense Department History of United States Decisionmaking on Vietnam. The Senator Gravel Edition, vol. 4 (Boston: Beacon Press, 1971), 21–29.

ing, and the government in Saigon continues to turn over. Pacification even in the Hop Tac area is making no progress. The government-to-VC ratio overall is now only 3-to-1, and in combat battalions only 1-to-1; government desertions are at a high rate, and the Vietnamese force build-up is stalled; the VC reportedly are trying to double their combat strength. There are no signs that the VC have been throttled by US/GVN inter-diction efforts; indeed, there is evidence of further PAVN build-up in the I and II Corps areas. The DRV/VC seem to believe that SVN is near collapse and show no signs of being interested in settling for less than a complete take-over.

Faced with this gloomy situation, the leading question on the U.S. agenda for Vietnam was a further major escalation of troop commitments, together with a call-up of reserves, extension of military tours, and a general expansion of the armed forces.

The question of intensifying the air war against the North was a subsidiary issue, but it was related to the troop question in several ways. The military view, as reflected in JCS proposals and proposals from the field, was that the war should be intensified on all fronts, in the North no less than in the South. There was political merit in this view as well, since it was difficult to publicly justify sending in masses of troops to slug it out on the ground without at least trying to see whether stronger pressures against NVN would help. On the other hand, there was con-tinued high-level interest in preventing a crisis atmosphere from developing, and in avoiding any over-reaction by NVN and its allies, so that a simultaneous esca-lation in both the North and the South needed to be handled with care. The bomb-ing of the North, coupled with the deployment of substantial forces should not look like an effort to soften up NVN for an invasion.

During the last days of June with U.S. air operations against North Vietnam well into their fifth month, with U.S. forces in South Vietnam embarking for the first time upon major ground combat operations, and with the President near a decision that would increase American troop strength in Vietnam from 70,000 to over 200,000, Under-Secretary of State George Ball sent to his colleagues among the small group of Vietnam "principals" in Washington a memorandum warning that the United States was poised on the brink of a military and political disaster. Nei-ther through expanded bombing of the North nor through a substantial increase in U.S. forces in the South would the United States be likely to achieve its objectives, Ball argued. Instead of escalation, he urged, "we should undertake either to ex-tricate ourselves or to reduce our defense perimeters in South Viet-Nam to accord with the capabilities of a limited US deployment."

"This is our last clear chance to make this decision," the Under-Secretary as-serted. And in a separate memorandum to the President, he explained why:

The decision you face now, therefore, is crucial. Once large numbers of US troops are committed to direct combat they will begin to take heavy casualties in a war they are ill-equipped to fight in a non-cooperative if not downright hostile countryside.

Once we suffer large casualties we will have started a well-nigh irreversible process. Our involvement will be so great that we cannot—without national humiliation—stop short of achieving our complete objectives. *Of the two possibilities I think humiliation would be more likely than the achievement of our objectives—even after we have paid terrible costs.*

"Humiliation" was much on the minds of those involved in the making of American policy for Vietnam during the spring and summer of 1965. The word, or phrases meaning the same thing, appears in countless memoranda. No one put it as starkly as Assistant Secretary of Defense John McNaughton, who in late March assigned relative weights to various American objectives in Vietnam. In McNaughton's view the principal U.S. aim was "to avoid a humiliating US defeat (to our reputation as a guarantor)." To this he assigned the weight of 70%. Second, but far less important at only 20% was "to keep SVN (and then adjacent) territory from Chinese hands." And a minor third, at but 10%, was "to permit the people of SVN to enjoy a better, freer way of life."

Where Ball differed from all the others was in his willingness to incur "humiliation" that was certain—but also limited and short-term—by withdrawing American forces in order to avoid the uncertain but not unlikely prospect of a military defeat at a higher level of involvement. Thus he entitled his memorandum "Cutting Our Losses in South Viet-Nam." In it and in his companion memorandum to the President ("A Compromise Solution for South Viet-Nam") he went on to outline a program, first, of placing a ceiling on U.S. deployments at present authorized levels (72,000 men) and sharply restricting their combat roles, and, second, of beginning negotiations with Hanoi for a cessation of hostilities and the formation in Saigon of a "government of National Union" that would include representatives of the National Liberation Front. Ball's argument was based upon his sense of relative priorities. As he told his colleagues:

The position taken in this memorandum does not suggest that the United States should abdicate leadership in the cold war. But any prudent military commander carefully selects the terrain on which to stand and fight, and no great captain has ever been blamed for a successful tactical withdrawal.

From our point of view, the terrain in South Viet-Nam could not be worse. Jungles and rice paddies are not designed for modern arms and, from a military point of view, this is clearly what General de Gaulle described to me as a "rotten country."

Politically, South Viet-Nam is a lost cause. The country is bled white from twenty years of war and the people are sick of it. The Viet Cong—as is shown by the Rand Corporation Motivation and Morale Study—are deeply committed.

Hanoi has a Government and a purpose and a discipline. The "government" in Saigon is a travesty. In a very real sense, South Viet-Nam is a country with an army and no government.

In my view, a deep commitment of United States forces in a land war
in South Viet-Nam would be a catastrophic error. If ever there was an
occasion for a tactical withdrawal, this is it.

Ball's argument was perhaps most antithetic to one being put forward at the
same time by Secretary of State Rusk. In a memorandum he wrote on 1 July, Rusk
stated bluntly: "The central objective of the United States in South Viet-Nam must
be to insure that North Viet-Nam not succeed in taking over or determining the
future of South Viet-Nam by force. We must accomplish this objective without a
general war *if possible*." Here was a statement that the American commitment to the
Vietnam war was, in effect, absolute, even to the point of risking general war. The
Secretary went on to explain why he felt that an absolute commitment was necessary:

> The integrity of the U.S. commitment is the principal pillar of peace
> throughout the world. If that commitment becomes unreliable, the com-
> munist world would draw conclusions that would lead to our ruin and
> almost certainly to a catastrophic war. So long as the South Vietnamese
> are prepared to fight for themselves, we cannot abandon them without
> disaster to peace and to our interests throughout the world.

In short, if "the U.S. commitment" were once seen to be unreliable, the risk
of the outbreak of general war would vastly increase. Therefore, prudence would
dictate risking general war, if necessary, in order to demonstrate that the United
States would meet its commitments. In either case, *some* risk would be involved,
but in the latter case the risk would be lower. The task of the statesman is to choose
among unpalatable alternatives. For the Under-Secretary of State, this meant an
early withdrawal from Vietnam. For the Secretary, it meant an open-ended commitment.

Ball was, of course, alone among the Vietnam principals in arguing for deescalation and political "compromise." At the same time that he and Rusk wrote
these papers, Assistant Secretary of State William Bundy and Secretary of Defense
McNamara also went on record with recommendations for the conduct of the war.
Bundy's paper, "A 'Middle Way' Course of Action in South Vietnam," argued for
a delay in further U.S. troop commitments and in escalation of the bombing campaign against North Vietnam, but a delay only in order to allow the American public time to digest the fact that the United States was engaged in a land war on the
Asian mainland, and for U.S. commanders to make certain that their men were, in
fact, capable of fighting effectively in conditions of counterinsurgency warfare without either arousing the hostility of the local population or causing the Vietnamese
government and army simply to ease up and allow the Americans to "take over"
their war.

For McNamara, however, the military situation in South Vietnam was too
serious to allow the luxury of delay. In a memorandum to the President drafted on
1 July and then revised on 20 July, immediately following his return from a week-
long visit to Vietnam, he recommended an immediate decision to increase the U.S.–

Third Country presence from the current 16 maneuver battalions (15 U.S., one Australian) to 44 (34 U.S., nine Korean, one Australian), and a change in the mission of these forces from one of providing support and reinforcement for the ARVN to one which soon became known as "search and destroy"—as McNamara put it, they were "by aggressive exploitation of superior military forces...to gain and hold the initiative...pressing the fight against VC/DRV main force units in South Vietnam to run them to ground and destroy them."

At the same time, McNamara argued for a substantial intensification of the air war. The 1 July version of his memorandum recommended a total quarantine of the movement of war supplies into North Vietnam, by sea, rail, and road, through the mining of Haiphong and all other harbors and the destruction of rail and road bridges leading from China to Hanoi; the Secretary also urged the destruction of fighter airfields and SAM sites "as necessary" to accomplish these objectives.

On 2 July the JCS, supporting the views in the DPM, reiterated a recommendation for immediate implementation of an intensified bombing program against NVN, to accompany the additional deployments which were under consideration. The recommendation was for a sharp escalation of the bombing, with the emphasis on interdiction of supplies into as well as out of NVN. Like the DPM, it called for interdicting the movement of "war supplies" into NVN by mining the major ports and cutting the rail and highway bridges on the LOCs from China to Hanoi; mounting intensive armed reconnaissance against all LOCs and LOC facilities within NVN; destroying the "war-making" supplies and facilities of NVN, especially POL; and destroying airfields and SAM sites as necessary to accomplish the other tasks. The JCS estimated that an increase from the then 2000 to about 5000 attack sorties per month would be required to carry out the program.

The elements of greater risk in the JCS proposals were obvious. The recommendation to mine ports and to strike airfields and SAM sites had already been rejected as having special Soviet or Chinese escalatory implications, and even air strikes against LOCs from China were considered dangerous. U.S. intelligence agencies believed that if such strikes occurred the Chinese might deliberately engage U.S. aircraft over NVN from bases in China. CIA thought the chances were "about even" that this would occur; DIA and the Service intelligence agencies thought the chances of this would increase but considered it still unlikely; and State thought the chances "better than even."

Apart from this element of greater risk, however, intelligence agencies held out some hope that an intensified bombing program like that proposed by the JCS (less mining the ports, which they were not asked to consider) would badly hurt the NVN economy, damage NVN's ability to support the effort in SVN, and even lead Hanoi to consider negotiations. An SNIE of 23 July estimated that the extension of air attacks only to military targets in the Hanoi/Haiphong area was not likely to "significantly injure the Viet Cong ability to persevere" or to "persuade the Hanoi government that the price of persisting was unacceptably high." Sustained interdiction of the LOCs from China, in addition, would make the delivery of Soviet and Chinese aid more difficult and costly and would have a serious impact on the NVN economy, but it would still not have a "critical impact" on "the Communist determination to persevere" and would not seriously impair Viet Cong capabilities in SVN, "at least for the short term." However:

> If, in addition, POL targets in the Hanoi-Haiphong area were destroyed by air attacks, the DRV's capability to provide transportation for the general economy would be severely reduced. It would also complicate their military logistics. If additional PAVN forces were employed in South Vietnam on a scale sufficient to counter increased US troop strength [which the SNIE said was "almost certain" to happen] this would substantially increase the amount of supplies needed in the South. The Viet Cong also depend on supplies from the North to maintain their present level of large-scale operations. The accumulated strains of a prolonged curtailment of supplies received from North Vietnam would obviously have an impact on the Communist effort in the South. They would certainly inhibit and might even prevent an increase in large-scale Viet Cong military activity, though they would probably not force any significant reduction in Viet Cong terrorist tactics of harassment and sabotage. These strains, particularly if they produced a serious check in the development of Viet Cong capabilities for large-scale (multi-battalion) operations might lead the Viet Cong to consider negotiations.

There were certain reservations with respect to the above estimate. The State and Army intelligence representatives on USIB registered a dissent, stating that even under heavier attack the LOC capacities in NVN and Laos were sufficient to support the war in SVN at the scale envisaged in the estimate. They also pointed out that it was impossible to do irreparable damage to the LOCs, that the Communists had demonstrated considerable logistic resourcefulness and considerable ability to move large amounts of war material long distances over difficult terrain by primitive means, and that in addition it was difficult to detect, let alone stop, sea infiltration. On balance, however, the SNIE came close to predicting that intensified interdiction attacks would have a beneficial effect on the war in the South.

Facing a decision with these kinds of implications, the President wanted more information and asked McNamara to go on another fact-gathering trip to Vietnam before submitting his final recommendations on a course of action. In anticipation of the trip, McNaughton prepared a memo summarizing his assessment of the problem. McNaughton wrote that "meaningful negotiations" were unlikely until the situation began to look gloomier for the VC, and that even with 200,000–400,000 U.S. troops in SVN the chances of a "win" by 1968 (i.e., in the next 2½ years) were only 50–50. But he recommended that the infiltration routes be hit hard, "at least to put a 'ceiling' on what can be infiltrated;" and he recommended that the limit on targets be "just short" of population targets, the China border, and special targets like SAM sites which might trigger Soviet or Chinese reactions.

McNamara left for Vietnam on July 14 and returned a week later with a revised version of his July 1st DPM ready to be sent to the President as a final recommendation. The impact of the visit was to soften considerably the position he had apparently earlier taken. His 20 July memorandum backed off from the 1 July recommendations—perhaps, although it is impossible to tell from the available materials—because of intimations that such drastic escalation would be unacceptable to the President. Instead of mining North Vietnam's harbors as a quarantine measure, the Secretary recommended it as a possible "severe reprisal should the VC or DRV commit a particularly damaging or horrendous act" such as "interdiction of the Saigon river." But he recommended a gradual increase in the number of strike sorties against North Vietnam from the existing 2,500 per month to 4,000 "or more," still "avoiding striking population and industrial targets not closely related to the DRV's supply of war material to the VC."

The urgency which infused McNamara's recommendations stemmed from his estimate that "the situation in South Vietnam is worse than a year ago (when it was worse than a year before that)." The VC had launched a drive "to dismember the nation and maul the army"; since 1 June the GVN had been forced to abandon six district capitals and had only retaken one. Transport and communications lines throughout the country were being cut, isolating the towns and cities and causing sharp deterioration of the already shaky domestic economy. Air Marshal Ky presided over a government of generals which had little prospect of being able to unite or energize the country. In such a situation, U.S. air and ground actions thus far had put to rest Vietnamese fears that they might be abandoned, but they had not decisively affected the course of the war. Therefore, McNamara recommended escalation. His specific recommendations, he noted, were concurred in by General Wheeler and Ambassador-designate Lodge, who accompanied him on his trip to Vietnam, and by Ambassador Taylor, Ambassador Johnson, Admiral Sharp, and General Westmoreland, with whom he conferred there. The rationale for his decisions was supplied by the CIA, whose assessment he quoted with approval in concluding the 1 July version of his memorandum. It stated:

> Over the longer term we doubt if the Communists are likely to change their basic strategy in Vietnam (i.e., aggressive and steadily mounting insurgency) unless and until two conditions prevail: (1) they are forced to accept a situation in the war in the South which offers them no prospect of an early victory and no grounds for hope that they can simply outlast the US and (2) North Vietnam itself is under continuing and increasingly damaging punitive attack. So long as the Communists think they scent the possibility of an early victory (which is probably now the case), we believe that they will persevere and accept extremely severe damage to the North. Conversely, if North Vietnam itself is not hurting, Hanoi's doctrinaire leaders will probably be ready to carry on the Southern struggle almost indefinitely. If, however, both of the conditions outlined above should be brought to pass, we believe Hanoi probably would, at least for a period of time, alter its basic strategy and course of action in South Vietnam.

McNamara's memorandum of 20 July did not include this quotation, although many of these points were made elsewhere in the paper. Instead, it concluded with an optimistic forecast:

The overall evaluation is that the course of action recommended in this
memorandum—if the military and political moves are properly integrated
and executed with continuing vigor and visible determination—stands
a good chance of achieving an acceptable outcome within a reasonable
time in Vietnam.

Never again while he was Secretary of Defense would McNamara make so optimistic a statement about Vietnam—except in public.

This concluding paragraph of McNamara's memorandum spoke of political,
as well as military, "vigor" and "determination." Earlier in the paper, under the
heading "Expanded political moves," he had elaborated on this point, writing:

Together with the above military moves, we should take political initiatives in order to lay a groundwork for a favorable political settlement
by clarifying our objectives and establishing channels of communications. At the same time as we are taking steps to turn the tide in South
Vietnam, we would make quiet moves through diplomatic channels (a)
to open a dialogue with Moscow and Hanoi, and perhaps the VC, looking first toward disabusing them of any misconceptions as to our goals
and second toward laying the groundwork for a settlement when the
time is ripe; (b) to keep the Soviet Union from deepening its military in
the world until the time when settlement can be achieved; and (c) to
cement support for US policy by the US public, allies and friends, and
to keep international opposition at a manageable level. Our efforts may
be unproductive until the tide begins to turn, but nevertheless they should
be made.

Here was scarcely a program for drastic political action. McNamara's essentially procedural (as opposed to substantive) recommendations amounted to little
more than saying that the United States should provide channels for the enemy's
discrete and relatively face-saving surrender when he decided that the game had
grown too costly. This was, in fact, what official Washington (again with the exception of Ball) meant in mid-1965 when it spoke of a "political settlement." (As
McNamara noted in a footnote, even this went too far for Ambassador-designate
Lodge, whose view was that "'any further initiative by us now [before we are strong]
would simply harden the Communist resolve not to stop fighting.'" In this view
Ambassadors Taylor and Johnson concurred, except that they would maintain "discreet contacts with the Soviets.")

McNamara's concluding paragraph spoke of "an acceptable outcome." Previously in his paper he had listed "nine fundamental elements" of a *favorable* outcome. These were:

(a) VC stop attacks and drastically reduce incidents of terror and sabotage.
(b) DRV reduces infiltration to a trickle, with some reasonably reliable method
     of our obtaining confirmation of this fact.
(c) US/GVN stop bombing of North Vietnam.

(d) GVN stays independent (hopefully pro-US, but possibly genuinely neutral).
(e) GVN exercises governmental functions over substantially all of South Vietnam.
(f) Communists remain quiescent in Laos and Thailand.
(g) DRV withdraws PAVN forces and other North Vietnamese infiltrators (not regroupees) from South Vietnam.
(h) VC/NLF transform from a military to a purely political organization.
(i) US combat forces (not advisors or AID) withdraw.

These "fundamental elements," McNamara said, could evolve with or without express agreement and, indeed, except for what might be negotiated incidental to a cease-fire they were more likely to evolve without an explicit agreement than with one. So far as the difference between a "favorable" and an "acceptable" outcome was concerned, he continued, there was no need for the present to address the question of whether the United States should "ultimately settle for something less than the nine fundamentals," because the force deployments recommended in the memorandum would be prerequisite to the achievement of *any* acceptable settlement; "a decision can be made later, when bargaining becomes a reality, whether to compromise in any particular."

In summary, then, McNamara's program consisted of first substantially increasing the pressure on the enemy by every means short of those, such as the bombing of population centers in the North, that would run sizeable risks of precipitating Soviet or Chinese direct intervention in the war, and then seeking a *de facto* political settlement essentially on US/GVN terms.

The July 20 memo to the President was followed up by two others on specific aspects of the problem before the end of July. On July 28, he replied to a series of eighteen points made by Senator Mansfield with respect to the Vietnam war. In so doing, Secretary McNamara informed the President of his doubts that even a "greatly expanded program" could be expected to produce significant NVN interest in a negotiated settlement "until they have been disappointed in their hopes for a quick military success in the South." Meanwhile he favored "strikes at infiltration routes" to impose a ceiling on what NVN could pour into SVN, "thereby putting a ceiling on the size of war that the enemy can wage there." He warned that a greatly increased program would create even more serious risks of "confrontations" with the Soviet Union and China.

McNamara stated that the current bombing program was on the way to accomplishing its purposes and should be continued. The future program, he said, should:

(a) *Emphasize the threat.* It should be structured to capitalize on fear of future attacks. At any time, "pressure" on the DRV depends not upon the *current* level of bombing but rather upon the credible threat of *future* destruction which can be avoided by agreeing to negotiate or agreeing to some settlement in negotiations.
(b) *Minimize the loss of DRV "face."* The program should be designed to make it politically easy for the DRV to enter negotiations and to make

concessions during negotiations. It may be politically easier for North Vietnam to accept negotiations and/or to make concessions at a time when bombing of their territory is not currently taking place.

(c) *Optimize interdiction vs. political costs.* Interdiction should be carried out so as to maximize effectiveness and to minimize the political repercussions from the methods used. Physically, it makes no difference whether a rifle is interdicted on its way into North Vietnam, on its way out of North Vietnam, in Laos or in South Vietnam. But different amounts of effort and different political prices may be paid depending on how and where it is done. The critical variables in this regard are (1) the type of targets struck (e.g., port facilities involving civilian casualties vs. isolated bridges), (2) types of aircraft (e.g., B-52s vs. F-105s), (3) kinds of weapons (e.g., napalm vs. ordinary bombs), (4) location of target (e.g., in Hanoi vs. Laotian border area), and (5) the accompanying declaratory policy (e.g., unlimited vs. a defined interdiction zone).

(d) *Coordinate with other influences on the DRV.* So long as full victory in the South appears likely, the effect of the bombing program in promoting negotiations or a settlement will probably be small. The bombing program now and later should be designed for its influence on the DRV at that unknown time when the DRV becomes more optimistic about what they can achieve by continuation of the war.

(e) *Avoid undue risks and costs.* The program should avoid bombing which runs a high risk of escalation into war with the Soviets or China and which is likely to appall allies and friends.

. . . Secretary McNamara's 5 principles prevailed. The bombing continued to expand and intensify, but there was no abrupt switch in bombing policy and no sudden escalation. The high-value targets in the Hanoi/Haiphong area were kept off limits, so as not to "kill the hostage." Interdiction remained the chief criterion for target selection, and caution continued to be exercised with respect to sensitive targets. The idea of a possible bombing pause, longer than the last, was kept alive. The Secretary refused to approve an overall JCS concept for fighting the Vietnam War which included much heavier ROLLING THUNDER strikes against key military and economic targets coordinated with a blockade and mining attack on NVN ports, and he also continued to veto JCS proposals for dramatic attacks on major POL depots, power plants, airfields, and other "lucrative" targets.

The expansion of ROLLING THUNDER during the rest of 1965 followed the previous pattern of step-by-step progression. . . .

13

PSYCHOLOGICAL
REALITY-WORLDS

RALPH K. WHITE

Since the 1960s social psychologist Ralph K. White has sought to "explore the psychological forces and rigidities that make war possible." In his book, Nobody Wanted War, *published in 1970, White discussed the two psychological "reality-worlds" of American prowar militants, reality-worlds that orbited around the assumption of the Munich syndrome. Comparing the mirror-image views that North Vietnamese and American militants held about the other's aggression in South Vietnam, White claimed that both sides were victims of misperception.*

REALITY-WORLDS OF THE RECLAIMERS AND ESCALATORS

Two central themes, common to both the reclaimers and the escalators, are that the North Vietnamese Communists have committed unequivocal aggression against their South Vietnamese neighbor, and that we must resist their aggression in order to avoid the tragic blunder of appeasement, and to deter further Communist aggression.

Probably these two themes, Communist aggression and anti-appeasement (which assumes Communist aggression) have been more prominent than any others in the public statements of our leaders of both parties. President Johnson has said: "The first reality is that North Vietnam has attacked the independent nation of South Vietnam. Its object is total conquest....Let no one think for a moment that retreat from Vietnam would bring an end to the conflict. The battle would be renewed in one country and then another. The central lesson of our time is that the appetite of aggression is never satisfied."[1] Secretary McNamara has said: "The prime aggressor is North Vietnam."[2] Secretary Rusk has said: "What we are seeking to achieve in South Vietnam is part of a process that has continued for a long time—a process of preventing the expansion and extension of Communist domination by the use of force against the weaker nations on the perimeter of Communist power."[3] Richard Nixon has emphasized the analogy of Hitler and Munich: "To negotiate with the enemy before we have driven him out of the South would be like negotiating with Hitler before the German armies had been driven from France.... The Communists claim it is a civil war. Actually it is naked aggression on the part of North Vietnam."[4]

Often the militant American feels he has a ready, convincing answer to every argument raised against either of these two central themes. He may ask: Can you deny that North Vietnam has sent troops and weapons to the South? Can you deny that the Viet Cong is essentially an arm of the North Vietnamese government? Can you deny that war by assassination in the villages is aggression, in principle, as much as is war by invasion? And can you deny that rewarding aggression is likely to encourage further aggression, as experience after Munich proved? When he finds that his opponent does not try to deny any of these statements, the militant is likely to feel he has established his case.

In his eyes, appeasement would endanger our two most important objectives: preserving peace and preserving freedom in the Free World where it still exists. We are confronted with a brutal fact: Communist aggression. As he sees it, we must determine our response to that brutal fact in the light of an unquestionable lesson of history: that allowing aggression to be rewarded by success only whets the appetite of the aggressor and makes it necessary to fight a bigger war on less favorable terms somewhere else. The domino process, in some form, begins to operate. This means we cannot allow the Communists to end the war with *any* territorial gain. The so-called holding strategy or enclave theory would leave perhaps half or more than half of South Vietnam in Communist hands; that would be appeasement.

To resist aggression and to push back the would-be conqueror to his starting point is not only right and wise from our own standpoint. From the militant's standpoint, it is also our commitment to the people of South Vietnam, whose opportunity to achieve some measure of self-determination in the near future and whose long-run possibility of developing genuine democracy and independence would be ruled out if the Communists took over. We have given them our promise. We cannot welch on it and preserve either self-respect, or the credibility of our promises to anti-Communists in other countries, or the credibility of present and future warnings to the Communists. Honor and interest therefore coincide. It is a matter of honor to fulfill our commitment, and interest dictates that our future commitments should be completely credible.

[1] Johnson, in Marcus G. Raskin and Bernard B. Fall, eds., *The Vietnam Reader* (New York: Random House, 1965), pp. 344–45.

[2] Robert McNamara, in ibid., p. 196.

[3] Dean Rusk, Testimony to Foreign Relations Committee, February 18, 1966, *Washington Post*, February 19, p. A10.

[4] Richard M. Nixon, "Why Not Negotiate in Vietnam?" *Reader's Digest*, December 1965, pp. 50, 53.

It is at this point that the two militant reality worlds, that of the reclaimers and that of the escalators, begin to diverge. The reclaimers (that is, those who want to do whatever is necessary to reclaim all South Vietnam for an anti-Communist government, but without more escalation in the North) are likely to argue somewhat as follows:

"Important as it is to avoid appeasement, it is also important to avoid nuclear war. We must therefore exercise restraint. We do not want to risk much greater Communist Chinese or Russian involvement, nor do we want to cause avoidable suffering on the part of the innocent common people of North Vietnam. We should therefore refrain from any ground attack on the North, and should confine our bombing to military targets and to what is strictly necessary for our essential defensive enterprise of winning in the South. If we exercise restraint we will not only avoid the catastrophic possibilities of a larger war; we will also greatly reduce the negative impact of the war on other countries. We will not deeply alienate the Russians, nor drive them into the arms of the Chinese, nor deeply split the Western alliance, nor alienate most of the neutralists in the developing countries. This is the sane middle path, the only one that will simultaneously achieve three major goals of our foreign policy: to preserve the freedom of the Free World, to prevent a major war (both directly by avoiding escalation and indirectly by avoiding appeasement), and to preserve reasonably good relations with all the rest of the world."

The reality world of the escalators is much less familiar to non-militant Americans than that of the reclaimers, and in approaching it a conscious effort to listen and to empathize is therefore, for them, much more necessary.

Those who favor escalation are not "war-makers" in their own eyes. On the conscious level, at least, most of them feel that their desire for peace is as great as anyone's, but that they care more about freedom than some of the appeasers do, have more courage, and, above all, have a more realistic view of the brutal realities of the present situation. Even the "reclaimers," as seen by the escalators, are not fully realistic. Their own objective, as they see it, is exactly the same as that of the reclaimers: to win a decisive victory in the South. Neither has any desire to attack the North for the sake of attacking; both regard any operations in the North as strictly a means to an end, the end being the defensive one of decisively driving out the Communist aggressors in South Vietnam. As the escalators see it, the war in the South has bogged down and become an interminable, indecisive stalemate. A decisive victory in the South that would end the loss of American and Vietnamese lives, preserve South Vietnam's freedom and teach Communists all over the world to stay where they belong is simply not possible unless we have the courage and realism to strike at the heart of the beast, in Hanoi. That can be done—with some danger, but with no great danger—and it would quickly end the war. Let's get it over with. If we're going to fight, let's fight to win.

An impressive, clearly reasoned case along this line has been presented by the *New York Times* military specialist, Hanson Baldwin.[5] Like a great many of his countrymen, but even more intensely, he rejects a pull-out. "Given the pledges of three Presidents, and the political, psychological, and military catastrophe that would

---

[5] Hanson Baldwin, "The Case for Escalation," *New York Times Magazine*, February 27, 1966, pp. 22–82.

result from such a surrender [pulling out], this course is unthinkable, even to most opponents of the war. Such a course would mean not only that the United States had decided to abdicate as a great power, not only that it was dropping the global struggle to contain Communism, not only that it reneged on its pledged word, but that it conceded complete defeat and was reconciled to withdrawal from Asia and the Western Pacific."[6] He then argues that we should both increase our forces considerably beyond their present level and "intensify the bombing and interdiction of North Vietnam and Laos (while at the same time holding open the prospect of an *acceptable* negotiated peace)." Any course of action short of this "would mean indefinite stalemate–deferred defeat, defeat on the installment plan."

Baldwin acknowledges the possibility of Chinese Communist intervention but regards it as minimal for a number of reasons: the logistic difficulties of Chinese troops fighting in Vietnam, the reluctance of the North Vietnamese to permit it, the vulnerability of China to "devastating attack" by our air power. Similarly, he sees Russian intervention as only a remote possibility. "Would Russia risk her developed economy for the sake of Ho Chi Minh? And is Russia, at dagger's points with Peking, likely to invoke nuclear arms in a war, to her, remote in space and interest? The idea is preposterous. We scare ourselves with shadows."[7]

CONTROVERSIAL IMPLICIT ASSUMPTIONS

Like many other reality-worlds, that of the typical American militant contains some important assumptions that are taken so completely for granted that they are seldom put into words. To him they seem so obvious, so self-evident, that there is no need to discuss or even mention them. They are not "unconscious"; if challenged, they leap into the full light of consciousness and are vigorously defended. But as a rule they are unchallenged, and remain implicit.

A curious thing about these implicit assumptions, as a general human phenomenon, is that actually they are often controversial. Members of a conflicting group may actually regard the opposite assumptions as self-evident, and fail to argue for them on that account. It is quite possible, therefore, for two conflicting groups to "talk past each other," each defending itself and denouncing the other on the basis of assumptions that seem self-evident to it, while to the other side the same assumptions seem too fantastic to be taken seriously. In such a case, conflict-resolution is impossible until each side at least recognizes its own implicit assumptions, makes them explicit, and treats them as a legitimate subject of discussion....

In Chapter 3 the "mirror-image" phenomenon has been described at some length. On the level of public, verbal discussion and propaganda, each side calls the other an aggressor, accuses it of various other crimes, asserts its own peacefulness, speaks of "the people" as being obviously with it, asserts its own manhood and courage, vows to drive out the aggressors no matter how long it takes or how much sacrifice it involves, etc. What now needs to be brought out is that the implicit

[6] Ibid., p. 79.
[7] Ibid., p. 82.

assumptions on each side also tend to be mirror-images of those on the opposite side. Specifically:

Communist	*Militant American*
The land that the enemy (American imperialism and its lackeys) have taken is obviously not theirs. It is ours (the Vietnamese people's).	The land that the enemy (the Communists) have taken is obviously not theirs. It belongs to our allies (the non-Communists in South Vietnam).
To be a Man obviously means to drive out completely those who invade one's own land, regardless of the cost.	To be a Man obviously means to drive out completely those who invade one's own land, regardless of the cost.
The idea that we (North Vietnamese Communists) are on *their* land is fantastic.	The idea that we (Americans) are on *their* land is fantastic.

No one of these assumptions appears in anything very close to this form in the quotations from Communists... or in the quotations from militant Americans.... But it will be noted that a denial of all three would thoroughly undercut the case presented explicitly by either side. Suppose for instance that Americans were to grant that South Vietnam "belonged to" the Communists in the same sense in which North Vietnam does; suppose we felt that *even if* "invaders" were on South Vietnamese territory our manhood in no way required us to drive them out; and suppose we were to grant that we Americans were trespassers on Vietnamese soil in the first place, starting in 1950 or in 1954. Our case would not wholly disappear, perhaps, but a great deal of the psychological force that now supports it would dissolve.

The rest of this chapter will attempt to make some progress in separating the kernels of truth from the husks of misperception in these three implicit assumptions in the minds of militant Americans as well as in their explicit arguments.

OVERLAP AND CONFLICT OF TERRITORIAL SELF-IMAGES

Students of animal behavior have often remarked on how quickly an animal will spring to the defense of a piece of territory with which he has identified himself and which he perceives to be invaded by outsiders.[8] "Territoriality" is a major basis of animal fighting. Similarly, history is full of examples of human warfare originating from the fact that more than one human group has identified itself with the same patch of land. Bosnia and other Yugoslav territory under Austrian rule, plus Serbia herself when Austria claimed a right to punish her, constituted the initial focus of

[8] Elton B. McNeil, ed., *The Nature of Human Conflict* (Englewood Cliffs, N.J.: Prentice-Hall, 1965), p. 17; Robert Ardrey, *African Genesis* (New York: Atheneum, 1963), pp. 33–58; N. Collias, "Aggressive Behavior among Vertebrae Animals," *Physiol. Zoology*, 1944, *17*, pp. 83–123; C. Ray Carpenter, "Behavior and Social Relations of the Howling Monkey," *Comparative Psychology Monthly* (Baltimore: Johns Hopkins University Press, 1934); Konrad Lorenz, *On Aggression* (New York: Harcourt, Brace & World, 1966).

World War I. The Polish Corridor, claimed by both Poland and Germany, and Danzig, an internationalized German city, were the initial focus of World War II. Both Germans and Czechs identified with the Sudetenland; Alsace-Lorraine long poisoned the relationship between France and Germany; Israelis and Arabs claim Israel; Pakistanis and Indians claim Kashmir; French and Algerians identified with Algeria (some striking quotations from French writers suggest that for them Algeria was almost a part of their own body); French and Indochinese claimed Indochina; Communist China and "the Free World" identify with Taiwan (both Communist and Nationalist Chinese treat it as self-evident that Taiwan is an integral part of China, though most of the Taiwanese feel differently). Areas along the Sino-Indian border have caused fighting and great bitterness on both sides, each side feeling that its own land had been infringed upon. Egypt claims the Strait of Tiran while others call it international. With the growth of nationalism during the past century, irredentism in scores of places has become a potent source of conflict.

It is somewhat surprising that psychologists have paid so little attention to the territorial self-images of human groups, when these bulk so large in both animal behavior and human history. Although there have been studies of the factors determining national identification,[9] they have not stressed this aspect of the problem. A study is needed of two distinct psychological processes: the process by which a human group comes to identify firmly with a given piece of land and to assume implicitly that it is "our" land, and the process by which strong emotions, some of which are probably unconscious, become mobilized when the territorial self-image is impinged upon by "outsiders."

The way in which feelings about manhood and virility become an integral part of the territorial self-image would be particularly interesting. Presumably, such feelings enter into both phases. In the first phase, the strength or potency of the national self-image is felt to be enhanced by expanding it into all territories actually subject to dispute and ambiguity. India, for instance, feels that its manhood would be diminished if it weakly gave up its claim to all Kashmir. There is pain at the thought of accepting a diminished image of one's own nation on the map, and map makers push their own nation's claims to the limit of what is plausible. In the second phase, once a given territorial image has become thoroughly identified with the national self, it is almost as if the territorial image becomes an image of the nation's physical body. Infringements upon it are reacted to as an individual might react to violations of his own body. The nation's territorial self-image becomes its body-image. The presence on one's "own" land of the "outsiders" who have conflicting claims to it is then perceived as obvious aggression, a challenge to one's manhood, requiring even the risks and costs of war in order to drive them out.

Although this emphasizes the importance of land, it should be noted that it is not an economic interpretation of war in the usual sense. According to this hypothesis, it is not the economic, or even the military, significance of the land, rationally considered, that matters. What matters is its symbolic importance as part of the national body-image. What counts emotionally in this context is not pros-

[9] Karl Deutsch, *Nationalism and Social Communication* (New York: Wiley, 1953); Leonard W. Doob, *Patriotism and Nationalism: Their Psychological Foundations* (New Haven: Yale University Press, 1966).

perity or even national power—there may be very little desire for power beyond the nation's own borders, as the nation itself conceives those borders—but national integrity and self-respect, symbolized by driving all invaders out of "our" territory.

The way this applies to the North Vietnamese is similar to the various examples above. They see South Vietnam as part of their national body, and our presence there as self-evidently a violation of it, and a challenge to their manhood. We have stepped over the boundary of their land with guns in our hands.

The way this applies to American militants is a variation on the usual pattern, since Americans do not regard South Vietnam as American land at all. We mean it when we say we have no territorial ambitions there. We see ourselves as defending the right of a small, weak nation to its own land and its own integrity. But it can be argued that we nevertheless have identified with the soil of South Vietnam. Since 1945, we have seen ourselves as the champion of the entire Free World in its attempt to defend itself against Communist aggression; in a sense, therefore, our national body-image has expanded until it has become co-extensive with our conception of the Free World itself, visualized as having a definite outer boundary that we feel we must defend at all costs, much as a nation feels it must defend its own boundary. In the eyes of American militants, that boundary in Vietnam is obviously the 17th Parallel.

Those who regard this boundary as part of the natural order of things may forget (or perhaps they have never learned) certain historical facts that are psychologically important enough to call for review at this point: The great majority of the Vietnamese were elated by what they thought was independence under Ho Chi Minh's leadership immediately after World War II. With much trickery and bloodshed, the French tried to reimpose Western, white rule upon Vietnam. Our own form of Western, white influence (which we have never regarded as "rule" but which a great many Vietnamese naturally assimilated to their perception of French trickery, French warmaking, and French rule) began to be exerted in 1950, when we began giving major financial help to the French, and became predominant after we contributed to setting up Diem's regime. During Diem's later years, while we still supported him, his regime became quite generally hated. The Catholics, of whom he was one and who were as a rule the most militant anti-Communists, were widely regarded by non-Catholics as semi-foreign and sometimes as the stooges of foreigners. Most of the present military leaders are tainted by association with the French during the period of the long war for independence from France, while Ho Chi Minh is the chief symbol of the struggle and of its final victory. The Communists' victory in 1954 gave them (and almost everyone else) the expectation that the whole country would in 1956 revert to the Communist government it had in 1945. The North Vietnamese made peace—giving up at the conference table what they could then have won rather easily on the battlefield—on the basis of what they took to be a general agreement, to be enforced by the French, that all-Vietnamese elections would be held in 1956;[10] chiefly because of actions by Diem and his American backers, this expectation was never fulfilled. This must have appeared to the Communists as a confession by Diem that the people would not support him.

---

[10] Phillippe Devillers, "The Struggle for Unification of Vietnam," *China Quarterly*, January–March, 1962, pp. 211–12.

All of this makes psychologically interesting the apparent assumption of a great many American militants that South Vietnam is self-evidently "our" (the Free World's) territory, that North Vietnamese Communists who cross the line as we have defined it are self-evidently invading "another country" rather than, as they claim, trying to "liberate" their countrymen from foreign rule, and that to regard our presence in Vietnam (from 1950 to the present) as an infringement on Vietnamese soil is fantastic.

Among the militants who care greatly about peace—and there are many such—an additional factor clearly has psychological importance: Many have hoped that peace between East and West might be preserved by an increasing tacit acceptance, on both sides, of the existing boundary line between the two worlds. Irrational as it may be at certain points (especially where it cuts a nation in two) it is the only clear line we have had. We respected it when the Hungarian uprising gave us a moral right to intervene on behalf of a people most of whom seemed to be greatly distressed and clearly hostile to Soviet rule. We cared more about peace, then, than about extending "our" territory (the Free World) or liberating a people who wanted to be liberated. In Korea we defended the line, and since then many of us have thought of "holding the line" as one of the two essential ingredients in keeping the equilibrium between East and West, the other essential ingredient being that our military power should at least equal that of the Communists. In 1954 we said to ourselves, in effect: Now the boundary line between the two worlds, as far as Vietnam is concerned, is the 17th Parallel; it has been divided as Korea was, and our job as keepers of the peace is to hold that line as we held the line in Korea.

In other words, we identified "ourselves" (the Free World) with South Vietnam, defined as a separate, non-Communist country. Very few of us were clearly aware, at that time, of the historical facts and of the psychological situation in Vietnam that made this a highly questionable identification. Partly because of the seeming analogy with Korea it became very firm in our minds before we were given any strong reason to challenge it. Many of us have used it ever since then as a fixed image and frame of reference for deciding who is "the aggressor," without challenging it at all.

At the same time, we have kept another standard for judging what is the legitimate government of a given country: the principle of national self-determination. That principle is still very much alive, as is shown by our present commitment to let the people of South Vietnam determine their own destiny. If this means that a country on our side of the East-West boundary line can freely "go Communist" if it wants to, then we have two criteria, one geographical and one psychological, that are capable of clashing. If and when they clash we may be forced to choose between them, instead of continuing to assume implicitly that it is always possible to retain both.

FOUR MEANINGS OF "AGGRESSION"

Since the assumption of Communist aggression is central in the reality-world of the typical American militant, while the assumption that there has been no clear, one-sided aggression is central in that of the typical non-militant, our most important question of "misperception" is: Which side is more nearly right? Has there been clear, one-sided Communist aggression or not? The answer depends partly on what we mean by "aggression."

Like many other intractable arguments in human affairs, this one has a semantic aspect that has to be grappled with before the relevant empirical questions can be asked in a clear, answerable way. About two central facts there is little disagreement: North Vietnamese troops and weapons have unquestionably been on South Vietnamese soil at least since 1960, and the general fact of control of the Viet Cong by the North Vietnamese Communists is also unquestioned (though there has been a good deal of doubt in the minds of Georges Chaffard, Bernard Fall, Sanford Gottlieb, and others as to the absoluteness of Hanoi's control). But as to the words to be used in describing these facts there is much disagreement depending on the definitions used, the criteria applied, and the interpretation given to certain other important facts.

We have just considered one definition that is probably implicit in much of the thinking of American militants: Aggression exists when either side uses force on the other side of the East-West boundary line that *we* regard as clear and well-established. In Vietnam, this is the 17th Parallel. Since there are North Vietnamese fighting south of that line, we assume that North Vietnam must have committed aggression. For convenience, let us call this the *boundary-line* definition of aggression. (Since the Communists think of the shoreline of South Vietnam as their boundary, they apply the boundary-line definition quite differently. Our landing troops on their shore may be to them an act of aggression.)

But at least three other definitions are possible, and perhaps all of them have been implicit in militant American thinking:

One is that aggression exists when any government uses force on a neighboring territory against the government of that territory. Since North Vietnam has quite clearly used force on the territory of South Vietnam against the present government of South Vietnam, by this definition it has clearly committed aggression. This can be called the *force-against-government* definition. (In their eyes, our bombing the North is aggression by the same definition.)

Another is that aggression exists when any government uses force on a neighbor's territory against the people of that territory (or the majority of the people, or the majority of those people who take sides). It can be called the *force-against-people* definition. Since the question of whether North Vietnam has done this is controversial and ambiguous, the question of whether North Vietnam has committed aggression by this definition is also controversial and ambiguous. One thing is clear, however: They do not think they have. They believe most of the people in the South are on their side. By this definition, also, they undoubtedly believe that America has committed aggression on a very large scale, since they believe America has been using force on the territory of South Vietnam against the people of South Vietnam since 1950.

Finally, one could say that if two governments are both using force on the territory of a third government, the one that first began to use force is the aggressor. This can be called the *first-use-of-force* definition.

According to a typical American militant's view of the facts, the first to intervene with force in South Vietnam was North Vietnam, because it either ordered or permitted the Viet Cong to start its campaign of assassination in 1957. North Vietnam officially declared war against the South Vietnamese government in 1960, and it has been intervening more and more openly, on a larger and larger scale, since then. Meanwhile, according to this view of the facts, America did not use actual force on any great scale until early 1965.

However, the Communists have a radically different picture of who used violence first. As they see it, violence was first used against the Vietnamese by white men from overseas in the late nineteenth century when France first conquered the country. It was used again when France tried to reconquer the country (with much American help after 1950) in the war of 1946–54. As they see it, force has been used by Americans ever since 1954 in the form of massive economic and military aid which Diem turned against "the people" in a brutal witch hunt that precipitated the militant reaction of the Viet Cong in 1957. By the first-use-of-force definition, then, it would be fair to say that the question of who is the aggressor is at least controversial.

These differing interpretations illustrate the general type of irrationality that Osgood has called "psycho-logic" or "the Neanderthal mentality."[11] In this type of thinking, exactly the same behavior is interpreted as moral if *we* do it (whoever the *we* may be) but as immoral and aggressive if *they* do it (whoever the *they*—the enemy—may be).

Vietnam provides a prime example. The physical fact is that North Vietnamese and American troops are both fighting on South Vietnamese soil, but the interpretations put on that fact are radically different. The Communist interprets the presence of American troops as self-evidently aggressive and the presence of his own as moral, legitimate self-defense. The militant American interprets the presence of North Vietnamese troops as self-evidently aggressive and the presence of his own as moral, legitimate defense of the Free World.

The black-and-white picture produced by psycho-logic is, however, the end result of a rather complex psychological process. At the moment we are concerned only with the semantic aspect of it. That semantic aspect is important as a necessary preliminary to a discussion of the assumptions about reality that are relevant to the central problem of how perceptions of aggression can be so radically different. The definitions of aggression that are at least implicit in a given person's mind constitute necessary connecting links, psychologically as well as logically, between his beliefs about the facts and his judgment about who the aggressor is.

In addition, the semantic differences between the Communists and the militant Americans may supply a part (though probably only a minor part) of the answer to the question of why their reality-worlds are so different, each feeling so sure that the other is the aggressor. To some extent the choice of definition may itself reflect the black-and-white picture, and contribute to maintaining it. A militant

---

[11] Charles E. Osgood, *An Alternative to War or Surrender* (Urbana: University of Illinois Press, 1962), pp. 18–36.

American, for instance, can buttress his interpretation that the North Vietnamese Communists are the aggressors by focusing on that one definition of aggression according to which they are most clearly aggressors: the "force-against-government" definition. Given the unchallenged fact that North Vietnamese troops are opposing the South Vietnamese government on land it claims as its own, the implicit adoption of this definition necessarily leads to the unconsciously desired conclusion— that the North Vietnamese are aggressors. On the other hand, since the North Vietnamese evidently think most of the people in the South are against America and its lackeys in Saigon, they can achieve the psychologically necessary black-and-white picture most easily by implicitly adopting the force-against-people definition.

THE ASSUMPTION OF COMMUNIST AGGRESSION

We are now in a better position to tackle the central, decisive issue: *Are* the Vietnamese Communists aggressors, or not? Is this a misperception in the minds of American militants, or not?

One thing seems certain: The answer is not self-evident. Those who have treated it as such stand convicted of self-evident superficiality, ignorance of essential historical facts, and self-protective inattention. Any candid, open-minded approach, with even minimal attention to the most important historical facts, would immediately disclose that it is a complex issue, full of ambiguities and capable of being honestly interpreted in radically different ways. Those who see one answer as self-evident are exhibiting a rather extreme degree of intolerance of ambiguity, inability to suspend judgment, and selective inattention to the evidence that does not fit their preconceptions.

An early statement by President Nixon provides an example of such intolerance of ambiguity: "This goes to the heart of what the Vietnam war is all about. The Communists claim it is a civil war. Actually it is naked aggression on the part of North Vietnam."[12] Mr. Nixon does not examine the rather elementary logical possibility that it might be both—both a civil war and naked aggression. He also refrains from discussing the definition of aggression according to which the intervention of North Vietnam (which is unquestioned) must be called naked aggression while that of the United States (which is also unquestioned, which began sooner and which has been on a larger scale) is regarded as a moral imperative. As a matter of fact, the evidence...would seem to make plain that it is a civil war, whatever else it may be in addition. If our definition of a civil war is a conflict in which the *primary* motivating forces come from within a specified area rather than from outside, then there can be little doubt that it is a civil war.[13]

Another thing seems certain or almost certain:...the Communists do not regard themselves as aggressors. Their picture of the situation is in this respect close

---

[12] Nixon, "Why Not Negotiate in Vietnam?" p. 53.

[13] For evidence of consensus of experts on this point, see Arthur M. Schlesinger, Jr., *The Bitter Heritage* (New York: Fawcett Crest Books, 1967), p. 50.

to a mirror-image of that of the militant Americans, since all the evidence suggests that they feel as sure of their innocence as the militant American is of ours, and as sure of our aggression as the militant American is of theirs. For many practical purposes, such as predicting the response of the North Vietnamese to bombing or to a ground-force attack by us, this is what matters most.

Perhaps still another thing can be pinned down as definite: In the eyes of most of the rest of the world, the answer to the question of who is the aggressor is not self-evident.... The rest of the world recognizes ambiguity where many Americans do not. If anything, those who leap to the conclusion that we are now playing an imperialist role like that of the French, and that this war is an aggressive "colonial war" of white against non-white, probably outnumber considerably those who assume, as militant Americans do, that it is a clear case of Communist aggression. There are some, especially in small neighbors of Communist China (South Korea, Taiwan, Thailand, Malaya, the Philippines, Australia, New Zealand), whose overriding preoccupation is a fear of conquest by Communist China, and who see the war as militant Americans do, but they are the exceptions. The majority in most of the rest of the world either see the situation as ambiguous, with blame often attached equally to Communist China and to the United States, or as a clear case of "a colonial war" waged by America.

For many practical purposes this too is a thing we Americans need to know. For example, if we are wondering whether most of the world would regard us as "appeasers" in case we settled for a holding operation, the answer is clear: They would not. Not assuming as we do that the Communists are obvious aggressors, they would see a compromise peace not as a dishonorable temporizing with aggression but as a statesmanlike ending, on more or less equal terms, of a war that has threatened to spread and engulf the whole world. There is little doubt that a compromise peace would be met by most of the politically conscious people in the world not with scorn for our weakness, but with respect for our reasonableness, and with an enormous sigh of relief.

This is relevant also to the way we should talk about the issue in discussing it with people in other countries. If in talking with them we take the line that militants habitually take in the United States, that the central issue is whether we have the courage to resist a clear case of Communist aggression, they are not likely to respect our courage; they are likely, rather, to question our candor or our intelligence. In their eyes, any reference to Communist aggression is merely begging the essential question: Which side is actually the aggressor? If we want to win their respect we will meet that issue head-on and discuss it candidly rather than seeming to ignore or evade it.

The insistent question remains: Apart from what various people think, which side is *really* the aggressor? After the ambiguities are clarified and the evidence weighed, what is the answer? Each reader will answer that question for himself—with, one may hope, a clear choice of some definition or definitions of the word "aggression," and with due attention to the most relevant historical facts.

There is a deeper semantic question that must finally be considered: Is there any real meaning or practical importance in the question of which side is "really" the aggressor, when obviously each side is utterly convinced that it is not and the other side is? Aren't both sides innocent, in that they are not guilty of conscious wrongdoing but only, at worst, of misperception? Aren't both sides guilty of gross misperception in failing to see that the other side, in its own eyes, is fighting a defensive war? The question itself, "Which side is the aggressor?" carries with it the controversial implicit assumption that one side must be "the aggressor," with all that that term implies of deliberate wrongdoing and of obligatory resistance to "aggression" in order to avoid appeasement and keep the peace of the world. If the North Vietnamese see themselves—however mistakenly—as carrying on a desperate struggle to defend their homeland against American aggression, are we obligated to "resist" them as we were obligated to resist Hitler? The term "the aggressor" carries with it a cloud of historical associations and moral imperatives, among which the Munich analogy and the feeling of obligation to "resist" aggression are central. If the situation is actually basically different from Munich, don't we beg the question when in our own thinking we seriously use the term "the aggressor" at all?

In the light of these considerations, how can we answer now the central question of this chapter: Is the major assumption of American militants—the assumption that the Communists have committed aggression—a misperception or not?

One answer would be: It is a misperception in so far as they assume Communist aggression to be self-evident when it is not. In glossing over—not resolving but simply glossing over—all the complexities and ambiguities, the typical American militant is indulging in an extreme form of selective inattention and is basically misperceiving the issue. It is a misperception also in so far as he fails to realize how completely the North Vietnamese Communists regard themselves as innocent and regard us as the aggressor. Finally, and most basically, it is a misperception in that it assumes the existence of an aggressor in the Munich sense of that word when, psychologically, the contrast with Munich is very great. In this ambiguous, inbetweenish war there is not necessarily a full-blown devil anywhere. . . .

THE ASSUMPTION OF AMERICAN NON-AGGRESSION

To almost any American the most emotionally unacceptable thought about Vietnam is probably the thought that we ourselves might have in some way committed aggression. Yet, as every psychoanalyst knows, the most unthinkable thought may be precisely the one that most needs to be brought up into the sunlight and calmly, rationally examined if it and related problems are to be realistically understood and grappled with. An intensely unthinkable thought not only sinks below the level of clear consciousness itself; it tends to pull down with it into murky obscurity, in varying degrees, a whole network of related thoughts. There is partial, peripheral repression of, or selective inattention to, a number of ideas that are merely associated with a more deeply repressed idea.

In the case of Vietnam, if the most unthinkable thought is that we might have committed aggression, then we would be wise to try to react to the question not with moral indignation against those who ask it—which is a frequent indication of psychological vulnerability and one of the more immature responses to a psychological threat—but with a tough-minded willingness to consider the question factually, on its merits, letting the chips fall where they may....

From a psychological standpoint, though, one fact is striking: the selective inattention that Americans have given to the whole question of whether our actions were aggressive. The points on this side of the argument have been rather thoroughly ignored and glossed over in the thinking of the great majority of the American people and probably, to a lesser extent, in the thinking of our decision-making leaders also. At any rate they have seldom if ever been publicly discussed by our leaders in these terms. Like the Austrians in 1914, we as a country have simply never candidly asked ourselves whether what we were doing could be legitimately called aggression. In this massive absence of thought there is strong support for the hypothesis that repression of an intolerable idea has been going on, on a very large scale.

A further psychological hypothesis is that when this most intolerable thought has been pushed down into unconsciousness (or, in our own terms, selectively inattended), it has dragged down with it a closely associated thought: that the Vietnamese Communists firmly *believe* we are aggressors, and firmly believe they are defending their homeland against our aggression. The lack of attention to this further thought, in the minds of most Americans, is perhaps even more remarkable in view of the fact that the evidence in favor of it is so very strong.... Whatever the actual rights and wrongs of this complex, ambiguous situation may be, it seems almost certain that the Communist leaders believe themselves to be right, in the very simple terms of foreign invasion and self-defense. But few militant Americans seem to have thought about this; most of them continually give evidence that they have not thought about it when they speak as if it were self-evident that the North Vietnamese are aggressors and have committed aggression by fighting in the South. (A person who believes he is defending his homeland may be tragically deluded, but he cannot be fairly called an aggressor without at least mentioning his delusions.)...

14

LIBERAL IDEALISM

GRAHAM GREENE

In this excerpt from The Quiet American, *Graham Greene's classic 1955 novel about the Vietnam War and early American involvement in it, Fowler, a cynical British journalist, argues with Pyle, an optimistic American employee of the U.S. Economic Aid Mission to the French-supported State of Vietnam. Their car having run out of gasoline in the countryside, Fowler and Pyle have taken refuge for the night in a watchtower garrisoned by two State of Vietnam soldiers, who are nervous about a possible nighttime attack by the "Viets," the Vietminh. In their conversation, Fowler, the narrator, ridicules Pyle's liberal idealism and the mental concepts of York Harding, Pyle's favorite political author, whose books had inspired him to try to save the East for democracy.*

...Now that we too had settled on the floor, the Vietnamese relaxed a little. I felt some sympathy for them; it wasn't an easy job for a couple of ill-trained men to sit up here night after night, never sure of when the Viets might creep up on the road through the fields of paddy. I said to Pyle, "Do you think they know they are fighting for democracy? We ought to have York Harding here to explain it to them."

"You always laugh at York," Pyle said.

"I laugh at anyone who spends so much time writing about what doesn't exist—mental concepts."

"They exist for him. Haven't you got any mental concepts? God, for instance."

"I've no reason to believe in a God. Do you?"

"Yes. I'm a Unitarian."

"How many hundred million Gods do people believe in? Why, even a Roman Catholic believes in quite a different God when he's scared or happy or hungry."

"Maybe if there is a God, he'd be so vast he'd look different to everyone."

"Like the great Buddha in Bangkok," I said. "You can't see all of him at once. Anyway, *he* keeps still."

"I guess you're just trying to be tough," Pyle said. "There must be something you believe in. Nobody can go on living without some belief."

"Oh, I'm not a Berkeleian. I believe my back's against this wall. I believe there's a sten gun over there."

"I didn't mean that."

"I even believe what I report, which is more than most of your correspondents do."

"Cigarette?"

"I don't smoke—except opium. Give one to the guards. We'd better stay friends with them." Pyle got up and lit their cigarettes and came back. I said, "I wish cigarettes had a symbolic significance, like salt."

"Don't you trust them?"

"No French officer," I said, "would care to spend the night alone with two scared guards in one of these towers. Why, even a platoon have been known to hand over their officers. Sometimes the Viets have a better success with a megaphone than a bazooka. I don't blame them. They don't believe in anything either. You and your like are trying to make a war with the help of people who just aren't interested."

"They don't want communism."

"They want enough rice," I said. "They don't want to be shot at. They want one day to be much the same as another. They don't want our white skins around telling them what they want."

"If Indochina goes—"

"I know that record. Siam goes. Malaya goes. Indonesia goes. What does 'go' mean? If I believed in your God and another life, I'd bet my future harp against your golden crown that in five hundred years there may be no New York or London, but they'll be growing paddy in these fields, they'll be carrying their produce to market on long poles, wearing their pointed hats. The small boys will be sitting on the buffaloes. I like the buffaloes, they don't like our smell, the smell of Europeans. And remember—from a buffalo's point of view you are a European too."

"They'll be forced to believe what they are told; they won't be allowed to think for themselves."

"Thought's a luxury. Do you think the peasant sits and thinks of God and democracy when he gets inside his mud hut at night?"

"You talk as if the whole country were peasant. What about the educated? Are they going to be happy?"

"Oh, no," I said, "we've brought them up in *our* ideas. We've taught them dangerous games, and that's why we are waiting here, hoping we don't get our throats cut. We deserve to have them cut. I wish your friend York was here too. I wonder how he'd relish it."

"York Harding's a very courageous man. Why, in Korea—"

"He wasn't an enlisted man, was he? He had a return ticket. With a return ticket, courage becomes an intellectual exercise, like a monk's flagellation. How much can I stick? Those poor devils can't catch a plane home. Hi," I called to them, "what are your names?" I thought that knowledge somehow would bring them into the circle of our conversation. They didn't answer, just glowered back at us behind the stumps of their cigarettes. "They think we are French," I said.

"That's just it," Pyle said. "You shouldn't be against York, you should be against the French. Their colonialism."

"Isms and ocracies. Give me facts. A rubber planter beats his labourer—all right, I'm against him. He hasn't been instructed to do it by the Minister of the Colonies. In France I expect he'd beat his wife. I've seen a priest, so poor he hasn't a change of trousers, working fifteen hours a day from hut to hut in a cholera epidemic, eating nothing but rice and salt fish, saying his Mass with an old cup—a wooden platter. I don't believe in God and yet I'm for that priest. Why don't you call that colonialism?"

"It *is* colonialism. York says it's often the good administrators who make it hard to change a bad system."

"Anyway, the French are dying every day—that's not a mental concept. They aren't leading these people on with half-lies like your politicians—and ours. I've been in India, Pyle, and I know the harm liberals do. We haven't a liberal party any more—liberalism's infected all the other parties. We are all either liberal conservatives or liberal socialists; we all have a good conscience. I'd rather be an exploiter who fights for what he exploits, and dies with it. Look at the history of Burma. We go and invade the country; the local tribes support us; we are victorious; but like you Americans we weren't colonialists in those days. Oh no, we made peace with the king and we handed him back his province and left our allies to be crucified and sawn in two. They were innocent. They thought we'd stay. But we were liberals and we didn't want a bad conscience."

"That was a long time ago."

"We shall do the same thing here. Encourage them and leave them with a little equipment and a toy industry."

"Toy industry?"

"Your plastic."

"Oh yes, I see."

"I don't know what I'm talking politics for. They don't interest me and I'm a reporter. I'm not engagé."

"Aren't you?" Pyle said.

"For the sake of an argument—to pass this bloody night, that's all. I don't take sides. I'll be still reporting whoever wins."

"If they win, you'll be reporting lies."

"There's usually a way round, and I haven't noticed much regard for truth in our papers either."

I think the fact of our sitting there talking encouraged the two soldiers; perhaps they thought the sound of our white voices—for voices have a colour too: yellow voices sing and black voices gargle, while ours just speak—would give an impression of numbers and keep the Viets away. They picked up their pans and began to eat again, scraping with their chopsticks, eyes watching Pyle and me over the rim of the pan.

"So you think we've lost?"

"That's not the point," I said. "I've no particular desire to see you win. I'd like those two poor buggers there to be happy—that's all. I wish they didn't have to sit in the dark at night, scared."

"You have to fight for liberty."

"I haven't seen any Americans fighting around here. And as for liberty, I don't know what it means. Ask them." I called across the floor in French to them. "La liberté—qu'est-ce que c'est la liberté?" They sucked in the rice and stared back and said nothing.

Pyle said, "Do you want everybody to be made in the same mould? You're arguing for the sake of arguing. You're an intellectual. You stand for the importance of the individual as much as I do—or York."

"Why have we only just discovered it?" I said. "Forty years ago no one talked that way."

"It wasn't threatened then."

"Ours wasn't threatened, oh no, but who cared about the individuality of the man in the paddy field—and who does now? The only man to treat him as a man is the political commissar. He'll sit in his hut and ask his name and listen to his complaints; he'll give up an hour a day to teaching him—it doesn't matter what, he's being treated like a man, like someone of value. Don't go on in the East with that parrot cry about a threat to the individual soul. Here you'd find yourself on the wrong side—it's they who stand for the individual and we just stand for Private 23987, unit in the global strategy."

"You don't mean half what you are saying," Pyle said uneasily.

"Probably three-quarters. I've been here a long time. You know, it's lucky I'm not engagé; there are things I might be tempted to do—because here in the East—well, I don't like Ike. I like—well, these two. This is their country. What's the time? My watch has stopped."

"It's turned eight-thirty."

"Ten hours and we can move."

"It's going to be quite chilly," Pyle said and shivered. "I never expected that."

"There's water all round. I've got a blanket in the car. That will be enough."

"Is it safe?"

"It's early for the Viets."

"Let me go."

"I'm more used to the dark."

When I stood up, the two soldiers stopped eating. I told them, "Je reviens tout de suite." I dangled my legs over the trapdoor, found the ladder, and went down. It is odd how reassuring conversation is, especially on abstract subjects; it seems to normalize the strangest surroundings. I was no longer scared; it was as though I had left a room and would be returning there to pick up the argument— the watch-tower was the rue Catinat, the bar of the Majestic, or even a room off Gordon Square.

I stood below the tower for a minute to get my vision back. There was starlight, but no moonlight. Moonlight reminds me of a mortuary and the cold wash of an unshaded globe over a marble slab, but starlight is alive and never still; it is almost as though someone in those vast spaces is trying to communicate a message of good will, for even the names of the stars are friendly. Venus is any woman we love, the Bears are the bears of childhood, and I suppose the Southern Cross, to those, like my wife, who believe, may be a favourite hymn or a prayer beside the bed. Once I shivered, as Pyle had done. But the night was hot enough; only the shallow stretch of water on either side gave a kind of icing to the warmth. I started out towards the car, and for a moment when I stood on the road I thought it was no longer there. That shook my confidence, even after I remembered that it had petered out thirty yards away. I couldn't help walking with my shoulders bent; I felt more unobtrusive that way.

I had to unlock the car boot to get the blanket, and the click and squeak startled me in the silence. I didn't relish being the only noise in what must have been a night full of people. With the blanket over my shoulder I lowered the boot more carefully than I had raised it, and then, just as the catch caught, the sky towards Saigon flared with light and the sound of an explosion came rumbling down the road. A bren spat and spat and was quiet again before the rumbling stopped. I thought, Somebody's had it; and very far away heard voices crying with pain or fear or perhaps even triumph. I don't know why, but I had thought all the time of an attack coming from behind, along the road we had passed, and I had a moment's sense of unfairness that the Viet should be there ahead, between us and Saigon. It was as though we had been unconsciously driving towards danger instead of away from it, just as I was now walking in its direction, back towards the tower. I walked because it was less noisy than to run, but my body wanted to run....

15

ARROGANCE OF POWER

J. WILLIAM FULBRIGHT

A conservative Democratic senator from Arkansas, chair of the Senate Committee on Foreign Relations, sponsor of the Gulf of Tonkin Resolution, and friend and supporter of President Johnson, J. William Fulbright nonetheless became one of the most influential establishment critics of Johnson's policy of escalation in Vietnam. In 1966 he spoke and wrote about the "arrogance of power," which, he argued, had inadvertently brought America to Vietnam. American arrogance was rooted in excessive military and economic power, vaulting pride, and a missionary instinct. Even though Fulbright thought U.S. foreign policy aims were well-meaning, he believed that Americans' arrogant idealism was condescending toward third world peoples, produced "fatal impacts" on their societies, and brought Americans into conflict with other nations.

...The attitude above all others which I feel sure is no longer valid is the arrogance of power, the tendency of great nations to equate power with virtue and major responsibilities with a universal mission. The dilemmas involved are pre-eminently American dilemmas, not because America has weaknesses that others do not have but because America is powerful as no nation has ever been before, and the discrepancy between her power and the power of others appears to be increasing. One may hope that America, with her vast resources and democratic traditions, with her diverse and creative population, will find the wisdom to match her power; but one can hardly be confident because the wisdom required is greater wisdom than any great nation has ever shown before. It must be rooted, as Dr. Chisholm says, in the re-examination of "all of the attitudes of our ancestors."

It is a tall order. Perhaps one can begin to fill it by an attempt to assess the attitudes of Americans toward other peoples and some of the effects of America's power on small countries whom she has tried to help.

INNOCENTS ABROAD

There are signs of the arrogance of power in the way Americans act when they go to foreign countries. Foreigners frequently comment on the contrast between the behavior of Americans at home and abroad: in our own country, they say, we are hospitable and considerate, but as soon as we get outside our own borders something seems to get into us and wherever we are we become noisy and demanding and we strut around as if we owned the place. The British used to say during the war that the trouble with the Yanks was that they were "overpaid, oversexed, and over here." During a recent vacation in Mexico, I noticed in a small-town airport two groups of students on holiday, one group Japanese, the other American. The Japanese were neatly dressed and were talking and laughing in a manner that neither annoyed anybody nor particularly called attention to themselves. The Americans, on the other hand, were disporting themselves in a conspicuous and offensive manner, stamping around the waiting room in sloppy clothes, drinking beer, and shouting to each other as if no one else were there.

This kind of scene, unfortunately, has become familiar in many parts of the world. I do not wish to exaggerate its significance, but I have the feeling that just as there was once something special about being a Roman or a Spaniard or an Englishman, there is now something about the consciousness of being an American abroad, something about the consciousness of belonging to the biggest, richest country in the world, that encourages people who are perfectly well behaved at home to become boorish when they are in somebody else's country and to treat the local citizens as if they were not really there.

One reason Americans abroad may act as though they "own the place" is that in many places they very nearly do: American companies may dominate large segments of a country's economy; American products are advertised on billboards and displayed in shop windows; American hotels and snack bars are available to protect American tourists from foreign influence; American soldiers may be stationed in the country, and even if they are not, the population are probably well aware that their very survival depends on the wisdom with which America uses her immense military power.

I think that when any American goes abroad, he carries an unconscious knowledge of all this power with him and it affects his behavior, just as it once affected the behavior of Greeks and Romans, of Spaniards, Germans, and Englishmen, in the brief high noons of their respective ascendancies. It was the arrogance of their power that led nineteenth-century Englishmen to suppose that if they shouted at a foreigner loud enough in English he was bound to understand, or that now leads Americans to behave like Mark Twain's "innocents abroad," who reported on their travels in Europe that

> The people of those foreign countries are very, very ignorant. They looked curiously at the costumes we had brought from the wilds of America. They observed that we talked loudly at table sometimes. . . . In Paris they just simply opened their eyes and stared when we spoke to them in

French! We never did succeed in making these idiots understand their own language.[1]

THE FATAL IMPACT

Reflecting on his voyages to Polynesia in the late eighteenth century, Captain Cook later wrote that "It would have been better for these people never to have known us." In a book on European explorations of the South Pacific, Alan Moorehead relates how the Tahitians and the Australian aborigines were corrupted by the white man's diseases, alcohol, firearms, laws, and concepts of morality, by what Moorehead calls "the long down-slide into Western civilization." The first missionaries to Tahiti, says Moorehead, were "determined to recreate the island in the image of lower-middle-class Protestant England.... They kept hammering away at the Tahitian way of life until it crumbled before them, and within two decades they had achieved precisely what they set out to do."[2] It is said that the first missionaries to Hawaii went for the purpose of explaining to the Polynesians that it was sinful to work on Sunday, only to discover that in those bountiful islands nobody worked on any day.

Even when acting with the best of intentions, Americans, like other Western peoples who have carried their civilizations abroad, have had something of the same "fatal impact" on smaller nations that European explorers had on the Tahitians and the native Australians. We have not harmed people because we wished to; on the contrary, more often than not we have wanted to help people and, in some very important respects, we have helped them. Americans have brought medicine and education, manufactures and modern techniques to many places in the world; but they have also brought themselves and the condescending attitudes of a people whose very success breeds disdain for other cultures. Bringing power without understanding, Americans as well as Europeans have had a devastating effect in less advanced areas of the world; without knowing they were doing it, they have shattered traditional societies, disrupted fragile economies and undermined peoples' self-confidence by the invidious example of their own power and efficiency. They have done this in many instances simply by being big and strong, by giving good advice, by intruding on people who have not wanted them but could not resist them.

The missionary instinct seems to run deep in human nature, and the bigger and stronger and richer we are, the more we feel suited to the missionary task, the more indeed we consider it our duty. Dr. Chisholm relates the story of an eminent cleric who had been proselyting the Eskimos and said: "You know, for years we couldn't do anything with those Eskimos at all; they didn't have any sin. We had to teach them sin for years before we could do anything with them."[3] I am reminded of the three Boy Scouts who reported to their scoutmaster that as their good deed for the day they had helped an old lady to cross the street.

"That's fine," said the scoutmaster, "but why did it take three of you?"

[1] Mark Twain, *The Innocents Abroad* (New York: The Thistle Press, 1962), p. 494.

[2] Alan Moorehead, *The Fatal Impact* (New York: Harper & Row, 1966), pp. 61, 80–81.

[3] Brock Chisholm, *Prescription for Survival* (New York: Columbia University Press, 1957), pp. 55–56.

"Well," they explained, "she didn't want to go."

The good deed above all others that Americans feel qualified to perform is the teaching of democracy. Let us consider the results of some American good deeds in various parts of the world.

Over the years since President Monroe proclaimed his doctrine, Latin Americans have had the advantages of United States tutelage in fiscal responsibility, in collective security, and in the techniques of democracy. If they have fallen short in any of these fields, the thought presents itself that the fault may lie as much with the teacher as with the pupils.

When President Theodore Roosevelt announced his "corollary" to the Monroe Doctrine in 1905, he solemnly declared that he regarded the future interventions thus sanctified as a "burden" and a "responsibility" and an obligation to "international equity." Not once, so far as I know, has the United States regarded itself as intervening in a Latin American country for selfish or unworthy motives—a view not necessarily shared, however, by the beneficiaries. Whatever reassurance the purity of our motives may give must be shaken a little by the thought that probably no country in human history has ever intervened in another except for motives it regarded as excellent.

For all our noble intentions, the countries which have had most of the tutelage in democracy by United States Marines have not been particularly democratic. These include Haiti, which is under a brutal and superstitious dictatorship; the Dominican Republic, which languished under the brutal Trujillo dictatorship for thirty years and whose second elected government since the overthrow of Trujillo is threatened, like the first, by the power of a military oligarchy; and of course Cuba, which, as no one needs to be reminded, has replaced its traditional right-wing dictatorships with a communist dictatorship.

Maybe, in the light of this extraordinary record of accomplishment, it is time for us to reconsider our teaching methods. Maybe we are not really cut out for the job of spreading the gospel of democracy. Maybe it would profit us to concentrate on our own democracy instead of trying to inflict our particular version of it on all those ungrateful Latin Americans who stubbornly oppose their North American benefactors instead of the "real" enemies whom we have so graciously chosen for them. And maybe—just maybe—if we left our neighbors to make their own judgments and their own mistakes, and confined our assistance to matters of economics and technology instead of philosophy, maybe then they would begin to find the democracy and the dignity that have largely eluded them, and we in turn might begin to find the love and gratitude that we seem to crave.

Korea is another example. We went to war in 1950 to defend South Korea against the Russian-inspired aggression of North Korea. I think that American intervention was justified and necessary: we were defending a country that clearly wanted to be defended, whose army was willing to fight and fought well, and whose government, though dictatorial, was patriotic and commanded the support of the people. Throughout the war, however, the United States emphasized as one of its war aims the survival of the Republic of Korea as a "free society," something which it was not then and is not now. We lost 33,629 American lives in that war and have since spent $5.61 billion on direct military and economic aid and a great deal more on indirect aid to South Korea. The country, nonetheless, remained until recently in a condition of virtual economic stagnation and political instability. Only now is economic progress being made, but the truly surprising fact is that having fought a war for three years to defend the freedom of South Korea, most Americans quickly lost interest in the state of the ward for whom they had sacrificed so much. It is doubtful that more than a handful of Americans now know or care whether South Korea is a "free society."

We are now engaged in a war to "defend freedom" in South Vietnam. Unlike the Republic of Korea, South Vietnam has an army which fights without notable success and a weak, dictatorial government which does not command the loyalty of the South Vietnamese people. The official war aims of the United States government, as I understand them, are to defeat what is regarded as North Vietnamese aggression, to demonstrate the futility of what the communists call "wars of national liberation," and to create conditions under which the South Vietnamese people will be able freely to determine their own future.

I have not the slightest doubt of the sincerity of the President and the Vice-President and the Secretaries of State and Defense in propounding these aims. What I do doubt, and doubt very much, is the ability of the United States to achieve these aims by the means being used. I do not question the power of our weapons and the efficiency of our logistics; I cannot say these things delight me as they seem to delight some of our officials, but they are certainly impressive. What I do question is the ability of the United States or any other Western nation to go into a small, alien, undeveloped Asian nation and create stability where there is chaos, the will to fight where there is defeatism, democracy where there is no tradition of it, and honest government where corruption is almost a way of life.

In the spring of 1966 demonstrators in Saigon burned American jeeps, tried to assault American soldiers, and marched through the streets shouting "Down with American imperialists," while a Buddhist leader made a speech equating the United States with the communists as a threat to South Vietnamese independence. Most Americans are understandably shocked and angered to encounter expressions of hostility from people who would long since have been under the rule of the Viet Cong but for the sacrifice of American lives and money. Why, we may ask, are they so shockingly ungrateful? Surely they must know that their very right to parade and protest and demonstrate depends on the Americans who are defending them.

The answer, I think, is that "fatal impact" of the rich and strong on the poor and weak. Dependent on it though the Vietnamese are, American strength is a reproach to their weakness, American wealth a mockery of their poverty, American success a reminder of their failures. What they resent is the disruptive effect of our strong culture upon their fragile one, an effect which we can no more avoid having than a man can help being bigger than a child. What they fear, I think rightly, is that traditional Vietnamese society cannot survive the American economic and cultural impact.

The evidence of that "fatal impact" is seen in the daily life of Saigon. A *New York Times* correspondent reported—and his information matches that of other observers on the scene—that many Vietnamese find it necessary to put their wives or daughters to work as bar girls or to peddle them to American soldiers as mistresses; that it is not unusual to hear a report that a Vietnamese soldier has committed suicide out of shame because his wife has been working as a bar girl; that Vietnamese have trouble getting taxicabs because drivers will not stop for them, preferring to pick up American soldiers who will pay outrageous fares without complaint; that as a result of the American influx bar girls, prostitutes, pimps, bar owners, and taxi drivers have risen to the higher levels of the economic pyramid; that middle-class Vietnamese families have difficulty renting homes because Americans have driven the rents beyond their reach, and some Vietnamese families have actually been evicted from houses and apartments by landlords who prefer to rent to the affluent Americans; that Vietnamese civil servants, junior army officers, and enlisted men are unable to support their families because of the inflation generated by American spending and the purchasing power of the G.I.s. One Vietnamese explained to the *New York Times* reporter that "Any time legions of prosperous white men descend on a rudimentary Asian society, you are bound to have trouble." Another said: "We Vietnamese are somewhat xenophobe. We don't like foreigners, any kind of foreigners, so that you shouldn't be surprised that we don't like you."[4]

Sincere though it is, the American effort to build the foundations of freedom in South Vietnam is thus having an effect quite different from the one intended. "All this struggling and striving to make the world better is a great mistake," said George Bernard Shaw, "not because it isn't a good thing to improve the world if you know how to do it, but because striving and struggling is the worst way you could set about doing anything."[5]

One wonders how much the American commitment to Vietnamese freedom is also a commitment to American pride—the two seem to have become part of the same package. When we talk about the freedom of South Vietnam, we may be thinking about how disagreeable it would be to accept a solution short of victory; we may be thinking about how our pride would be injured if we settled for less than we set out to achieve; we may be thinking about our reputation as a great power, fearing that a compromise settlement would shame us before the world, marking us as a second-rate people with flagging courage and determination.

Such fears are as nonsensical as their opposite, the presumption of a universal mission. They are simply unworthy of the richest, most powerful, most productive, and best educated people in the world. One can understand an uncompromising attitude on the part of such countries as China or France: both have been struck low in this century and a certain amount of arrogance may be helpful to them in recovering their pride. It is much less comprehensible on the part of the United States— a nation whose modern history has been an almost uninterrupted chronicle of success, a nation which by now should be so sure of its own power as to be capable of magnanimity, a nation which by now should be able to act on the proposition that, as George Kennan said, "there is more respect to be won in the opinion of the world

---

[4] Neil Sheehan, "Anti-Americanism Grows in Vietnam," *The New York Times*, April 24, 1966, p. 3.
[5] George Bernard Shaw, *Cashel Byron's Profession* (1886), Chapter 5.

by a resolute and courageous liquidation of unsound positions than in the most stubborn pursuit of extravagant or unpromising objectives."[6]

The cause of our difficulties in Southeast Asia is not a deficiency of power but an excess of the wrong kind of power, which results in a feeling of impotence when it fails to achieve its desired ends. We are still acting like Boy Scouts dragging reluctant old ladies across streets they do not want to cross. We are trying to remake Vietnamese society, a task which certainly cannot be accomplished by force and which probably cannot be accomplished by any means available to outsiders. The objective may be desirable, but it is not feasible. As Shaw said: "Religion is a great force—the only real motive force in the world; but what you fellows don't understand is that you must get at a man through his own religion and not through yours."[7]

With the best intentions in the world the United States has involved itself deeply in the affairs of developing nations in Asia and Latin America, practicing what has been called a kind of "welfare imperialism." Our honest purpose is the advancement of development and democracy, to which end it has been thought necessary to destroy ancient and unproductive modes of life. In this latter function we have been successful, perhaps more successful than we know. Bringing skills and knowledge, money and resources in amounts hitherto unknown in traditional societies, the Americans have overcome indigenous groups and interests and become the dominant force in a number of countries. Far from being bumbling, wasteful, and incompetent, as critics have charged, American government officials, technicians, and economists have been strikingly successful in breaking down the barriers to change in ancient but fragile cultures.

Here, however, our success ends. Traditional rulers, institutions, and ways of life have crumbled under the fatal impact of American wealth and power but they have not been replaced by new institutions and new ways of life, nor has their breakdown ushered in an era of democracy and development. It has rather ushered in an era of disorder and demoralization because in the course of destroying old ways of doing things, we have also destroyed the self-confidence and self-reliance without which no society can build indigenous institutions. Inspiring as we have such great awe of our efficiency and wealth, we have reduced some of the intended beneficiaries of our generosity to a condition of dependency and self-denigration. We have done this for the most part inadvertently: with every good intention we have intruded on fragile societies, and our intrusion, though successful in uprooting traditional ways of life, has been strikingly unsuccessful in implanting the democracy and advancing the development which are the honest aims of our "welfare imperialism."

AMERICAN EMPIRE OR AMERICAN EXAMPLE?

Despite its dangerous and unproductive consequences, the idea of being responsible for the whole world seems to be flattering to Americans and I am afraid it is

[6] George F. Kennan, "Supplemental Foreign Assistance Fiscal Year 1966—Vietnam," *Hearings Before the Committee on Foreign Relations*, United States Senate, 89th Congress, 2nd Session on S. 2793, Part I (Washington: U.S. Government Printing Office, 1966), p. 335.
[7] George Bernard Shaw, *Getting Married* (1911).

turning our heads, just as the sense of universal responsibility turned the heads of ancient Romans and nineteenth-century British.

In 1965 Henry Fairlie, a British political writer for *The Spectator* and *The Daily Telegraph,* wrote what he called "A Cheer for American Imperialism."[8] An empire, he said, "has no justification except its own existence." It must never contract; it "wastes treasure and life"; its commitments "are without rhyme or reason." Nonetheless, according to Fairlie, the "American empire" is uniquely benevolent, devoted as it is to individual liberty and the rule of law, and having performed such services as getting the author released from a Yugoslav jail simply by his threatening to involve the American Consul, a service which he describes as "sublime."

What romantic nonsense this is. And what dangerous nonsense in the age of nuclear weapons. The idea of an "American empire" might be dismissed as the arrant imagining of a British Gunga Din except that it surely strikes a responsive chord in at least a corner of the usually sensible and humane American mind. It calls to mind the slogans of the past about the shot fired at Concord being heard 'round the world, about "manifest destiny" and "making the world safe for democracy," and the demand for "unconditional surrender" in World War II. It calls to mind President McKinley taking counsel with the Supreme Being about his duty to the benighted Filipinos.

The "Blessings-of-Civilization Trust," as Mark Twain called it, may have been a "Daisy" in its day, uplifting for the soul and good for business besides, but its day is past. It is past because the great majority of the human race is demanding dignity and independence, not the honor of a supine role in an American empire. It is past because whatever claim America may make for the universal domain of her ideas and values is balanced by the communist counter-claim, armed like our own with nuclear weapons. And, most of all, it is past because it never should have begun, because we are not God's chosen saviour of mankind but only one of mankind's more successful and fortunate branches, endowed by our Creator with about the same capacity for good and evil, no more or less, than the rest of humanity.

An excessive preoccupation with foreign relations over a long period of time is more than a manifestation of arrogance; it is a drain on the power that gave rise to it, because it diverts a nation from the sources of its strength, which are in its domestic life. A nation immersed in foreign affairs is expending its capital, human as well as material; sooner or later that capital must be renewed by some diversion of creative energies from foreign to domestic pursuits. I would doubt that any nation has achieved a durable greatness by conducting a "strong" foreign policy, but many have been ruined by expending their energies in foreign adventures while allowing their domestic bases to deteriorate. The United States emerged as a world power in the twentieth century, not because of what it had done in foreign relations but because it had spent the nineteenth century developing the North American continent; by contrast, the Austrian and Turkish empires collapsed in the twentieth century in large part because they had so long neglected their internal development and organization.

If America has a service to perform in the world—and I believe she has—it is in large part the service of her own example. In our excessive involvement in the

[8] *The New York Times Magazine,* July 11, 1965.

affairs of other countries we are not only living off our assets and denying our own people the proper enjoyment of their resources, we are also denying the world the example of a free society enjoying its freedom to the fullest. This is regrettable indeed for a nation that aspires to teach democracy to other nations, because, as Edmund Burke said, "Example is the school of mankind, and they will learn at no other."[9]

The missionary instinct in foreign affairs may, in a curious way, reflect a deficiency rather than an excess of national self-confidence. In America's case the evidence of a lack of self-confidence is our apparent need for constant proof and reassurance, our nagging desire for popularity, our bitterness and confusion when foreigners fail to appreciate our generosity and good intentions. Lacking an appreciation of the dimensions of our own power, we fail to understand our enormous and disruptive impact on the world; we fail to understand that no matter how good our intentions—and they are, in most cases, decent enough—other nations are alarmed by the very existence of such great power, which, whatever its benevolence, cannot help but remind them of their own helplessness before it.

Those who lack self-assurance are also likely to lack magnanimity, because the one is the condition of the other. Only a nation at peace with itself, with its transgressions as well as its achievements, is capable of a generous understanding of others. Only when we Americans can acknowledge our own past aggressive behavior—in such instances, for example, as the Indian wars and the wars against Mexico and Spain—will we acquire some perspective on the aggressive behavior of others; only when we can understand the human implications of the chasm between American affluence and the poverty of most of the rest of mankind will we be able to understand why the American "way of life" which is so dear to us has few lessons and limited appeal to the poverty-stricken majority of the human race.

It is a curiosity of human nature that lack of self-assurance seems to breed an exaggerated sense of power and mission. When a nation is very powerful but lacking in self-confidence, it is likely to behave in a manner dangerous to itself and to others. Feeling the need to prove what is obvious to everyone else, it begins to confuse great power with unlimited power and great responsibility with total responsibility: it can admit of no error; it must win every argument, no matter how trivial. For lack of an appreciation of how truly powerful it is, the nation begins to lose wisdom and perspective and, with them, the strength and understanding that it takes to be magnanimous to smaller and weaker nations.

Gradually but unmistakably America is showing signs of that arrogance of power which has afflicted, weakened, and in some cases destroyed great nations in the past. In so doing we are not living up to our capacity and promise as a civilized example for the world. The measure of our falling short is the measure of the patriot's duty of dissent.

[9] Edmund Burke, "On a Regicide Peace" (1796).

16

MORAL ANTICOMMUNISM

NORMAN PODHORETZ

After the war the editor of Commentary *magazine, Norman Podhoretz, became one of the stoutest defenders of America's involvement in Vietnam against those who accused it of immorality. To Podhoretz, America's imprudent idealism and the impracticality of involvement were proof that the United States had gone to Vietnam for moral, altruistic purposes, which included saving South Vietnam from what he considered were the evils of communism.*

...[S]tupid though the American way of war no doubt was in the political context of Vietnam—where it served to arouse the hostility of the very people whose "hearts and minds" were being courted and whose support was a necessary ingredient of victory—it could not reasonably be considered immoral. Nor could it even be considered extraordinarily brutal. Writing in 1970, not, obviously, to defend the United States, but out of the expectation that things might yet get worse both in Vietnam and elsewhere, Daniel Ellsberg warned his fellow activists in the antiwar movement that "an escalation of rhetoric can blind us to the fact that Vietnam is...no more brutal than other wars in the past—and it is absurdly unhistorical to insist that it is...."[1]

Even granting to writers like the sociologist Peter L. Berger that "the war was marked by a distinctive brutality...flowing in large measure from its character as a war of counterinsurgency,"[2] Ellsberg's point was so obviously true that it poses a difficult intellectual problem. One can easily enough understand how the young of the 1960s—who were in general notoriously deficient in historical knowledge or understanding, and who therefore tended to look upon all the ills around them, including relatively minor ones, as unique in their evil dimension—would genu-

From Norman Podhoretz, *Why We Were in Vietnam.* Copyright © 1982 by Norman Podhoretz. Reprinted by permission of Simon & Schuster, Inc.

[1] Daniel Ellsberg, in *War Crimes and the American Conscience*, ed. Erwin Knoll and Judith Nies McFadden (New York: Holt, Rinehart & Winston, 1970), p. 82.

[2] Peter L. Berger, "Indochina and the American Conscience," *Commentary*, Feb. 1980.

inely imagine that never in all of human experience had there been anything to compare in cruelty and carnage with the war in Vietnam. But how did it happen that so many of their elders and teachers, who did have historical perspective and had even lived through two earlier and bloodier wars, should have taken so "absurdly unhistorical" a view of Vietnam? The answer is, quite simply, that they opposed—or had turned against—the American effort to save South Vietnam from Communism. Being against the end, they could not tolerate the very means whose earlier employment in Korea and in World War II they had not only accepted but applauded.

In World War II, as Lewy says, "despite the fact that the Allies...engaged in terror-bombing of the enemy's civilian population and generally paid only minimal attention to the prevention of civilian casualties—even during the liberation of Italy and France—hardly anyone on the Allied side objected to these tactics." The reason was that "the war against Nazism and fascism was regarded as a moral crusade in which the Allies could do no wrong...."[3]

So, too, with the Korean War, in which practically all the major population centers were leveled, dams and irrigation systems were bombed, napalm was used, and enormous numbers of civilians were killed. Yet there was no morbidly fascinated dwelling on those horrors in the press, and very little moral outrage expressed. For the Korean War was seen as an extension of World War II not merely in the strategic sense of representing a new phase in the resistance to aggression through the principle of collective security, but also in being part of a moral crusade against Communism. As such it was a continuation of the struggle against totalitarianism, whose first battles had been fought and won in the Second World War.

The fact that this aspect of the Korean War was rarely emphasized in the official pronouncements, which tended to dwell upon the strategic element, does not mean that it was considered less important. It means rather that it was taken so entirely for granted as to need little if any explicit stress. The consensus of the period was that Communism represented an evil comparable to and as great as Nazism. This was the feeling in the country at large, and it was even the prevalent view within the intellectual community where Communism was regarded—not least by many who had earlier embraced it—as the other great embodiment of totalitarianism, the twentieth century's distinctive improvement upon the despotisms and tyrannies of the past. In one of the most influential books of the Korean War period, *The Origins of Totalitarianism*, Hannah Arendt brought Nazism and Communism together under the same rubric as systems of total control (in contrast to the traditional despotisms which exercised lesser degrees of domination over the individuals living under them). Indeed, Arendt went even further, arguing that Hitler, for all his anti-Communist passion, had looked admiringly to Lenin and Stalin for lessons in the practical implementation of his own brand of totalitarianism.

To go to war in order to contain the spread of Communism was therefore on the same moral plane as going to war against Nazism had been, "and those who fought such a war could do no wrong" either. "There was hideous bloodletting in

[3] Guenter Lewy, *America in Vietnam* (New York: Oxford University Press, 1978), p. 223.

Korea," wrote Richard H. Rovere in 1967, "and few liberals protested it";[4] he himself...celebrated the Korean War as "a turning point in the world struggle against Communism."[5] Having then believed that "we had an obligation" to go to the aid of the government in South Vietnam when it was threatened by a combination of internal and external Communist aggression, by 1967 he had come to feel that the American role was indefensible. "People who used to say there are things worse than war now say there are things worse than Communism and that the war in Vietnam is one of them."[6] Rovere himself was clearly one of those people, and their number was now legion. It was because they no longer thought that Communism was so great an evil that they saw the American war against it as a greater evil than it truly was, either by comparison with other wars, or more emphatically, in relation to the political system whose extension to South Vietnam the war was being fought to prevent.

Here then we arrive at the center of the moral issue posed by the American intervention into Vietnam.

The United States sent half a million men to fight in Vietnam. More than 50,000 of them lost their lives, and many thousands more were wounded. Billions of dollars were poured into the effort, damaging the once unparalleled American economy to such an extent that the country's competitive position was grievously impaired. The domestic disruptions to which the war gave rise did perhaps even greater damage to a society previously so self-confident that it was often accused of entertaining illusions of its own omnipotence. Millions of young people growing to maturity during the war developed attitudes of such hostility toward their own country and the civilization embodied by its institutions that their willingness to defend it against external enemies in the future was left hanging in doubt.

Why did the United States undertake these burdens and make these sacrifices in blood and treasure and domestic tranquillity? What was in it for the United States? It was a question that plagued the antiwar movement from beginning to end because the answer was so hard to find. If the United States was simply acting the part of an imperialist aggressor in Vietnam, as many in the antiwar movement professed to believe, it was imperialism of a most peculiar kind. There were no raw materials to exploit in Vietnam, and there was no overriding strategic interest involved. To Franklin Roosevelt in 1941 Indochina had been important because it was close to the source of rubber and tin, but this was no longer an important consideration. Toward the end of the war, it was discovered that there was oil off the coast of Vietnam and antiwar radicals happily seized on this news as at last providing an explanation for the American presence there. But neither Kennedy nor Johnson knew about the oil, and even if they had, they would hardly have gone to war for its sake in those pre-OPEC days when oil from the Persian Gulf could be had at two dollars a barrel.

[4] Richard H. Rovere, in "Liberal Anti-Communism Revisited," *Commentary*, Sept. 1967.

[5] Richard H. Rovere, quoted in William Manchester, *American Caesar* (New York: Dell Publishing Co., 1979), p. 808.

[6] Richard H. Rovere, in "Liberal Anti-Communism Revisited," *Commentary*, Sept. 1967.

In the absence of an economic interpretation, a psychological version of the theory of imperialism was developed to answer the maddening question: *Why are we in Vietnam?* This theory held that the United States was in Vietnam because it had an urge to dominate—"to impose its national obsessions on the rest of the world," in the words of a piece in the *New York Review of Books,*[7] one of the leading centers of antiwar agitation within the intellectual community. But if so, the psychic profits were as illusory as the economic ones, for the war was doing even deeper damage to the national self-confidence than to the national economy.

Yet another variant of the psychological interpretation, proposed by the economist Robert L. Heilbroner, was that "the fear of losing our place in the sun, of finding ourselves at bay,... motivates a great deal of the anti-Communism on which so much of American foreign policy seems to be founded." This was especially so in such underdeveloped countries as Vietnam, where "the rise of Communism would signal the end of capitalism as the dominant world order, and would force the acknowledgment that America no longer constituted the model on which the future of world civilization would be mainly based."[8]

All these theories were developed out of a desperate need to find or invent selfish or self-interested motives for the American presence in Vietnam, the better to discredit it morally. In a different context, proponents of one or another of these theories—Senator Fulbright, for example—were not above trying to discredit the American presence politically by insisting that *no* national interest was being served by the war. This latter contention at least had the virtue of being closer to the truth than the former. For the truth was that the United States went into Vietnam for the sake not of its own direct interests in the ordinary sense but for the sake of an ideal. The intervention was a product of the Wilsonian side of the American character— the side that went to war in 1917 to "make the world safe for democracy" and that found its contemporary incarnations in the liberal internationalism of the 1940s and the liberal anti-Communism of the 1950s. One can characterize this impulse as naive; one can describe it, as Heilbroner does (and as can be done with any virtuous act), in terms that give it a subtly self-interested flavor. But there is no rationally defensible way in which it can be called immoral.

Why, then, were we in Vietnam? To say it once again: because we were trying to save the Southern half of that country from the evils of Communism....

In May 1977, two full years after the Communist takeover, President Jimmy Carter—a repentant hawk, like many members of his cabinet, including his Secretary of State and his Secretary of Defense—spoke of "the intellectual and moral poverty" of the policy that had led us into Vietnam and had kept us there for so long. When Ronald Reagan, an unrepentant hawk, called the war "a noble cause" in the course of his ultimately successful campaign to replace Carter in the White House, he was accused of having made a "gaffe." Fully, painfully aware as I am that the American effort to save Vietnam from Communism was indeed beyond our intellectual and moral capabilities, I believe the story shows that Reagan's "gaffe"

---

[7] Jason Epstein, "The CIA and the Intellectuals," *New York Review of Books.* Apr. 20, 1967.

[8] Robert L. Heilbroner, "Counterrevolutionary America," *Commentary,* Apr. 1967.

was closer to the truth of why we were in Vietnam and what we did there, at least until the very end, than Carter's denigration of an act of imprudent idealism whose moral soundness has been so overwhelmingly vindicated by the hideous consequences of our defeat.

17

CREDIBILITY AND LIMITED WAR

JONATHAN SCHELL

In The Time of Illusion *journalist and writer Jonathan Schell described the decade of 1965 to 1975 as one of deep political crisis, which "diverted the nation's energy and attention from virtually all other business, embittered every aspect of public life, and finally brought the American Constitutional system to the edge of a break-down."* At the root of the crisis was America's involvement in Vietnam, and at the root of the involvement was the aim of protecting U.S. "credibility," a strategic doctrine "that formed the basis for all strategic thinking in the nineteen-sixties—the doctrine of nuclear deterrence."†*

...If one examines the covert record, as it appears in the Pentagon Papers and in other secret memoranda, and ignores the public justifications that were put forward only for reasons of propaganda, a remarkable consistency of purpose emerges; and

From *The Time of Illusion* by Jonathan Schell. Copyright © 1975 by Jonathan Schell. Reprinted by permission of Alfred A. Knopf, Inc.
*Jonathan Schell, *The Time of Illusion* (New York: Alfred A. Knopf, 1976), p. 5.
†Ibid., p. 9.

if guiding principles in government policy are to be found in the years in which the American democracy experienced its crisis, they are buried here, in the realm of strategic theory. For from January of 1961, when John Kennedy took office, until August of 1974, when Richard Nixon was forced to leave office, the unvarying dominant goal of the foreign policy of the United States was the preservation of what policymakers throughout the period called the credibility of American power. (And, indeed, since President Nixon's fall the preservation of American credibility has remained the dominant goal of United States foreign policy.) The various policymakers phrased the aim in many ways. To have a formidable "psychological impact...on the countries of the world" is how the Joint Chiefs of Staff put it in a memo to Secretary of Defense Robert McNamara in January of 1962.[1] To prevent a situation from arising in which "no nation can ever again have the same confidence in American promise or in American protection" is how President Johnson put it at a news conference in July of 1965. To "avoid humiliation" is how Assistant Secretary of Defense John McNaughton put it in a memo in January of 1966. To shore up "the confidence factor" is how Assistant Secretary of State William Bundy put it in a speech in January of 1967. To prevent "defeat and humiliation" is how President Nixon put it in a speech in November of 1969. To demonstrate America's "will and character" is how President Nixon put it in a speech in April of 1970. To prevent the United States from appearing before the world as a "pitiful, helpless giant" is another way that President Nixon put it in that speech. To maintain "respect for the office of President of the United States" is how President Nixon put it in a speech in April of 1972. To win an "honorable" peace or a "peace with honor" is how President Nixon put it from time to time. But, whatever words it was couched in, the aim was always the same: to establish in the minds of peoples and their leaders throughout the world an image of the United States as a nation that possessed great power and had the will and determination to use it in foreign affairs. In the name of this objective, President Kennedy sent "advisers" to Vietnam in the early nineteen-sixties, and President Johnson escalated the Vietnam war in secrecy and persisted in carrying on the war in the face of growing public opposition. In the name of this objective, also, President Nixon sent planes and troops into Cambodia, sent an aircraft carrier into the Indian Ocean at the time of the India-Pakistan war, mined North Vietnamese ports in the spring of 1972, and carpet-bombed North Vietnam during the Christmas season of 1972. In the pursuit of this objective, massacres were condoned, hundreds of thousands of lives were lost, dictatorial governments were propped up, nations friendly to the United States were turned into adversaries, the domestic scene was thrown into turmoil, two Presidents were forced from office, the Constitution was imperilled, and the entire world was repeatedly brought to the verge of war.

---

[1] All the quotations of officials of the Kennedy and Johnson years are taken from *The Pentagon Papers* (Beacon, 1971) which includes a useful chronologically arranged catalogue of public statements by government officials concerning the war. Henry Kissinger's *Nuclear Weapons and Foreign Policy* has come out in two editions—one brought out in 1957 by Harper & Row, and the other by Norton in 1969. The Norton edition is abridged, and readers who wish to have a full and accurate impression of Kissinger's thinking in 1957 should make sure to read the original edition.

The doctrine of credibility, far from being a fanatical ideology, was a coldly reasoned strategic theory that was designed to supply the United States with effective instruments of influence in an age dominated by nuclear weapons. The doctrine did not take shape all at once but evolved gradually as the full sweep of American military policy, including, especially, nuclear policy, was subjected to a reexamination, which got under way outside the government in the late nineteen-fifties and was carried forward within the government in the early nineteen-sixties, after President Kennedy took office. When Kennedy entered the White House, the nation's nuclear policy had remained all but unchanged since the end of the Korean war, in 1953. In fact, although the conditions under which men lived and conducted their politics were altered more drastically by the invention of nuclear weapons than by any previous single invention, nuclear weapons had never become the subject of intensive public debate. In the aftermath of the Second World War, the United States had made a brief effort at the United Nations to bring the new weapons under some form of international control, but the atmosphere of the Cold War had soon settled in and the effort had been abandoned. Then, in the nineteen-fifties, the nation's attention had been further distracted from the new peril by rising levels of consumption, which quickly climbed beyond the highest expectations. In the United States, unprecedented wealth and ease came to coexist with unprecedented danger, and a sumptuous feast of consumable goods was spread out in the shadow of universal death. Americans began to live as though on a luxuriously appointed death row, where one was free to enjoy every comfort but was uncertain from moment to moment when or if the death sentence might be carried out. The abundance was very much in the forefront of people's attention, however, and the uncertainty very much in the background; and in the government as well as in the country at large the measureless questions posed by the new weapons were evaded. As far as any attempt to find a way out of the nuclear dilemma was concerned, the time was one of sleep. But in the late nineteen-fifties, as the reexamination of the American military position gathered momentum, a few men began to think through the whole subject of nuclear strategy anew. Among them were two men whose writings proved to be of special importance, not only because the ideas expressed were influential in themselves but because each man was to take a high post in government in the years ahead. One was Henry Kissinger, who was a professor at Harvard during the nineteen-fifties and nineteen-sixties, and whose book *Nuclear Weapons and Foreign Policy* appeared in 1957. The other was General Maxwell Taylor, who was the Army Chief of Staff under President Eisenhower, and whose book *The Uncertain Trumpet* appeared in 1960.

Both men were disturbed by a paradox that seemed to lie near the heart of the nuclear question. It was that nuclear weapons, the most powerful instruments of violence ever invented, tended to immobilize rather than strengthen their possessors. This paradox was rooted in the central fact of the weapons' unprecedented destructive force, which made mankind, for the first time in its history, capable of annihilating itself. Nuclear weapons, Kissinger and Taylor realized, were bound to have a chilling effect on any warlike plans that their possessors, including the United States, might entertain. Wars were supposedly fought for ends, but a war fought with nuclear arms might well obliterate any end for which a war could be fought. Not only that but it might obliterate all means as well, and, for that matter, obliterate the only earthly creature capable of thinking in terms of means and ends. As Kissinger put it in his book, "the destructiveness of modern weapons deprives victory in an all-out war of its historical meaning." He decided that "all-out war has therefore ceased to be a meaningful instrument of policy." Thenceforward, the United States would be in the position of having to fear its own power almost as much as it feared the power of its foes. Taylor, in his book, described his doubts about the usefulness of nuclear weapons in somewhat different language. The notion that "the use or the threatened use of atomic weapons of mass destruction would be sufficient to assure the security of the United States and its friends," he wrote, was "The Great Fallacy" in the prevailing strategic thinking of the day. The new strategists were saying that nuclear weapons, instead of making the nuclear powers more formidable, appeared to be casting a pall of doubt over their military policies. The doubt did not concern the amounts of military power at their disposal; it concerned their willingness, in the face of the dread of extinction, to unleash that power. Kissinger wrote, "Both the horror and the power of modern [nuclear] weapons tend to paralyze action: the former because it will make few issues seem worth contending for; the latter because it causes many disputes to seem irrelevant to the over-all strategic equation"—which had to do with the victory of one side or the other. In strength, it had turned out, lurked weakness; in omnipotence, impotence.

Kissinger and Taylor, working separately, set out to frame a foreign policy that would take into account the implications of nuclear weapons. Each of them began to think through a policy that would accommodate two broad aims. One aim was to prevent the extinction of the world in a nuclear war, and the other aim was to prevent the domination of the world—naturally, including the domination of the United States—by Communist totalitarian forces. It was clear to the two men that these aims conflicted at many points. The aim of preventing human extinction, which was peculiar to the nuclear age, seemed to call for unprecedented restraint in military matters, but the aim of preventing global Communist totalitarian rule seemed to call for unceasing military efforts on an unprecedented scale. On the one hand, nuclear dread inhibited the United States from using its military power aggressively; on the other hand, the ambitions, ideals, and fears that have traditionally impelled powerful nations onto the world stage impelled the United States to use its military power aggressively. Kissinger wrote, "The dilemma of the nuclear period can, therefore, be defined as follows: the enormity of modern weapons makes the thought of war repugnant, but the refusal to run any risks would amount to giving the Soviet rulers a blank check." The aim of standing firm in the face of Soviet power, which of course, corresponded to the broad aim of preventing world domination by Communist totalitarian forces, struck a responsive chord in the thinking of American politicians of the late nineteen-fifties. American political life had been dominated at least since the decade began by a conviction that the freedom and independence of nations all over the world was threatened by a unified, global Communist conspiracy that was under the control of the Soviet Union. Since then, "anti-Communism" not only had been the mainspring of American foreign policy but for a time—when Senator Joseph McCarthy hunted for Communists in the United States—had also been the central preoccupation of domestic politics. In this atmosphere, a reluctance to give Soviet leaders "a blank check" was quickly understood. However, the second aim recognized by Kissinger and Taylor—the avoidance of a nuclear catastrophe—was harder for the politicians of that time to grasp; and it was in championing this aim that the two men had to do the greater part of their explaining. (Something that helped them greatly in getting a hearing on the nuclear question was the fact that the anti-Communism of each of them was so strong as to be above suspicion.) The military, in particular, was difficult to persuade. The notion that an increase in military strength might, in effect, enfeeble the nation was a paradox not to the liking of the military mind. It was therefore difficult at first for the military to agree that, as Kissinger put it, in the nuclear age "the more powerful the weapons . . . the greater becomes the reluctance to use them"—in other words, the greater the power, the greater the paralysis.

Kissinger and Taylor, however, had an answer to those who were afraid that a recognition of the paralyzing influence of nuclear weapons might weaken the nation. While the two men were prepared to point out that reliance upon nuclear weapons might lead to a sort of impotence, they were far from willing to accept the condition. In fact, they were convinced that by failing to take cognizance of the danger the government was actually making the United States weaker in world affairs than it need be. In the late nineteen-fifties, the Eisenhower administration was relying almost exclusively on the threat of nuclear attack to cope with military challenges around the world. As Kissinger observed, American military policy was governed by the belief that "the chief deterrent to Soviet aggression resides in United States nuclear superiority." The policy was deliberate, and had been framed in response to the nation's experience in the early nineteen-fifties, during the Korean war. At that time, the public had shown that it reacted unenthusiastically to the sacrifice of American ground troops in inconclusive small wars fought far from the United States for goals that were difficult to grasp; and in 1954, after the war was brought to an end, Secretary of State John Foster Dulles had established a policy of using the threat of nuclear retaliation to achieve the sort of limited, local objective for which ground troops had been used in Korea. In a speech in January of that year, he said that in responding to a Communist challenge in any part of the world the United States would "depend primarily upon a great capacity to retaliate instantly by means and at places of our choosing," and he pointed out that a policy of reliance upon the nuclear threat not only would keep the troops at home but would be less expensive than ground operations. The Dulles policy became known as the policy of "massive retaliation," and also as "brinksmanship." It required the United States to rush toward the brink of nuclear war each time a crisis broke out somewhere in the world, and then to draw back at the last moment, having, it was hoped, frightened the foe into complying with American wishes. The strategy assumed, of course, that the Communist movement was a single force, controlled by the Soviet Union, and that a threat of nuclear retaliation against the Soviet Union would serve to stop Communist moves in, say, the Far East. Kissinger and Taylor were no less firm believers than Dulles in the unity of World Communism, and they did not oppose the Dulles policy on this point. Their charge was that his policy ignored the implications of the all-encompassing destructive force of nuclear weapons. Kissinger, employing a word that was just beginning to come into vogue, observed that a threat to use nuclear weapons in each minor crisis around the world would lack "credibility." What worried him was not only that the United States might make a misstep at the brink; it was also that the Communists might not be adequately deterred by a threat of massive nuclear retaliation. He was afraid that the Communists would find it implausible that the United States should be willing to risk nuclear annihilation merely to serve some minor purpose thousands of miles from home, and that they would therefore be unafraid to oppose the United States. For in the strategy of massive retaliation the government seemed to take the use of nuclear force almost lightly, as though nuclear weapons were ordinary, readily usable instruments of policy rather than engines of doom. The danger was, as Kissinger saw it, that "every move on [the Soviet bloc's] part will...pose the appalling dilemma of whether we are willing to commit suicide to prevent encroachments, which do not, each in itself, seem to threaten our existence directly but which may be steps on the road to our ultimate destruction." Kissinger was attempting to work out the implications of the distressing fact that once both adversaries were armed with nuclear weapons, a decision to use nuclear weapons was as dangerous to oneself as it was to the foe, for the result might be "suicide." And a threat to commit suicide was not a very convincing way of deterring a foe. Kissinger was suggesting that the policy of brinksmanship menaced the world with both great dangers of the period: global totalitarianism *and* human extinction. On the one hand, that policy threatened to transform every small crisis into a major nuclear crisis, and, on the other hand, it left the United States without "credible" instruments of force in situations where the stakes were too small to justify any risk of "suicide." The need was for a policy that would steer a middle course between the two dangers—for a policy that would, in Kissinger's words, "provide a means to escape from the sterility of the quest for absolute peace, which paralyzes by the vagueness of its hopes, and of the search for absolute victory, which paralyzes by the vastness of its consequences."

A middle course was available, both Kissinger and Taylor believed, in a strategy of limited war. "A strategy of limited war," Kissinger wrote, "would seek to escape the inconsistency of relying on a policy of deterrence [that is, massive retaliation], whose major sanction involves national catastrophe." And Taylor wrote, "The new strategy would recognize that it is just as necessary to deter or win quickly a limited war as to deter general war." Kissinger, for his part, believed that even in the nuclear age the freedom actually to use force rather than merely to threaten the use of force was indispensable to the maintenance of international order. He derided "the national psychology which considers peace as the 'normal' pattern of relations among states," and, while granting that "the contemporary revolution cannot be managed by force alone," he maintained that "when there is no penalty for irresponsibility, the pent-up frustrations of centuries may seek an outlet in the international field." Therefore, "to the extent that recourse to force has become impossible the restraints of the international order may disappear as well." In his view, dangerous as the use of force was in the nuclear age, the United States would have to overcome its uneasiness and thus "face up to the risks of Armageddon." And limited war, he believed, was both a more acceptable and a more effective way of facing up to these risks than was massive retaliation. For a strategy of limited war would rescue the use of force from nuclear paralysis. It would provide "credible" means of threatening the foe. It would make the world safe again for war.

More specifically, there were, in Kissinger's view, "three reasons...for developing a strategy of limited war." He listed them as follows: "First, limited war represents the only means for preventing the Soviet bloc, at an acceptable cost, from overrunning the peripheral areas of Eurasia. Second, a wide range of military capabilities may spell the difference between defeat and victory even in an all-out war. Finally, intermediate applications of our power offer the best chance to bring about strategic changes favorable to our side." (By "victory even in an all-out war" Kissinger meant the survival after nuclear war of enough conventional forces in the United States to impose America's will on the surviving remnant of the Soviet population.) His reference to "the best chance to bring about strategic changes favorable to our side" had to do with what he saw as the possibility that on occasion limited war might be used offensively as well as defensively, and would place the United States in a position to reduce "the Soviet sphere." These aims—the defense of a perimeter, the attainment of "victory" in all-out hostilities, and the attainment of improved strategic positions that would reduce "the Soviet sphere"—were straightforward military aims of a traditional kind. They can be called the tangible objectives of limited war.

One aim of the strategy of limited war, then, was to free the use of military force from nuclear paralysis, so that the United States might still avail itself of its arms to stop Communism from spreading around the globe. But there was also a second aim. It was to help in preventing a nuclear war. It was Kissinger's hope that the new policy could "rescue mankind from the horrors of a thermonuclear holocaust by devising a framework of war limitation." Or, in Taylor's words, the new policy "is not blind to the awful dangers of general atomic war; indeed, it takes as its primary purpose the avoidance of that catastrophe." By assigning largely to limited war the achievement of the tangible objectives in the fight against Communist enemies, the policy opened the way to a crucial shift in the mission of the American nuclear force. Secretary of State Dulles had sought to use the threat of nuclear war to work America's will in small crises around the world, but if limited-war forces could take over this job, the nuclear force, relieved of its provocative, belligerent role, could be retired into the purely passive one of deterring nuclear attack. Thereafter, the role of the nuclear force would simply be that of threatening retaliation in order to dissuade the Soviet Union from using its nuclear force in a first strike. Neither Taylor nor Kissinger spelled out the possibility of this shift, but it was implicit in their writings, and was later adopted as policy, under the name of deterrence. The strategy of limited war was thus a necessary companion to the policy of deterrence. In fact, it had been designed, in part, to wean the United States from its perilous sole reliance on the threat of massive nuclear retaliation. The policies of nuclear deterrence and limited war represented a division of labor, in which nuclear weapons would take on the defensive role in military policy and the limited-war forces would take on the offensive role. Taylor, describing a proposal along these lines he had made to the National Security Council in 1958, wrote, "Our atomic deterrent forces would be the shield under which we must live from day to day with the Soviet threat. This shield would provide us protection, but not a means of maneuver. It was rather to the so-called limited-war forces that we henceforth must look for the active elements of our military strategy."

The limited-war strategy would dovetail with nuclear strategy in another way, too. It would give the United States a new opportunity to make demonstrations of its "will" or "resolve" to use force in the world. It would, that is, give the nation a chance to demonstrate its credibility. This objective of limited war can be called the psychological objective. In a passage setting forth some of the fundamental reasoning behind the policy of limited war, Kissinger described the importance of the psychological objective to the whole of American strategic policy:

> Deterrence is brought about not only by a physical but also by a psychological relationship: deterrence is greatest when military strength is coupled with the willingness to employ it. It is achieved when one side's readiness to run risks in relation to the other is high; it is least effective when the willingness to run risks is low, however powerful the military capability. It is, therefore, no longer possible to speak of military superiority in the abstract. What does "being ahead" in the nuclear race mean if each side can already destroy the other's national substance?...It is the task of strategic doctrine to strike a balance between the physical and the psychological aspects of deterrence, between the desire to pose a maximum threat and the reality that no threat is stronger than the belief of the opponent that it will in fact be used....The reliance on all-out war as the chief deterrent inhibits the establishment of this balance. By identifying deterrence with maximum power it tends to paralyze the will. Its concern with the physical basis of deterrence neglects the psychological aspect. Given the power of modern weapons, a nation that relies on all-out war as its chief deterrent imposes a fearful psychological handicap on itself. The most agonizing decision a statesman can face is whether or not to unleash all-out war; all pressures will make for hesitation, short of a direct attack threatening the national existence. In any other situation he will be inhibited by the incommensurability between the cost of the war and the objective in dispute. And he will be confirmed in his hesitations by the conviction that, so long as his retaliatory force remains intact, no shift in the territorial balance is of decisive significance....The psychological equation, therefore, will almost inevitably operate against the side which can extricate itself from a situation *only* by the threat of all-out war. Who can be certain that, faced with the catastrophe of all-out war, even Europe, long the keystone of our security, will seem worth the price? As the power of modern weapons grows, the threat of all-out war loses its credibility.

A strategy of limited war would help overcome the deficiency in the psychological equation and restore credibility. By advertising America's strength to the world at levels below the brink, it would hold the world a few steps back from nuclear extinction and at the same time would deter the Communists from aggressive moves. New room for military maneuvering would open up. Whereas under the strategy of massive retaliation there was only one step on the ladder between peace and the holocaust, under the strategy of limited war there would be many steps, and at each step the superpowers would have the opportunity to take stock of each other's intentions, to send each other clear signals of their "resolve," and, perhaps, to draw back before things got out of hand. In a passage that compared the opportunities for demonstrating credibility which were offered by the strategy of massive retaliation (in which only threats were possible) with the opportunities offered by a strategy of limited war (in which actual military efforts were possible), Kissinger wrote, "It is a strange doctrine which asserts that we can convey our determination to our opponent by reducing our overseas commitments, that, in effect, our words will be a more effective deterrent than our deeds." Under the policy he was proposing, America's deeds—its actions in limited wars—would "convey our determination." Taylor similarly underscored the psychological importance of limited war, writing, "There is also an important psychological factor which must be present to make this retaliatory weapon [the nuclear deterrent force] effective. It must be clear to the aggressor that we have the will and determination to use our retaliatory power without compunction if we are attacked. Any suggestion of weakness or indecision may encourage the enemy to gamble on surprise." And the best way to prevent "any suggestion of weakness or indecision" from appearing, he thought, was to prepare for limited war. The strategy would, in his words, guard against the danger that "repeated [Communist] success in creeping aggression may encourage a Communist miscalculation that could lead to general war."

The psychological objective was to be sharply distinguished from the tangible objectives. The tangible objectives grew out of an effort to escape the paralyzing influence of nuclear strategy, but the psychological objective was part and parcel of the nuclear strategy. In the new scheme, the attainment of the tangible objectives would belong wholly to the limited-war forces, but the attainment of the psychological objective of maintaining credibility, though it was also an important aim of limited war, would still belong primarily to the nuclear retaliatory force. For it was the inherent futility of ever using the nuclear retaliatory force—a futility that threatened military paralysis—that had driven the policymakers to rely so heavily on credibility in the first place. It was dread of extinction in a nuclear war that had placed in doubt the "will" of the United States to use its undeniably tremendous nuclear arsenal. Of course, there were additional factors that might paralyze America's will to use its military forces. One was the element of isolationism that had long existed in American political life, and another was the natural revulsion of any peaceful people against warfare. Yet these obstacles had been overcome in times of danger in the past. The dread of nuclear war was a paralyzing influence of new dimensions. Now, even if the public should develop a will to victory, a clear upper limit had been placed on the usefulness of violence as an instrument in foreign affairs. The strategists were preoccupied with the question of how to demonstrate America's will—or "resolve," or "determination," or "toughness," as it was variously put. How to make demonstrations of credibility was, above all, a problem of public relations, since what counted was not the substance of America's strength or the actual state of its willingness but the image of strength and willingness. To put it more precisely, the substance of the nation's strength was useful only insofar as it enhanced the image of strength. In Kissinger's words, "Soviet reactions to what we do will depend not on what we intend but on what the Soviet leaders think we intend." Or, as he also wrote, "until power is used, it is...what people think it is." The strategy of massive retaliation had been one way of maintaining credibility—the technique in that case being to attest to America's will to go to war by *almost* going to war—but it was in the doctrine of nuclear deterrence that the doctrine of credibility found its purest expression. The deterrent force was real, but its entire purpose was to *appear* so formidable that the Soviet Union would hesitate to take aggressive actions that might provoke the United States into retaliating. The deterrent was not meant for use, because its use would lead to the utter futility of mutual extinction. Appearances, therefore, were not merely important to deterrence—they were everything. If the deterrent was used, deterrence would have failed. If the image did not do its preventive work and there was a resort to action, the whole purpose of the policy would have been defeated, and the human race, with all its policies and purposes, might be lost. In the strategy of nuclear deterrence, the "psychological relationship" was the whole relationship. If power, until it was used, was what people thought it was, then nuclear power could never be anything more than what people thought it was, for its use was forever ruled out, except in retaliation. The strategy of nuclear deterrence presented the nuclear dilemma in the form of pure paradox. It provided for weapons of limitless power whose whole purpose was to prevent their ever having to be used. It called for ceaseless preparations for a war whose prevention was the preparations' whole aim.

    This arrangement was what opened up the fissure dividing image and substance which characterized American policy in the Vietnam years. The United States, blocked by nuclear dread from using its military forces on a scale commensurate with its global aims, began to use its power to strike poses and manufacture images. In the strategy of deterrence, the very survival of mankind was made to depend upon an image. An image, however, was a distressingly undependable thing on which to rest the species' hope of escaping extinction. And the image that was required in this case was even more undependable than most. In the first place, the system of deterrence was aimed at producing an impression of certainty in the minds of America's foes about the mental state of the American people; and mental states are inherently obscure. In the second place, the mental state involved was a future one, concerning what the United States *would* do *if* such-and-such a train of events chanced to occur; and therefore it was highly changeable. And, in the third place, the future mental state to be depicted in the image was a willingness to risk destroying the human race, and this willingness was in its very nature open to question. The policymakers might declare their willingness to "face up to the risks of Armageddon," but the meaning of such a declaration was far from transparent. After all, what *did* it mean to "face up" to the extinction of the race? And what did their willingness say about the men who declared it? Clearly, this intention was one of the least "credible" ones imaginable. The doubts became especially keen as soon as one tried to imagine what a President really would do once the Soviet Union had launched a first strike—once deterrence had failed. Would he retaliate, out of pure revenge, and risk completing the annihilation of the human race for no reason? And if he would not, then what became of the doctrine of credibility, which rested on the assumption that the President would do just that? Since the whole system was so shaky, with its cross-currents of belligerence and dread of annihilation, it was perhaps not surprising that the strategists turned in any direction they could, including the direction of limited war, to find theatres where the crucial but elusive quantity of "credibility" might be demonstrated. Certainly limited wars were among the last places where the appearance of "weakness or indecision" which Taylor feared so much could be tolerated. For, in this system, if the credibility of American power should be destroyed in a limited war, then the middle ground between global extinction and global totalitarianism would be lost, and the government would be forced once again to choose between the risk of giving the Soviet leaders "a blank check" and the risk of committing suicide.

In considering the origins and the character of the war in Vietnam, the extent of the theoretical preparations for limited war in general must be kept in mind. Today, the notion that the war was a "quagmire" into which successive Administrations were sucked, against their will, has won wide acceptance. The metaphor is apt insofar as it refers to the policymakers' undoubted surprise, year after year, at the way their policies were turning out in Vietnam, and to the evident reluctance of both President Kennedy and President Johnson to get involved there; but it is misleading insofar as it suggests that the United States merely stumbled into the war, without forethought or planning. In 1960, Taylor recommended the establishment of a "Limited War Headquarters"—and this was before the nation began fighting in Vietnam. Rarely has such a large body of military theory been developed in advance of an outbreak of hostilities. The war in Vietnam was, in a sense, a theorists' war *par excellence*. The strategists of the late nineteen-fifties were only slightly interested in the question of which country or countries might be the scene of a limited war. When they turned their attention to questions of geography— which they did only rarely—they tended to speak blurrily of "peripheral areas" around the Soviet Union and China which stretched from Japan, in the east, through India and the Middle East, in the south, to Europe, in the west. A reader in the nineteen-seventies of Kissinger's and Taylor's books is struck by how seldom Vietnam is mentioned. Today, the very word "Vietnam" is so rich in association and so heavily laden with historical significance that an atmosphere of inevitability—almost of fate—hangs over it, and it is difficult to imagine oneself back in a time when few Americans even knew of that nation's existence. Instead of speaking in terms of particular wars, whether in Vietnam or elsewhere, the theorists tended to speak in terms of types of wars. One type that came under discussion was limited nuclear war. The strategists drew a sharp distinction between limited nuclear war and all-out nuclear war. Kissinger devoted a chapter of *Nuclear Weapons and Foreign Policy* to limited nuclear war. What might be called the fear of the fear of nuclear weapons was one of the keystones of the policy he was proposing, and he wrote, "The greater the horror of our destructive capabilities, the less certain has it become that they will in fact be used"—a situation that he evidently contemplated with alarm, for he saw it as undermining American credibility. The use of nuclear weapons in limited war, he thought, would help to overcome this dangerous uncertainty. As he put it, "in this task of posing the maximum *credible* threat, limited nuclear war seems a more suitable deterrent than conventional war." Another way he suggested of combatting the paralyzing effect of the fear of nuclear arms was to fashion "a diplomacy which seeks to break down the atmosphere of special horror which now surrounds the use of nuclear weapons, an atmosphere which has been created in part by skillful Soviet 'ban-the-bomb' propaganda." Kissinger, however, was not strictly consistent on this point, for it had been precisely the "special horror" of nuclear weapons which had inspired him in the first place to recommend the shift from the policy of massive retaliation to the policy of limited war, and in another passage in *Nuclear Weapons and Foreign Policy* he wrote that "a thermonuclear attack may...become the symbol of the vanity of all human strivings"—a statement that might be thought to add to the atmosphere of "special horror" surrounding nuclear weapons. Another type of limited war that the new strategists recommended would rely on conventional forces that could be flown to troubled areas around the globe at a moment's notice in a fleet of special transport planes, whose construction the strategists counselled. In virtually all the planning for limited war, the speed of the American reaction was seen as crucial. The strategists of the time apparently believed that limited war would be not only limited but short.

Once one has worked out the strategy and the goals of a war, and has gone as far as to contemplate setting up a "headquarters" from which to fight it, the step to actual hostilities is not necessarily a very large one; in the early nineteen-sixties the abstractions in Kissinger's and Taylor's books came to life in the hostilities in Vietnam. John Kennedy found the arguments of the limited-war strategists persuasive, and in February of 1960, while he was still a senator, he stated, "Both before and after 1953 events have demonstrated that our nuclear retaliatory power is not enough. It cannot deter Communist aggression which is too limited to justify atomic war. It cannot protect uncommitted nations against a Communist takeover using local or guerrilla forces. It cannot be used in so-called brushfire peripheral wars. In short, it cannot prevent the Communists from gradually nibbling at the fringe of the free world's territory and strength, until our security has been steadily eroded in piecemeal fashion—each Red advance being too small to justify massive retaliation, with all its risks.... In short, we need forces of an entirely different kind to keep the peace against limited aggression, and to fight it, if deterrence fails, without raising the conflict to a disastrous pitch." Kennedy was saying that the limited-war forces would accomplish the two great objectives of policy that Kissinger and Taylor had set forth in their books: the prevention of global totalitarianism and the prevention of human extinction. By using limited forces to push back "limited aggression," the United States would be able to oppose the spread of Communism, and at the same time avoid confrontation at the brink. Kennedy, moreover, had become persuaded that the outcome of a limited war would be important not only for tangible objectives that might be attained but for the psychological objective of demonstrating America's "will" to oppose Communism, and after he became President he often referred to the hostilities in Vietnam as a "test case" of America's determination to protect its allies.

The spirit of the Kennedy Administration was activist, and the policymakers set about their tasks in a mood of high excitement. In April of 1961, three months after his inauguration, Kennedy made a speech to the American Society of Newspaper Editors in which he defined the nature of the challenge that lay ahead:

> We face a relentless struggle in every corner of the globe that goes far beyond the clash of armies or even nuclear armaments. The armies are there, and in large number. The nuclear armaments are there. But they serve primarily as the shield behind which subversion, infiltration, and a host of other tactics steadily advance, picking off vulnerable areas one by one. . . . We dare not fail to see the insidious nature of this new and deeper struggle. We dare not fail to grasp the new concepts, the new tools, the new sense of urgency we will need to combat it—whether in Cuba or South Vietnam. . . . The message of Cuba, of Laos, of the rising din of Communist voices in Asia and Latin America—these messages are all the same. The complacent, the self-indulgent, the soft societies are about to be swept away with the debris of history. Only the strong, only the industrious, only the determined, only the courageous, only the visionary who determine the real nature of our struggle can possibly survive. No greater task faces this country or this Administration. No other challenge is more deserving of our every effort and energy. . . . We intend to reexamine and reorient our forces of all kinds—our tactics and our institutions here in this community. . . . For I am convinced that we in this country and in the free world possess the necessary resources, and the skill, and the added strength that comes from a belief in the freedom of man. And I am equally convinced that history will record the fact that this bitter struggle reached its climax in the late nineteen-fifties and the early nineteen-sixties. Let me then make clear as the President of the United States that I am determined upon our system's survival and success, regardless of the cost and regardless of the peril.

One of the members of President Kennedy's staff was Maxwell Taylor, who had been appointed Military Representative of the President, and in the fall of 1961 he was sent to Vietnam to take stock of the situation there. In Vietnam, the strategists of limited war, who had been thinking mainly in global terms, found themselves face to face with the challenge of guerrilla warfare. They quickly set about devising techniques to meet the challenge. Turning to the manuals of the Communist foe for guidance, they came up with the concept of "counterinsurgency" war. Men in the Pentagon began to regard themselves as potential guerrilla soldiers, and soon they were repeating such Maoist phrases as "The soldiers are the fish and the people are the sea." And in the early nineteen-sixties it was not only in the military area that the theories of professors were being translated into governmental policy in the struggle against Communism. During that period, a new breed of professor, trained in the social sciences and eager to test theories in the laboratory

of real societies, came forward to offer "models" of economic and social development with which the government could rival the Communist "model."

In spite of all the expertise that was being brought to bear on the war, however, the reports from the field in Vietnam, when they began to come in, were
discouraging. The long, sad tale of optimistic predictions followed by military reverses, to be followed, in turn, by increasingly drastic military measures, began to
unfold, and by the mid-nineteen-sixties it was plain that the war would be far longer
and far more difficult to end than any of the professors or policymakers had foreseen. The theory of limited war had been abstract and general, but Vietnam was a
particular country, with a particular history and a particular society, and these particularities turned out to be more important than the strategists had ever dreamed
they could be. Awed, perhaps, by the magnitude of America's global power and
global responsibilities, the strategists had overlooked the possibility that purely local events, not controlled by a centralized, global conspiracy, might pose serious
obstacles to their plans. Yet it was on the local events, and not on the balance of
nuclear forces, that the outcome in Vietnam was proving to depend. For Vietnamese
life had its own tendencies, which not even the power of the United States could
alter. Moreover, the strategic theory had it that human beings behaved according
to certain laws—that if people were punished sufficiently, they could be deflected
from their goals, even if they had not been defeated outright. Accordingly, the
strategists had fashioned a policy known as escalation, in which the level of violence
would be raised, notch by notch, until the foe, realizing that America's instruments
of pain were limitless and its will to inflict pain unshakable, would reach the breaking point and desist. The Vietnamese revolutionaries, however, did not behave in
this way at all. Their will stiffened under punishment. And many Americans at
home, too, behaved in an unexpected way. Their will to inflict the punishment
began to falter. The material resources for inflicting punishment were indeed nearly
limitless, but the capacity of the American spirit for inflicting punishment, although
great, did have limits. The stubborn uniqueness of the situation in Vietnam was
perhaps even more devastating to the plans of the theorists than the unexpected
stiffness of the opposition. It meant not only that the war was going to be difficult
to win but that it was not the war they had thought it was—that the United States
might have sent its troops into the wrong country altogether. For if the Vietnam war
was primarily a local affair, rather than a rebellion under the control of World
Communism, then it was not a test case of anything. Then, instead of being one of
those limited wars between global forces of freedom and global forces of totalitarianism which the theorists had foreseen in their books, it was just a civil war in a
small country.

If the war had been planned only to achieve the tangible objectives that
Kissinger assigned to limited war in 1957, the unexpected intractability of Vietnamese
affairs and the revelation that the Vietnamese forces were not under the control of
World Communism might well have inspired a reappraisal of the American effort,
and perhaps a withdrawal. After all, even if Vietnam *had* been the right place to
oppose World Communism, only a limited tangible advantage could have been gained
there: at best, the freedom of one-half of one small country could be protected. And

when the situation had deteriorated to the point where the possible strategic gains were outweighed by the manifold costs of the war effort, a strict accounting logic would have dictated that the United States should cut its losses and leave. In the mid-nineteen-sixties, that point was apparently reached. However, the war was not being fought only for the tangible objectives. It was being fought also for the psychological objective of maintaining American credibility—an aim that was bound up in the strategists' thinking with the prevention of nuclear war and the prevention of global totalitarianism. The war had a symbolic importance that was entirely separate from any tangible objective that might or might not be achieved. The policymakers were divided on many points, but they were united on this one. In both their private and their public statements, they unwaveringly affirmed the absolute necessity of preserving the integrity of America's image in the fighting in Vietnam. For the Joint Chiefs of Staff, the importance of the war lay in "the psychological impact that a firm position by the United States will have on the countries of the world—both free and Communist," according to the memo they sent Secretary of Defense McNamara in 1962. For Assistant Secretary of Defense John McNaughton, writing a memo in 1965, the aim of the war was to "avoid harmful appearances which will affect judgments by, and provide pretexts to, other nations regarding how the US will behave in future cases of particular interest to those nations—regarding US policy, power, resolve, and competence." For President Johnson, in a speech in April of 1965, the United States was in Vietnam because it had "a promise to keep." He went on, "We are also there to strengthen world order. Around the globe, from Berlin to Thailand, are people whose well-being rests in part on the belief that they can count on us if they are attacked. To leave Vietnam to its fate would shake the confidence of all these people in the value of an American commitment and in the value of America's word. The result would be increased unrest and instability, and even wider war." By 1966, the aim of upholding credibility had become virtually the sole aim of the war. In January of that year, McNaughton wrote the memo in which he said, *"The present U.S. objective in Vietnam is to avoid humiliation*. The reasons why we *went into* Vietnam to the present depth are varied; but they are now largely academic. Why we have *not withdrawn* is, by all odds, *one* reason. (1) To preserve our reputation as a guarantor, and thus to preserve our effectiveness in the rest of the world. We have not hung on (2) to save a friend, or (3) to deny the Communists the added acres and heads (because the dominoes don't fall for that reason in this case), or even (4) to prove that 'wars of national liberation' won't work (except as our reputation is involved)." In this memo, McNaughton affirmed the aim of upholding credibility ("to preserve our reputation as guarantor") and specifically dismissed the tangible aims ("to deny the Communists the added acres and heads"). The aim of upholding American credibility superseded any conclusions drawn from a simple accounting of tangible gains and tangible losses, and it dictated that the war must go on, for it was on American credibility, the strategists thought, that the safety of the whole world depended. Secretary of State Dean Rusk wrote in a letter to a hundred student leaders in January of 1967, "We are involved in Vietnam because we know from painful experience that the minimum condition for order on our planet is that aggression must not be permitted to succeed. For when it does succeed, the consequence is not peace, it is the further expansion of aggression. And those who have borne responsibility in our country since 1945 have not for one moment forgotten that a third world war would be a nuclear war." Nor did the question of whether or not Vietnam was the wrong country to be fighting in matter much in this thinking. The fact that the United States was fighting there made it the right country; America's presence in Vietnam invested the war with the global significance that it lacked intrinsically, for if the United States involved itself in a war, its credibility was by that very action placed at stake. An analyst representing the Joint Chiefs of Staff wrote in commenting upon a draft paper of a Project Outline on Courses of Action in Southeast Asia, which had been prepared by a National Security Council "working group," "It is *our* judgment, skill, capability, prestige, and national honor which are at stake, and we put them there." And Secretary Rusk wrote in his letter to the student leaders, "We are involved because the nation's word has been given that we would be involved."

Limited war had been conceived in part as a way for the United States to do bold things in an age when nuclear dread made the doing of bold things—particularly if they were violent things—especially dangerous. But now all hope of *doing* anything was abandoned. That aim was now considered to be, in McNaughton's phrase, "largely academic." What remained was proving something, to friends and foes alike: America's will and determination. The tangible objectives of limited war had been completely eclipsed by the psychological objective. The war had become an effort directed entirely toward building up a certain image by force of arms. It had become a piece of pure theatre. The purpose of the enterprise now was to put on a performance for what John McNaughton called "audiences." In the memo in which he mentioned the need to avoid harmful appearances, he went on to say, "In this connection, the relevant audiences are the Communists (who must feel strong pressures), the South Vietnamese (whose morale must be buoyed), our allies (who must trust us as 'underwriters'), and the US public (which must support our risk-taking with US lives and prestige)." The triumph of the doctrine of credibility had introduced into the actual conduct of the war the gap between image and substance which characterized the doctrine of nuclear deterrence. The whole aim of having a nuclear retaliatory force for deterrence was to create an image of the United States as a nation not to be trifled with, and so to forestall challenges that could lead to a nuclear holocaust. Now a real and bloody war was being fought for precisely the same end. As the paper of the National Security Council "working group" put it, the loss of South Vietnam could lead to "the progressive loss of other areas or to taking a stand at some point where there would almost certainly be major conflict and perhaps the great risk of nuclear war." Those who were opposed to the war tirelessly pointed out the disparity between the Johnson Administration's depiction of South Vietnam as a free country battling international Communist aggression and their own impression that the South Vietnamese government was a corrupt dictatorship that, supported by foreign arms and foreign money, was fighting a civil war against indigenous Communist forces. What those opposed to the war did not know was that the Johnson Administration had largely lost interest in Vietnam *per se.* What primarily interested the Johnson Administration from the mid-sixties on was not what was going on in Vietnam but how what was going on in Vietnam was perceived by what the Joint Chiefs referred to as the "countries of the world." In fact, so important were appearances in the official thinking that as things went from bad to worse on the battlefield the policymakers began to dream of completely separating the nation's image from what happened in the war, in order that even in the face of failure the desired image of American "will" might be preserved. The effort to rescue the national image from the debacle conditioned the tactics of the war from the mid-nineteen-sixties on. On one occasion in 1965, McGeorge Bundy, a special assistant to the President for national-security affairs, discussing a plan for *"sustained reprisal* against North Vietnam," wrote, "It may fail....What we can say is that even if it fails, the policy will be worth it. At a minimum, it will damp down the charge that we did not do all that we could have done, and this charge will be important in many countries, including our own. Beyond that, a reprisal policy—to the extent that it demonstrates U.S. willingness to employ this new norm in counterinsurgency—will set a higher price for the future upon all adventures of guerrilla warfare." To Bundy, a disastrous war effort was better than no war effort, because even a disastrous war effort would "demonstrate" the crucial "willingness" to use force in the nuclear age, and so would enhance American credibility. John McNaughton, writing in the same vein in a draft of a memo to Secretary of Defense McNamara in March of 1965, advised, "It is essential—however badly SEA [Southeast Asia] may go over the next 1–3 years—that US emerge as a 'good doctor.' We must have kept promises, been tough, taken risks, gotten bloodied, and hurt the enemy very badly." McNaughton may have been one of the first military advisers ever to suggest that getting bloodied should in itself be an objective of an army in the field. (He was telling men that they must get wounded or killed even though they knew they could not win.) Only in a war fought for credibility could the question of victory or defeat ever seem so immaterial.

The men in charge of the government were struggling to work out what the uses of military force might be in the age of nuclear weapons. The dilemma in which they found themselves was expressed in a memo that Walt Rostow, chairman of the State Department Policy Planning Council, wrote to Secretary of State Rusk in November of 1964, in which he mentioned "the real margin of influence...which flows from the simple fact that at this stage of history, we are the greatest power in the world—if we behave like it." Rostow's qualifying phrase "if we behave like it" summed up the maddening predicament of the great power in the nuclear age. For in reality "the fact" that the United States was "the greatest power in the world" was not "simple" at all. It was endlessly complicated, and contained deep, and perhaps irreconcilable, ambiguities. The reality was that the United States could by no means "behave like" the greatest power in the world if that meant acting the way great powers had acted on the world stage in the past. And it was not only idealism or moral scruple that stood in the way (although one can hope that these factors, too, did have a restraining influence) but also the unprecedented destructiveness, and self-destructiveness, of nuclear war. In October of 1964, in a paper titled "Aims and Options in Southeast Asia," McNaughton wrote that the United

States must create an appearance of success in its operations in Vietnam in order
to show that the nation was not "hobbled by restraints." But, whatever appearance
the United States might create in Vietnam, or anywhere else, the fact was that the
United States *was* hobbled by restraints—the very restraints inherent in the possession of nuclear weapons which Kissinger and Taylor had tried to come to grips
with in their books in the late nineteen-fifties. Indeed, it was these restraints that
had given rise to the doctrine of credibility, which now dominated government
policy. It is true that before the development of nuclear weapons powerful nations
had sought to cultivate aspects of their power which were similar to what the American
policymakers meant when they spoke of credibility. In military affairs, a nation
would often make a show of force in the hope of having its way without resorting
to arms. The appearance of a gunboat in a harbor might be used to bring a rebellious
colony back in line, or a troop movement on a border might be used to deter an
attack. But in any matter of the first importance the show of force would give way
to the use of force. The situation of a great power in the nuclear age was altogether
different. A nuclear power was stuck on the level of show. When nuclear powers
confronted one another over an important issue, major use of force was ruled out,
since the unrestrained use of force could lead to national "suicide," and even to
human extinction. Nuclear powers were in the situation—unprecedented in military history—of always having more power in their possession than they were free
to use. The question of "will," which in former times was a question of a nation's
capacity for making great sacrifices in order to protect itself, now became a question
of a nation's willingness to approach the point of suicide. For the closer a nation was
willing to come to that point, the more force it could permit itself to unleash. According to the doctrine of credibility, a nation that wished to have its way in international affairs was obliged, in a sense, to make demonstrations of indifference
to its own survival, for it was obliged constantly to show its willingness not just to
unleash force on others but to put the gun to its own head and pull the trigger—its
willingness, that is, to "face up to the risks of Armageddon." Perhaps for this reason, policymakers of the time often announced that it was an aim of American
policy to cultivate a reputation for "unpredictability." The ultimate in unpredictability, of course, would be to blow up the world, oneself included. Leaving the
question of unpredictability aside, the will to victory in the nuclear age was tempered by the realization that victory could be a worse disaster than defeat. This new
circumstance had a shaping influence on every phase of the warfare in Vietnam—on
the limits of the war effort, on the justifications for the war, and on the atmosphere
engendered in the home country by the war. The nuclear predicament forced the
great powers to take military action only within a narrowed sphere, and always to
behave with extreme caution and trepidation, not because they were weak but because they were too strong, and it taught them to rely more on the reputation of
power—on show—than on the use of power. Still, the level of show was not without
its possibilities. It provided the military strategists with what they regarded as an
entire new sphere of action—the image world, in which battles were fought not to
achieve concrete ends but to create appearances. Through actions taken to buttress
the image of the United States, the strategists believed, the nation might still lay

claim to the "margin of influence" that flowed from being the greatest power in the world. The United States might still have its way in international affairs, they thought, by fighting the admittedly militarily useless but presumably psychologically effective war in Vietnam. The image world was not the world of borders defended, of strategic positions won or lost, of foes defeated in great and bloody battles; it was the world of "reputations," of "psychological impact," of "audiences." It was, in a word, the world of credibility. . . .

It has not been the purpose of these remarks to blame theorists of the nineteen-fifties for the calamities of the nineteen-sixties and the nineteen-seventies, or to suggest that when they devised the strategies that would rule American politics in the years ahead they should have foreseen the bizarre events that unfolded. Many Americans found these events all but unbelievable even as they occurred. Moreover, the strategists' attention was concentrated on a dilemma that overarched all particular events. This dilemma—the dilemma of nuclear warfare—remains entirely unresolved to this day. And it can also be said that the combined strategies of limited war and nuclear deterrence still seem an improvement over the strategy of massive retaliation, which to the contemporary eye seems to have been an exceptionally reckless and shortsighted way of handling the question of human survival. On the other hand, it is not the purpose of these remarks to in any way excuse the political actors of the period—some of whom were also key strategists—from responsibility on the ground that they did what they did in the cause of human survival. All governments have their burdens to bear and their decisions to make, and if the heaviness of the responsibilities were to be considered justification for repressive action, no country would remain free. A free country does not place responsibilities in one of the scales and the liberties of the people in the other. It holds to the faith that only in an atmosphere of freedom can the responsibilities be squarely met. Moreover, precisely because the United States is a free country, choices were at all times open to the government in the Vietnam years. At each stage, alternative policies were offered—sometimes by men in high positions in the government. In the Kennedy and Johnson years, the names of George Kennan, William Fulbright, George Ball, John Kenneth Galbraith, and Clark Clifford are among those that come to mind. In the Nixon years, the name of Walter Hickel comes to mind. And, what was of greater importance, millions of ordinary citizens, making use of their freedom, raised their voices to insist that the war be brought to an end. In fact, their voices finally prevailed. And of still greater importance was the broad political coalition that forced President Nixon from office. There is every reason to believe that if this coalition had not been successful, the United States, by then a Presidential dictatorship, would still be pursuing credibility in Vietnam. For nothing in the record suggests that President Nixon was anything but dead serious both when he promised President Thieu that the United States would "respond with full force" if the North Vietnamese attempted to take over the South and when he told John Dean, speaking of his struggle with his domestic "enemies," "This is war."

However, if the record of American statesmanship in the Vietnam years, with its sheer mendacity, fumbling, and brutality—not to mention the apparent dementia in the White House which first made its appearance in the Johnson years and emerged fully into public view in President Nixon's last days in office—has a tragic aspect as well, it lies in the fact that in those years the nation experienced the defeat of its first sustained, intellectually coherent attempt to incorporate the implications of nuclear weaponry into national policy. For today it is clear that the doctrine of credibility has failed. It has failed not only in the terms of those who opposed it but also in its own terms. The doctrine of credibility did not provide the United States with an effective means of promoting its interests and ideals at levels of violence below the brink of nuclear war; instead, it provided the notorious quagmire in Vietnam into which the United States poured its energy and power uselessly for more than a decade. The doctrine of credibility, though different from the doctrine of massive retaliation, did not spare mankind from confrontations at the brink between the nuclear powers; far from freezing hostilities at a low level of the escalatory ladder, it led the United States up the ladder, step by step, until, in May of 1972, President Nixon felt obliged to lay down a frontal challenge to the Soviet Union and China by mining North Vietnamese ports against their ships. Finally, the doctrine of credibility failed to enhance American credibility; instead of enabling the United States to "avoid harmful appearances" and to create "respect for the office of President of the United States," it engendered appearances not only of helplessness, irresolution, and incompetence but of duplicity and ruthlessness—and precipitated a wave of disrespect for a particular President which culminated in his forced resignation from office. Nor did the doctrine of credibility merely fail; it was a catastrophe in its own right, which led to the needless devastation of the Indo-Chinese peninsula and the assault on Constitutional government in the United States....

PART THREE

The Process of Involvement

Stumbling into the Quagmire or Knowingly Accepting Stalemate?

In South Vietnam, the U.S. had stumbled into a bog. It would be mired down there a long time.
— Soviet Premier Nikita Krushchev, 1962

The basic alternatives for Vietnam are . . . a nightmare. . . . We are caught in the quagmire.
— David Halberstam, *The Making of a Quagmire*, 1965

Mr. Lovett made the point that it was not useful to talk about "victory," that what was really involved was preventing the expansion of Communism by force; in a sense, avoiding defeat. This view seemed to be generally shared.
— Notes of a meeting of the U.S. Department of State "Vietnam Panel," 8 July 1965

We are in an escalating military stalemate.
— Assistant Secretary of Defense John McNaughton, 1966

18

THE POLITICS OF INADVERTENCE

ARTHUR M. SCHLESINGER, JR.

To Arthur M. Schlesinger, Jr.—well-known historian and White House special assistant in the Kennedy administration—a key phase in the march toward an expanding American war was the period from late 1963 to 1965, which included the deaths of Diem and Kennedy, Johnson's ascendancy to the presidency, the election of 1964, and the escalations of 1965. Writing in 1966, Schlesinger claimed that policymakers had been blind to the long-term consequences of progressive, piecemeal escalations and walked unsuspectingly into the trap that was Vietnam. Founded on false assumptions and ignorance of Vietnam's political and military realities, theirs was a "policy of 'one more step'—each new step always promising the success which the previous last step had also promised but had unaccountably failed to deliver."

...Finally the South Vietnamese army brought off its coup, killed Diem and Nhu, and the war entered a new phase. Three weeks later Kennedy too was dead, and a new President inherited the trouble. Vietnam was still not a top problem. In his first State of the Union message, President Johnson hardly mentioned Vietnam.[1] In his 1965 message, Vietnam received hardly more than 100 words. Even his 1966 message took thirty-five minutes before there was any extended discussion of Vietnam. It is important to remember how long it was before Vietnam emerged as the all-consuming and all-dominating issue it is today.

[1] The two references in the message of January 8, 1964, were speechwriter's reflexes: "Today Americans of all races stand side by side in Berlin and in Vietnam" (in a passage on civil rights) and "In 1964 we will be better prepared than ever before to defend the cause of freedom—whether it is threatened by outright aggression or by the infiltration practiced by those in Hanoi and Havana" (in a passage on national security policy).

It did, however, play a role in the 1964 election, largely because of Senator Goldwater's advocacy of an aggressive northern strategy. President Johnson replied:

> Some others are eager to enlarge the conflict. They call upon us to supply American boys to do the job that Asian boys should do. They ask us to take reckless actions which might risk the lives of millions and engulf much of Asia.
>
> (August 12)

> I have had advice to load our planes with bombs and to drop them on certain areas that I think would enlarge the war and result in committing a good many American boys to fighting a war that I think ought to be fought by the boys of Asia to help protect their own land. And for that reason I haven't chosen to enlarge the war.
>
> (August 29)

> There are those that say you ought to go north and drop bombs, to try to wipe out the supply lines, and they think that would escalate the war. We don't want our American boys to do the fighting for Asian boys. We don't want to get involved in a nation with 700 million people and get tied down in a land war in Asia.
>
> (September 25)

> We are not going north and we are not going south; we are going to continue to try to get them to save their own freedom with their own men, with our leadership and our officer direction, and such equipment as we can furnish them.
>
> (September 28)

> We are not going to send American boys nine or ten thousand miles away from home to do what Asian boys ought to be doing for themselves.
>
> (October 21)

...Campaign speeches are not sacred covenants with the people; they are expressions of intent and hope, and there is no reason to question the honesty of President Johnson's 1964 statements.[2] What the President apparently did not allow for was a continued decay in the military situation. Things became so desperate in the early months of 1965—or so we were later told—that only the February decision to start bombing the north, followed by the commitment of American combat forces the next month, averted total collapse. If the situation was really all that grave, the administration did not confide this fact at the time to the American people; in ret-

---

[2] However, Charles Roberts, the White House correspondent of *Newsweek,* wrote in his book, *LBJ's Inner Circle,* "The President...told me in May 1965 that he had made the decision to bomb [North Vietnam]...four months before Pleiku." This would place the decision in October 1964. But the President's wording may have been loose or his memory faulty; for I know of no other indication that the decision was in fact taken that early.

rospect, one simply does not know whether this story is actuality or myth. If actuality, it might surely have called Washington's attention to the political weaknesses of the Saigon regime; for the South Vietnamese Army at this point still outnumbered the Viet Cong by at least six to one, and its capitulation would have been more an expression of political demoralization than of military inferiority.

In any case, the President now felt he had no alternative but to begin to supply American boys to do the job that he had thought a few months before Asian boys should do. The number of American troops doubled, and doubled again; by August 1965 there were 125,000. The bombing steadily grew, except for a meaningless six-day pause in May. As we increased our activity, Hanoi reciprocated. According to our estimates, the enemy amounted to 90,000 in March 1964; 100,000 in January 1965; and, after the active American entry into the war, 135,000 by April and 170,000 by August. In December 1965 the United States instituted a second bombing pause. After thirty-seven days, the process of escalation resumed. By the end of 1966 the number of American troops was rising toward 400,000. As for the bombing of the north, there were 1935 missions in February 1966, 5183 in April, 7357 in June, 9765 in July, 12,673 in September.

And so the policy of 'one more step' lured the United States deeper and deeper into the morass. In retrospect, Vietnam is a triumph of the politics of inadvertence. We have achieved our present entanglement, not after due and deliberate consideration, but through a series of small decisions. It is not only idle but unfair to seek out guilty men. President Eisenhower, after rejecting American military intervention in 1954, set in motion the policy of support for Saigon which resulted, two Presidents later, in American military intervention in 1965. Each step in the deepening of the American commitment was reasonably regarded at the time as the last that would be necessary. Yet, in retrospect, each step led only to the next, until we find ourselves entrapped today in that nightmare of American strategists, a land war in Asia—a war which no President, including President Johnson, desired or intended. The Vietnam story is a tragedy without villains. No thoughtful American can withhold sympathy as President Johnson ponders the gloomy choices which lie ahead.

Yet each President, in the words of Andrew Jackson, remains "accountable at the bar of public opinion for every act of his administration." President Johnson has made his ultimate objective very clear: he does not seek, he has said, total military victory or the unconditional surrender of North Vietnam,[3] but a negotiated settlement. He has also made very clear his judgment that the way to achieve a political solution is by intensifying military pressure until a battered and reeling Hanoi agrees to negotiate—or, at least, pulls out its forces and allows the war to fade away. By continually increasing what the Pentagon calls the "quotient of pain," we can, according to the administration theory, force Hanoi at each new stage of widening the war to reconsider whether the war is worth the price.

This has been the persistent administration course since February 1965. New experiments in escalation are first denied, then disowned, then discounted and fi-

---

[3] One must discount flourishes like the presidential exhortation to the combat commanders in the officers' club at Camranh Bay: "Come home with that coonskin on the wall."

nally undertaken. Thus in the early winter of 1965 the Secretary of Defense told Congress that bombing the petroleum facilities near Haiphong was of "no fundamental consequence"; in the spring the Secretary of the Air Force explained why we were not going to bomb Hanoi and Haiphong; on June 26, the Under Secretary of State denied that any decision had been taken to bomb the oil storage depots; on June 29, the bombing began. For a moment Washington put out stories suggesting that this was going to be some sort of turning point in the war. High officials cited unidentified intelligence dispatches reporting the decline of morale in North Vietnam. But in the months since it has become evident that, once again, the newest step in escalation made no more difference than the previous steps.

So, once again, the demand arises for 'just one *more* step.' As past medicine fails, all we can apparently think to do is to double the dose. Plenty of room remains for widening the war: the harbors of North Vietnam, the irrigation dikes, the steel plants, the factories, the power grid, the crops, the civilian population, the Chinese border. The fact that we excluded such steps yesterday is, alas, no guarantee that we will not pursue them tomorrow. And if bombing will not bring Ho Chi Minh to his knees or stop his support of the Viet Cong in South Vietnam, there is always the resort of invasion. General Ky has already told us that we must invade North Vietnam to win the war. In an August press conference, the Secretary of State twice refused to rule out this possibility. And beyond invasion lies the field of nuclear weapons—weapons which General Eisenhower, who declined the conventional bombing of Dien Bien Phu in 1954, would not exclude in 1966.

The theory, of course, is that widening the war will shorten it. This theory appears to be based on three convictions: first, that the war will be decided in North Vietnam; second, that the risk of Chinese or Soviet entry is negligible; and third, that military 'victory' in some sense is possible—not perhaps total victory over North Vietnam but suppression of resistance in South Vietnam. Perhaps these premises are correct, and in another year or two we may all be saluting the wisdom and statesmanship of the American government. In so enigmatic a situation, no one can be confident about his doubt and disagreement. Nonetheless, to many Americans these propositions constitute a terribly shaky basis for action which has already carried the United States into a ground war in Asia and which may well carry the world to the brink of the third world war.

The illusion that the war in South Vietnam can be decided in North Vietnam is evidently a result of listening too long to our own propaganda. "The war," the Secretary of State has solemnly assured us, "is clearly an 'armed attack,' cynically and systematically mounted by the Hanoi regime against the people of South Vietnam." Our government has insisted so often that the war in South Vietnam is, in President Johnson's phrase, "a vicious and illegal aggression across this little nation's frontier," that it has come to believe itself that the war was started in Hanoi and can only be stopped there.

Yet the best evidence remains that the war began as an insurrection within South Vietnam which, as it has gathered momentum, has attracted increasing support and direction from the north. In August 1966, four correspondents who had been covering the Vietnam war—Malcolm Browne of the Associated Press (whose book on Vietnam, *The New Face of War,* had won the Pulitzer Prize), Jack Foisie of the *Los Angeles Times* (who is the Secretary of State's brother-in-law), Charles Mohr of the *New York Times* and Dean Brelis of the National Broadcasting Company—discussed this point:

BROWNE: Of course, it is a civil war, by the Webster definition of the thing.
NIVEN (moderator): So you all agree?
FOISIE: I think it is.
BRELIS: Yes, I agree.
MOHR: Yes, a special kind of civil war.

Even today the North Vietnamese regulars in South Vietnam amount to only a small fraction of the total enemy force (and to an even smaller fraction of the American army in South Vietnam). We could follow the genial prescription of General LeMay and bomb North Vietnam back to the Stone Age—and the war would still go on in South Vietnam. To reduce this war to the simplification of a wicked regime molesting its neighbors, and to suppose that it can be ended by punishing the wicked regime, is surely to misconceive not only the political but even the military character of the problem....

19

DISCOVERING THE QUAGMIRE

HENRY KISSINGER

Henry A. Kissinger, President Nixon's assistant for national security and later secretary of state, described Vietnam as "that distant monochromatic land, of green

From *White House Years* by Henry Kissinger. Copyright © 1979, by Henry A. Kissinger. By permission of Little, Brown and Company.

mountains and fields merging with an azure sea, that for millennia has acted as a magnet for foreigners who sought glory there and found frustration, who believed that in its rice fields and jungles some principle was to be established and entered them only to recede in disillusion."* Kissinger was a foreign policy realist with a gloomy view of American policy. He thought that U.S. "entry into the war had been the product...of a naive idealism" and believed that the process of involvement had been "imperceptibly gradual and progressively sobering," paralleling his own slow education about the conflict.† His ideas about how the United States got involved, which he described in "My Exposure to the Quagmire," a section of his memoir, White House Years, *resembled the views of David Halberstam and Arthur Schlesinger, Jr. Kissinger, like Schlesinger, implied that decision makers had been blind to the long-term consequences of incremental escalation and had walked unawares into the quagmire trap. Like Halberstam, Kissinger had been influenced by Lieutenant Colonel John Paul Vann, a U.S. military adviser in Vietnam, and he wrote of the policy dilemmas caused by diplomatic folly, administrative self-delusion, and strategic errors during the Kennedy and Johnson years. He believed, for example, that the Johnson administration had possessed no clear conception of how to win the war or to conclude it. A supporter of maintaining the credibility of the U.S. commitment, however, he sought to develop military and diplomatic strategies that would enable the Nixon administration to achieve an "honorable outcome" while escaping from the quagmire.*

My own exposure to Vietnam was imperceptibly gradual and progressively sobering; it paralleled the simplifications that led our government into an adventure whose ultimate cost proved out of proportion to any conceivable gain. I shared the gradual disillusionment.

In the early Sixties I did not pay much attention to Vietnam. Europe, strategy, and arms control were my academic specialties. Insofar as I held any views, I shared the conventional wisdom that the war was an effort by North Vietnam to take over South Vietnam by military force. This I continue to believe. In the early Sixties the possibility of sending American combat troops did not occur to me. ...[T]he Johnson Administration saw Peking as masterminding the Vietnam aggression. The Kennedy Administration, which had sent the first 16,000 American military advisers to Vietnam, had also been fascinated by the phenomenon of guerrilla war, though it tended to see the inspiration in a January 1961 speech by Nikita Krushchev endorsing "wars of national liberation."

When the Kennedy Administration sent those 16,000 advisers to Vietnam, I remember asking Walt Rostow, then Director of the Policy Planning Staff of the State Department, what made him think we would succeed with that number when the French had failed with several hundred thousand. ... The French, he explained, as if teaching the alphabet to an illiterate, did not understand guerrilla warfare; they

---

*Henry Kissinger, *White House Years* (Boston: Little, Brown, 1979), p. 226.
†Ibid., p. 230.

lacked the mobility of the American forces. I did not pursue the matter, as my interest in Vietnam in those days was rather superficial.

It was not until November 1963 that I took strong exception to a government policy and then it was on a matter that enjoyed wide support. I was appalled by the direct role the United States had evidently played in the overthrow of South Vietnam's President Ngo Dinh Diem, which led to his assassination. This folly committed us to a course we could not foresee while undermining the political base for it; in the purge following, the country was bereft of almost its entire civil administration. For us to be seen to connive in the overthrow of a friendly government was bound to shake the confidence of other allies in Southeast Asia. I questioned the assumptions that had led us into such a gamble. Ngo Dinh Diem had to be overthrown, so argued his opponents, including much of the press corps in Saigon, because the war against the Communists would never be pursued with adequate energy or popular support while Diem was in office. His brother was accused of seeking a compromise with the Communists—precisely what seven years later became the orthodoxy of many of the same critics and for the refusal of which they now wanted to overthrow Diem's successor, Nguyen Van Thieu. But since the war concerned the legitimacy of the non-Communist government in South Vietnam, to overturn that government was a novel way to win it. The presumed military gains could not outweigh the loss of political authority. And we would be much more deeply committed morally to the government we had brought to office. We know today that Hanoi reached the same conclusion. While it had actively supported guerrilla warfare, it did not commit its regular forces until after the overthrow of Diem. I was in the process of writing an article along these lines, predicting a drastic deterioration in Vietnam, when President Kennedy was assassinated. I decided it would be in bad taste to proceed.

In 1964 I encouraged Governor Rockefeller to speak strongly on Vietnam in his primary campaign. Neither he nor I had a clear-cut view of an appropriate strategy and neither he nor I envisioned sending American combat troops. By 1965, however, I belonged to the silent majority that agreed with the Johnson Administration's commitment of combat forces to resist Hanoi's now clear direct involvement.

I ceased being a spectator in early August 1965 when Henry Cabot Lodge, an old friend then serving as Ambassador to Saigon, asked me to visit Vietnam as his consultant. I toured Vietnam first for two weeks in October and November 1965, again for about ten days in July 1966, and a third time for a few days in October 1966—the last trip was made at the request of Averell Harriman. Lodge gave me a free hand to look into any subject of my choice; he put the facilities of the Embassy at my disposal.

I soon realized that we had involved ourselves in a war which we knew neither how to win nor how to conclude. The enemy's sanctuaries in Laos and Cambodia prevented the achievement of the classic military objective of war—the destruction of the military power of the enemy. In North Vietnam we were engaged in a bombing campaign powerful enough to mobilize world opinion against us but too half-hearted and gradual to be decisive. Thus our adversary was in a position to control the pace of military operations and the level of casualties, both his and ours. And the level of American casualties was to become a pivotal element in American public opinion.

I became convinced that in a civil war, military "victories" would be meaningless unless they brought about a political reality that could survive our ultimate withdrawal. Negotiations would occur only when Hanoi realized that it faced the progressive loss of its political influence over the local population the longer the war lasted. This was a monumental task. The North Vietnamese and Viet Cong, fighting on familiar terrain, needed only to hang on to keep in being forces sufficiently strong to dominate the population after the United States tired of the war. Our challenge was much more complex: We had to fight the war and simultaneously strengthen the South Vietnamese to survive without us—in other words, to make ourselves dispensable. It is a cardinal principle of guerrilla warfare that the guerrilla wins if he does not lose; the regular army loses unless it wins. We were fighting a military war against an elusive enemy; our adversary fought a political one against a stationary population. From the first I doubted that our planners had grasped this. On my way to Vietnam in October 1965, I stopped at our Pacific headquarters in Hawaii. After my first formal briefing on Vietnam, I wrote in my diary:

> I was impressed by the fact that no one could really explain to me how even on the most favorable assumptions about the war in Vietnam the war was going to end.... I do not think we have even begun to solve the basic problem which is psychological. It seems to me that the Viet Cong and the North Vietnamese must be saying to themselves that even though their hopes for a victory this year were disappointed [because of American intervention], there is a possibility, even a probability, that if they can prolong the war sufficiently they will exhaust us. How does one convince a people that one is prepared to stay indefinitely 10,000 miles away against opponents who are fighting in their own country?... If we fail in our Pacific operations it will not be because of a failure in the technical realm, but because of a difficulty of synchronizing political and military objectives in a situation for which this enormously complex military establishment is not designed.

It seemed to me that regular North Vietnamese units, which were the chief target of our military operations, played the role of the matador's cape: they tempted our forces to lunge into politically insignificant areas while the Viet Cong infrastructure undermined the South Vietnamese government in the populated countryside. After a visit to a Vietnamese province on October 21, 1965, I wrote in my diary:

> It is obvious that there are two separate wars going on here: (1) reflected in the army statistics about security of military units; and (2) that which affects the population. The two criteria do not match. For the army a road is open when it can travel in convoy along it. For the villager a road is open when he can travel it without paying taxes. For the army a vil-

lage is secure when it can station its forces there. For the population a village is secure when it has protection not only from attacks by organized VC units but also from VC terrorism.

In the absence of criteria of success, self-delusion took the place of analysis. When I visited the province of Vinh Long in October 1965, I asked the province chief what percentage of his province was pacified; he proudly told me 80 percent. When I visited Vietnam for the second time in July 1966, I made a point of visiting the same provinces in order to assess the changes. In Vinh Long the same province chief told me that enormous progress had been made since my earlier visit. When I asked him how much of the province was now pacified, he proudly told me 70 percent!

I summed up my views of my first visit in a letter to Henry Cabot Lodge dated December 3, 1965:

> Overshadowing everything is a social or maybe even philosophical problem: The Vietnamese have a strong sense of being a distinct people but little sense of nationhood. Our deepest challenge then is to discover how a nation can be built when the society is torn by internal schisms and in the middle of a civil war. All new countries have had the problem of achieving political cohesion; none have had to do so in the face of such overwhelming pressures as Vietnam.

On August 18, 1966, after my second visit to Vietnam, I wrote another letter to Lodge: "Candor compels me to say that I did not find any substantial change in the provinces...." The attempt by American officials to judge security in the countryside was an attempt to quantify intangibles. Perhaps because of the inexperience of our province advisers (whose tour of duty was so short that by the time they learned their job they had to leave), our effort lacked political perspective. For example, some areas listed as pacified might have been so because the Viet Cong found it convenient to leave agriculture undisturbed as a source of supply for themselves, because they were regularly collecting the taxes. I added some recommendations: that the Embassy should attempt a more accurate assessment of the security situation, that local government should be strengthened, and that priorities should be firmly established. Also, we urgently needed a strategy for the negotiations for which the Administration constantly proclaimed its eagerness. For a negotiation would be the beginning, not the end, of our difficulties.

And I had had some limited experience in dealing with the North Vietnamese. Between July and October 1967, at the request of the Johnson Administration, I served as an intermediary in an effort to get negotiations started. I conveyed messages through two French intellectuals I knew, one of whom had befriended Ho Chi Minh in the Forties, offering him the hospitality of his house when Ho was in Paris to negotiate with the French. I was authorized to encourage my friends to visit Hanoi to offer compromise terms for a halt to American bombing as a prelude to a negotiation. They went and met with Ho Chi Minh. For several months I traveled to Paris at intervals to convey or receive messages from the North Vietnamese.

Eventually the effort aborted, though it was a step in the direction of the agreement that produced a bombing halt and the opening of peace talks a year later.

After these negotiations had at last begun, at the end of 1968 I published my assessment in an article in *Foreign Affairs*.[1] It was written before I was appointed security adviser but published afterward. I expressed my basic conclusions:

- that our military strategy was incapable of producing victory;
- that our military operations had to be geared to clearly defined negotiating objectives;
- that the South Vietnamese government could survive only if it developed a political program to which non-Communist South Vietnamese could rally;
- that the United States must cede increasing responsibility for the conduct of the war to the South Vietnamese; and
- that if in negotiations "Hanoi proves intransigent and the war goes on, we should seek to achieve as many of our objectives as possible unilaterally;"
- that in our negotiations we should concentrate on military issues such as cease-fire while leaving the distribution of political power to the Vietnamese parties.

To some extent, I agreed with critics on both sides of the political spectrum. The Johnson Administration, by its conduct of the war, had abandoned whatever prospect of a conventional military victory existed; it had set a ceiling on our force levels and accepted a bombing halt. An honorable outcome depended on our ability to create political incentives for Hanoi to compromise—which would be impossible unless we could convert our military position on the ground into a durable political structure. Our negotiating position had to enlist enduring public support at home in order to make it clear to Hanoi that it would not gain by enmeshing us in protracted talks. To hold all these pieces in place while disengaging would be the task of any new Administration.

But while by January of 1969 I had become profoundly uneasy about the war, I differed with many of the critics in several respects. I did not favor an unconditional withdrawal. By 1969 the over half-million American forces, the 70,000 allied forces, and the 31,000 who had died there had settled the issue of whether the outcome was important for us and those who depended on us. Nor did I go along with the many critics of the war who acted as if peace depended above all on *our* goodwill. The hard men in Hanoi, having spent their lives in struggle, did not consider compromise a moral category. Driven by the epic saga of Vietnamese history—a history of wars against the Chinese, the French, the Japanese, and now us—they had sustained their undoubted heroism by the dream of victory; they would settle for compromise only on the basis of calculation and necessity. A negotiated peace would result from the reckoning of risks on both sides, not from a burst of sentiment. This judgment would forever separate me from many of the protesters—even when I agreed with their analysis that the war was draining our national strength and had to be liquidated. . . .

---

[1] "The Viet Nam Negotiations," *Foreign Affairs*, vol. 47, no. 2 (January 1969), pp. 211–34.

20

HOW THE SYSTEM WORKED

LESLIE H. GELB

In a paper first published in 1971, Leslie H. Gelb challenged that view which portrayed decision makers as sleepwalkers who had stumbled into the quagmire of Vietnam. Instead, the decision-making process was one influenced by a mechanism he and Daniel Ellsberg called "the stalemate machine." Gelb had been a deputy director of policy planning in the Defense Department from 1967 to 1968, a deputy assistant secretary of policy planning from 1968 to 1969, and the director of Secretary of Defense Robert McNamara's Vietnam Study Task Force from 1967 to 1969, which compiled the Pentagon Papers.

The story of United States policy toward Vietnam is either far better or far worse than generally supposed. Our Presidents and most of those who influenced their decisions did not stumble step by step into Vietnam, unaware of the quagmire. U.S. involvement did not stem from a failure to foresee consequences.

Vietnam was indeed a quagmire, but most of our leaders knew it. Of course there were optimists and periods where many were genuinely optimistic. But those periods were infrequent and short-lived and were invariably followed by periods of deep pessimism. Very few, to be sure, envisioned what the Vietnam situation would be like by 1968. Most realized, however, that "the light at the end of the tunnel" was very far away—if not finally unreachable. Nevertheless, our Presidents persevered. Given international compulsions to "keep our word" and "save face," domestic prohibitions against "losing," and their personal stakes, our leaders did "what was necessary," did it about the way they wanted, were prepared to pay the costs, and plowed on with a mixture of hope and doom. They "saw" no acceptable alternative.

Three propositions suggest why the United States became involved in Vietnam, why the process was gradual, and what the real expectations of our leaders were:

Reprinted with permission from *Foreign Policy* no. 3 (Summer 1971). Copyright 1971 by the Carnegie Endowment for International Peace.

First, U.S. involvement in Vietnam is not mainly or mostly a story of step by step, inadvertent descent into unforeseen quicksand. It is primarily a story of why U.S. leaders considered that it was vital not to lose Vietnam by force to Communism. Our leaders believed Vietnam to be vital not for itself, but for what they thought its "loss" would mean internationally and domestically. Previous involvement made further involvement more unavoidable, and, to this extent, commitments were inherited. But judgments of Vietnam's "vitalness"—beginning with the Korean War—were sufficient in themselves to set the course for escalation.

Second, our Presidents were never actually seeking a military victory in Vietnam. They were doing only what they thought was minimally necessary at each stage to keep Indochina, and later South Vietnam, out of Communist hands. This forced our Presidents to be brakemen, to do less than those who were urging military victory and to reject proposals for disengagement. It also meant that our Presidents wanted a negotiated settlement without fully realizing (though realizing more than their critics) that a civil war cannot be ended by political compromise.

Third, our Presidents and most of their lieutenants were not deluded by optimistic reports of progress and did not proceed on the basis of wishful thinking about winning a military victory in South Vietnam. They recognized that the steps they were taking were not adequate to win the war and that unless Hanoi relented, they would have to do more and more. Their strategy was to persevere in the hope that their will to continue—if not the practical effects of their actions—would cause the Communists to relent.

Each of these propositions is explored below.

I. ENDS: "WE CAN'T AFFORD TO LOSE"

Those who led the United States into Vietnam did so with their eyes open, knowing why, and believing they had the will to succeed. The deepening involvement was not inadvertent, but mainly deductive. It flowed with sureness from the perceived stakes and attendant high objectives. U.S. policy displayed remarkable continuity. There were not dozens of likely "turning points." Each postwar President inherited previous commitments. Each extended these commitments. Each administration from 1947 to 1969 believed that it was necessary to prevent the loss of Vietnam and, after 1954, South Vietnam by force to the Communists. The reasons for this varied from person to person, from bureaucracy to bureaucracy, over time and in emphasis. For the most part, however, they had little to do with Vietnam itself. A few men argued that Vietnam had intrinsic strategic military and economic importance, but this view never prevailed. The reasons rested on broader international, domestic, and bureaucratic considerations.

Our leaders gave the *international* repercussions of "losing" as their dominant explicit reason for Vietnam's importance. During the Truman Administration, Indochina's importance was measured in terms of French-American relations and Washington's desire to rebuild France into the centerpiece of future European security. After the cold war heated up and after the fall of China, a French defeat in

Indochina was also seen as a defeat for the policy of containment. In the Eisenhower years, Indochina became a "testing ground" between the Free World and Communism and the basis for the famous "domino theory" by which the fall of Indochina would lead to the deterioration of American security around the globe. President Kennedy publicly reaffirmed the falling domino concept. His primary concern, however, was for his "reputation for action" after the Bay of Pigs fiasco, the Vienna meeting with Khrushchev, and the Laos crisis, and in meeting the challenge of "wars of national liberation" by counterinsurgency warfare. Under President Johnson, the code word rationales became Munich, credibility, commitments and the U.S. word, a watershed test of wills with Communism, raising the costs of aggression, and the principle that armed aggression shall not be allowed to succeed. There is every reason to assume that our leaders actually believed what they said, given both the cold war context in which they were all reared and the lack of contradictory evidence.

With very few exceptions, then, our leaders since World War II saw Vietnam as a vital factor in alliance politics, U.S.-Soviet-Chinese relations, and deterrence. This was as true in 1950 and 1954 as it was in 1961 and 1965. The record of United States military and economic assistance to fight Communism in Indochina tells this story quite clearly. From 1945 to 1951, U.S. aid to France totaled over $3.5 billion. Without this, the French position in Indochina would have been untenable. By 1951, the U.S. was paying about 40 percent of the costs of the Indochina war and our share was going up. In 1954, it is estimated, U.S. economic and technical assistance amounted to $703 million and military aid totaled almost $2 billion. This added up to almost 80 percent of the total French costs. From 1955 to 1961, U.S. military aid averaged about $200 million per year. This made South Vietnam the second largest recipient of such aid, topped only by Korea. By 1963, South Vietnam ranked first among recipients of military assistance. In economic assistance, it followed only India and Pakistan.

The *domestic* repercussions of "losing" Vietnam probably were equally important in Presidential minds. Letting Vietnam "go Communist" was undoubtedly seen as:

- opening the floodgates to domestic criticism and attack for being "soft on Communism" or just plain soft;
- dissipating Presidential influence by having to answer these charges;
- alienating conservative leadership in the Congress and thereby endangering the President's legislative program;
- jeopardizing election prospects for the President and his party;
- undercutting domestic support for a "responsible" U.S. world role; and
- enlarging the prospects for a right-wing reaction—the nightmare of a McCarthyite garrison state.

U.S. domestic politics required our leaders to maintain both a peaceful world and one in which Communist expansion was stopped. In order to have the public support necessary to use force against Communism, our leaders had to employ strong generalized, ideological rhetoric. The price of this rhetoric was consistency. How could our leaders shed American blood in Korea and keep large numbers of American troops in Europe at great expense unless they were also willing to stop Communism in Vietnam?

Bureaucratic judgments and stakes were also involved in defining U.S. interests in Vietnam. Most bureaucrats probably prompted or shared the belief of their leaders about the serious repercussions of losing Vietnam. Once direct bureaucratic presence was established after the French departure, this belief was reinforced and extended. The military had to prove that American arms and advice could succeed where the French could not. The Foreign Service had to prove that it could bring about political stability in Saigon and "build a nation." The CIA had to prove that pacification would work. AID had to prove that millions of dollars in assistance and advice could bring political returns.

The U.S. commitment was rationalized as early as 1950. It was set in 1955 when we replaced the French. Its logic was further fulfilled by President Kennedy. After 1965, when the U.S. took over the war, it was immeasurably hardened.

There was little conditional character to the U.S. commitment—except for avoiding "the big war." Every President talked about the ultimate responsibility resting with the Vietnamese (and the French before them). This "condition" seems to have been meant much more as a warning to our friends than a real limitation. In every crunch, it was swept aside. The only real limit applied to Russia and China. Our leaders were not prepared to run the risks of nuclear war or even the risks of a direct conventional military confrontation with the Soviet Union and China. These were separate decisions. The line between them and everything else done in Vietnam always held firm. With this exception, the commitment was always defined in terms of the objective to deny the Communists control over all Vietnam. This was further defined to preclude coalition governments with the Communists.

The importance of the objective was evaluated in terms of cost, and the perceived costs of disengagement outweighed the cost of further engagement. Some allies might urge disengagement, but then condemn the U.S. for doing so. The domestic groups which were expected to criticize growing involvement always were believed to be outnumbered by those who would have attacked "cutting and running." The question of whether our leaders would have started down the road if they knew this would mean over half a million men in Vietnam, over 40,000 U.S. deaths, and the expenditure of well over $100 billion is historically irrelevant. Only Presidents Kennedy and Johnson had to confront the possibility of these large costs. The point is that each administration was prepared to pay the costs it could foresee for itself. No one seemed to have a better solution. Each could at least pass the baton on to the next.

Presidents could not treat Vietnam as if it were "vital" without creating high stakes internationally, domestically, and within their own bureaucracies. But the rhetoric conveyed different messages:

To the Communists, it was a signal that their actions would be met by counteractions.

To the American people, it set the belief that the President would ensure that the threatened nation did not fall into Communist hands—although without the anticipation of sacrificing American lives.

To the Congress, it marked the President's responsibility to ensure that Vietnam did not go Communist and maximized incentives for legislators to support him or at least remain silent.

To the U.S. professional military, it was a promise that U.S. forces would be used, if necessary and to the degree necessary, to defend Vietnam.

To the professional U.S. diplomat, it meant letting our allies know that the U.S. cared about their fate.

To the President, it laid the groundwork for the present action and showed that he was prepared to take the next step to keep Vietnam non-Communist.

Words were making Vietnam into a showcase—an Asian Berlin. In the process, Vietnam grew into a test case of U.S. credibility—to opponents, to allies, but perhaps most importantly, to ourselves. Public opinion polls seemed to confirm the political dangers. Already established bureaucratic judgments about the importance of Vietnam matured into cherished convictions and organizational interests. The war dragged on.

Each successive President, initially caught by his own belief, was further ensnarled by his own rhetoric, and the basis for the belief went unchallenged. Debates revolved around how to do things better, and whether they could be done, not whether they were worth doing. Prior to 1961, an occasional senator or Southeast Asian specialist would raise a lonely and weak voice in doubt. Some press criticism began thereafter. And later still, wandering American minstrels returned from the field to tell their tales of woe in private. General Ridgway as Chief of Staff of the Army in 1954 questioned the value of Vietnam as against its potential costs and dangers, and succeeded in blunting a proposed U.S. military initiative, although not for the reasons he advanced. Under Secretary of State George Ball raised the issue of international priorities in the summer of 1965 and lost. Clark Clifford as Secretary of Defense openly challenged the winnability of the war, as well as Vietnam's strategic significance, and argued for domestic priorities. But no systematic or serious examination of Vietnam's importance to the United States was ever undertaken within the government. Endless assertions passed for analysis. Presidents neither encouraged nor permitted serious questioning, for to do so would be to foster the idea that their resolve was something less than complete. The objective of a non-Communist Vietnam, and after 1954 a non-Communist South Vietnam, drove U.S. involvement ever more deeply each step of the way.

II. MEANS: "TAKE THE MINIMAL NECESSARY STEPS"

None of our Presidents was seeking total victory over the Vietnamese Communists. War critics who wanted victory always knew this. Those who wanted the U.S. to get out never believed it. Each President was essentially doing what he thought was minimally necessary to prevent a Communist victory during his tenure in office. Each, of course, sought to strengthen the anti-Communist Vietnamese forces, but with the aim of a negotiated settlement. Part of the tragedy of Vietnam was that the compromises our Presidents were prepared to offer could never lead to an end of the war. These preferred compromises only served to reinforce the conviction of both Communist and anti-Communist Vietnamese that they had to fight to the finish in their civil war. And so, more minimal steps were always necessary.

Our Presidents were pressured on all sides. The pressures for victory came mainly from the inside and were reflected on the outside. From inside the administrations, three forces almost invariably pushed hard. *First,* the military establishment generally initiated requests for broadening and intensifying U.S. military action. Our professional military placed great weight on the strategic significance of Vietnam; they were given a job to do; their prestige was involved; and of crucial importance (in the 1960's)—the lives of many American servicemen were being lost. The Joint Chiefs of Staff, the MAAG (Military Assistance Advisory Group) Chiefs and later the Commander of U.S. forces in Vietnam were the focal points for these pressures. *Second,* our Ambassadors in Saigon, supported by the State Department, at times pressed for and often supported big steps forward. Their reasons were similar to those of the military. *Thirdly,* an ever-present group of "fixers" was making urgent demands to strengthen and broaden the Saigon government in order to achieve political victory. Every executive agency had its fixers. They were usually able men whose entire preoccupation was to make things better in Vietnam. From outside the administration, there were hawks who insisted on winning and hawks who wanted to "win or get out." Capitol Hill hawks, the conservative press, and, for many years, Catholic organizations were in the forefront.

The pressures for disengagement and for de-escalation derived mostly from the outside with occasional and often unknown allies from within. Small for most of the Vietnam years, these forces grew steadily in strength from 1965 onward. Isolated congressmen and senators led the fight. First they did so on anticolonialist grounds. Later their objections developed moral aspects (interfering in a civil war) and extended to non-winnability, domestic priorities, and the senselessness of the war. Peace organizations and student groups in particular came to dominate headlines and air time. Journalists played a critical role—especially through television reports. From within each administration, opposition could be found: (1) among isolated military men who did not want the U.S. in an Asian land war; (2) among some State Department intelligence and area specialists who knew Vietnam and believed the U.S. objective was unattainable at any reasonable price; and (3) within the civilian agencies of the Defense Department and isolated individuals at State and CIA, particularly after 1966, whose efforts were trained on finding a politically feasible way out.

Our Presidents reacted to the pressures as brakemen, pulling the switch against both the advocates of "decisive escalation" and the advocates of disengagement. The politics of the Presidency largely dictated this role, but the personalities of the Presidents were also important. None were as ideological as many persons around them. All were basically centrist politicians.

Their immediate aim was always to prevent a Communist takeover. The actions they approved were usually only what was minimally necessary to that aim. Each President determined the "minimal necessity" by trial and error and his own judgment. They might have done more and done it more rapidly if they were convinced that: (1) the threat of a Communist takeover were more immediate, (2) U.S.

domestic politics would have been more permissive, (3) the government of South Vietnam had the requisite political stability and military potential for effective use and (4) the job really would have gotten done. After 1965, however, the minimal necessity became the maximum they could get given the same domestic and international constraints.

The tactic of the minimally necessary decision makes optimum sense for the politics of the Presidency. Even our strongest Presidents have tended to shy away from decisive action. It has been too uncertain, too risky. They derive their strength from movement (the image of a lot of activity) and building and neutralizing opponents. Too seldom has there been forceful moral leadership; it may even be undemocratic. The small step that maintains the momentum gives the President the chance to gather more political support. It gives the appearance of minimizing possible mistakes. It allows time to gauge reactions. It serves as a pressure-relieving valve against those who want to do more. It can be doled out. Above all, it gives the President something to do next time.

The tactic makes consummate sense when it is believed that nothing will fully work or that the costs of a "winning" move would be too high. This was the case with Vietnam. This decision-making tactic explains why the U.S. involvement in Vietnam was gradual and step by step.

While the immediate aim was to prevent a Communist victory and improve the position of the anti-Communists, the longer term goal was a political settlement. As late as February 1947, Secretary of State Marshall expressed the hope that "a pacific basis of adjustment of the difficulties" between France and the Vietminh could be found.[1] After that, Truman's policy hardened, but there is no evidence to suggest that until 1950 he was urging the French not to settle with the Vietnamese Communists. Eisenhower, it should be remembered, was the President who tacitly agreed (by not intervening in 1954) to the creation of a Communist state in North Vietnam. President Kennedy had all he could do to prevent complete political collapse in South Vietnam. He had, therefore, little basis on which to compromise. President Johnson inherited this political instability, and to add to his woes, he faced in 1965 what seemed to be the prospect of a Communist military victory. Yet, by his standing offer for free and internationally supervised elections, he apparently was prepared to accept Communist participation in the political life of the South.

By traditional diplomatic standards of negotiations between sovereign states, these were not fatuous compromises. One compromise was, in effect, to guarantee that the Communists could remain in secure control of North Vietnam. The U.S. would not seek to overthrow this regime. The other compromise was to allow the Communists in South Vietnam to seek power along the lines of Communist parties in France and Italy, i.e. to give them a "permanent minority position."

But the real struggle in Vietnam was not between sovereign states. It was among Vietnamese. It was a civil war and a war for national independence.

Herein lies the paradox and the tragedy of Vietnam. Most of our leaders and their critics did see that Vietnam was a quagmire, but did not see that the real

---

[1] *New York Times*, February 8, 1947.

stakes—who shall govern Vietnam—were not negotiable. Free elections, local sharing of power, international supervision, cease-fires—none of these could serve as a basis for settlement. What were legitimate compromises from Washington's point of view were matters of life and death to the Vietnamese. For American leaders, the stakes were "keeping their word" and saving their political necks. For the Vietnamese, the stakes were their lives and their lifelong political aspirations. Free elections meant bodily exposure to the Communist guerrillas and likely defeat to the anti-Communists. The risk was too great. There was no trust, no confidence.

The Vietnam war could no more be settled by traditional diplomatic compromises than any other civil war. President Lincoln could not settle with the South. The Spanish Republicans and General Franco's Loyalists could not have conceivably mended their fences by elections. None of the post–World War II insurgencies—Greece, Malaya, and the Philippines—ended with a negotiated peace. In each of these cases, the civil differences were put to rest—if at all—only by the logic of war.

It is commonly acknowledged that Vietnam would have fallen to the Communists in 1945–46, in 1954, and in 1965 had it not been for the intervention of first the French and then the Americans. The Vietnamese Communists, who were also by history the Vietnamese nationalists, would not accept only part of a prize for which they had paid so heavily. The anti-Communist Vietnamese, protected by the French and the Americans, would not put themselves at the Communists' mercy.

It may be that our Presidents understood this better than their critics. The critics, especially on the political left, fought for "better compromises," not realizing that even the best could not be good enough, and fought for broad nationalist governments, not realizing there was no middle force in Vietnam. Our Presidents, it seems, recognized that there was no middle ground and that "better compromises" would frighten our Saigon allies without bringing about a compromise peace. And they believed that a neutralization formula would compromise South Vietnam away to the Communists. So the longer-term aim of peace repeatedly gave way to the immediate needs of the war and the next necessary step.

III. EXPECTATIONS: "WE MUST PERSEVERE"

Each new step was taken not because of wishful thinking or optimism about its leading to a victory in South Vietnam. Few of our leaders thought that they could win the war in a conventional sense or that the Communists would be decimated to a point that they would simply fade away. Even as new and further steps were taken, coupled with expressions of optimism, many of our leaders realized that more—and still more—would have to be done. Few of these men felt confident about how it would all end or when. After 1965, however, they allowed the impression of "winnability" to grow in order to justify their already heavy investment and domestic support for the war.

The strategy always was to persevere. Perseverance, it seemed, was the only way to avoid or postpone having to pay the domestic political costs of failure. Finally, perseverance, it was hoped, would convince the Communists that our will to continue was firm. Perhaps, then, with domestic support for perseverance, with bombing North Vietnam, and with inflicting heavy casualties in the South, the Communists would relent. Perhaps, then, a compromise could be negotiated to save the Communists' face without giving them South Vietnam.

Optimism was a part of the "gamesmanship" of Vietnam. It had a purpose. Personal-organizational optimism was the product of a number of motivations and calculations:

- Career services tacitly and sometimes explicitly pressured their professionals to impart good news.
- Good news was seen as a job well done; bad news as personal failure.
- The reporting system was set up so that assessments were made by the implementors.
- Optimism bred optimism so that it was difficult to be pessimistic this time if you were optimistic the last time.
- People told their superiors what they thought they wanted to hear.
- The American ethic is to get the job done.

Policy optimism also sprang from several rational needs:

- To maintain domestic support for the war.
- To keep up the morale of our Vietnamese allies and build some confidence and trust between us and them.
- To stimulate military and bureaucratic morale to work hard.

There were, however, genuine optimists and grounds for genuine optimism. Some periods looked promising: the year preceding the French downfall at Dienbienphu; the years of the second Eisenhower Presidency when most attention was riveted on Laos and before the insurgency was stepped up in South Vietnam; 1962 and early 1963 before the strategic hamlet pacification program collapsed; and the last six months of 1967 before the 1968 Tet offensive.

Many additional periods by comparison with previous years yielded a sense of real improvement. By most conventional standards—the size and firepower of friendly Vietnamese forces, the number of hamlets pacified, the number of "free elections" being held, the number of Communists killed, and so forth—reasonable men could and did think in cautiously optimistic terms.

But comparison with years past is an illusory measure when it is not coupled with judgments about how far there still is to go and how likely it is that the goal can ever be reached. It was all too easy to confuse short-term breathing spells with long-term trends and to confuse "things getting better" with "winning." Many of those who had genuine hope suffered from either a lack of knowledge about Vietnam or a lack of sensitivity toward politics or both.

The basis for pessimism and the warning signals were always present. Public portrayals of success glowed more brightly than the full range of classified reporting. Readily available informal and personal accounts were less optimistic still. The political instability of our Vietnamese allies—from Bao Dai through Diem to President Thieu have always been apparent. The weaknesses of the armed forces of our

Vietnamese allies were common knowledge. Few years went by when the fighting did not gain in intensity. Our leaders did not have to know much about Vietnam to see all this.

Most of our leaders saw the Vietnam quagmire for what it was. Optimism was, by and large, put in perspective. This means that many knew that each step would be followed by another. Most seemed to have understood that more assistance would be required either to improve the relative position of our Vietnamese allies or simply to prevent a deterioration of their position. Almost each year and often several times a year, key decisions had to be made to prevent deterioration or collapse. These decisions were made with hard bargaining, but rapidly enough for us now to perceive a preconceived consensus to go on. Sometimes several new steps were decided at once, but announced and implemented piecemeal. The whole pattern conveyed the feeling of more to come.

With a tragic sense of "no exit," our leaders stayed their course. They seemed to hope more than expect that something would "give." The hope was to convince the Vietnamese Communists through perseverance that the U.S. would stay in South Vietnam until they abandoned their struggle. The hope, in a sense, was the product of disbelief. How could a tiny, backward Asian country *not* have a breaking point when opposed by the might of the United States? How could they not relent and negotiate with the U.S.?

And yet, few could answer two questions with any confidence: Why should the Communists abandon tomorrow the goals they had been paying so dear a price to obtain yesterday? What was there really to negotiate? No one seemed to be able to develop a persuasive scenario on how the war could end by peaceful means.

Our Presidents, given their politics and thinking, had nothing to do but persevere. But the Communists' strategy was also to persevere, to make the U.S. go home. It was and is a civil war for national independence. It was and is a Greek tragedy....

VIII. WHERE DO WE GO FROM HERE?

If Vietnam were a story of how the system failed, that is, if our leaders did not do what they wanted to do or if they did not realize what they were doing or what was happening, it would be easy to package a large and assorted box of policy-making panaceas. For example: Fix the method of reporting from the field. Fix the way progress is measured in a guerrilla war. Make sure the President sees all the real alternatives. But these are all third-order issues, because the U.S. political-bureaucratic system did not fail; it worked.

Our leaders felt they had to prevent the loss of Vietnam to Communism, and they have succeeded so far in doing just that. Most of those who made Vietnam policy still believe that they did the right thing and lament only the domestic repercussions of their actions. It is because the price of attaining this goal has been so dear in lives, trust, dollars, and priorities, and the benefits so intangible, remote, and often implausible, that these leaders and we ourselves are forced to seek new answers and new policies.

Paradoxically, the way to get these new answers is not by asking why did the system fail, but why did it work so tragically well. There is, then, only one first-order issue—how and why does our political-bureaucratic system decide what is vital and what is not? By whom, in what manner, and for what reasons was it decided that all Vietnam must not fall into Communist hands?

Almost all of our leaders since 1949 shared this conviction. Only a few voices in the wilderness were raised in opposition. Even as late as mid-1967, most critics were arguing that the U.S. could not afford to lose or be "driven from the field," that the real problem was our bombing of North Vietnam, and that this had to be stopped in order to bring about a negotiated settlement. Fewer still were urging that such a settlement should involve a coalition government with the Communists. Hardly anyone was saying that the outcome in Vietnam did not matter.

There is little evidence of much critical thinking about the relation of Vietnam to U.S. security. Scholars, journalists, politicians, and bureaucrats all seem to have assumed either that Vietnam was "vital" to U.S. national security or that the American people would not stand for the loss of "another" country to Communism.

Anti-Communism has been and still is a potent force in American politics, and most people who were dealing with the Vietnam problem simply believed that the Congress and the public would "punish" those who were "soft on Communism." Our leaders not only anticipated this kind of public reaction, but believed that there were valid reasons for not permitting the Communists to take all of Vietnam by force. In other words, they believed in what they were doing on the national security "merits." The domino theory, which was at the heart of the matter, rested on the widely shared attitude that security was indivisible, that weakness in one place would only invite aggression in others.

What can be done?

The President can do more than Presidents have in the past to call his national security bureaucracy to task. He can show the bureaucracy that he expects it to be more rigorous in determining what is vital or important or unimportant. Specifically, he can reject reasoning which simply asserts that security is indivisible, and he can foster the belief that while the world is an interconnected whole, actions can be taken in certain parts of the world to compensate for actions which are not taken elsewhere. For example, if the real concern about Vietnam were the effect of its loss on Japan, the Middle East and Berlin, could we not take actions in each of these places to mitigate the "Vietnam fallout"?

None of these efforts with the bureaucracy can succeed, however, unless there is a change in general political attitudes as well. If anti-Communism persists as an overriding domestic political issue it will also be the main bureaucratic issue. Altering public attitudes will take time, education, and political courage—and it will create a real dilemma for the President. If the President goes "too far" in re-educating public and congressional opinions about Communism, he may find that he will have little support for threatening or using military force when he believes that our se-

curity really is at stake. In the end, it will still be the President who is held responsible for U.S. security. Yet, if our Vietnam experience has taught us anything,
it is that the President must begin the process of re-education despite the risks.

21

CYCLES OF OPTIMISM
AND PESSIMISM

DANIEL ELLSBERG

*Daniel Ellsberg shared Gelb's view of a decision-making process dominated by the
stalemate machine. Both had read the documents and analyses in the* Pentagon
Papers. *But Ellsberg differed with Gelb on several related issues, including the
degrees of optimism and pessimism among decision makers, the relative influence of
domestic politics, and the morality of the war. In the excerpt below, taken from a
much longer piece, Ellsberg argued that the quagmire theory concealed executive
deception of Congress and the public, and he described how this deception, in turn,
caused them to deceive themselves, leading them through cycles of optimism and
pessimism. Ellsberg had been in the Marine Corps, worked for the Rand
Corporation, and served as special assistant for international security affairs, liaison
officer for the American embassy in Saigon, and member of Gelb's Study Task
Force. With Anthony J. Russo, another Rand employee, Ellsberg leaked the*
Pentagon Papers *to the* New York Times *in 1971.*

...[D]eceptive practices bring us...to the quagmire myth and to the question of
why it seems so plausible to the public.

From Daniel Ellsberg, "The Quagmire Myth and the Stalemate Machine," *Papers on the War*. Copyright © 1972 by Daniel Ellsberg. Reprinted by permission of Simon & Schuster, Inc.

Part of the answer is that the Presidents themselves choose to foster impressions, when new crises and requirements emerge, that their past Vietnam decision-making has been subject to a quicksand process.

This is the effect of repeatedly announcing very limited measures—usually less than is expected privately to be needed, sometimes less than is definitely planned—as if they were believed adequate to achieve ambitious publicly announced goals. By doing so they win public support for programs that will, in fact, assure avoidance of short-term defeat, though probably not much more than that; at the same time they avoid public pressures that could result from frankness on prospects, pressures either to take much riskier measures to win and get the problem over with, or to get out of Vietnam, accepting a defeat that might cut losses for the country but might mean eventual disaster for the Administration, even if the initial public reaction were relief. To these risks of candor, Presidents prefer the risks of concealment and deception.

They do so despite the unfavorable implications—when their aims appear repeatedly frustrated and "hopes" disappointed—of inadvertence, ignorance, inattention, lack of Presidential control, lack of realistic planning, lack of expertise, overly ambitious aims for the means used, overly optimistic expectations. They choose to encourage these particular criticisms—even when these are both damaging and misguided—because either a different substantive policy or a more accurate public understanding of their actual policy seems to them to pose even greater disadvantages and risks.

All very calculated, this. But, it turns out, this posture of secrecy and deception toward Congress and the public, maintained over time, takes its internal toll. An ironic result is that all of the above imputed flaws and limitations increasingly do characterize the Executive decision-making process. And for a number of reasons, as the chosen policy begins to be implemented, internal operational reporting, program analyses, and high-level expectations do gradually drift in the direction of the public optimism expressed constantly from the outset.

Thus real hopes—ill-founded hopes—follow hard upon the crisis choices, eventually replacing phony and invalid optimism with genuine invalid optimism.

Again, the aftermath of the November, 1961, decision is typical. Schlesinger reports it well: the striking advent of optimism in official expectations during 1962, a reversal which the public misread as a vindication of earlier estimates. U.S. combat troops, it now appeared, had not been "essential" after all. (If the President had, indeed, suspected that earlier, he was the only one who seemed vindicated.) But no recriminations blossomed in this atmosphere; only mutual congratulations that the long shot was paying off.[1]

Roger Hilsman reports a meeting in Honolulu in April, 1963:

General Harkins gave us all the facts and figures—the number of strategic hamlets established, number of Viet Cong killed, operations initiated by government forces, and so on. He could not, of course, he said,

---

[1] Arthur Schlesinger, Jr., *A Thousand Days: John F. Kennedy in the White House* (Boston: Houghton Mifflin, 1965), p. 508, and *The Bitter Heritage: Vietnam and American Democracy, 1941–1966* (Boston: Houghton Mifflin, 1967), pp. 41, 42.

give any guarantees, but he thought he could say that *by Christmas it would be all over*. The Secretary of Defense was elated. He reminded me that I had attended one of the very first of these meetings, *when it had all looked so black—and that had been only a year and a half ago.*[2]

Why the fast reversal? There were several reasons, none peculiar to this case. First, the new programs had been implemented in Vietnam by new American officials directed to carry them to success. They were as unaware as the public of the different recommendations made only a few months before by Taylor and others, and the pessimistic predictions made for the actual courses they were attempting to implement. The recommendations, in particular, had been "closely held" and later denied even within the system, so they were part of no institutional "memory" below the highest levels; and old intelligence estimates are rarely consulted by those with operational responsibilities. Ignorant of past predictions and current realities in Vietnam, they had no strong reason to assume that the tasks they had been given were infeasible with the means at hand. And they quickly learned that Washington tended to rely on reporting up through the chain of operational command; which is to say, their performance in their jobs would be evaluated by their own reports of "progress." As an American division commander told one of his district advisors, who insisted on reporting the persistent presence of unpacified VC hamlets in his area: "Son, you're writing our own report card in this country. Why are you failing us?"

Even when this did not lead to conscious dishonesty at the higher levels in Saigon, it created a bias toward accepting and reporting favorable information from subordinates and from their Vietnamese counterparts, neither of whom failed to provide it.

Thus, it was more mechanism than coincidence that in 1962 and early 1963, as Schlesinger notes, the strategy of unconditional support of Diem combined with the military advisor system seemed to be working—or so at least the senior American officials in Saigon assured the President.[3] Such assurances said nothing more than that the two officials themselves—Ambassador Nolting and General Harkins—were "working"—succeeding—in the two programs they had been sent by Kennedy respectively to manage:

> Ngo Dinh Nhu made the strategic hamlet program his personal project and published glowing reports of spectacular success. One might have wondered whether Nhu was just the man to mobilize the idealism of the villages; but Ambassador Nolting and General Harkins listened uncritically to his claims and passed them back to Washington as facts, where they were read with elation.[4]

One might also have wondered—but no one ever seemed to—whether Nhu was just the man uniquely to report upon "his personal project"; or whether Nolting was just the man to report the effects and value of reassuring Diem and Nhu, or Harkins the success of the military advisor system, their own respective personal projects.

---

[2] Roger Hilsman, *To Move a Nation* (New York: Doubleday, 1967), pp. 466–67.

[3] *The Bitter Heritage*, p. 45.

[4] *The Bitter Heritage*, p. 40.

But to emphasize the role of bureaucratic optimism in this process of internal self-deception is to underrate the influence of the President himself, and of his top advisors. They, too, like Nolting, Harkins, or Nhu, had their personal projects, larger ones, on which they reported to those who controlled their budgets and their tenure: Congress and the public. And they too, thanks to the security system and Executive privilege, "wrote their own report cards": with a little help from their subordinates.

Precisely as at lower levels, but with enormously broader impact, the needs of the President and the Secretaries of State and Defense to use "information" to reassure Congress and the public had its effect on the internal flow of information up to the President. Reports and analyses that supported the Administration's public position and could be released or leaked to that end were "helpful" and welcome, while "pessimism" was at best painful, less "useful," if not even dangerous to put down on paper. Executive values like these (vastly sharpened in 1966–1968, when skeptics and critics were more numerous and vocal, and had to be refuted) translate into powerful incentives at lower levels to give the Chief what he so obviously wants.

Moreover, human wishfulness, a factor at all levels, probably had its greatest impact at the highest. Repeatedly we have seen that a President felt compelled to adopt and promote policies that his chief advisors or official intelligence estimates told him were inadequate, while he told the public otherwise. He could only hope that these best-informed perceptions would prove wrong, and that what he had been telling the public would turn out, for the good of all, to have been correct. In hoping, one finds indications (especially from highly dependent subordinates) that support one's hopes.

At other levels, the same mechanisms. In periods like 1956 or 1962, when the policy "seemed to be working" despite its neglect of factors that had been considered by some experts critical to success, it was easy for all to doubt and gradually forget the earlier warnings. In general, pessimism regarding an ongoing policy is a fragile, unstable phenomenon within a large bureaucracy.

Ironically, even the VC and the GVN (earlier, the Viet Minh and French) played their roles, too, in providing indicators of allied "progress" and intervals when things "seemed to be working." In 1951, 1956, 1962, and 1965, bureaucratic optimism was catalyzed by the actual effects of the new programs on allies and opponents in the desired direction. "In the field," these effects proved very temporary, whereas our reading of them did not. As Kennedy had predicted, the effects of any one "small drink" on friend and opponent faded quickly. What he may not fully have foreseen was the far more lasting afterglow in our own system.

In each case, the aftermath of escalation was an increased emphasis on military factors, and an accompanying alteration of mood from gloom to elation. Thus, when U.S. combat units flooded into Vietnam from 1965 on, the pessimism of late 1964 gave way increasingly to buoyant hopes by 1967 of a military victory, just as it had in the past, as early as 1951, after U.S. matériel and American liaison teams had made their way to Tonkin to join a failing French effort.[5]

---

[5] See Senator John F. Kennedy's speech in 1954, cited in Schlesinger, *The Bitter Heritage*, p. 27, on official optimism underlying a Truman-Eisenhower "credibility gap" in Indochina.

Meanwhile, the Viet Minh, and later the VC, had a characteristic response to a new U.S./GVN strategy or to an escalation of our involvement which further encouraged our shift to unbounded optimism. After suffering initial setbacks, they would lie low for an extended period, gather data, analyze experience, develop, test, and adapt new strategies, then plan and prepare carefully before launching them. (Nothing, our Vietnam experience tells us, could be more un-American.)

Since so great a part of U.S. and GVN knowledge of enemy activities comes from operational contacts, there seems to be an irresistible tendency for U.S. commanders to believe that data concerning contacts reveals enemy capabilities, i.e., that lessened VC combat operations indicate lessened capability. Another mechanism, then: U.S. optimism grows during VC "inactivity"—periods when VC activities are of a sort we do not observe—reaching a peak, ironically, when extreme VC quiescence reflects intense preparations for an explosion.

Crisis periods, then, are typically preceded by high points in U.S. official expectations. Thus, peaks of U.S. optimism occurred in late 1953 (just before Dien Bien Phu), 1958 (when guerrilla warfare was about to recommence), early 1963 (when the VC had been studying the vulnerabilities of the strategic hamlet program, and meanwhile infiltrating massively), and late 1967 (during last-minute recruiting and preparations for the Tet offensive, including feints at the borders).

If a fever chart of U.S. expectations could be drawn meaningfully for the last twenty years, it would have a recurrent sawtooth shape: an accelerating rise of optimism just before an abrupt decline (Figure 1 is a conceptual sketch of such a graph).[6] Our perceptual and emotional experience in Vietnam can be regarded as a sequence of two-phase cycles, in which Phase B—optimism—evolves causally in large part from decisions that follow Phase A, a crisis period of pessimism.

(The B-phases in Figure 1 have been drawn with a reverse S-shape, signifying three subphases: an initial period in which the VC suffers real reverses and the GVN stabilizes on the basis of new programs; then a period in which, in reality, the VC have adapted and the GVN is declining, but U.S. expectations remain at a plateau instead of being reduced; finally, a period when the VC begin quietly preparing for a major offensive, causing U.S. hopes to soar.)

If major escalating decisions—enlarging the nature of our involvement, not merely the scale—had actually been made during the B-phases, that would conform to the quagmire model. This has never been the case.

However, although no new major policies or commitments are introduced during the B-phases, U.S. aims may change significantly in the atmosphere of optimism, especially in the last stage, going beyond the goal of avoiding defeat (dominant aim in Phase A and the early Phase B) to that of achieving a victory. At the same time, real optimism leads officials to be much less cautious in public aims and predictions; to give commanders more leeway; to monitor operations less closely; and to indulge in operations that are costly (in many terms) and of low effectiveness but that may speed the coming win. All of these responses lead to toleration of

---

[6] The question mark placed at the end of the latest Phase B when this graph was first drawn (in September, 1970) can now be replaced by the heading: NVA offensive, April, 1972.

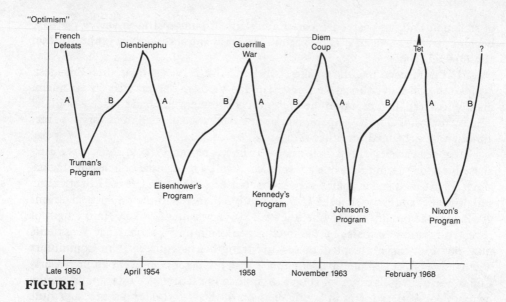

FIGURE 1

rapidly rising costs, and hence to a feeling, when a new crisis brings the return of Phase A, that the stakes, the investment, the commitment have become still higher than before, the need to avoid "defeat" being now even greater.

Nevertheless, this post-escalation euphoria, or "quagmire phase" of the cycle, seems to play no essential role in the escalation process. It simply reinforces the Presidential tendency to escalate if and as necessary to avoid an imminent "defeat." As Leslie Gelb has put it: "Each Administration was prepared to pay the costs it could foresee for itself." Political, along with strategic, motives underlying that tendency were already strong enough in 1950 to induce the initial U.S. commitment without any prior or current period of American optimism. And they almost surely were felt strongly enough in subsequent years to have induced much greater escalation than occurred if that had appeared both necessary and effective in the short run.

Consciously oriented as escalating decisions actually were, when chosen, to the defensive aim of averting an immediate Communist takeover, *each of these decisions of the past two decades can be said to have achieved its initial, internal aim.*

In Gelb's phrase: "The system worked," not in terms of publicly avowed long-range aims, but in terms of the successive short-range aims and expectations that were actually—it is inferred here—salient in the White House. In fact, these Presidential policies and tactics, in sequence, had the effect of holding South Vietnam out of Communist hands "cheaply"—i.e., without sizable numbers of U.S. combat troops—for fifteen years, from 1950 to 1965.

Whether efforts and sacrifices, by Americans and Vietnamese, of even these limited but increasing magnitudes could easily have been justified to various parts of the electorate in terms of such limited aims—in starkest terms, the restoration of stalemate and the postponement of a possible Communist takeover in Vietnam beyond the date of the next U.S. election—is another question. No Administration chose to find out.

In this respect, too, the policies "worked." Until 1968 at least, each President avoided the kinds of political damages related to Vietnam that his tactics were meant mainly to avert. In fact, up to the present, no President has had to face a political penalty for losing South Vietnam. Not even LBJ will be blamed in history for that, although he is blamed for other things.

Yet the earlier "cheap victories" year by year from 1950 to 1965, were purchased at a long-term price, one not yet paid in full. Presidential policies and tactics actively sustained and encouraged over that period a high estimate of U.S. strategic stakes in the conflict within the U.S. Executive branch and the military, the Congress, and the public. Meanwhile, they failed—as was highly likely, in the light of repeated internal estimates by the intelligence community, though the Presidents may not fully have accepted these—to strengthen adequately non-Communist Vietnamese efforts; to modify Communist aims; to deter or prevent an increase in Communist capabilities; or, of course, to induce the acceptance by Hanoi's leaders or the revolutionary forces in South Vietnam of the U.S. role, presence, and aims in South Vietnam, or those of the U.S.-supported Saigon regime.

Thus, a hypothetical observer who adopted the view of Presidential motives presented here, and at the same time accepted the view of GVN and DRV/VC behavior regularly presented by the intelligence community, could have calculated during most of that fifteen-year period that there was a high probability that large numbers of U.S. troops would end up fighting in South Vietnam, with U.S. planes bombing throughout Indochina. He would have predicted that they would be sent if necessary to avert defeat, and that they would be necessary.

This is what is meant by saying that there is, I believe, a mechanism at work, a "stalemate machine": not perfectly determinate, but with stable tendencies well-enough established so that one can say usefully, on the basis of an understanding of it, *how to bet*, at various moments and with respect to various activities.

This is *not* to say that any of the Presidents concerned would have bet the same way, with respect to the long run: i.e., that they accepted this model of the "stalemate machine." Almost surely they did not. For example, George Ball is quoted as having told President Kennedy in 1961 that General Taylor's 8,000-man task force "could lead in five years' time to an involvement of 300,000 men." The President answered him, "George, you're crazy as hell!"[7]

Four years later, Ball told Kennedy's successor, on the eve (July 1, 1965) of President Johnson's decision to expand from 75,000 men to an open-ended commitment:

> The South Vietnamese are losing the war to the Viet Cong. No one can
> assure you that we can beat the Viet Cong or even force them to the
> conference table on our terms, no matter how many hundred thousand

[7] Martin Agronsky, TV broadcast, June 27, 1971.

white, foreign (U.S.) troops we deploy.... The decision you face now, therefore, is crucial. Once large numbers of U.S. troops are committed to direct combat...[and] once we suffer large casualties, we will have started a well-nigh irreversible process. Our involvement will be so great that we cannot—without national humiliation—stop short of achieving our complete objectives. *Of the two possibilities I think humiliation would be more likely than the achievement of our objectives—even after we have paid terrible costs.* [*PP*, IV, 615–16; italics added.]

The President's answer, if any, is not recorded.

So the future, and even the process, was visible—to some officials. Why not to the Presidents? Probably for two reasons. Ball stressed the first of these as he explained to Agronsky Kennedy's answer to his prediction:

What he was saying to me was—look, I'm not going to do this, I'm not going to let it escalate. I think that he was aware of the fact that when he moved up from the 600 to 700 advisors that we had [to] a very much larger number that he might be starting a process. But I think that he felt that it was a process that he could control.

Johnson in mid-'65, on the other hand, knew he was taking no "small step," knew he was starting a process not easily controlled, and knew that the intelligence analysts offered little promise of victory ever, while no one (except, most of the time, Walt Rostow) promised it quickly. But in terms of his longer-range expectations, Schlesinger's guess about Johnson is probably right:

I still believe he found it viscerally inconceivable that what Walt Rostow kept telling him was "the greatest power in the world" could not dispose of a collection of night-riders in black pajamas.[8]

Thus, neither of these Presidents chose "knowingly"[9] the actual future of a half-million U.S. troops and twelve million tons of shells and bombs. Contrary to the quagmire model, they did know at the moment of their escalating decisions that new crises or challenges to larger efforts would *probably* return. But each of them undoubtedly believed—like Truman and Eisenhower before them—that at some stage long before the actual 1968–72 levels of violence were reached he, or his successor, would have chosen *either* to Win or to Leave: i.e., would have finally accepted one of the two alternatives both of which he was postponing at the moment in favor of Staying: avoiding defeat, regaining a stalemate. What none probably imagined was that he himself, and his successors, would go on making the same conceptual choice again and again—Winning always looking too risky or infeasible, the other side never cracking; but it seeming always the wrong time to Leave. None may have guessed that "buying time," postponing a defeat, would *always* look like

[8] "The Quagmire Papers (Cont.)," *New York Review of Books*, December 16, 1971, p. 41.

[9] My use of this word in the earlier version of this paper was somewhat misconstrued by Schlesinger (in "Eyeless in Indochina," *New York Review of Books*, October 21, 1971, pp. 23–32) but it was, I now feel, misleading; and I am indebted to Schlesinger's critique, and to several conversations with him, for stimulating me to rethink and modify this passage.

a lesser evil to an American President than ending the war as a failure, despite escalation of the stalemate and of the human costs to awful levels.

So we need not infer of any of our five Presidents who have made this war that he acted in full knowledge or acceptance of what it would finally mean to America and Indochina; just that at each juncture in the quarter-century, each chose knowingly to *prolong* the war, and in most cases to expand it. Each always paid the necessary price—in the lives and resources of others—to "stay in the game," always preserving the options to go Up while making it more costly and unlikely for himself and his successors ever to go Out. That pattern covers a generation of Presidents; all the Presidents within the lifetime of a recent college graduate.

Will the tradition of choosing probable stalemate end with the current President? How many more could it encompass? Nothing in the generalizations we have abstracted in this paper from the experience of the last two decades gives a clear hint of a definite breaking point, or a foreseeable change in basic motives and values either for the Communist-led forces or the U.S. Government. That may be a limitation of the analysis, a characteristic—perhaps a defect—of the model suggested.

But perhaps it is a property of reality.

If so, it is a human and political reality, and humans can, in principle, change it. But change would not be easy. Rule 1 has deep roots in politicians' fears and motives, and in public responses, that have been powerfully influential for twenty years, through some hard times and challenges. There is little indication yet that it will not speak commandingly to Presidents after this one. (Of its authority for the present one, there can be no real doubt.)[10]

Improved Presidential foresight—even the awareness that might be attained from this analysis—would not probably supersede Rule 1. If anything, it might serve to relax the constraining influence of Rule 2.*

In the spring of 1965 President Johnson is reported to have received calls almost daily from one of his closest advisers, telling him (what no one had to tell him): "Lyndon, don't be the first American President to lose a war."

It is true that such advisers omitted warnings of other deadly errors. They neglected to caution him: Don't, over more than one or two years, lie to the public; or mislead and bypass Congress; or draft and spend and kill and suffer casualties at the rate your military will propose; or abort negotiations; or, even once, allow your generals to describe the enemy as defeated on the eve of their major offensive.[11]

---

[10] The discussion has gone only through 1968; no attempt is made here to apply the conjectures and generalizations of this paper to the statements and actions of the current Administration. That is left as an exercise to the reader.

Nothing in the past attitudes and history of the current President, or any of his public statements or official actions so far in office, suggests in any way that these generalizations should be less applicable to him than to any of his predecessors; thus this extrapolation should be a fair test. One might, for example, address the question: Which year between now and 1977 might Richard Milhous Nixon consider an acceptable one, for him, to lose South Vietnam to Communist control?

*[Rule 1 = Do not lose Vietnam to communism before the next election. Rule 2 = Do not commit U.S. troops to a land war in Asia.—Ed. note]

[11] No advisor is perfect. There are things Presidents have to learn for themselves. One supposes no one told President Nixon, before the event: "Don't condone the shooting of white students by National

But if they had, and if he had seen the cogency of their warning: Would he then have decided to lose the war? Or would he, mindful of the time constraints, have tried to *win* it within them? The same question applies to earlier Presidents; and later.

Theodore Draper has observed of the Bay of Pigs that it was that rare political/military event, "a perfect failure." If U.S. policy in Vietnam is at all to be seen as a tragedy—rather than a mechanical process, or a criminal one—it might be because its failures have all been imperfect: a series of achievements seen by our Presidents as adequate—though limited and temporary—successes as well as partial failures, each drawing them ever deeper into...a Sea of Pigs.

THE FACES IN THE QUAGMIRE

Looking at where their policies and tactics have brought us so far, it is easy to understand why the past four Presidents would want, before and after, to conceal and deprecate their own foreknowledge and intentions.[12] And it is no harder to guess why—perhaps unconsciously—participant-observers of one or another of these Administrations have promoted the same lenient interpretation of foresight and purpose, values and priorities, influence and responsibility, respecting their past colleagues within and outside government. Indeed, they make no secret of the conclusion they wish to convey by the quagmire metaphor and model concerning the responsibility of individuals and groups.

Thus, Townsend Hoopes, acutely and perceptively critical of the policies under Johnson and earlier Presidents, extends what Richard Falk has called "the circle of responsibility" widely indeed, in explicit purpose to relieve the burden of those seemingly at its center. Traumatized by a suggestion made by two reporters from the *Village Voice* that he himself, as Assistant Secretary of the Air Force under Johnson, might have been guilty of war crimes (their subsequent article was titled: "The War Criminals Hedge Their Bets"),[13] Hoopes has published several rejoinders and discussions of the problem of responsibility. In the first of these, he describes his chief concern in the disturbing conversation to be "the broad question of how the *entire nation* had stumbled down the long slippery slope of self-delusion into the engulfing morass." Hoopes then concludes:

> The tragic story of Vietnam is not, in truth, a tale of malevolent men
> bent upon conquest for personal gain or imperial glory. It is the story
> of an entire generation of leaders (and an entire generation of
> followers).... [Johnson's] principal advisers were, almost uniformly,

Guardsmen just after crossing a national border with troops without consulting Congress, the public, or the country invaded."

[12] No event, and no Presidential decision, of course, occurred because it "had" to, in any sense of certainty or absolute determinism. What does? On the other hand, in every major case, from the perspective of existing, inside knowledge and opinion years earlier, what actually occurred in the way of Presidential decision and of resulting developments in Vietnam would have seemed the way to bet.

[13] Judith Coburn and Geoffrey Cowan, *Village Voice*, December 4, 1969.

those considered when they took office to be among the ablest, the best, the most humane and liberal men that could be found for public trust. No one doubted their honest, high-minded pursuit of the best interests of their country, and indeed of the whole non-Communist world, as they perceived those interests.[14]

Arthur Schlesinger, Jr., less generous in his appreciation of some of Kennedy's and Johnson's civilian lieutenants, is no less reluctant to single out them or their Chief as "guilty" in any special way for their role in our vast national undertaking. In the "quagmire" (literally, "morass") passage previously cited in this paper, he asserts:

It is not only idle but unfair to seek out guilty men. . . . We find ourselves entrapped today in . . . a war which no President, including President Johnson, desired or intended. The Vietnam story is *a tragedy without villains*. No thoughtful American can withhold sympathy as President Johnson ponders the gloomy choices which lie ahead.[15]

One can read some of these passages as reflections of the sentiment Hoopes expresses: "What the country needs is not retribution, but therapy. . . ." (It is just possible that both are needed, at this point, in the interests of our country and of others.) He completes the sentence, plausibly—"therapy in the form of deeper understanding of our problems and each other"; but in all of these passages and the larger arguments in which they are embedded, one senses that the drive to exculpate, to ward off retribution, is seriously setting back the cause of understanding.

Both the substance of the tentative conclusions in this paper, and my experience of the heuristic process that gradually pointed toward them, warn that a deeper analytical understanding of these well-guarded data and controverted events is not likely to be reached by a searcher committed and determined to see the conflict and our part in it as "a tragedy without villains": war crimes without criminals, lies without liars, a process of immaculate deception.

Many former officials are particularly concerned to defend American institutions and legitimate authority (and surely some of their leaders and colleagues, if not themselves) from the most extreme charges and sanctions: "Lyndon Johnson,

[14] Townsend Hoopes, "The Nuremberg Suggestion," *Washington Monthly*, December, 1969; italics added. Reprinted, with reply, in "The Hoopes Defense," by Judith Coburn and Geoffrey Cowan, *Village Voice*, January 29, 1970. See also the cogent comment by lawyer Peter Weiss (with reply by Hoopes), *Washington Monthly*, June, 1970, pp. 4–8.

In none of his comments (nor in his later *Foreign Affairs* article, "Legacy of the Cold War in Indochina," July, 1970) does Hoopes dissent from this general evaluation of the aims and values of the Johnson advisers, although it would seem fair to reexamine these on the basis of their official performance as it becomes increasingly known, and on their sense of social responsibility for events, shown after leaving office.

[15] *The Bitter Heritage*, pp. 47, 48; italics added. Schlesinger's more recent comments, quoted earlier— "At every stage of our descent into the quagmire, the military have played the dominant role. . . . At each point along the ghastly way, the generals promised . . ."—do, of course, add villains to the tragedy, although not civilian ones. If he no longer thinks it idle to seek out guilty men, he has nevertheless managed to be unfair.

though disturbingly volatile," Hoopes remarks, "was not in his worst moments an evil man in the Hitlerian sense." This leads them as analysts to adopt and promulgate a view of the process, roles, and motives involved that is grossly mistaken—as should be known to them from their own experience and access to information as officials.

Thus, an effort—in alleged pursuit of "objective judgment"—to defend against self-perceptions or accusations by others of "immorality" leads in this case to historical and analytical error. And it has political consequences: It underwrites deceits that have served importantly a succession of Presidents to maintain support for their substantive policies of intervention in Vietnam.

Of course, to promulgate a view is not necessarily to have it accepted. But this one has a powerful appeal. We can suspect that the quagmire image speaks for deeper, more emotional concerns when it is presented regularly in the broad strokes of political cartoons in mass-circulation newspapers. That was particularly evident on the nation's editorial pages during the Cambodian invasion.

That week, while photographs on the front page showed unwonted images of *blitzkrieg*—tanks in formation driving across fields trailing plumes of dust, and locust swarms of American armed helicopters moving across new borders—and while reporters offered verbal pictures of the Cambodian village of Snoul being destroyed and looted, the drawings on the editorial pages were of Uncle Sam's and GI Joe's engulfed, bemused, floundering from a swamp marked "Vietnam" to one marked "Cambodia." Images, curiously, of impotence, passivity: ironically contrasting both with the news and the photographs of what Americans in Southeast Asia were actually doing and with the President's announced intent to expunge any notions of America as a "pitiful, helpless giant."

One cartoon, reproduced in *Time,* showed the "U.S. citizen" in tatters on a raft, confronting three enormous, wide-mouthed whales, labeled: "Vietnam," "Cambodia," and "Laos."

Whales?

The imagery, pressed far enough, reveals its key. The relative scale of the parties, and the direction of the menace, have simply been reversed. The actual role of America and Americans in and toward Indochina has been distorted, to a staggering degree, in the very process of suggesting that it be reconsidered. And looking back to the quicksand cartoons, one sees their self-pity, their preoccupation with Uncle Sam's predicament, and one finally asks: Where are the Asians? Where are the Cambodians, the Laotians, the Vietnamese in these drawings?

Presumably—there is no other sign—they are the particles of the bog, bits of the porridgey quagmire that has seized GI Joe and will not free him. . . .

It is not, after all, only Presidents and Cabinet members who have a powerful need and reason to deny their responsibility for this war. And who succeed at it. It is true that the fact of Executive deception gives the quagmire model a reality with respect to the *public,* and even the Congress, that it lacks for the Presidents; the responsibility of those lied to—even given a persistent "need-not-to-know"—is not as great as that of the liars. Nevertheless, just as Presidents and their partisans find comfort and political safety in the quicksand image of the *President-as-victim,* so Americans at large are reassured in sudden moments of doubt by the same image drawn large, *America-as-victim*. It is no more real than the first, and neither national understanding nor extrication truly lie that way.

To understand the war process as it emerges in the documents behind public statements, the concerns never written down that moved decisions, the history scratched on the minds of bureaucrats: to translate that understanding into images that can guide actions related closely to reality, one must begin by seeing that it is Americans, our leaders and ourselves, that build the bog, a trap much more for other victims: *our* policies, our politics the quagmire in which Indochina drowns.

PART FOUR

The Buck Stops Here
The President as Primary Cause

Kings had always been involving and impoverishing their people in wars....This our Convention understood to be the most oppressive of all kingly oppressions.

—Abraham Lincoln, 1848

A constitutional principle is involved. It is dangerous to give to any President an unchecked power...to make war.

—Senator Wayne Morse, 1965

The Executive can bootstrap the nation into any war by sending one American soldier into hostile territory....The Vietnam war escalated in precisely this context.

—Legal brief, *Berk v. Laird*, 1970

22

JFK: A "CAN-DO" PRESIDENT

THOMAS G. PATERSON, J. GARRY CLIFFORD, AND KENNETH J. HAGAN

In their popular textbook on American foreign policy, Thomas G. Paterson, J. Garry Clifford, and Kenneth J. Hagan saw the period of John F. Kennedy's presidential term from 1961 to 1963 as pivotal to American involvement in Vietnam. To them JFK was a President who shared with other Presidents a belief in counterrevolution, globalism, the domino principle, and other tenets of the cold war mind-set. In addition, JFK brought a verve, charisma, and romantic toughness to the executive office, along with a strategy of counterinsurgency, a policy of nation building, and a group of "action intellectuals" who possessed a can-do confidence in their ability to handle the crisis in Vietnam.

...Kennedy said he did not mind being called Truman with a Harvard accent. Born in 1917 to wealthy, Catholic, politically active parents, John Fitzgerald Kennedy graduated from Harvard College and served with honor in World War II. In 1940, at the time his father was ambassador to Great Britain, his senior thesis was published as *Why England Slept*, with the theme that England should have demonstrated a willingness to use force in resisting Nazi aggression, rather than embracing weakness. For Kennedy's generation, the Munich agreement became the "Munich syndrome" or appeasement lesson. During the Cuban Missile Crisis, Kennedy tapped that historical legacy for a policy rationale: "The 1930s taught us a clear lesson: aggressive conduct, if allowed to go unchecked and unchallenged, ultimately leads to war."[1] He also remembered the experience of the 1940s. As presidential assistant and grand theorist Walt Whitman Rostow reported, the "first charge of the Kennedy

From *American Foreign Policy*, vol. II by Thomas G. Paterson, J. Garry Clifford, and Kenneth J. Hagan. Copyright © 1988 by D. C. Heath and Company. Reprinted by permission of the publisher.

[1] *Public Papers, John F. Kennedy, 1962* (Washington: Government Printing Office, 1963), p. 807.

Administration in 1961—somewhat like the challenge faced by the Truman Administration in 1947—was to turn back the Communist offensive."[2] History both tugged at the Kennedy advisers and pushed them.

So did the distinctive style and personality of the young President. "All at once you had something exciting," recalled a student campaigner in comparing the Eisenhower and Kennedy days. "You had a young guy who had kids, and who liked to play football on his front lawn. He was a real human being. He was talking about pumping some new life into the country... just giving the whole country a real shakedown and a new image.... Everything they did showed that America was alive and active.... To run a country it takes more than just mechanics. It takes a psychology."[3] Call it psychology, charisma, charm, image, mystique, or cult, Kennedy had it. Photogenic and quick-witted, he became a television star. Observers marveled at his speed-reading abilities. Decrying softness in the American people, he challenged their egos by launching a physical fitness program. Handsome, articulate, ingratiating, dynamic, energetic, competitive, athletic, cultured, bright, self-confident, cool, analytical, mathematical, zealous—these were the traits universally ascribed to the President. People often listened not to what he said, but to how he said it, and he usually said it with verve and conviction. He simply overwhelmed. Dean Rusk remembered him as an "incandescent man. He was on fire, and he set people around him on fire."[4] For historian-politician and presidential assistant Arthur M. Schlesinger, Jr., JFK had "enormous confidence in his own luck," and "everyone around him thought he had the Midas touch and could not lose."[5]

Style and personality are usually important to the conduct of diplomacy; how we behave obviously affects how others read us and respond to us, and our personal characteristics and needs generate measurable behavior. Many of his friends have commented that John F. Kennedy was driven by a desire for power, because power ensured winning. Furthermore, he personalized issues, converting them into tests of will. Diplomacy became a matter of crises and races. His father, Joseph P. Kennedy, demanded excellence. As political scientist James Barber has pointed out, old Joe "pressed his children hard to compete, never to be satisfied with anything but first place. The point was not just to try; the point was to win."[6] John developed a thirst for victory and a self-image as the vigorous man. Aroused in the campaign of the 1960 by the stings of anti-Catholic bias, by misplaced right-wing charges that he was soft on communism, and by his narrow victory over Nixon, Kennedy, once in office, seemed eager to prove his toughness. He took up challenges with zest and soon Americans watched for box scores on the missile race, the arms race, and the space race. Kennedy and his advisers, it seems, thought that Premier Nikita Khrushchev and the Russians were testing them as men. In early

---

[2] Walt W. Rostow, "The Third Round," *Foreign Affairs*, XLII (October, 1963), 5-6.

[3] Don Ferguson in Peter Joseph, *Good Times: An Oral History of America in the Nineteen Sixties* (New York: William Morrow, 1974), p. 4.

[4] *Ibid.*, p. 54.

[5] Arthur M. Schlesinger, Jr., *A Thousand Days: John F. Kennedy in the White House* (Boston: Houghton Mifflin, 1965), p. 259.

[6] James Barber, *The Presidential Character* (Englewood Cliffs, N.J.: Prentice-Hall, 1972), p. 298.

1961, when they discussed the possibility of a summit meeting with Khrushchev, Kennedy asserted that "I have to show him that we can be as tough as he is.... I'll have to sit down with him, and let him see who he's dealing with."[7] John F. Kennedy and his aides feared to be thought fearful.

With these psychic needs and with their high intellectual talents, the Kennedy officials came to Washington, "swashbuckling" and suffering from "auto-intoxication," commented one observer.[8] Cocky, thinking themselves the "right" people, they were, as skeptical Under Secretary of State Chester Bowles later complained, "sort of looking for a chance to prove their muscle." They were "full of belligerence."[9] Schlesinger captured the mood: "Euphoria reigned; we thought for a moment that the world was plastic and the future unlimited."[10] Kennedy's alarmist Inaugural Address reflected the new spirit. Its swollen Cold War language was matched only by its pompous phrasing: "the torch has been passed to a new generation." He paid homage to historical memories when he noted that his generation had been "tempered by war" and "disciplined by a hard and bitter peace." Then came those moving, but in hindsight rather frightening words: "Let every nation know that we shall pay any price, bear any burden, meet any hardship, support any friend, oppose any foe to assure the survival and the success of liberty."[11] No halfway measures here. Kennedy and his assistants, impatient and tough, thought they could lick anything—or anyone.

The Kennedy people considered themselves "can-do" types, who with rationality and careful calculation could revive an ailing nation and world. Theodore H. White tagged them "the Action Intellectuals."[12] "Management" became one of the catchwords of the time. With adequate data, and they had an inordinate faith in data, they were certain they could succeed. When an heretical White House assistant attempted to persuade Secretary of Defense Robert McNamara, the "whiz kid" from the Ford Motor Company, that the Vietnam venture was doomed, the efficiency-minded McNamara shot back: "Where is your data? Give me something I can put in the computer. Don't give me your poetry."[13] There were dangers in a heavy reliance on quantified information. "Ah, *les statistiques*," said a Vietnamese general to an American official. "We Vietnamese can give him [McNamara] all he wants. If you want them to go up, they will go up. If you want them to go down, they will go down."[14] Nonetheless, with its faith in formulas and the computer, the Kennedy "can-do" team brought a freshness to American foreign policy, if not in substance, at least in slogans: "The Grand Design" for Europe; the "New Africa"

---

[7] Quoted in Kenneth P. O'Donnell and David F. Powers, *"Johnny, We Hardly Knew Ye": Memoirs of John Fitzgerald Kennedy* (Boston: Little, Brown, 1972), p. 287.

[8] Midge Decter, "Kennedyism," *Commentary*, XLIX (January, 1970), 21.

[9] Oral History Interview by Chester Bowles, pp. 49, 90, John F. Kennedy Library, Massachusetts.

[10] Schlesinger, *A Thousand Days*, p. 217.

[11] *Public Papers, Kennedy, 1961* (Washington: Government Printing Office, 1962), pp. 1–3.

[12] Theodore H. White, "The Action Intellectuals," *Life*, LXII (June, 1967), 43.

[13] Quoted in David Halberstam, "The Programming of Robert McNamara," *Harper's Magazine*, CCXLII (February, 1971), 62.

[14] Quoted in Roger Hilsman, *To Move a Nation: The Politics of Foreign Policy in the Administration of John F. Kennedy* (Garden City, N.Y.: Doubleday, 1967), p. 523.

policy; "Flexible Response" for the military; the "Alliance for Progress" for Latin America; and the "New Frontier" at home.

Kennedy's Secretary of State, Dean Rusk, was somewhat uneasy with the crusading "action intellectuals," but he was a loyal member of the team. A Rhodes Scholar, Rusk had been a military intelligence officer in Asia during World War II, a political science instructor, an assistant secretary of state under Truman, and in the 1950s president of the Rockefeller Foundation. Truman warhorses Robert Lovett and Dean Acheson enthusiastically recommended Rusk to Kennedy, who liked Rusk's quiet, modest, and unflappable manner. The President wanted to design his own foreign policy and did not desire a secretary of state who was too independent-minded or outspoken. The relatively unknown Rusk fit the bill. "The gentle, gracious Rusk," presidential assistant Theodore C. Sorenson later noted, "deferred almost too amiably to White House initiatives and interference."[15] . . .

Continued unrest in Laos and Vietnam placed those Asian trouble spots high on the "action intellectuals'" list for the remedial magic of counterinsurgency and nation building. Rostow saw an opportunity to use "our unexploited counterguerrilla assets"—helicopters and Special Forces units. "In Knute Rockne's old phrase," he told President Kennedy, "we are not saving them for the Junior Prom."[16] The landlocked agricultural nation of Laos, wracked by civil war, seemed to provide a testing ground. Granted independence at Geneva in 1954, Laos chose neutralism in the Cold War when nationalist leader Souvanna Phouma organized a coalition government of neutralists and the pro-Communist Pathet Lao in 1957. The Eisenhower Administration opposed the neutralist government and initiated a major military aid program to build up the rightist and corrupt Laotian army; by 1961, $300 million had been spent. The money helped only slightly to improve the army's desire or ability to fight, but it did disrupt the Laotian economy through inflation and graft. In 1958 CIA-funded rightists helped displace Souvanna and shape a pro-American government without Pathet Lao participation. Washington soon dispatched military advisers to the new but shaky regime.

Souvanna Phouma returned to power after a coup in August, 1960, but the United States undermined him by again equipping rightist forces. Seeking a counterweight to American influence, Souvanna received assistance from Moscow and North Vietnam. But in December he fled his country. "The Americans say I am a Communist," he sighed. "All this is heartbreaking. How can they think I am a Communist? I am looking for a way to keep Laos non-Communist."[17] Unwilling to accept neutralism, the United States had helped convert a civil war into a big power confrontation. For Eisenhower the problem was simple: "the fall of Laos to Communism would mean the subsequent fall—like a tumbling row of dominoes—of its still-free neighbors, Cambodia and South Vietnam and, in all probability, Thailand and Burma. Such a chain of events would open the way to Communist

---

[15] Theodore C. Sorensen, *Kennedy* (New York: Harper & Row, 1965), p. 270.

[16] Memorandum for the President by Walt W. Rostow, March 29, 1961, Box 193, National Security Files, Kennedy Papers, Kennedy Library.

[17] Quoted in Schlesinger, *A Thousand Days*, p. 330.

seizure of all Southeast Asia."[18] The neutralists and the Pathet Lao, it appeared to Eisenhower, were simply part of a global Communist conspiracy.

The incoming Kennedy Administration did not perceive the Laotian problem much differently, although Kennedy was miffed over having to deal with it. In a re-phrasing of the "domino theory," adviser Arthur M. Schlesinger, Jr. later explained that "If Laos was not precisely a dagger pointed at the heart of Kansas, it was very plainly a gateway to Southeast Asia."[19] In March Kennedy blotched the historical record by blaming the Pathet Lao for preventing the creation of a neutral Laos. As conspicuous Soviet aid flowed to the Pathet Lao, Kennedy determined to halt the im-minent collapse of the pro-American government. He ordered the Seventh Fleet into the South China Sea, alerted American forces in Okinawa, and moved 500 Marines with helicopters into Thailand a short distance from the Laotian capital. Then the Bay of Pigs disaster struck. Fearing to appear weak with one arm tied down in Cuba, Ken-nedy flexed the other in Laos. The President instructed the several hundred American military advisers in Laos, heretofore involved in covert operations, to discard their civilian clothes and dress in more ostentatious military uniforms as a symbol of Amer-ican resolve. The Soviets wanted no fight in Laos. In April, 1961 they endorsed Kennedy's appeal for a cease-fire. But the Soviets were unable to control the indepen-dent-minded Pathet Lao, who battled on. Kennedy asked the joint chiefs of staff if an American military expedition could succeed. The military experts demurred. However, "if we are given the right to use nuclear weapons," remarked JCS Chair-man General Lyman L. Lemnitzer, "we can guarantee victory."[20] Somebody in the room incredulously suggested the President ask the general what he meant by "vic-tory." Kennedy adjourned the meeting, wondering what to do.

The answer came in Geneva, where a conference on Laos began in May, 1961. Although it took deft diplomatic pressure from W. Averell Harriman, continued bloodshed in Laos, and hard bargaining lasting until June, 1962, the major powers did sign a Laotian agreement. Laos would be neutral; it could not enter military alliances or permit foreign military bases on its soil. Souvanna Phouma headed the new government. Bernard Fall, veteran observer of Southeast Asia, measured the results of the United States involvement in Laos by looking at the difference be-tween the neutralist government of the 1950s that the United States had subverted and that of 1962: "Instead of two communists in Cabinet positions, there would be four now; instead of having to deal with 1,500 poorly armed Pathet Lao fighters, there were close to 10,000 now well-armed with new Soviet weapons."[21] Still, peace did not come to that ravaged land. In late 1962, in clear violation of the agreement it had just signed, Washington secretly began arms shipments to Souvanna's gov-ernment, which increasingly turned to the right. The pretext was the presence of

[18] Dwight D. Eisenhower, *The White House Years: Waging Peace, 1956–1961* (Garden City, N.Y.: Doubleday, 1965), p. 607.

[19] Schlesinger, *A Thousand Days*, p. 324.

[20] Quoted *ibid.*, p. 338.

[21] Bernard Fall, *Anatomy of a Crisis: The Laotian Crisis of 1960-1961* (Garden City, N.Y.: Doubleday, 1969), p. 229.

small numbers of North Vietnamese soldiers in the north, but it seems evident that Washington had not given up its goal of building a sturdy pro-American outpost in Indochina. Unbeknownst to the American people, the United States began in 1964 secret bombing raids against Pathet Lao forces, after a right-wing coup had diminished Souvanna's authority. By then Laos' major problem was that it lay too close to Vietnam, where American intervention had also escalated under Kennedy.

"This is the worst one we've got, isn't it," Kennedy asked Rostow. "You know, Eisenhower never mentioned it. He talked at length about Laos, but never uttered the word Vietnam."[22] For the next decade Vietnam would indeed become America's "worst one." Some Kennedy watchers have suggested that his intervention in Vietnam and his bold action in the Cuban missile crisis stemmed from his reaction to the criticism of the joint chiefs of staff and such hawks as columnist Joseph Alsop that he had weakened over Laos, and that, in turn, his success in the missile episode further emboldened him in Vietnam. Whatever the relationship of events, Kennedy shared America's antirevolutionary and globalist attitudes. Early in his Administration he decided to apply counterinsurgency methods in Vietnam to gain a triumph over communism. Washington soon kept a "box score" on counterinsurgency efforts. Vietnam was beset by a nasty civil war between the National Liberation Front and the Diem regime. The Kennedy advisers considered the conservative, vain Premier Ngo Dinh Diem a liability, but as Vice-President Lyndon B. Johnson put it privately—after having publicly annointed Diem the Winston Churchill of Asia—"Sh—, man, he's the only boy we got out there."[23]

Kennedy was cautious about Vietnam, hardly wanting to tie American fate to a faltering Diem or to tread the disastrous path already traveled by the French. He said he did not want to launch a white man's war in Asia and that Asians had to fight their own battles. But because he accepted the "domino theory," interpreted all Communists as part of an international conspiracy, thought that China lay behind the Vietnamese turmoil, and believed that "nation building" promised success, he expanded the American presence. "We have a very simple policy in Vietnam," Kennedy told a news conference in September, 1963. "We want the war to be won, the Communists to be contained, the Americans to go home."[24] Asked that year if he would reduce aid to South Vietnam, the President replied that he would not. "Strongly in our mind is what happened in the case of China at the end of World War II, where China was lost.... We don't want that."[25] In January, 1961, Kennedy authorized $28.4 million to enlarge the South Vietnamese army and another $12.7 million to improve the civil guard. In May he sent Vice-President Johnson to Saigon. That veteran Texas politician stated the problem in extreme terms: either "help these countries... or throw in the towel in the area and pull back our defenses to San Francisco and a 'Fortress America.'"[26] That month Kennedy also ordered 400 Special Forces soldiers and another 100 military "advisers" to South Vietnam. Mean-

---

[22] Quoted in Walt W. Rostow, *The Diffusion of Power* (New York: Macmillan, 1972), p. 265.

[23] Quoted in David Halberstam, *The Best and the Brightest* (Greenwich, Conn.: Fawcett, 1973), p. 167.

[24] *Public Papers, Kennedy, 1963*, p. 673.

[25] *Ibid.*, p. 659.

[26] New York Times, *Pentagon Papers*, p. 129.

while the Vietcong captured more territory and accelerated the violence through a bloody campaign of assassinations of village chiefs. In October a United States intelligence report indicated that 80–90 percent of the 17,000 Vietcong in South Vietnam were recruited in the South, and hence were not from North Vietnam, and that most of their supplies were also Southern. Although this estimate exploded the theory of advisers like Walt Rostow that the Vietnamese crisis was a case of aggression by North Vietnam, the report apparently made only a slight impact on Kennedy.

The President was, however, troubled by conflicting viewpoints, so in October he dispatched two hawks, General Maxwell Taylor and Walt Rostow, to South Vietnam to study the war firsthand. Diem naturally asked for more American military aid, and when Taylor returned to Washington he urged the President to send American combat troops. Rusk questioned such advice, arguing that Diem must first reform his conservative government; and the intelligence agencies suggested that sending such military assistance would likely arouse a North Vietnamese counterresponse. McNamara and the joint chiefs of staff supported Taylor and Rostow. Conscious that his decision violated the Geneva Accords but unwilling to say so publicly, Kennedy authorized in November a large increase in American forces of "advisers" in South Vietnam. By the end of 1961 there were 3,205; at the start of the year the figure had been about 900. During 1962 the figure jumped to 9,000, and at the time of Kennedy's death in November, 1963 the number had reached 16,700. American troops, helicopter units, minesweepers, and air reconnaissance aircraft went into action. In 1962, 109 Americans died and in 1963, 489. A "strategic hamlet" program was initiated to fortify villages and isolate them from Vietcong influence. This population control through barbed wire, however, proved disruptive and unpopular with villagers and permitted the Vietcong to appear as Robin Hoods. Then, too, many of the American weapons actually ended up in Vietcong hands. From New Delhi, a doubting Ambassador John Kenneth Galbraith asked the President a telling question: "Incidentally, who is the man in your administration who decides what countries are strategic? I would like to have his name and address and ask him what is so important about this real estate in the space age. What strength do we gain from alliance with an incompetent government and a people who are largely indifferent to their own salvation?"[27] To allay such questioning, the Administration issued optimistic statements. In February of 1963 Rusk announced that the "momentum of the Communist drive has been stopped."[28]

In May, 1963 the difficulties of "nation building" were exposed when South Vietnamese troops attacked protesting and unarmed Buddhists in Hué, massacring nine. The incident erupted after Diem, a Catholic, had banned the flying of Buddhist flags. Vietnam was a nominally Buddhist country governed by Catholics; the remnants of French colonialism were evidenced in various privileges, including education, for Catholics. Although the Buddhist demonstrations were a vehicle for the expression of long-standing nationalist sentiments, Diem soon equated Buddhism

[27] John Kenneth Galbraith, *Ambassador's Journal: A Personal Account of the Kennedy Years* (Boston: Houghton Mifflin, 1969), p. 311 (March 2, 1962).
[28] U.S. Senate, *Foreign Assistance Act of 1968—Part I—Vietnam*, p. 218.

with communism. The Vietcong were actually as surprised as Diem with the Buddhist uprising. On June 10 a Buddhist monk sat in a Saigon street, poured fuel over his body, and immolated himself. The appalling sight led Diem's callous sister-in-law Madame Nhu to chortle about "Buddhist barbecues." During the late summer and fall the protest spread; so did Diem's military tactics, including an attack upon Hué's pagoda. Also, thousands of students were arrested, including the children of many of Diem's own civil and military officers. Kennedy publicly chastised Diem and exerted pressure by reducing aid. Senior South Vietnamese generals, now aware that Diem was no longer in American favor, asked American officials how they would respond to a coup d'état. The new Ambassador, Henry Cabot Lodge, unsuccessful Republican vice-presidential candidate in 1960, was ready to dump Diem in order to get on with the war, but officials in Washington were divided. McNamara sent a new study mission. Marine General Victor H. Krulak and State Department officer Joseph Mendenhall took a hurried tour; Krulak reported that the war was going well despite the Buddhist squabble, and Mendenhall argued that the Vietnamese were more displeased with Diem than with the Vietcong. A puzzled Kennedy asked: "You two did visit the same country, didn't you?"[29]

Washington continued cool relations with Diem, who proved more and more resistant to American advice. In early October the Vietnamese generals informed the CIA that they were going to overthrow the recalcitrant premier. Lodge did not discourage them from the undertaking, a signal the generals fully appreciated. The White House was less eager than Lodge for the coup, fearing a failure. On November 1 the generals surrounded the Saigon palace with troops, took Diem prisoner, and murdered him. The assassination shocked Kennedy. "I had not seen him so depressed since the Bay of Pigs," Schlesinger recalled.[30] A few weeks later, on November 22, Kennedy himself was assassinated in Dallas. Some observers have suggested that after the presidential election of 1964, when he no longer suffered political vulnerability and was less fearful of right-wing charges of softness on communism, Kennedy would have withdrawn from Vietnam. We can never know for sure. We know only what he *did* for his 1,000 days in office....

[29] Quoted in George C. Herring, *America's Longest War* (New York: Knopf, 1986). p. 100.
[30] Schlesinger, *A Thousand Days*, p. 997.

23

ACCIDENTS OF HISTORY: JFK AND LBJ COMPARED

BERNARD BRODIE

In the early 1970s, while exploring the many causes for American involvement, strategic analyst Bernard Brodie drew special attention to the nature of the decision maker and, in particular, to the "personality and character of the President in power when the basic decisions were made." He argued that Kennedy's temperament and his comprehension of the conflict would probably have prevented him from expanding America's commitment in Vietnam in the way that his successor Johnson did. Having made a case for the importance of accidents in shaping history—in this case the "accidents" of personality and assassination—Brodie thus contributed to speculation about what might have happened in Vietnam had Kennedy lived.

...Given the circumstances prevailing, did it matter much or relatively little who was President? What the journalist and usually the historian take for granted we have to discuss seriously, because this issue is rather deliberately evaded in some learned discussions of what got us involved in Vietnam....

There are always important latitudes of choice within existing patterns of thought. And there can be few decisions more crucial than that of deciding whether or not to go to war. Within any given climate, one man may decide for one course and another man for the opposite course, and surely it should be redundant to say that it matters which of them is in control. Why each makes his choice the way he does depends in large part on things internal to him, including significantly the unconscious aspects of his motivation. To adopt this conception means to be ready to accept the notion that caprice may play a significant part in the destinies of great nations and thus of the world—for when a man like Lyndon B. Johnson can become President of the United States by virtue of the fact that an otherwise insignificant person full of rage happened to be able to fire a rifle bullet accurately, or another some five years later can achieve the authority because he won by a majority of 313,000 popular votes with only 43 per cent of the electorate, that victory being partly the result of a second assassination, then surely we are dealing with a large measure of caprice. This is hard on "theorists." Actually the point of view I am expressing is itself only a different kind of theory, but with much less accent on tidiness....

We have already paid our respects to the currents of thought and of doctrine that would have affected the judgments of any United States President holding office in the 1950's and 1960's and that certainly influenced deeply those who did hold office. However, it is also necessary to observe the relevant differences in insight as well as other aspects of personality and character among those who held it.

There were...important differences between Eisenhower and his successor, but we might also speculate briefly on whether it would have made a substantial difference to the decisions made in 1964 and thereafter had President Kennedy stayed alive to make them (in view of his great and growing popularity there can be small doubt that he would have been reelected in 1964). It is not an easy thing to do. We have to make judgments on the basis of deeply conflicting evidence, relying only on intuition to tell us which is the most significant among several widely varying indications of how a man's mind inclines. We feel the frustration of forever lacking any final and decisive proof. Also, we can have no idea at all how a third or a fourth or a fifth person in the same post would have acted. Presidents Kennedy and Johnson were each in his own way very special persons, and as examples of possible Presidential behavior they offer at best limited statistics. These are among the reasons why some rationalize away the importance of the problem. We shall never know conclusively how President Kennedy, had he lived, would have acted differently from his successor. Nor is there publicly available anything like an adequate body of insight into the psychological makeup of either of these two men, and there may never be one. The personality and character of some of the greatest figures of our national history have until now persistently eluded their biographers.[1]

The waters would be muddied enough, but we now are additionally blessed with something called the "New Left," which differs from the old left mostly in that it seems to lack entirely any integrating doctrine and that its adherents insist on the absence of any significant differentiation among any politicians outside their own vaguely defined camp. They naturally find it excessively easy to wipe out *any* distinction between Lyndon Johnson and his 1964 electoral opponent Senator Barry Goldwater, though the public statements that the latter was continuing to make into

---

[1] I am particularly sensitized to this point by the biographical work of my wife, Fawn M. Brodie, who is currently engaged on a volume on Thomas Jefferson aimed at recapturing his essential personality and character—which have been entirely blanked out by all his major biographers thus far. The basic reasons for the latter phenomenon appear to be two-fold. First, biographers of great national heroes like Jefferson tend to be primly protective of the man who is their subject, apparently feeling that a child-like adulation is the only right attitude with which to approach him. Second, all but a very few of them live in a world unsullied by any of the psychological notions developed by Freud and others.

1972 suggest strongly that had he won that election the levels of violence in Vietnam would have gone sharply higher than they did, quite possibly including the use of nuclear weapons. With the New Left marches also the new "cold war revisionism," according to which Harry Truman and his successors were guilty not simply of errors of judgment, which included exaggerated fears of Soviet intentions, but of a conspiratorial villainy! In a sudden Vietnam-induced paroxysm of disillusionment with former hero John F. Kennedy they suddenly discover that the very words they had been wont to quote approvingly from his inaugural speech demonstrate his commitment to the cold war, as indeed they do. His "missile-gap" warnings in his 1960 campaign speeches are paraded as wilful deception when we know they were due to an error in intelligence shared by the Administration in power. Such is the environment in which we must attempt a tentative appraisal.

The record is not simple and one-sided, but we do have many important hints. We notice one in Schlesinger's ... statement concerning Kennedy's behavior during and after the Bay of Pigs fiasco. We know from others, too, that he immediately admitted to his friends and staff members and shortly thereafter to the world at large that he had made a tragic mistake: "Not only were our facts in error, but our policy was wrong because the premises on which it was built was wrong."[2] One cannot remotely imagine President Johnson saying any such thing, publicly *or* privately. Does this reflect merely a difference in personal style, or does it go much deeper? There is quite enough known publicly about both men to suggest that we are dealing with a basic and vital character difference.

We know from many sources, including the books he had written when he came to office (for example, *Why England Slept; Profiles in Courage*), that Kennedy was deeply affected by the thinking of his time on international affairs. We know also that he immensely admired dynamism of character and personal courage, both physical and moral. Partly for those reasons he yielded to what he felt to be massive pressures shortly after his inauguration in permitting to go into execution that harebrained plan *developed and implemented under his predecessor* by the CIA and approved by the Joint Chiefs to have some 1,200 refugee Cubans invade their native land against Castro's 200,000; but he determined after its failure that he would never again so yield. Eighteen months later he carried off, without violence, the tremendous triumph of the missile crisis, the "Cuban Trafalgar" of October 1962. He was profoundly concerned with what was happening in Indochina and in his somewhat less than three years in office he increased the number of "military advisers" in Vietnam from about 600 to almost 17,000. We can also charge Kennedy with responsibility for appointing those officials who were to guide his successor down the path of major military intervention in Vietnam, including Secretary of State Dean Rusk, Secretary of Defense Robert McNamara, General Maxwell Taylor, McGeorge Bundy, and Walt W. Rostow—none of whom, it should be noticed, projected himself in 1960–1961 as a particularly warlike character. In October 1961

---

[2] Clark Clifford quotes the late President as using these words to him just after the Bay of Pigs disaster. See his article, "Set a Date in Vietnam ... " in *Life*, May 22, 1970. But see especially Arthur M. Schlesinger, Jr., *A Thousand Days* (Boston: Houghton Mifflin, 1965), pp. 265–273.

he sent Taylor and Rostow to Vietnam to report on the situation there. Their report elicited from J. Kenneth Galbraith, then Ambassador to India, the following remark: "It is a curious document. The recommendations are for vigorous action. The appendices say it cannot possibly succeed given the present government in Saigon."[3]

This looks rather like a man who could easily have done what President Johnson did in early 1965, and naturally the data on this side could be greatly expanded. However, there is another large side to the story. Kennedy had toured Indochina in 1951 and 1953, had also read considerably about it, and had expressed the belief that Communism could be defeated in Asia only by the force of nationalism. "Without the support of the native population," he had stressed, "there is no hope of success in any of the countries in Southeast Asia." To attempt to halt Communist advance "apart from and in defiance of innately nationalistic aims spells foredoomed failure."[4]

When in office he impressed those around him with the conviction that he did not approve the commitment of American ground troops. However, Roger Hilsman, who expresses this thought, also adds: "In an interesting example of one type of gambit in the politics of Washington policy-making, the President avoided a direct 'no' to the proposal for introducing troops to Vietnam. He merely let the decision slide, at the same time ordering the government to set in motion all the preparatory steps for introducing troops."[5] The latter remark is not too reassuring, but we also learn that the President frequently remarked concerning the Vietnamese: "In the final analysis, it is their war." And in one of his statements of that opinion he added, "...I don't think the war can be won unless the people support the effort."[6]

More directly significant, no doubt, is the fact that although the Taylor-Rostow report of November 1961 specifically urged a "hard commitment to the ground" made persuasive by the immediate introduction into Vietnam of some American combat forces, and although this recommendation was supported by the Joint Chiefs and by Rusk and McNamara—the latter in his memorandum talked of going as high as 205,000 men—the President flatly refused to do it. The statement that Kennedy approved omitted the key opening sentence of the Rusk-McNamara rec-

---

[3] See Galbraith's *Ambassador's Journal: A Personal Account of the Kennedy Years* (Boston: Houghton Mifflin, 1969), p. 254. Galbraith saw the Taylor-Rostow report in Washington, but after stopping off in Saigon on his way to his post at New Delhi, he sent President Kennedy on November 20 and 21, 1961 cables eloquently and cogently urging against further escalation of our action in Vietnam and specifically against commitment of combat forces. See *The Pentagon Papers*, Gravel ed., vol. 2, pp. 121–125. See also Galbraith's memorandum to the President of April 4, 1962, reproduced in part in *Ambassador's Journal*, pp. 342–344. The compilers of the Pentagon Papers in their connecting narrative seem to me to be quite in error when they interpret Galbraith's view as being "optimistic" and as seeing "no alternative to continuing to support Vietnam." Galbraith could not, after all, wholly condemn the President's existing policy in his communication to him; the obvious thrust of his remarks was for holding back.

[4] From a Senate speech, quoted by Roger Hilsman, *To Move a Nation* (New York: Doubleday, 1967), p. 423.

[5] Ibid., p. 424. See also pp. 504, 536.

[6] In a televised interview with Walter Cronkite of CBS, on September 2, 1963, reported in the *New York Times* for the following day.

ommendations, that "we now take the decision to commit ourselves to the objective of preventing the fall of South Viet-Nam to Communism. . . ." Schlesinger reports the President as telling him at that time:

> They want a force of American troops. They say it's necessary in order to restore confidence and maintain morale. But it will be just like Berlin. The troops will march in; the bands will play; the crowds will cheer; and in four days everyone will have forgotten. Then we will be told we have to send in more troops. It's like taking a drink. The effect wears off, and you have to take another.

The war in Vietnam, the President added (and here the words are Schlesinger's, no longer using the direct quote), "could be won only so long as it was their war. If it were ever converted into a white man's war, we would lose as the French had lost a decade earlier."[7]

It is also interesting that his brother, Attorney General Robert Kennedy, in whose judgment the President reposed much confidence, was dubious throughout about the wisdom of introducing American fighting forces. He was sure that a Communist takeover could not be successfully resisted with the Diem government then in power, and he felt that no one had enough information to answer the question whether it could be successfully resisted with *any* government.[8]

Hilsman also records a most significant conversation with President Kennedy early in 1962 in which the President, taking up the former's statement that it would be impossible to cut off the infiltration routes completely in Vietnam, added an extraordinarily penetrating and prophetic observation. The President thought it was really worse than that. In Hilsman's words:

> Even if the flow was choked down to a trickle, he went on to say, we would still have to carry a political burden. It was not that anyone would actually lie, but every time things went badly in the future, there would be more reports about increased use of the trails, and people in Saigon and Washington would take them seriously. "No matter what goes wrong or whose fault it really is, the argument will be that the Communists have stepped up their infiltration and we can't win unless we hit the north. Those trails are a built-in excuse for failure, and a built-in argument for escalation."[9]

What is revealed here is not only exceptional insight but also a confidence in his own judgment and in his understanding of both foreign and military affairs that his successor completely lacked. Even in the Bay of Pigs disaster, he had intervened in the existing plan at the last minute to eliminate the air strike that would have made United States participation too open and blatant—a decision that has been absurdly charged with being responsible for the failure of a plan that had no pos-

---

[7] Schlesinger, *A Thousand Days*, p. 505. On the Taylor-Rostow report and the follow-on Rusk and McNamara memoranda and recommendations, see *The Pentagon Papers*, Gravel ed., vol. 2, pp. 84–120.

[8] Hilsman, *To Move a Nation*, p. 501.

[9] Ibid., p. 439.

sibility of success even with a hundred times the originally planned air strikes. After that affair, and after experiencing the highly variable estimates of the Joint Chiefs of Staff concerning the requirements for an intervention in Laos, he was not again prepared to stake very much politically on what is sometimes called (usually by those who acknowledge themselves to possess it) "mature military judgment." Apart from his own direct experience in World War II as a junior naval officer, he had served on the Senate Armed Services Committee at a time of great ferment in strategic thinking and had been an avid reader in the considerable literature expressing that new thought. He thus had some basis for being properly critical or skeptical of military advice that he felt to be illogical or presumptuous—as it all too often is—and this is a marvelous quality for any President to have.[10] It served him well in the Cuban missile crisis of 1962.

Schlesinger relates one episode in the discussions over Laos that eloquently portrays this quality. Having earlier recommended that 60,000 men would be sufficient to guarantee success in Laos, the Joint Chiefs were chastened by the Bay of Pigs disaster and were now implying that they did not want to intervene at all "unless they could send at least 140,000 men equipped with tactical nuclear weapons." They were also trying to set down "the impossible condition that the President agree in advance to every further step they deemed sequential, including, on occasion, nuclear bombing of Hanoi and even Peking." At this point there occurred a meeting of the National Security Council with the President, at which General Lyman L. Lemnitzer, Chairman of the Joint Chiefs,

> outlined the process by which each American action would provoke a Chinese counteraction, provoking in turn an even more drastic American response. He concluded: "If we are given the right to use nuclear weapons we can guarantee victory." The President sat glumly rubbing his upper molar saying nothing. After a moment someone said, "Mr. President, perhaps you would have the General explain to us what he means by victory." Kennedy grunted and dismissed the meeting. Later he said, "Since he couldn't think of any further escalation, he would *have* to promise us victory."[11]

Kennedy apparently assumed in 1961 and 1962 that the war in Vietnam was going well, but, according to Henry Brandon

> at the end of 1962, in a conversation with Roswell Gilpatrick [Deputy Secretary of Defense], he talked in a restless and impatient way about how the U.S. had been sucked into Vietnam little by little. By the autumn of 1963 he seemed sick of it, and frequently asked how to be rid of the commitment. He began talking about the need to reduce the size of American forces in Europe and extricate the U.S. from Southeast

---

[10] In using the word *presumptuous* I mean that the military are wont to speak with an unwarranted certitude of prediction. No doubt it is partly because it is expected of them.

[11] Schlesinger, *A Thousand Days*, pp. 315 f. General Lemnitzer was shortly thereafter sent to Paris to relieve General Lauris Norstad as Supreme Commander, Allied Forces Europe (SACEUR).

Asia. Just before his death, he gave Mike Forrestal [of McGeorge Bundy's staff], in private conversation, odds of a hundred-to-one that the U.S. could not win. But he also knew that he could not get out of Vietnam before the elections in November 1964 without inviting his own political eclipse.[12]

Perhaps the clinching point, confirmed in the Pentagon Papers but hardly mentioned in the voluminous discussion of those papers, is the fact that shortly before his death President Kennedy approved a plan for the phased withdrawal of U.S. military personnel from Vietnam. They were supposed to be reduced to about 12,000 by the middle of 1964, bottoming out by the middle of 1968 at the level of 1,500, which would simply provide for a headquarters for the Military Assistance Advisory Group (MAAG). The functions of the men removed were to be taken over by the Vietnamese. The removal of the first 1,000 was to be completed before the end of 1963, and almost that number were in fact withdrawn in the month following Kennedy's assassination on November 22 of that year.[13] To be sure, this withdrawal plan was drawn up and approved during a period when things seemed to be going well, and it is possible that Kennedy might have been as willing to reverse the process as his successor was when things began to turn ill again in March 1964. But, again, the assumption that he would in fact have done so is based on the doubtful premise that with respect to Vietnam, Kennedy and Johnson would respond to any new situation in practically identical fashion.

It is clear, however, that John F. Kennedy had a basically different comprehension as well as temperament, in various ways that deeply mattered, from the man who succeeded him. It was not that the latter was originally bellicose about Vietnam, anxious to prove his virility and muscle. The bellicosity developed later, after he felt himself fully committed and under attack. As a politician President Johnson was at home in domestic affairs. Foreign affairs were indeed foreign to him, and so for that matter were military affairs. Nor was he one to buck the opinion of experts, the latter being rather narrowly defined as the persons holding appropriate office.

When in May 1961 Kennedy had sent him as Vice President to Vietnam, Lyndon Johnson, influenced no doubt by Ambassador Frederick Nolting, Jr., among others, returned uttering the clattering sounds of falling dominoes.[14] Time was

[12] Brandon, *Anatomy of Error* (London: Andre Deutsch, 1970), p. 30. The sources for this important statement obviously include Gilpatrick and Forrestal. The reference to marking time until the next election will no doubt shock some readers, but we are not here dealing with the question of moral issues in domestic politics, or of the divergence between Kennedy and Johnson in *this* respect.

[13] *The Pentagon Papers*, Gravel ed., vol. 2, pp. 160–200.

[14] Of the four ambassadors we have had in Vietnam during the critical years since the early days of the Kennedy Administration—Frederick Nolting, Jr., Henry Cabot Lodge, Maxwell Taylor, and Ellsworth Bunker—only Lodge can be regarded as having served his President with even a relatively detached view of events in Vietnam. The others were strongly prointervention and generally supported in their reports and behavior the government in power in Saigon. Nolting had been sent out early in 1961 because his predecessor was considered too anti-Diem, and he in turn had to be relieved by Lodge in 1963 because he was clearly too pro-Diem.

running out, he said, and, with characteristic exaggeration, added that if we did not go ahead with a full, forward strategy, the United States would have to "pull back our defenses to San Francisco and a 'Fortress America' concept."[15] His succession to the Presidency did not find him eager to rush into war, but he was not one to question seriously the unanimous recommendations of people like McGeorge Bundy, General Taylor, and Secretaries Rusk and McNamara, as well as numerous others at the Pentagon and the State Department. When he made the fateful decision to send combat forces to Vietnam, beginning in March 1965 with some battalions of Marines, he publicly stressed the *continuity* of his action with what his three predecessors had been doing and emphasized that nothing was really changed. In this he was of course either deceptive or enormously wrong. Up to that point a retreat and a liquidation of commitment would have been relatively easy. From then on retreat would have been difficult for any man, and for a Lyndon B. Johnson close to impossible.

Early in his administration he gave instructions for everyone in his entourage to ask himself each day what he had done toward victory and reminded everyone "that Vietnam was 'the only war we've got.'"[16] When he got well launched into the war he became obsessed, as was to be true also of his successor, with the attitude that he was not going to be the first American president to lose a war. Then, as more and more troops were needed, as casualties mounted, as month followed month without a definitive improvement in the situation, he became increasingly the man at bay, insisting not only on the absolute rightness of the decisions he had made but also on having around him none who might cause him even a moment's self-doubt. Thus he brought Walt Rostow back from the State Department to become a constant shield between him and reality and to give every untoward turn of events its optimistic interpretation. Those about him who became doubters left of their own accord or were cast out. As James Reston of the *New York Times* put it in late 1967: "The President is being told by a shrinking company of intimates that the Communist aggression in Vietnam is the same as the Nazi aggression in the Rhineland, Austria and Czechoslovakia, and he is holding the line; as Churchill defended freedom in Europe, so Johnson is holding the bridge in Asia...."[17]

It took much more than the shock of the Tet offensive of February 1968, mounted after three years of American combat and of troop buildup to numbers reaching over half a million, to jar his confidence in the rightness of his course. He was quite ready to fulfill General William C. Westmoreland's request for more troops, a request actually initiated by General Earl Wheeler, Chairman of the Joint Chiefs,

---

[15] *The Pentagon Papers*, Gravel ed., vol. 2, pp. 55–59.

[16] Hilsman, *To Move a Nation*, p. 534.

[17] Quoted in Hoopes, *The Limits of Intervention* (New York: Doubleday, 1967), p. 100. Though it would have been of no help to inform them so, neither Johnson nor Nixon could possibly have been the first American President to lose a war. That was James Madison's distinction. The War of 1812 cannot by any stretch of the imagination be considered as having been won by the United States. That war ended with American ports under tight blockade, and none of the reasons for which we ostensibly went to war were mentioned in the peace treaty signed at Ghent in 1815.

who wanted a global total of 206,000 additional troops, which would have necessitated what Wheeler had long been pressing for—the calling up of the reserves.[18] President Johnson's instructions to outgoing McNamara and incoming Clark Clifford were simply to look into how it should be done. Things began to break only when a certified hawk like Clifford, after undergoing his own profound conversion, set about in a real saga of determination and forensic skill to induce the President *not* to escalate further and to agree to a halting of the bombing of North Vietnam. Even so, Clark Clifford could not have done it alone. He needed and received the support and assistance of dedicated and gifted subordinates like Paul Nitze, Townsend Hoopes, and others, as well as the concurring opinion of several others of credentials similar to those he originally possessed, notably Dean Acheson, whom the President, in Hoopes' words, "held in the highest regard as a brilliant mind, a courageous and distinguished former Secretary of State, and the toughest of Cold Warriors." Hoopes reports a conversation in February 1968 between the President and Acheson concerning some briefings the latter had been given by JCS officers: "'With all due respect, Mr. President, the Joint Chiefs of Staff don't know what they are talking about.' The President said that was a shocking statement. Acheson replied that, if such it was, then perhaps the President ought to be shocked."[19]

That was not yet the end. The President continued "to lash out in a kind of emotional tantrum." In mid-March he flew to the Midwest to deliver two thoroughly truculent speeches, in the drafting of which Rostow and fellow hawk Abe Fortas (whose position on the Supreme Court did not prevent his doubling as the President's alter-ego) had had a major hand. The battle continued to the very end of March, with the President sustaining continued shocks from the obvious defections among his Senior Advisory Group on Vietnam, an *ad hoc* group of the country's most distinguished Presidential advisors with Acheson at their head. Finally, at the very last minute before the President was to give his major speech of March 31, 1968, the break came. The President had been presented with two drafts—a war speech and a peace speech. He used the latter, announcing the halting of the bombing north of the 20th parallel—and his own withdrawal from the forthcoming Presidential election.

From all this, and of course much more of like nature than can be included here, the following judgments seem reasonable. Although it is most unlikely that Kennedy would have followed the path that led Johnson in March 1965 to lay on the "Rolling Thunder" bombing program of North Vietnam and in the same month

[18] Wheeler went to Saigon and apparently cautioned Westmoreland not to let the outcome of the Tet offensive look too much like an American victory, which was the latter's inclination. Wheeler wanted to use the event as leverage to get his way finally on the matter of calling up the reserves. See John B. Henry II, "February, 1968," *Foreign Policy*, no. 4 (Fall 1971), pp. 3–33. Note especially that Henry received the approval of the person quoted for each of his direct quotations as published, which is astonishing in view of what they reveal. From this article (part of a bachelor's thesis at Harvard!) it is difficult to escape the conclusion that Wheeler engaged in some deception of his superiors, the Secretary of Defense and the President of the United States. If so, the results backfired on him.

[19] Hoopes, *Limits of Intervention*, pp. 204 f.

to land Marines in South Vietnam, thereby making it an American war, one cannot deny the possibility that he would have done so.[20] What seems to this writer next to impossible to imagine, however, is President Kennedy stubbornly escalating the commitment thereafter and persisting in a course that over time abundantly exposed its own bankruptcy, not only in its failure to accomplish the desired results and in its fantastically disproportionate costs to the United States, but also in the fact that it completely betrayed what he knew to be the basic principle of guerrilla warfare: that the object is not the killing of enemy soldiers but rather the winning of the allegiance of the people. Neither can one imagine him continuing to believe the unvarying optimistic reports and constantly disproved predictions of a General Westmoreland, or permitting a Walt Rostow to be a monitor for the kind of uniformly biased reports that the latter thought appropriate for the President's eyes,[21] or long outlasting in hawkishness a McGeorge Bundy and a Robert McNamara, or giving Clark Clifford so difficult a time in accomplishing as late as 1968 the mere beginning of deescalation of what was by then a wholly catastrophic war.

The last point above is especially important. If we ask who in government supported intervention in 1964 and 1965, the answer is almost everyone. At least, the opponents were neither many nor conspicuous. The Tonkin Bay Resolution in the Senate in August 1964 had but two negative votes, those of Wayne Morse and Ernest Gruening, both of whom were to lose their seats in the 1968 election. (Other reasons may have contributed; Gruening was over 81 years old; nevertheless, both lost.) The floor manager for putting through the Resolution was Senator J. William Fulbright (who reassured doubting senators with his own firm belief that it would not be used in the way it subsequently was used). Among those associated with the Executive at the time of the March 1965 intervention, we find opposing that intervention only Vice President Hubert Humphrey, Undersecretary of State George W. Ball, W. Averell Harriman, and Ambassador to the Soviet Union Llewellyn Thompson. Outside the government, but distinguished former members of it, were ex-Ambassadors George F. Kennan and J. Kenneth Galbraith. These were persons who might be listened to, but none was in a commanding position (Humphrey was in fact quickly brought to heel). Also, they were exceedingly few against many. The significant story lies in the subsequent steady erosion of support at the top, marked by a series of quiet defections. Whether or not they stayed in the Administration—most of

[20] It is somewhat unclear just when President Johnson took the most decisive step in shifting to a combat role. The Administration leadership seemed to feel the critical date was April 2, 1965, with the issuance of National Security Action Memorandum (NSAM) 328, directing that the Marine battalions already deployed to South Vietnam be shifted from a static defense role to one of active combat operations. See *The Pentagon Papers*, Gravel ed., vol. 3, pp. 345–354. It is, incidentally, quite wrong to assume, as the *New York Times* encouraged its readers to assume in its publication of a portion of the Pentagon Papers, that when he was campaigning as the peace candidate in the 1964 election against Senator Goldwater, President Johnson had already made up his mind to commit the nation to a combat role in Vietnam.

[21] When he sent Rostow to the State Department in late 1961, President Kennedy said of him to some intimates: "Walt has ten ideas every day, nine of which would lead to disaster but one of which is worth having, and this makes it important to have a filter between the President and Rostow." Brandon, *Anatomy of Error*, p. 28.

them did who were not in the White House—former supporters of subcabinet rank became first doubters, then alarmed disbelievers.[22] President Johnson thus has to be placed among the very last to give way.

When even McNamara began in late 1966, and increasingly through 1967, to feel disenchantment with what his revered statistics had been telling him, President Johnson surely had reason to suspect that he, too, needed desperately to reconsider the whole situation. Instead, he concluded automatically that McNamara had to go. He thought he had a reliably hawkish replacement for him in Clark Clifford, but as we have seen, the latter's accession to office coincided with the Tet offensive of February 1968. Johnson rewarded Clifford for his noble and difficult accomplishment with what seems to have been a massive bitterness, which he subsequently revealed publicly to his own discredit.[23]

The conclusion is unavoidable that Kennedy had a far more subtle intelligence than his successor, that he was decidedly less naive with respect to the advice of "experts," military and otherwise, and especially that he was free of the personal pigheadedness and truculence that Johnson so markedly betrayed. There can thus be little doubt that his conduct concerning Vietnam would have been critically and basically different.

Johnson was himself succeeded in the Presidency by a man who as Vice President had favored our intervention at the time of Dien Bien Phu, along with John Foster Dulles, Admiral Radford, and practically no one else, and who in early 1961 had called on the newly inaugurated Kennedy to urge intervention in Laos.[24] In 1965 Richard Nixon had written a letter to the *New York Times* with the astounding declaration that "victory for the Vietcong... would mean ultimately the destruction of freedom of speech for all men for all time, not only in Asia but in the United States as well."[25] The same man as President referred in his speech of November 3, 1969 to the "great stakes involved in Vietnam," asserting that they were no less than the maintenance of the peace "in the Middle East, in Berlin, eventually even in the Western Hemisphere." We are hearing here the crashing fall of dominoes to the last syllable of recorded time.

---

[22] In government circles doubters and opponents of current policy do not normally beat drums to call attention to their opposition, and may thus remain in part unknown to each other. Townsend Hoopes, who was Undersecretary of the Air Force at the time, speaks thus of the events of February 1968: "In the Pentagon, the Tet offensive performed the curious service of fully revealing the doubters and the dissenters to each other, in a lightning flash." Among the civilians these turned out to be numerous and to include officials of high rank, including Paul H. Nitze, then Deputy Secretary of Defense. See Hoopes, *Limits of Intervention*, p. 145.

[23] I am referring here to the second of the two television interviews, that of February 6, 1970, which former President Johnson had with Walter Cronkite of CBS. In it the former President tried to give to Dean Rusk the credit that should have gone to Clark Clifford. See, regarding that interview, Townsend Hoopes, "Standing History on Its Head: LBJ's Account of March, 1968," *The New Republic*, March 14, 1970.

[24] See Schlesinger, *A Thousand Days*, p. 314.

[25] This sentence is quoted in Clark Clifford's article in *Life* (footnote 2, above). It perhaps explains the extreme waspishness of President Nixon's reference to Clifford in a press conference shortly after publication of the article.

In the 1968 election Nixon won by a hair's breadth over Vice President Hubert Humphrey, a man of very different feelings about Vietnam,[26] and if Robert Kennedy, who by then was totally opposed to the Vietnam War, had not been felled by an assassin a few months earlier, he would very likely have won the Democratic nomination and also the election. One may conclude, therefore, that the United States at a crucial stage in its history has been the victim of cruel and capricious chance, that two small bullets have cost the American and the Vietnamese people exceedingly dear—the rifle bullet that killed President John F. Kennedy and the .22 calibre pistol bullet that five years later took the life of his brother. Those two bullets, too well aimed, have to be accounted an important part of the reason why we made the 1965 commitment to the war in Vietnam and why we are still there at this writing some seven years later.

[26] Hoopes has the following to say about Humphrey's position early in 1965: "Immediately following the February attack on Pleiku, but before retaliatory action had been ordered, Vice-President Humphrey returned urgently to Washington from a trip to Georgia, to make a last-ditch attempt to prevent escalation. He gave the President his view that bombing the North could not resolve the issue in the South, but that it would generate an inexorable requirement for U.S. ground forces in the South to protect airfields and aircraft.... His views were received at the White House with particular coldness, and he was banished from the inner councils for some months thereafter, until he decided to 'get back on the team,'" *Limits of Intervention*, p. 31. Brandon supports this view of Humphrey, see *Anatomy of Error*, pp. 35, 50 f. Humphrey was perhaps too anxious to "get back on the team," but as a Vice President he could have little choice and anyway this kind of dissent was not in his temperament. Besides, it must have been no help to the independence of his thinking to sit regularly in the meetings of the National Security Council. During the 1968 election campaign he freely expressed in semiprivate meetings his opposition to the ABM, but, knowing President Johnson's feelings on the matter, was markedly guarded about references to Vietnam. At a decent interval after he lost the election Humphrey began in his public utterances, especially as an occasional newspaper columnist, to attack the slowness of President Nixon's rate of deescalation.

24

LBJ AND PRESIDENTIAL MACHISMO

DAVID HALBERSTAM

Arriving in Saigon in September 1962 as a reporter for the New York Times, *David Halberstam grew steadily gloomier about the prospects for American victory. At first blaming the Diem regime for losing the war, he came to believe that the "sickness went far deeper.... The failings of the American-Diem side grew out of the French Indochina war, in which the other side had captured the nationalism of the country and become a genuine revolutionary force....Instead of believing that there was a right way of handling our involvement in Vietnam, in the fall of 1963 I came to the conclusion that it was doomed and that we were on the wrong side of history."* In this spirit he wrote* The Making of a Quagmire (1965). *Back in the United States, in 1969 Halberstam turned his attention to the Kennedy-Johnson intellectuals, the decisions they made, and the institutions in which they operated. Heralded as the best and the brightest, very little had been written about them. Halberstam found men possessed of hubris, yet men who misunderstood the war and did not want to learn. After Kennedy's death, the new President inherited many of Kennedy's action intellectuals, but he consulted his own men inside and outside of the White House as well. In the excerpt below from his 1972 book* The Best and the Brightest, *Halberstam describes how Johnson's powerful, complex personality and his interactions with the "boys" and "men" among his advisers would contribute to America's escalating involvement in Vietnam after the NLF attacked the U.S. base at Pleiku in February 1965.*

Lyndon Johnson had to decide. The pressures were enormous both ways, there was going to be no easy way out. A few friends like Dick Russell were warning him not

*David Halberstam, *The Best and the Brightest* (New York: Random House, 1972), p. 670.

to go ahead, that it would never work; Russell had an intuitive sense that it was all going to be more difficult and complicated than the experts were saying, but his doubts were written off as essentially conservative and isolationist, and it was easily rationalized that Russell, like Fulbright, did not care about colored people. Besides, Johnson had bettered Russell in the Senate and now here was Johnson surrounded by truly brilliant men (years later when there were free fire zones in the South—areas where virtually uncontrolled air and artillery could be used—which led to vast refugee resettlement, Russell would pass on his doubts about the wisdom of this as policy to the White House, saying, "I don't know those Asian people, but they tell me they worship their ancestors and so I wouldn't play with their land if I were you. You know whenever the Corps of Engineers has some dam to dedicate in Georgia I make a point of being out of state, because those people don't seem to like the economic improvements as much as they dislike being moved off their ancestral land"). But even Russell was telling the President that he had to make a decision, that he had better move, get off the dime, and Russell would support the flag.

Men who knew Johnson well thought of him as a man on a toboggan course in that period. Starting the previous November and then month by month as the trap tightened, he had become increasingly restless, irritable, frustrated, more and more frenetic, more and more difficult to work with. He was trapped and he knew it, and more than anyone else around him he knew that he was risking his great domestic dreams; it was primarily his risk, not theirs. The foreign policy advisers were not that privy to or that interested in his domestic dreams, and his domestic advisers were not that privy to the dangers ahead in the foreign policy. As a politician Johnson was not a great symbolic figure who initiated deep moral stirrings in the American soul, a man to go forth and lead a country by image, but quite the reverse, and he knew this better than most. His image and his reputation and his posture were against him; at his ablest he was a shrewd infighter. Despite the bombast he was a surprisingly cautious man (in guiding the Senate against McCarthy he had been the epitome of caution, so cautious as to not receive any credit for it, which was probably what he wanted, it was not an issue to be out in front on). He was very good at measuring his resources, shrewdly assessing what was needed for a particular goal: was it there, was it available, was the price of accomplishing it too high? He had advised against going into Dienbienphu in 1954, not because he thought there was anything particularly wrong with intervention, but because he felt that immediately after the Korean War the country simply could not absorb and support another Asian land war; indeed, it was the very psychology of exhaustion with the Korean War which had put Eisenhower into office.

Now he was facing fateful decisions on Vietnam just as he was getting ready to start the Great Society. With his careful assessment of the country, he was sure the resources were there, that the country was finally ready to do something about its long-ignored social problems. The time was right for an assault on them, and he, Lyndon Johnson, would lead that assault, cure them, go down in history as a Roosevelt-like figure. He was keenly aware of these resources, and in late 1964 and early 1965 he began to use the phrase "sixty months of prosperity" as a litany, not just as party propaganda to get credit for the Democrats, but as a way of reminding the country that it had been having it good, very good, that it was secure and affluent, that it now had to turn its attention to the needs of others. Yet he knew he would not have the resources for both the domestic programs and a real war, and as a need for the latter became more and more apparent, he became restless and irritable, even by Johnsonian standards irascible, turning violently on the men around him. Those who knew him well and had worked long for him knew the symptoms only too well; it was, they knew, part of the insecurity of the man, and they talked of it often and gradually among themselves, since they all were subject to the same abuse. Unable to bear the truth about himself if it was unpleasant, he would transfer his feelings and his anger at himself to others, lashing out at Lady Bird, or George Reedy, or Bill Moyers, or particularly poor Jack Valenti, but really lashing out at himself. And so in early 1965 this great elemental man, seeing his great hopes ahead and sensing also that they might be outside his reach, was almost in a frenzy to push his legislation through, a restless, obsessed man, driving himself and those around him harder and harder, fighting a civil war within himself.

He knew it would not be easy, that the bombing was a tricky business, not as tricky as ground troops, there was, after all, an element of control in bombing ("If they [the Air Force] hit people I'll bust their asses," he said at the start) but tricky nonetheless. And yet, and yet. "If I don't go in now and they show later I should have gone, then they'll be all over me in Congress. They won't be talking about my civil rights bill, or education or beautification. No sir, they'll push Vietnam up my ass every time. Vietnam. Vietnam. Vietnam. Right up my ass." Cornered, and having what he would consider the Kennedy precedent to stand in Vietnam, a precedent which Kennedy set, but probably never entirely believed, and with all the Kennedy luminaries telling him to go ahead, even Rusk's uneasiness having been resolved ("He would look around him," said Tom Wicker later, "and see in Bob McNamara that it was technologically feasible, in McGeorge Bundy that it was intellectually respectable, and in Dean Rusk that it was historically necessary"), he went forward. Of course he would; after all, it could be done. He was a can-do man surrounded by other can-do men. If we set our minds to something, we did not fail. If Europeans were wary of this war, if the French had failed, and thus were warning the Americans off, it was not because they had lived more history and seen more of the folly of war, it was because they had become cynical, they had lost the capacity to believe in themselves, they were decadent. We were the first team.

So it all came down to Lyndon Johnson, reluctant, uneasy, but not a man to be backed down. Lyndon would not cut and run, if it came to that; no one was going to push Lyndon Johnson around. Lyndon Johnson knew something about people like this, like the Mexicans back home, they were all right, the Mexicans, but "if you didn't watch they'll come right into your yard and take it over if you let them. And the next day they'll be right there on your porch, barefoot and weighing one hundred and thirty pounds, and they'll take that too. But if you say to 'em right at the start, 'Hold on, just wait a minute,' they'll know they're dealing with someone who'll stand up. And after that you can get along fine." Well, no one would push Lyndon Johnson of Texas around. This was Lyndon Johnson representing the United States of America, pledged to follow in the tradition of Great

Britain and Winston Churchill—Lyndon Johnson, who, unlike Jack Kennedy, was a believer, not a cynic about the big things. Honor. Force. Commitments. Who believed in the omnipotence of American power, the concept of the frontier and using force to make sure you were clearly understood, believing that white men, and in particular Americans, were just a bit superior, believing in effect all those John Wayne movies, a cliché in which real life had styled itself on image (paint the portrait of Johnson as a tall tough Texan in the saddle, he had told Pierre Salinger, although he was not a good rider). And in the Dominican crisis he sent word through McGeorge Bundy for Colonel Francisco Caamano Deno, the rebel leader: "Tell that son of a bitch that unlike the young man who came before me I am not afraid to use what's on my hip."

For *machismo* was no small part of it. He had always been haunted by the idea that he would be judged as being insufficiently manly for the job, that he would lack courage at a crucial moment. More than a little insecure himself, he very much wanted to be seen as a man; it was a conscious thing. He was very much aware of *machismo* in himself and those around him, and at a moment like this he wanted the respect of men who were tough, real men, and they would turn out to be the hawks. He had always unconsciously divided the people around him between men and boys. Men were activists, doers, who conquered business empires, who acted instead of talked, who made it in the world of other men and had the respect of other men. Boys were the talkers and the writers and the intellectuals, who sat around thinking and criticizing and doubting instead of doing. There were good boys, like Horace Busby and for a time Dick Goodwin, who used their talent for him, and there were snot noses, and kids who were to be found at the State Department or in the editorial rooms of the Washington *Post* or the *New York Times* using their talents against him. Bill Moyers was a boy who was halfway to becoming a man, a writer who was moving into operational activities. Hubert Humphrey, Vice President or no, was still a boy, better than most liberals, but too prone to talk instead of act, not a person that other *men* would respect in a room when it got down to the hard cutting; real men just wouldn't turn to Hubert, he didn't have the weight, and so when Humphrey voiced his doubts on Vietnam he was simply excluded from the action until he muffled his dissent.

Now, as Johnson weighed the advice he was getting on Vietnam, it was the boys who were most skeptical, and the men who were most sure and confident and hawkish and who had Johnson's respect. Hearing that one member of his Administration was becoming a dove on Vietnam, Johnson said, "Hell, he has to squat to piss." The *men* had, after all, done things in their lifetimes, and they had the respect of other men. Doubt itself, he thought, was an almost feminine quality, doubts were for women; once, on another issue, when Lady Bird raised her doubts, Johnson had said of course she was doubtful, it was like a woman to be uncertain. Thus as Vietnam came to the edge of decision, the sides were unfair, given Johnson's make-up. The doubters were not the people he respected; the men who were activists were hawks, and he took sustenance and reassurance that the real men were for going ahead. Of the doves, only George Ball really had his respect. Ball might be a dove, but there was nothing soft about him. He had made it in a tough and savage world of the big law firms, and his approach was tough and skeptical. He did not talk about doing good or put Johnson off by discussing the moral thing to do, rather he too was interested in the exercise of power and a real world that Johnson could understand. He was a doer, an activist, and Johnson would tell him again and again, even as Ball dissented, "You're one of these can-do fellows too, George."

Thus the dice were loaded; the advocates of force were by the very nature of Johnson's personality taken more seriously, the doubters were seen by their very doubts as being lesser men. So he would go ahead, despite his own inner instincts, that the rosy predictions were in fact not likely to be so rosy, that it was likely to be tougher and darker, that George Ball's doubts had a real basis. The thrust to go forward was just too great. Everyone else seemed so convinced of America's invincibility. Even Ball, arguing at the time that it was the right moment to cut our losses, sensed this feeling of American invincibility and will, and would write that by negotiating out, the United States could become a "wiser and more mature nation." But those lessons would have to come the hard way; there were too few restraints. All the training of two decades had been quite the reverse. They had come to the end of one path. They were cornered by bad policies on Asia which they had not so much authored as refused to challenge, both in the fifties when out of power, and in the sixties when in power. And so now they bombed. They did this in place of combat troops, and they believed that it would not last long, perhaps a few months.

A few days later, after the bombing campaign had begun, a White House reporter came across Bundy in the White House barbershop. Bundy was sitting there being lathered, and since he could not easily escape, the reporter thought it was a good time to ask Bundy something that had been bothering him since the incident. "Mac," he said, "what was the difference between Pleiku and the other incidents?"

Bundy paused and then answered, "Pleikus are like streetcars" (i.e., there's one along every ten minutes).

25

NIXON AND THE IMPERIAL PRESIDENCY

ARTHUR M. SCHLESINGER, JR.

In 1973, the year that the last American troops left Vietnam but before revelations about the Watergate scandal, Arthur M. Schlesinger, Jr., published The Imperial Presidency, *a history of the shift in the constitutional balance between Congress and the President from the Founding Fathers to Nixon. He placed emphasis on the war-making power of the President, who by the early 1970s, he said, "had become on issues of war and peace the most absolute monarch (with the possible exception of Mao Tse-tung of China) among the great powers of the world."* In his chapter on the Vietnam War, Schlesinger described how the inherent powers of the executive office, the personalities of LBJ and Nixon, and the acquiescence of Congress had not only helped cause the war but had brought about a revolutionary challenge to the doctrine of separation of powers. In the excerpt below, he discusses Nixon as commander in chief.*

Lincoln had said that the view that one man had the power of bringing the nation into war placed our Presidents where Kings had always stood. If Johnson construed the high prerogative more in the eighteenth-century style of the British monarch than of the republican executive envisaged by the Constitution, his successor carried the inflation of presidential authority even further. For President Nixon stripped away the fig leaves which his predecessor had draped over his assertion of unilateral presidential power. The SEATO treaty was returned to the oblivion from which the State Department had plucked it in 1966. The Tonkin Gulf resolution was dis-

*Arthur M. Schlesinger, Jr., *The Imperial Presidency* (Boston: Houghton Mifflin, 1973), p. ix.

owned by the administration in 1970[1] and revoked by Congress in January 1971; strict constructionists like Sam Ervin even voted against repeal on the ground that it deprived the President of his legal right to carry on the war. The claim of exclusive presidential authority now rested squarely on the powers of the Commander in Chief, especially his power to do whatever he thought necessary to protect American troops.

"I shall meet my responsibility as Commander in Chief of our Armed Forces," Nixon said in his announcement of the invasion of Cambodia in 1970, "to take the action necessary to defend the security of our American men." "The legal justification," he later explained, ". . . is the right of the President of the United States under the Constitution to protect the lives of American men." "As Commander in Chief, I had no choice but to act to defend those men. And as Commander in Chief, if I am faced with that decision again, I will exercise that power to defend those men."[2]

The repeated use of the term Commander in Chief, as if it were an incantation, would have confounded the Founding Fathers. As we have seen, the office through most of American history had a strictly technical connotation: it meant no more than the topmost officer in the armed forces. Lincoln in special circumstances had used it as a source of extra authority; but the Civil War could serve as precedent only for another civil war. Then the Second World War had given the title new glamor; and, beginning with the Truman Presidency, the Commander in Chief clause began to serve a variety of secular purposes. A President facing an unpopular decision, whether firing General MacArthur or seizing the steel plants, no doubt felt he could get away with it better if he wrapped himself in his military robe. For Truman's successor, donning the military robe was doing what came naturally. In any case, the growing militarization of American life under both the realities and the delusions of the Cold War increased the resonance of the office.

By the 1970s the title Commander in Chief had acquired almost a sacramental aura, translating its holder from worldly matters into an ineffable realm of higher duty. A dithyramb by Senator Goldwater in 1971 evokes the process of transfiguration. "We come," Goldwater said, "to the President's power as Commander in Chief. . . . Just why the founding fathers saw fit to confer this title on him and to invest him with these powers, I've never quite been able to understand; but I have a growing feeling that with the recognized and infinite wisdom of the founding fathers, they realized that a single man with these powers who would not be disturbed by the politics of the moment would use them more wisely than a Congress which is constantly looking toward the political results." The Founding Fathers, he continued, foreseeing the day when a divided Congress could not agree on a

[1] Cf. letter from the Acting Secretary of State to Senator Fulbright, May 30, 1970: "In his letter to you of March 12, 1970, Mr. [Horace] Torbert [Deputy Secretary for Congressional Relations] stated that the Administration does not depend on the Tonkin Gulf Resolution as legal or constitutional authority for its present conduct of foreign relations, or its contingency plans." *Congressional Record*, April 2, 1973, S6287.

[2] Richard M. Nixon, *A New Road For America: Major Policy Statements, March 1970 to October 1971* (New York, 1972), 38, 675, 683.

"single American course," must in their wisdom have arranged that "the power of war and peace might better be vested in a single man. . . . I believe it would offer an explanation of a means by which our forefathers and we ourselves were meant to become a single people with a single purpose."[3]

For Nixon his authority as Commander in Chief, conjoined with the principle of troop protection and the model of the missile crisis, was all he needed. In his announcement of the incursion into Cambodia, he compared himself to Kennedy who, "in his finest hour," had sat in the identical room in the White House and made "the great decision" that removed the missiles from Cuba. Later Nixon used the missile crisis to justify his failure to consult Congress over Cambodia. "I trust we don't have another Cuban missile crisis. I trust we don't have another situation like Cambodia, but I do know that in the modern world, there are times when the Commander in Chief. . . will have to act quickly. I can assure the American people that this President is going to bend over backward to consult the Senate and consult the House whenever he feels it can be done without jeopardizing the lives of American men. But when it is a question of the lives of American men or the attitudes of people in the Senate, I am coming down hard on the side of defending the lives of American men."[4]

One can only wonder whether Nixon seriously believed that Cuba and Cambodia were equal situations—equal in their danger to the security of the United States, equal in their need for secrecy, equal in their lack of time for congressional consideration. The enemy bases and the threat to American forces had existed in Cambodia for years; there was no sudden emergency in April 1970; indeed the enemy had already largely evacuated the sanctuary areas by the time the invasion began. There was ample time for congressional consultation. There was even more time within the executive branch for a canvass of the sort Kennedy had conducted in the infinitely more imperious case of the missiles in Cuba.

Indeed, so astute a student of the Presidency as Richard Neustadt had just argued that debate within the executive branch could replace Congress as the means of check and balance in the nuclear age. "Any modern President," Neustadt had written in a discussion of the missile crisis, "stands at the center of a watchful circle with whose members he cannot help but consult. . . . He is no freer than he would have been with Congress to ignore them."[5] But Nixon did ignore them. He had already cut the State Department out of serious policy, looking instead to a mini-State Department in the White House under the direction of his Assistant for National Security Affairs, Henry A. Kissinger. And in the case of Cambodia, Nixon,

---

[3] *Congressional Record,* April 26, 1971, S5640. Cf. Senator Goldwater in another mood (1964): "Some of the current worship of powerful executives may come from those who admire strength and accomplishment of any sort. Others hail the display of Presidential strength. . . simply because they approve of the *result* reached by the use of power. . . . If ever there was a philosophy of government totally at war with that of the Founding Fathers, it is this one"; Marcus Cunliffe, *American Presidents and the Presidency* (London, 1969), 112.

[4] Nixon, *New Road For America,* 39, 687.

[5] Afterword by R. E. Neustadt and Graham Allison in Norton paperback edition of Robert F. Kennedy, *Thirteen Days* (New York, 1971), 118–19.

instead of exposing himself to a candid discussion among even his closest colleagues, seems to have withdrawn into solitude and spring his unilateral decision on them as well as on the world.

As for the Constitution, Nixon showed no more interest in the location of the war-making power than his immediate predecessors, though, as the first lawyer to sit in the White House since Franklin Roosevelt, he might have had at least a professional curiosity about the subject. But his own public remarks on the question have already been reproduced nearly in their entirety; and the matter weighed so little on his mind that, according to the *New York Times,* he did not ask the State Department lawyers to prepare the legal case for the invasion of Cambodia until four days after it began.[6] For a systematic constitutional defense of his actions in Cambodia, Nixon relied on an Assistant Attorney General, William Rehnquist.

Rehnquist's argument was that the Commander in Chief clause was "a grant of substantive authority" which had enabled Presidents throughout American history to send troops "into conflict with foreign powers on their own initiative" and even to deploy "armed forces outside of the United States on occasion in a way which invited hostile retaliation." Congress had acquiesced in such presidential initiative, and the courts, he claimed, had repeatedly approved it. As for Indochina, war there had been authorized by the Tonkin Gulf resolution. (It is interesting that, in Nixon's case as in Johnson's, their lawyers clung to documents the principals had thrown overboard.) In carrying the war into Cambodia as a means of assuring the safety of American armed forces in the field, Nixon had made "precisely the sort of tactical decision traditionally confided to the commander-in-chief in the conduct of armed conflict."

Whatever merits Rehnquist possessed as a President's lawyer, he displayed few, in this instance at least, as a legal scholar. The Commander in Chief clause gave a President only the substantive powers that the office in top command of the armed forces would have had if he were not President. The idea that the clause gave a President authority beyond this was a product not of the Constitutional Convention but of the years after the Second World War. Rehnquist's judicial precedents were marked by a comparable indifference to history. Thus he cited the case of *Durand v. Hollins,* where Justice Nelson had upheld the bombardment of a Nicaraguan town by an American naval vessel. Rehnquist, who oddly thought the case was called *Durand v. Hollis* and even more oddly thought Nelson was "later a Justice of the Supreme Court" (Nelson had been on the Supreme Court for fifteen years at the time of *Durand v. Hollins*), now tried to transform unilateral executive action against what President Pierce had carefully defined as "not . . . an organized political society" into a precedent for President Nixon's invasion of the sovereign state of Cambodia. With the same disdain for context, he even cited the Prize Cases, as if Cambodia were a Confederate state in rebellion against the Union.

Most of the Rehnquist case was persiflage. His serious argument derived from the proposition, which no one disputed, that the Commander in Chief has full power

[6] *New York Times,* June 30, 1970.

to conduct a war once begun. But did this wartime power of command authorize a Commander in Chief, as Rehnquist contended, to invade neutral countries on his personal finding that they housed a potential danger to American forces? As a claim under international law, this was not impressive. The Nixon administration itself might not have been deeply moved if Brezhnev had said that the Red Army was perfectly justified in invading a neutral country in order to secure the safety of Russian forces. In such a case Americans would have denounced the argument as self-serving and specious. Was the same argument less self-serving on American lips? A century and a half before the incursion into Cambodia, Chief Justice Marshall had laid down the rule: "An army marching into the dominions of another sovereign may justly be considered as committing an act of hostility; and, if not opposed by force, acquires no privilege by its irregular and improper conduct."[7] This was the position the American government had taken in 1957 when French forces in Algeria, acting on the troop-protection principle, attacked a guerrilla sanctuary in Tripoli, as it was the continuing American position when Israeli forces attacked Arab guerrilla sanctuaries beyond the frontier of Israel.

As a claim under American law, the Nixon-Rehnquist proposition was even more troubling. Cambodia was not a threat to the security of the United States. Since the danger to American forces in South Vietnam had become less great than it had been for several years, it was hard to claim a sudden emergency. It was not a case of hot pursuit; nor could Rehnquist cite any previous occasion when a President ordered a massive attack on a neutral country to protect American troops in a third country. And what were the limits on this theory of presidential war? If Nixon could invade Cambodia and later bomb Laos without congressional consent on this principle, could he not also on the same principle attack China and Russia without congressional consent? Herndon had written to Lincoln that, if it should become necessary to repel invasion, the President could cross the line and invade a neighboring country, and that the President was the sole judge of the necessity. If this were so, Lincoln had replied, "Study to see if you can fix *any limit* to his power in this respect, after you have given him so much as you propose." Now Nixon claimed this power, not just in the case of a neighboring country or an imminent invasion of the United States, but in the case of a country on the other side of the world. He thereby equipped himself with so expansive a theory of the power of the Commander in Chief and so elastic a theory of defensive war that he could freely, on his own initiative, without a national emergency, without reference to Congress, as a routine employment of unilateral executive authority, go to war against any country containing any troops that might in any conceivable circumstances be used in an attack on American forces. And Rehnquist (whom Nixon soon elevated to the Supreme Court in what he hilariously called a strict-constructionist appointment) even contended ominously that the invasion of Cambodia was only the mildest exertion of presidential prerogative: "one need not approach anything like the

[7] *The Exchange v. McFaddon*, 7 Cranch 116, 140–41 (1812). I owe this quotation to the excellent article by F. D. Wormuth, "The Nixon Theory of the War Power: A Critique," *California Law Review*, May 1972, 650.

outer limits of his power, as defined by judicial decision and historical practice, in order to conclude that it supports the action he took in Cambodia."[8]

Both Johnson and Nixon had indulged in presidential war-making beyond the boldest dreams of their predecessors. Those who had stretched the executive war power to what had seemed its "outer limits" in the past had done so in the face of visible and dire threat to national survival: Lincoln confronted by rebellion, Roosevelt by Hitler. Neither had pretended to be exercising routine powers of the Commander in Chief. Johnson and Nixon had surpassed all their predecessors in claiming that inherent and exclusive presidential authority, unaccompanied by emergencies threatening the life of the nation, unaccompanied by the authorization of Congress or the blessing of an international organization, permitted a President to order troops into battle at his unilateral pleasure.

There were interesting differences, however, between the Johnson and Nixon theories of the presidential war power. Johnson's theory was more sweeping in principle but more confined in practice. His administration had argued that an attack on a country far from American shores could impinge "directly" on the nation's security and thereby sanction unilateral presidential action, where Nixon made his case on the presumably narrower ground of potential attack on American forces. But Johnson had restricted his unilateral action to a country with which the United States was in a state of *de facto* war. He had rejected recommendations from his military leaders that he carry the war into the neutral states of Cambodia and Laos.

Now in justifying the commitment of American troops to battle in neutral states with no gesture at all toward (in the words of Andrew Jackson) previous understanding with that body by whom war could alone be declared and by whom all the provisions for sustaining its perils must be furnished—in doing this, Nixon cited no emergency that denied time for congressional action, expressed no doubt about the perfect legality of his personal extension of the war into two new countries, and showed no interest even in retrospective congressional ratification. The authority claimed by Nixon appeared indefinitely extensible so long as a President could declare American forces anywhere in the world in danger of attack. It appeared extinguishable only when an American military withdrawal ended the hazard of such attack.

Though Congress was reluctant to use the power of the purse to stop the war in Vietnam, it did in 1969 and 1970 vote to deny funds for American ground combat troops in Laos, Thailand and, after the fact, Cambodia. In 1971 it added an amendment to the Defense Procurement Authorization Act declaring it "the policy of the United States to terminate at the earliest practicable date all military operations of the United States in Indochina." This declaration, especially in conjunction with the repeal of the Tonkin Gulf resolution, could be considered a cancellation by

[8] W. H. Rehnquist, "The President and Cambodia: His Constitutional Authority," *New York Law Journal*, June 8–9, 1970, reprinted in Senate Foreign Relations Committee, *War Powers Legislation*, 827–32.

Congress of its implicit authorization of further war in Indochina. But, since the amendment contained nothing, such as a fund cut-off, to give it substance, Nixon, on signing the bill, could say with impunity that the congressional declaration did "not represent the policies of the Administration," that it was "without binding force or effect" and that "my signing of the bill that contains this section...will not change the policies I have pursued." There was ample precedent for this disavowal of hortatory congressional resolutions, even if the tone seemed unnecessarily contemptuous. But Senator Church also had a point when he commented, "A century ago, it is inconceivable that a chief executive would have disregarded a statute, let alone dismiss its provisions in such an abrupt and peremptory way. That Mr. Nixon felt no compunction in doing so is a reflection of the low estate to which the Congress had fallen."[9]

Nixon's troop-protection doctrine hinged, however, on one factual requirement: there had to be American troops to protect. It was on this premise, and this premise alone, that the Nixon administration, having abandoned SEATO and the Tonkin Gulf resolution and the Johnson shrunken-world theory of defensive war, had rested its constitutional justification for the continuation of warfare in Indochina. Nixon repeated in 1971 that he would "use American airpower any place in North Vietnam, or in Southeast Asia, where I found that it would be necessary for the purpose of protecting American forces....The justification was, and *must always be*, the defense of American forces in South Vietnam."[10] If this thesis was not very convincing, at least it was a thesis. But what would happen once American forces were withdrawn? On March 28, 1973, this was the situation. Yet the Nixon administration, unperturbed, began to bomb Cambodia more intensively than ever and on occasion threatened renewing bombing in Vietnam. By what authority did it now claim to send Americans into battle?

When Henry Kissinger was asked, after the conclusion in January 1973 of the Paris Agreement on Ending the War and Restoring Peace in Vietnam, if there were "no inhibitions" on the renewal of American bombing in Vietnam, he replied, "That is legally correct. We have the right to do this."[11] Presumably he meant that the American government had a unilateral right under international law to resume bombing in case of violations of the Paris Agreement. If so, that right was short-lived. On March 2 the Declaration of the International Conference on Vietnam, signed by, among others, the American Secretary of State, pledged the signatories, if the Agreement were violated, to consult "either individually or jointly...with the other parties to this Act with a view to determining necessary remedial measures."

It is hard to believe that Kissinger, who after all was once a professor of government at Harvard, could have meant in addition that the President of the United States had the unilateral right under the American Constitution to resume warfare

[9] *Congressional Record*, May 5, 1972, S7386.

[10] Interview with Howard K. Smith, March 22, 1971. Emphasis added.

[11] Interview with Marvin Kalb, *The Listener*, March 1, 1973.

in Indochina. For powers conferred by international law on the government as a whole, President and Congress together, were not necessarily powers at the independent disposal of the President. In Washington members of Congress pressed the constitutional issue for some weeks in vain. One rather sympathized with the administration. The problem of finding legal grounds for the bombing of Cambodia was not easy. Not only were there no troops left to defend, but Cambodia had long since rejected any claim to protection under SEATO, as the administration had conceded to Congress in 1970.[12] Moreover, Congress itself had prohibited the sending of American military advisers or ground troops into Cambodia and had stipulated that other forms of aid to Cambodia could "not be construed as a commitment by the United States to Cambodia for its defense."[13]

Nevertheless the new Secretary of Defense in 1973 (this was Elliot Richardson, who had once served as Justice Frankfurter's law clerk and later as Attorney General of the state in whose constitution John Adams had inserted the phrase "a government of laws, and not of men"; soon he became Attorney General of the United States) now spoke of the Lon Nol government in Cambodia as an "ally." This perplexed members of Congress. It was, Senator McGovern commented, "a fascinating question of law how a country which has refused protection under a treaty, a country whose defense by the United States is prohibited by law, none the less qualifies as an 'ally.'" Indeed, McGovern continued, Cambodia was evidently more than an ally, since Richardson seemed to feel that Lon Nol's "request" for American air strikes gave the President authority to mount those strikes. The Lon Nol regime would therefore seem "a kind of super-ally, with an active role, superseding that of Congress...in our constitutional processes."[14]

Richardson, who was an able lawyer, had obviously had an off day. But the administration did not vouchsafe a considered explanation until April 30, 1973, when Secretary of State Rogers presented a memorandum to the Senate Foreign Relations Committee. The Secretary now denied that the withdrawal of American forces had "created a fundamentally new situation in which new authority must be sought by the President from Congress to carry out air strikes in Cambodia." The Paris Agreement, Rogers said, not only provided for a cease-fire in Vietnam but in Article 20 contemplated a cease-fire in Cambodia. Article 20 in consequence legalized the continuation of air strikes in Cambodia "until such time as a cease-fire could be brought into effect." If it were said that the constitution required the "immediate cessation" of air strikes in Cambodia, this would imply "a Constitution that contains an automatic self-destruct mechanism designed to destroy what has been so painfully achieved." Rogers therefore concluded that the President's executive powers were adequate "to prevent such a self-defeating result."[15]

[12] Elliot Richardson to J. W. Fulbright, May 30, 1970, *Congressional Record*, April 2, 1973, S6287.

[13] Section 6 of the Supplementary Foreign Assistance Act of 1970.

[14] *Congressional Record*, May 17, 1973, S9371.

[15] *New York Times*, May 1, 1973.

This was a feeble argument.[16] Article 20 of the Paris Agreement did not call for a cease-fire in Cambodia. By bringing this up three months later, Rogers seemed to be stating a new condition for the end of American warfare in Indochina. Nor did Article 20 give any of the signatories unilateral authority to enforce the settlement in Cambodia. Nor did Rogers say anything about the consultation required by the Declaration of the International Conference on Vietnam that he himself had signed eight weeks earlier. Nor, indeed, had the Paris Agreement ever been submitted by the President to the Senate as a treaty or to Congress as a joint resolution. When the Geneva Accords of 1954 brought the French war in Indochina to an end, Premier Pierre Mendès-France did submit the Accords to the National Assembly, even though French constitutional practice did not clearly oblige him to do so. The Assembly approved the Accords and commended the government. Mendès-France also promised that, if violation should necessitate a reintroduction of force, he would consult with the Assembly before sending French troops into battle.[17] It was a measure of the difference between the Fourth Republic of 1954 and the American republic of 1973 that the American President, unlike the French Premier, saw no need to include the American Congress in these decisions. (There was less difference, perhaps, between the American republic of 1973 and the Fifth Republic of General de Gaulle.) And, even if the Paris Agreement had been submitted to Congress, the congressional war-making power could hardly be transferred to the executive by an international compact.

All this fiddling, one feels, was by the way. The Deputy Assistant Secretary of State for Far Eastern Affairs probably put the administration view more bluntly when he was asked about the President's legal authority at a congressional briefing. "It is interesting you should ask me about that," he said. "I have got a couple of lawyers working on it." After a moment he added, "The justification is the re-election of President Nixon." "By that theory," the *Washington Post* commented, "he could level Boston."[18]

The Nixon theory of presidential war, above all in its post-troop-protection version, had effectively liquidated the constitutional command that the power to authorize war belonged to the Congress. Nixon had thereby erased the most solemn written check on presidential war. He had not, like Lincoln, confessed to the slightest misgiving about the legality of his course; nor, like Franklin Roosevelt, had he

---

[16] It also had at least one passage of notable dishonesty. The Rogers memorandum claimed that the decision of the United States Court of Appeals in *Mitchell v. Laird* "makes it clear that the President has the constitutional power" to bomb Cambodia for the purpose of bringing the military conflict to an end. "In the words of Judge Wyzanski the President properly acted 'with a profound concern for the durable interests of the nation—its defense, its honor, its morality.'" Wyzanski made no such judgment. What he said was very different: "President Nixon's duty did not go beyond trying to bring the war to an end as promptly as was consistent with a profound concern for the durable interests of the nation—its defense, its honor, its morality. *Whether President Nixon did so proceed is a question which at this stage in history a court is incompetent to answer.*" (Emphasis added.) *Congressional Record*, May 16, 1973, S9259.

[17] Library of Congress, "Congress and the Termination of the Vietnam War," Senate Foreign Relations Committee Print, 93 Cong., I Sess. (1973), 10.

[18] *New York Times*, March 28, 1973; *Washington Post*, March 30, 1973.

sought to involve Congress, if not in the decisions of war, then at least in the decisions of peace. He had aimed to establish as normal presidential power what previous Presidents had regarded as power justified only by extreme emergencies and employable only at their own peril.

With Nixon as with Johnson, the central role for Congress in foreign affairs was to provide aid and comfort to the Commander in Chief. He never sought its advice before major initiatives, and acknowledged its existence afterward mainly by inviting members of Congress to hear Henry Kissinger tell them in mass briefings what they had already read, if less stylishly expressed, in the newspapers....

The presumed requirements of a global and messianic foreign policy had thus begun to swallow up the congressional power to oversee international agreements as well as the congressional power to send armed force into battle against sovereign states. As the American Presidency came to conceive itself the appointed savior of a world whose interests and dangers demanded rapid and incessant deployment of men, arms and decisions, new power, reverence and awe flowed into the White House. Few Presidents had so much rejoiced in the exercise of power as Franklin D. Roosevelt; but even FDR had preferred, when possible, to act in concert and partnership with Congress. The presidential breakaway really came after the Second World War. The postwar Presidents, though Eisenhower and Kennedy markedly less than Truman, Johnson and Nixon, almost came to see the sharing of power with Congress in foreign policy as a derogation of the Presidency. Congress, in increasing self-abasement, almost came to love its impotence. The image of the President acting by himself in foreign affairs, imposing his own sense of reality and necessity on a waiting government and people, became the new orthodoxy.

As the Presidency pursued its independent course in foreign affairs, the constitutional separation of powers began to disappear in the middle distance. In 1967 an apprehensive Senate Judiciary Committee established a Subcommittee on Separation of Powers under the redoubtable chairmanship of Sam Ervin. Six years later the Ervin Subcommittee concluded that "the movement of the United States into the forefront of balance-of-power realpolitik in international matters has been accomplished at the cost of the internal balance of power painstakingly established by the Constitution." Whether this was a necessary cost, the Subcommittee did not say. It would be excessively gloomy, however, to suppose that moderate balance-of-power foreign policy was irreconcilable with the separation of powers. An immoderate balance-of-power foreign policy, however, involving the United States in useless wars and grandiose dreams, was another matter.

Certainly American foreign policy in the age of global intervention had steadily reduced the importance of Congress in the field of national security. Old Carl Vinson of Georgia, who first came to the House of Representatives in 1914, and who served as chairman of the Naval Affairs Committee under the second Roosevelt and as chairman of the Armed Services Committee thereafter, had had an intimate view of this process. The role of Congress, Vinson at last said, "has come to be that of a sometimes querulous but essentially kindly uncle who complains while furiously puffing on his pipe but who finally, as everyone expects, gives in and hands over the allowance, grants the permission, or raises his hand in blessing, and then re-

turns to his rocking chair for another year of somnolence broken only by an occasional anxious glance down the avenue and a muttered doubt as to whether he had
done the right thing."[19]

[19] Separation of Powers Subcommittee, *Congressional Oversight of Executive Agreements*, 93 Cong.,
I Sess. (1973), 1, 3.

PART FIVE

The Advisers
Managers and Bureaucrats

There have been many explanations of how we got into the Vietnam War....But all explanations come back to one. It was the result of a long series of steps taken in response to a bureaucratic view of the world.
—John Kenneth Galbraith, *How to Control the Military,* 1969

The more amiability and esprit de corps among the members of a policymaking in-group, the greater is the danger that independent critical thinking will be replaced by groupthink, which is likely to result in irrational and dehumanizing actions directed against out-groups.
—Irving L. Janis, *Groupthink,* 1982

26

AN AUTOPSY OF THE BUREAUCRACY

JAMES C. THOMSON, JR.

In 1968, attempting to explain America's calamitous involvement in Vietnam, historian and former bureaucrat James C. Thomson, Jr., put decision making in the context of the legacy of the anti-Communist politics of the 1950s and the counterinsurgency strategy of the early 1960s. But the focus of his analysis was on delineating the inner workings of the national security bureaucracy and its perceptions of foreign policy. These included the effectiveness trap, wishful thinking, and bureaucratic ignorance, confusion, and cowardice. Thomson warned of the rise of a class of technocratic ideologues.

As a case study in the making of foreign policy, the Vietnam War will fascinate historians and social scientists for many decades to come. One question that will certainly be asked: How did men of superior ability, sound training, and high ideals— American policy-makers of the 1960s—create such costly and divisive policy?

As one who watched the decision-making process in Washington from 1961 to 1966 under Presidents Kennedy and Johnson, I can suggest a preliminary answer. I can do so by briefly listing some of the factors that seemed to me to shape our Vietnam policy during my years as an East Asia specialist at the State Department and the White House. I shall deal largely with Washington as I saw or sensed it, and not with Saigon, where I have spent but a scant three days, in the entourage of the Vice President, or with other decision centers, the capitals of interested parties. Nor will I deal with other important parts of the record: Vietnam's history prior to 1961, for instance, or the overall course of America's relations with Vietnam.

Yet a first and central ingredient in these years of Vietnam decisions does involve history. The ingredient was *the legacy of the 1950s*—by which I mean the

From James C. Thomson, Jr., "How Could Vietnam Happen? An Autopsy," *Atlantic Monthly* 221 (April 1968): 47–53. Copyright © 1968 by James C. Thomson, Jr. Reprinted by permission of the author.

so-called "loss of China," the Korean War, and the Far East policy of Secretary of State Dulles.

This legacy had an institutional by-product for the Kennedy Administration: in 1961 the U.S. government's East Asian establishment was undoubtedly the most rigid and doctrinaire of Washington's regional divisions in foreign affairs. This was especially true at the Department of State, where the incoming Administration found the Bureau of Far Eastern Affairs the hardest nut to crack. It was a bureau that had been purged of its best China expertise, and of farsighted, dispassionate men, as a result of McCarthyism. Its members were generally committed to one policy line: the close containment and isolation of mainland China, the harassment of "neutralist" nations which sought to avoid alignment with either Washington or Peking, and the maintenance of a network of alliances with anti-Communist client states on China's periphery.

Another aspect of the legacy was the special vulnerability and sensitivity of the new Democratic Administration on Far East policy issues. The memory of the McCarthy era was still very sharp, and Kennedy's margin of victory was too thin. The 1960 Offshore Islands TV debate between Kennedy and Nixon had shown the President-elect the perils of "fresh thinking." The Administration was inherently leery of moving too fast on Asia. As a result, the Far East Bureau (now the Bureau of East Asian and Pacific Affairs) was the last one to be overhauled. Not until Averell Harriman was brought in as Assistant Secretary in December, 1961, were significant personnel changes attempted, and it took Harriman several months to make a deep imprint on the bureau because of his necessary preoccupation with the Laos settlement. Once he did so, there was virtually no effort to bring back the purged or exiled East Asia experts.

There were other important by-products of this "legacy of the fifties":

The new Administration inherited and somewhat shared *a general perception of China-on-the-march*—a sense of China's vastness, its numbers, its belligerence; a revived sense, perhaps, of the Golden Horde. This was a perception fed by Chinese intervention in the Korean War (an intervention actually based on appallingly bad communications and mutual miscalculation on the part of Washington and Peking; but the careful unraveling of that tragedy, which scholars have accomplished, had not yet become part of the conventional wisdom).

The new Administration inherited and briefly accepted *a monolithic conception of the Communist bloc*. Despite much earlier predictions and reports by outside analysts, policy-makers did not begin to accept the reality and possible finality of the Sino-Soviet split until the first weeks of 1962. The inevitably corrosive impact of competing nationalisms on Communism was largely ignored.

The new Administration inherited and to some extent shared *the "domino theory" about Asia*. This theory resulted from profound ignorance of Asian history and hence ignorance of the radical differences among Asian nations and societies. It resulted from a blindness to the power and resilience of Asian nationalisms. (It may also have resulted from a subconscious sense that, since "all Asians look alike," all Asian nations will act alike.) As a theory, the domino fallacy was not merely inaccurate but also insulting to Asian nations; yet it has continued to this day to beguile men who should know better.

Finally, the legacy of the fifties was apparently compounded by an uneasy sense of a worldwide Communist challenge to the new Administration after the Bay of Pigs fiasco. A first manifestation was the President's traumatic Vienna meeting with Khrushchev in June, 1961; then came the Berlin crisis of the summer. All this created an atmosphere in which President Kennedy undoubtedly felt under special pressure to show his nation's mettle in Vietnam—if the Vietnamese, unlike the people of Laos, were willing to fight.

In general, the legacy of the fifties shaped such early moves of the new Administration as the decisions to maintain a high-visibility SEATO (by sending the Secretary of State himself instead of some underling to its first meeting in 1961), to back away from diplomatic recognition of Mongolia in the summer of 1961, and most important, to expand U.S. military assistance to South Vietnam that winter on the basis of the much more tentative Eisenhower commitment. It should be added that the increased commitment to Vietnam was also fueled by a new breed of military strategists and academic social scientists (some of whom had entered the new Administration) who had developed theories of counterguerrilla warfare and were eager to see them put to the test. To some, "counterinsurgency" seemed a new panacea for coping with the world's instability.

So much for the legacy and the history. Any new Administration inherits both complicated problems and simplistic views of the world. But surely among the policymakers of the Kennedy and Johnson Administrations there were men who would warn of the dangers of an open-ended commitment to the Vietnam quagmire?

This raises a central question, at the heart of the policy process: Where were the experts, the doubters, and the dissenters? Were they there at all, and if so, what happened to them?

The answer is complex but instructive.

In the first place, the American government was sorely *lacking in real Vietnam or Indochina expertise*. Originally treated as an adjunct of Embassy Paris, our Saigon embassy and the Vietnam Desk at State were largely staffed from 1954 onward by French-speaking Foreign Service personnel of narrowly European experience. Such diplomats were even more closely restricted than the normal embassy officer—by cast of mind as well as language—to contacts with Vietnam's French-speaking urban elites. For instance, Foreign Service linguists in Portugal are able to speak with the peasantry if they get out of Lisbon and choose to do so; not so the French speakers of Embassy Saigon.

In addition, the *shadow of the "loss of China"* distorted Vietnam reporting. Career officers in the Department, and especially those in the field, had not forgotten the fate of their World War II colleagues who wrote in frankness from China and were later pilloried by Senate committees for critical comments on the Chinese Nationalists. Candid reporting on the strengths of the Viet Cong and the weaknesses of the Diem government was inhibited by the memory. It was also inhibited by some higher officials, notably Ambassador Nolting in Saigon, who refused to sign off on such cables.

In due course, to be sure, some Vietnam talent was discovered or developed. But a recurrent and increasingly important factor in the decision-making process was *the banishment of real expertise*. Here the underlying cause was the "closed politics" of policy-making as issues became hot: the more sensitive the issue, and the higher it rises in the bureaucracy, the more completely the experts are excluded while the harassed senior generalists take over (that is, the Secretaries, Undersecretaries, and Presidential Assistants). The frantic skimming of briefing papers in the back seats of limousines is no substitute for the presence of specialists; furthermore, in times of crisis such papers are deemed "too sensitive" even for review by the specialists. Another underlying cause of this banishment, as Vietnam became more critical, was the replacement of the experts, who were generally and increasingly pessimistic, by men described as "can-do guys," loyal and energetic fixers unsoured by expertise. In early 1965, when I confided my growing policy doubts to an older colleague on the NSC staff, he assured me that the smartest thing both of us could do was to "steer clear of the whole Vietnam mess"; the gentleman in question had the misfortune to be a "can-do guy," however, and is now highly placed in Vietnam, under orders to solve the mess.

Despite the banishment of the experts, internal doubters and dissenters did indeed appear and persist. Yet as I watched the process, such men were effectively neutralized by a subtle dynamic: *the domestication of dissenters*. Such "domestication" arose out of a twofold clubbish need: on the one hand, the dissenter's desire to stay aboard; and on the other hand, the nondissenter's conscience. Simply stated, dissent, when recognized, was made to feel at home. On the lowest possible scale of importance, I must confess my own considerable sense of dignity and acceptance (both vital) when my senior White House employer would refer to me as his "favorite dove." Far more significant was the case of the former Undersecretary of State, George Ball. Once Mr. Ball began to express doubts, he was warmly institutionalized: he was encouraged to become the inhouse devil's advocate on Vietnam. The upshot was inevitable: the process of escalation allowed for periodic requests to Mr. Ball to speak his piece; Ball felt good, I assume (he had fought for righteousness); the others felt good (they had given a full hearing to the dovish option); and there was minimal unpleasantness. The club remained intact; and it is of course possible that matters would have gotten worse faster if Mr. Ball had kept silent, or left before his final departure in the fall of 1966. There was also, of course, the case of the last institutionalized doubter, Bill Moyers. The President is said to have greeted his arrival at meetings with an affectionate, "Well, here comes Mr. Stop-the-Bombing. . . ." Here again the dynamics of domesticated dissent sustained the relationship for a while.

A related point—and crucial, I suppose, to government at all times—was *the "effectiveness" trap*, the trap that keeps men from speaking out, as clearly or often as they might, within the government. And it is the trap that keeps men from resigning in protest and airing their dissent outside the government. The most important asset that a man brings to bureaucratic life is his "effectiveness," a mysterious combination of training, style, and connections. The most ominous complaint that can be whispered of a bureaucrat is: "I'm afraid Charlie's beginning to lose his effectiveness." To preserve your effectiveness, you must decide where and when to fight the mainstream of policy; the opportunities range from pillow talk with your wife, to private drinks with your friends, to meetings with the Secretary of State or the President. The inclination to remain silent or to acquiesce in the presence of the great men—to live to fight another day, to give on this issue so that you can be "effective" on later issues—is overwhelming. Nor is it the tendency of youth alone; some of our most senior officials, men of wealth and fame, whose place in history is secure, have remained silent lest their connection with power be terminated. As for the disinclination to resign in protest: while not necessarily a Washington or even American specialty, it seems more true of a government in which ministers have no parliamentary backbench to which to retreat. In the absence of such a refuge, it is easy to rationalize the decision to stay aboard. By doing so, one may be able to prevent a few bad things from happening and perhaps even make a few good things happen. To exit is to lose even those marginal chances for "effectiveness."

Another factor must be noted: as the Vietnam controversy escalated at home, there developed *a preoccupation with Vietnam public relations as opposed to Vietnam policy-making*. And here, ironically, internal doubters and dissenters were heavily employed. For such men, by virtue of their own doubts, were often deemed best able to "massage" the doubting intelligentsia. My senior East Asia colleague at the White House, a brilliant and humane doubter who had dealt with Indochina since 1954, spent three quarters of his working days on Vietnam public relations: drafting presidential responses to letters from important critics, writing conciliatory language for presidential speeches, and meeting quite interminably with delegations of outraged Quakers, clergymen, academics, and housewives. His regular callers were the late A. J. Muste and Norman Thomas; mine were members of the Women's Strike for Peace. Our orders from above: keep them off the backs of busy policy-makers (who usually happened to be nondoubters). Incidentally, my most discouraging assignment in the realm of public relations was the preparation of a White House pamphlet entitled *Why Vietnam*, in September, 1965; in a gesture toward my conscience, I fought—and lost—a battle to have the title followed by a question mark.

Through a variety of procedures, both institutional and personal, doubt, dissent, and expertise were effectively neutralized in the making of policy. But what can be said of the men "in charge"? It is patently absurd to suggest that they produced such tragedy by intention and calculation. But it is neither absurd nor difficult to discern certain forces at work that caused decent and honorable men to do great harm.

Here I would stress the paramount role of *executive fatigue*. No factor seems to me more crucial and underrated in the making of foreign policy. The physical and emotional toll of executive responsibility in State, the Pentagon, the White House, and other executive agencies is enormous; that toll is of course compounded by extended service. Many of today's Vietnam policy-makers have been on the job for from four to seven years. Complaints may be few, and physical health may remain unimpaired, though emotional health is far harder to gauge. But what is most seriously eroded in the deadening process of fatigue is freshness of thought, imagination, a sense of possibility, a sense of priorities and perspective—those rare assets of a new Administration in its first year or two of office. The tired policy-maker becomes a prisoner of his own narrowed view of the world and his own clichéd rhetoric. He becomes irritable and defensive—short on sleep, short on family ties, short on patience. Such men make bad policy and then compound it. They have neither the time nor the temperament for new ideas or preventive diplomacy.

Below the level of the fatigued executives in the making of Vietnam policy was a widespread phenomenon: *the curator mentality* in the Department of State. By this I mean the collective inertia produced by the bureaucrat's view of his job. At State, the average "desk officer" inherits from his predecessor our policy toward Country X; he regards it as his function to keep that policy intact—under glass, untampered with, and dusted—so that he may pass it on in two to four years to his successor. And such curatorial service generally merits promotion within the system. (Maintain the status quo, and you will stay out of trouble.) In some circumstances, the inertia bred by such an outlook can act as a brake against rash innovation. But on many issues, this inertia sustains the momentum of bad policy and unwise commitments—momentum that might otherwise have been resisted within the ranks. Clearly, Vietnam is such as issue.

To fatigue and inertia must be added the factor of internal confusion. Even among the "architects" of our Vietnam commitment, there has been persistent *confusion as to what type of war we were fighting* and, as a direct consequence, *confusion as to how to end that war*. (The "credibility gap" is, in part, a reflection of such internal confusion.) Was it, for instance, a civil war, in which case counterinsurgency might suffice? Or was it a war of international aggression? (This might invoke SEATO or UN commitment.) Who was the aggressor—and the "real enemy"? The Viet Cong? Hanoi? Peking? Moscow? International Communism? Or maybe "Asian Communism"? Differing enemies dictated differing strategies and tactics. And confused throughout, in like fashion, was the question of American objectives; your objectives depended on whom you were fighting and why. I shall not forget my assignment from an Assistant Secretary of State in March, 1964: to draft a speech for Secretary McNamara which would, *inter alia*, once and for all dispose of the canard that the Vietnam conflict was a civil war. "But in some ways, of course," I mused, "it *is* a civil war." "Don't play word games with me!" snapped the Assistant Secretary.

Similar confusion beset the concept of "negotiations"—anathema to much of official Washington from 1961 to 1965. Not until April, 1965, did "unconditional discussions" become respectable, via a presidential speech; even then the Secretary of State stressed privately to newsmen that nothing had changed, since "discussions" were by no means the same as "negotiations." Months later that issue was resolved. But it took even longer to obtain a fragile internal agreement that negotiations might include the Viet Cong as something other than an appendage to Hanoi's delegation. Given such confusion as to the whos and whys of our Vietnam commitment, it is not surprising, as Theodore Draper has written, that policy-makers find it so difficult to agree on how to end the war.

Of course, one force—a constant in the vortex of commitment—was that of *wishful thinking*. I partook of it myself at many times. I did so especially during

Washington's struggle with Diem in the autumn of 1963 when some of us at State believed that for once, in dealing with a difficult client state, the U.S. government could use the leverage of our economic and military assistance to make good things happen, instead of being led around by the nose by men like Chiang Kai-shek and Syngman Rhee (and, in that particular instance, by Diem). If we could prove that point, I thought, and move into a new day, with or without Diem, then Vietnam was well worth the effort. Later came the wishful thinking of the air-strike planners in the late autumn of 1964; there were those who actually thought that after six weeks of air strikes, the North Vietnamese would come crawling to us to ask for peace talks. And what, someone asked in one of the meetings of the time, if they don't? The answer was that we would bomb for another four weeks, and that would do the trick. And a few weeks later came one instance of wishful thinking that was symptomatic of good men misled: in January, 1965, I encountered one of the very highest figures in the Administration at a dinner, drew him aside, and told him of my worries about the air-strike option. He told me that I really shouldn't worry; it was his conviction that before any such plans could be put into effect, a neutralist government would come to power in Saigon that would politely invite us out. And finally, there was the recurrent wishful thinking that sustained many of us through the trying months of 1965–1966 after the air strikes had begun: that surely, somehow, one way or another, we would "be in a conference in six months," and the escalatory spiral would be suspended. The basis of our hope: "It simply can't go on."

As a further influence on policy-makers I would cite the factor of *bureaucratic detachment*. By this I mean what at best might be termed the professional callousness of the surgeon (and indeed, medical lingo—the "surgical strike" for instance— seemed to crop up in the euphemisms of the times). In Washington the semantics of the military muted the reality of war for the civilian policy-makers. In quiet, air-conditioned, thick-carpeted rooms, such terms as "systematic pressure," "armed reconnaissance," "targets of opportunity," and even "body count" seemed to breed a sort of games-theory detachment. Most memorable to me was a moment in the late 1964 target planning when the question under discussion was how heavy our bombing should be, and how extensive our strafing, at some midpoint in the projected pattern of systematic pressure. An Assistant Secretary of State resolved the point in the following words: "It seems to me that our orchestration should be mainly violins, but with periodic touches of brass." Perhaps the biggest shock of my return to Cambridge, Massachusetts, was the realization that the young men, the flesh and blood I taught and saw on these university streets, were potentially some of the numbers on the charts of those faraway planners. In a curious sense, Cambridge is closer to this war than Washington.

There is an unprovable factor that relates to bureaucratic detachment: the ingredient of *cryptoracism*. I do not mean to imply any conscious contempt for Asian loss of life on the part of Washington officials. But I do mean to imply that bureaucratic detachment may well be compounded by a traditional Western sense that there are so many Asians, after all; that Asians have a fatalism about life and a disregard for its loss; that they are cruel and barbaric to their own people; and that they are very different from us (and all look alike?). And I *do* mean to imply that the upshot of such subliminal views is a subliminal question whether Asians, and particularly Asian peasants, and most particularly Asian Communists, are really people—like you and me. To put the matter another way: would we have pursued quite such policies—and quite such military tactics—if the Vietnamese were white?

It is impossible to write of Vietnam decision-making without writing about language. Throughout the conflict, words have been of paramount importance. I refer here to the impact of *rhetorical escalation* and to the *problem of oversell*. In an important sense, Vietnam has become of crucial significance to us *because we have said that it is of crucial significance*. (The issue obviously relates to the public relations preoccupation described earlier.)

The key here is domestic politics: the need to sell the American people, press, and Congress on support for an unpopular and costly war in which the objectives themselves have been in flux. To sell means to persuade, and to persuade means rhetoric. As the difficulties and costs have mounted, so has the definition of the stakes. This is not to say that rhetorical escalation is an orderly process; executive prose is the product of many writers, and some concepts—North Vietnamese infiltration, America's "national honor," Red China as the chief enemy—have entered the rhetoric only gradually and even sporadically. But there is an upward spiral nonetheless. And once you have *said* that the American Experiment itself stands or falls on the Vietnam outcome, you have thereby created a national stake far beyond any earlier stakes.

Crucial throughout the process of Vietnam decision-making was a conviction among many policy-makers: that Vietnam posed a *fundamental test of America's national will*. Time and again I was told by men reared in the tradition of Henry L. Stimson that all we needed was the will, and we would then prevail. Implicit in such a view, it seemed to me, was a curious assumption that Asians lacked will, or at least that in a contest between Asian and Anglo-Saxon wills, the non-Asians must prevail. A corollary to the persistent belief in will was a *fascination with power* and an awe in the face of the power America possessed as no nation or civilization ever before. Those who doubted our role in Vietnam were said to shrink from the burdens of power, the obligations of power, the uses of power, the responsibility of power. By implication, such men were soft-headed and effete.

Finally, no discussion of the factors and forces at work on Vietnam policy-makers can ignore the central fact of *human ego investment*. Men who have participated in a decision develop a stake in that decision. As they participate in further, related decisions, their stake increases. It might have been possible to dissuade a man of strong self-confidence at an early stage of the ladder of decision; but it is infinitely harder at later stages since a change of mind there usually involves implicit or explicit repudiation of a chain of previous decisions.

To put it bluntly: at the heart of the Vietnam calamity is a group of able, dedicated men who have been regularly and repeatedly wrong—and whose standing with their contemporaries, and more important, with history, depends, as they see it, on being proven right. These are not men who can be asked to extricate themselves from error.

The various ingredients I have cited in the making of Vietnam policy have created a variety of results, most of them fairly obvious. Here are some that seem to me most central:

Throughout the conflict, there has been *persistent and repeated miscalculation* by virtually all the actors, in high echelons and low, whether dove, hawk, or something else. To cite one simple example among many: in late 1964 and early 1965, some peace-seeking planners at State who strongly opposed the projected bombing of the North urged that, instead, American ground forces be sent to South Vietnam; this would, they said, increase our bargaining leverage against the North—our "chips"—and would give us something to negotiate about (the withdrawal of our forces) at an early peace conference. Simultaneously, the air-strike option was urged by many in the military who were dead set against American participation in "another land war in Asia"; they were joined by other civilian peace-seekers who wanted to bomb Hanoi into early negotiations. By late 1965, we had ended up with the worst of all worlds: ineffective and costly air strikes against the North, spiraling ground forces in the South, and no negotiations in sight.

Throughout the conflict as well, there has been *a steady give-in to pressures for a military solution* and only minimal and sporadic efforts at a diplomatic and political solution. In part this resulted from the confusion (earlier cited) among the civilians—confusion regarding objectives and strategy. And in part this resulted from the self-enlarging nature of military investment. Once air strikes and particularly ground forces were introduced, our investment itself had transformed the original stakes. More air power was needed to protect the ground forces; and then more ground forces to protect the ground forces. And needless to say, the military mind develops its own momentum in the absence of clear guidelines from the civilians. Once asked to save South Vietnam, rather than to "advise" it, the American military could not but press for escalation. In addition, sad to report, assorted military constituencies, once involved in Vietnam, have had a series of cases to prove: for instance, the utility not only of air power (the Air Force) but of supercarrier-based air power (the Navy). Also, Vietnam policy has suffered from one ironic by-product of Secretary McNamara's establishment of civilian control at the Pentagon: in the face of such control, interservice rivalry has given way to a united front among the military—reflected in the new but recurrent phenomenon of JCS unanimity. In conjunction with traditional congressional allies (mostly Southern senators and representatives) such a united front would pose a formidable problem for any President.

Throughout the conflict, there have been *missed opportunities, large and small, to disengage ourselves from Vietnam on increasingly unpleasant but still acceptable terms.* Of the many moments from 1961 onward, I shall cite only one, the last and most important opportunity that was lost: in the summer of 1964 the President instructed his chief advisers to prepare for him as wide a range of Vietnam options as possible for postelection consideration and decision. He explicitly asked that all options be laid out. What happened next was, in effect, Lyndon Johnson's slow-motion Bay of Pigs. For the advisers so effectively converged on one single option—juxtaposed against two other, phony options (in effect, blowing up the world, or scuttle-and-run)—that the President was confronted with unanimity for bombing the North from all his trusted counselors. Had he been more confident in foreign affairs, had he been deeply informed on Vietnam and Southeast Asia, and had he raised some hard questions that unanimity had submerged, this President could have used the largest electoral mandate in history to de-escalate in Vietnam, in the clear expectation that at the worst a neutralist government would come to power in Saigon and politely invite us out. Today, many lives and dollars later, such an alternative has become an elusive and infinitely more expensive possibility.

In the course of these years, another result of Vietnam decision-making has been *the abuse and distortion of history*. Vietnamese, Southeast Asian, and Far Eastern history has been rewritten by our policy-makers, and their spokesmen, to conform with the alleged necessity of our presence in Vietnam. Highly dubious analogies from our experience elsewhere—the "Munich" sellout and "containment" from Europe, the Malayan insurgency and the Korean War from Asia—have been imported in order to justify our actions. And more recent events have been fitted to the Procrustean bed of Vietnam. Most notably, the change of power in Indonesia in 1965–1966 has been ascribed to our Vietnam presence; and virtually all progress in the Pacific region—the rise of regionalism, new forms of cooperation, and mounting growth rates—has been similarly explained. The Indonesian allegation is undoubtedly false (I tried to prove it, during six months of careful investigation at the White House, and had to confess failure); the regional allegation is patently unprovable in either direction (except, of course, for the clear fact that the economies of both Japan and Korea have profited enormously from our Vietnam-related procurement in these countries; but that is a costly and highly dubious form of foreign aid).

There is a final result of Vietnam policy I would cite that holds potential danger for the future of American foreign policy: *the rise of a new breed of American ideologues who see Vietnam as the ultimate test of their doctrine*. I have in mind those men in Washington who have given a new life to the missionary impulse in American foreign relations: who believe that this nation, in this era, has received a threefold endowment that can transform the world. As they see it, that endowment is composed of, first, our unsurpassed military might; second, our clear technological supremacy; and third, our allegedly invincible benevolence (our "altruism," our affluence, our lack of territorial aspirations). Together, it is argued, this threefold endowment provides us with the opportunity and the obligation to ease the nations of the earth toward modernization and stability: toward a full-fledged *Pax Americana Technocratica*. In reaching toward this goal, Vietnam is viewed as the last and crucial test. Once we have succeeded there, the road ahead is clear. In a sense, these men are our counterpart to the visionaries of Communism's radical left: they are technocracy's own Maoists. They do not govern Washington today. But their doctrine rides high.

Long before I went into government, I was told a story about Henry L. Stimson that seemed to me pertinent during the years that I watched the Vietnam tragedy unfold—and participated in that tragedy. It seems to me more pertinent than ever as we move toward the election of 1968.

In his waning years Stimson was asked by an anxious questioner, "Mr. Secretary, how on earth can we ever bring peace to the world?" Stimson is said to have answered: "You begin by bringing to Washington a small handful of able men who believe that the achievement of peace is possible.

"You work them to the bone until they no longer believe that it is possible.

"And then you throw them out—and bring in a new bunch who believe that it is possible."

27

BUREAUCRACY'S CALL FOR U.S. GROUND TROOPS

GEORGE McTURNAN KAHIN

According to political scientist and Southeast Asia scholar George Kahin, officials in Washington were alarmed in spring 1965 over the deteriorating military and political situation in South Vietnam. The bombing of North Vietnam was ineffective, ARVN was on the defensive, and the Saigon government was unpopular and weak. In the excerpt below, Kahin describes the mentality of President Johnson's national security managers and the advice they gave him for increasing the commitment of U.S. ground troops and rejecting the path of a negotiated settlement. In addition to some civilian advisers, the Joint Chiefs of Staff, General William Westmoreland, and Admiral Ulysses G. Sharp pushed hard for escalation.

From *Intervention: How America Became Involved in Vietnam* by George McT. Kahin. Copyright © 1986 by George McT. Kahin. Reprinted by permission of Alfred A. Knopf, Inc.

...Taylor and Westmoreland were not alone in their alarm. That the military and political deterioration of the Saigon regime was accelerating was now, in fact, becoming a broadly based perception within the administration, and was eloquently reflected in a White House memorandum prepared for Chester Cooper on March 22.[1] This memorandum shows a striking preoccupation with the absence of indigenous political foundations for the U.S. military effort. Two of the "three major problem areas" it regarded as of "overriding importance in the precariousness" of the U.S. position related to this deficiency. "The lack of a political base for the GVN [Saigon government] of sufficient strength to counter Viet Cong political and psychologic superiorities" was perceived as being so great that, to compensate, an American effort was needed "of the scope undertaken by the U.S. in support of the Diem government in 1954–55." Coupled to this "political action effort," "psychological operations" would have to be mounted for "motivating the government administration, military forces and populace in support of the government."

There was, the memorandum continued, a "growing lack of confidence among the GVN leadership—political and military—and the populace in the ultimate success of the counterinsurgency." This was "a direct result of the apparent superiority of the Viet Cong in the military, political, and psychological fields." Neither "U.S. punitive expeditions against North Vietnam" nor "the limited deployment of U.S. ground forces to provide security for rear installations" had induced "the morale boost necessary to offset this lack of confidence." In view of all this, together with the Saigon forces' ineffectiveness in countering the threat posed by the Viet Cong main-force battalions and regiments, substantial reinforcements were needed. Otherwise there was likely to be "continued deterioration—possibly at an accelerating rate." Since the ARVN was already "too thinly spread," only by "abandoning wide areas," with a consequent "serious adverse impact on morale," could its forces be regrouped for a more effective confrontation of the Viet Cong. It was argued that the only alternative was "introducing additional forces from outside Vietnam." "If done on a sufficiently large scale [this] would have a substantial favorable impact on the military situation and on morale in South Vietnam, would adversely affect morale of the Viet Cong, and would clearly demonstrate to Hanoi and Peking the extent of U.S. determination and will to end Communist aggression in South Vietnam." About three divisions—the amount then being proposed by the JCS— were needed "to have the necessary impact on the military situation," and they "should be employed essentially in offensive and counteroffensive operations against major Viet Cong troop concentrations rather than in security or pacification missions."[2]

John McNaughton's draft memorandum for McNamara written during the period March 10–24 reveals the administration's state of mind as to military and political prospects in the South. It also makes more understandable why West-

[1] Memorandum for Chester Cooper, "Courses of Action in South Vietnam," March 22, 1965, White House Files: NSF, Vietnam, vol. 31.

[2] Recommendation of three divisions is in Memorandum for the President from McG. B[undy], "The History of Recommendations for Increased U.S. Forces in Vietnam," July 24, 1965.

moreland and the JCS succeeded in their now insistent campaign for introducing substantial U.S. ground combat forces.[3] Concerning the "deteriorating situation," McNaughton reported that "militarily, SVN has been cut in two with GVN [Saigon's] control in [the] north [of South Vietnam] reduced to enclaves" and "politically, 50% chance of coup within 3 weeks." In terms of basic U.S. objectives in Vietnam, his "Prognosis" forecast a progressive political and military deterioration leading to unmitigated disaster:

(a) GVN officials will adjust their behavior to an eventual VC takeover.
(b) Defections of significant military forces will take place.
(c) Whole integrated regions of the country will be totally denied to GVN.
(d) Neutral and/or left wing elements will enter the government.
(e) A popular-front regime will emerge which will invite the U.S. out.
(f) Fundamental concessions will be made to the VC.
(g) Accommodations to the DRV will put SVN behind the Curtain.

McNaughton's scenario depicted the perceived course of events if the existing level of U.S. power were not increased. He posited three possible alternative courses of action: "progressively squeeze North Vietnam; or add massive U.S. ground effort in South Vietnam; or downgrade the apparent stakes." The increasing bombing pressure and covert actions to implement the first course were already well under way, with the tonnage of bombing and scope of targets soon to grow. The ground effort envisaged in the second alternative was very soon to be approved and set in motion. But the third option, that of downgrading the stakes in Vietnam, was not given a serious hearing. Yet had this been followed in 1965, the United States might well have achieved at least as many of its objectives as it secured ten years later, and without the enormous losses of life that this delay entailed. The terms of this option should be noted.

If and when it is estimated that even the best US/GVN efforts mean failure (undesirable escalation or defeat), it will be important to act to minimize the damage to the U.S. effectiveness and image thereafter by such steps as these:

(a) Deliver ultimatum to coup-prone generals to "shape up or ship out," and when they patently fail to shape up, we ship out.
(b) Publicize uniqueness and congenital impossibility of SVN case (e.g., Vietminh held much of SVN in 1954, long uncontrollable borders, unfavorable terrain, absence of national tradition or administrators,

[3] Memorandum from Office of Assistant Secretary of Defense, by John McNaughton, March 10, 1965. This was apparently the first draft of his memorandum "Plan for Action for South Vietnam," of which a later draft (March 24) is reproduced in *PP* (*NYT*), pp. 432–40. (The authors of the *NYT* account are clearly incorrect in believing that the draft they cite was the first. The March 10 draft, from which I quote, bears the handwritten note on the cover page "Mac—A preliminary shot at an outline.") McNaughton held the post of assistant secretary of defense until July 19, 1967, when he died in an air crash in the United States. [Ed. note: *PP* (*NYT*)=Neil Sheehan, Hedrick Smith, E. W. Kenworthy, and Fox Butterfield, *The Pentagon Papers as Published by "The New York Times"* (Bantam Books, 1971).]

       mess left by French, competing factions, Communist LOC [line of
communications] advantage, late U.S. start, etc.).
(c) Create diversionary "offensives" elsewhere in the world (e.g., to
     shore up Thailand, Philippines, Malaysia, India, Australia); launch
     an "anti-poverty program" for underdeveloped areas.
(d) Enter multi-nation negotiations calculated to shift opinions and
     values.
(e) Shift to Saigon focus of decision and discussion.

    In his initial draft McNaughton did not append to this third option any men-
tion of the risks it might entail. However, two weeks later, presumably after feed-
back from McNamara and others, the new version did contain such a caveat, which
in its entirety reads, "Risks. With the physical situation and the trends as they are
the fear is overwhelming that an exit negotiated now would result in humiliation for
the US."[4]
    This fear of national humiliation, and the attendant damage to their own
prestige, remained at the forefront of the minds of the president's advisers and
of the president himself, and the same was to be true of Nixon's administration.
Moreover, most of the president's associates were apparently still confident that
through the injection of U.S. power they could engineer the survival of a separate state in the southern half of Vietnam, regardless of the continuing lack of
any significant indigenous foundation. With reservoirs of U.S. military might
still available, they were not interested in any serious exploration of a disengagement—whether negotiated or otherwise—at least until they could assess the
consequences of applying this additional power. They clearly hoped that the results would vindicate them and the advice they had already given the president,
while saving him, the country—and themselves—from the humiliation that they
believed would ensue from switching to a negotiations track at a time when their
South Vietnamese ward was so weak. Perhaps later, if the balance of internal
forces had been favorably affected by an injection of sufficient additional American
power, they would be willing to risk taking that route, but not now.

    In Robert McNamara's policy memorandum of mid-March 1964 the central
U.S. objective had been "an independent non-communist South Vietnam," which
had to be maintained both to keep the rest of Southeast Asia from falling under
communist dominance and to demonstrate to the rest of the world through this
"test case" the capacity of the United States "to help a nation meet a Communist
'war of liberation.'"[5]
    In the internal rationale of a year later, however, these considerations were
much less prominent; indeed, the fate of the South Vietnamese themselves seems

---

[4] In this version of March 24, 1965, the third option was subsumed within a section headed "Exit by
Negotiations." (*PP* [*NYT*]), pp. 437–38.)

[5] *Ibid.*, p. 278; *PP* (Gravel), 3:499–500. [Ed. note: *PP* (Gravel)=*The Pentagon Papers: The Defense
Department History of United States Decisionmaking on Vietnam: The Senator Gravel Edition*, 4 vols. (Beacon
Press, 1971).]

to have become a minor consideration. Partly because the administration had publicly endowed the struggle in Vietnam with enormous importance—through its apocalyptic rhetoric as well as its actions—the American involvement had become the focus of such a glaringly intense spotlight of worldwide attention that Johnson's advisers now placed much greater emphasis on how the United States looked in its efforts to manage events in this increasingly prominent part of the world. And both the president and his advisers often seemed to have difficulty in distinguishing between their personal prestige and that of the United States.[6] These advisers clearly believed that further American military escalation might work. In any case it was consistent with the primarily military approach with which they and their careers had already become so closely identified, and consistency is usually a prerequisite for protecting a public career.

Perhaps the most succinct articulation of the internal rationale that had now emerged was incorporated in the above-mentioned memorandum of McNaughton, an official upon whose judgment McNamara relied heavily. This weighted United States objectives in Vietnam as: "70% To avoid a humiliating U.S. defeat (to our reputation as a guarantor), 20% To keep SVN [South Vietnam] (and the adjacent) territory from Chinese hands, 10% To permit the people of SVN to enjoy a better, freer way of life." This preoccupation with the reputation of the United States, and of the administration in office and its top officials, was to influence American policy heavily during the next decade. Equally revealing of the paramount importance now attached to U.S. prestige was one of the concluding paragraphs in McNaughton's memorandum, captioned "Evaluation."

> It is essential—however badly SEA [Southeast Asia] may go over the next 1–3 years—that U.S. emerge as a "good doctor." We must have kept promises, been tough, taken risks, gotten bloodied and hurt the enemy very badly. We must avoid harmful appearances which will affect judgments by, and provide pretexts to, other nations regarding how the U.S. will behave in future cases of particular interest to those nations— regarding U.S. policy, power, resolve and competence to deal with their problems. In this connection, the relevant audiences are the Communists (who must feel strong pressures), the South Vietnamese (whose morale must be buoyed), our allies (who must trust us as "underwriters") and the U.S. public (which must support our risk-taking with U.S. lives and prestige).

McNaughton's category of "humiliating defeat" was, of course, relevant not only to audiences outside the United States, but also to the domestic political considerations so ingrained in the minds of the president and his advisers as to be taken for granted and require no explicit articulation in a strictly internal

---

[6] This difficulty in distinguishing personal from U.S. prestige was emphasized by George Ball in a discussion with the author, January 1965, and by James Thomson, who during this period served as senior White House aide. (Seminar, Cornell University, November 5, 1979. See also his "How Could Vietnam Happen?" *Atlantic Monthly*, April 1968.)

memorandum. This was the political calculation that failure to keep South
Vietnam free of communist control would leave the Democratic Party open to
a Vietnamese analogue of the damaging "loss of China" charge. That consideration had been pertinent even in Truman's approach to Vietnam, and for
Johnson as well as Kennedy it remained an abiding obsession that any administration that could be charged with responsibility for "losing" more Asian territory to communist control would stand vulnerable to serious domestic political
attack.

The rationales the administration presented for its Vietnam policy inter-
nally and publicly diverged widely. For the public the relative importance of
McNaughton's three objectives was reversed (and, of course, the "loss of China"
syndrome was not referred to). Thus, conspicuous in Lyndon Johnson's major
speech of April 7 was self-determination—albeit highly qualified and built on
the premise of there being an "independent nation of South Vietnam." The
American objective was that the Vietnamese "be allowed to guide their own
country in their own way," and "free from outside interference." (However
bizarre such an objective must have seemed to the South Vietnamese people in
view of the heavy American political presence among them, this proposition had
appeal for an American citizenry that had only recently begun to focus on Vietnam
and was still largely ignorant of the political dimension of the U.S. involvement
there.) "The first reality," the president asserted, was aggression against "the
independent nation of South Vietnam." And containment of the power of communist China remained a central concern, for Peking was accused not only of
urging on Hanoi against South Vietnam, but also of "helping the forces of violence in almost every continent," its role in Vietnam merely "part of a wider
pattern of aggressive purposes." Eisenhower's domino theory and the lesson of
Munich were still very much alive: if the United States retreated from Vietnam,
"the battle would be renewed in one country and then another," for "the appetite of aggression is never satisfied." As it had done in Europe, the United
States had to draw a line in Southeast Asia against the spread of communist
power. And then, more akin to his administration's internal rationale, the president affirmed that over many years America had made a commitment, "a national pledge to help South Vietnam defend its independence." To leave that
nation to its fate would shake the confidence of people "around the globe, from
Berlin to Thailand," in the value of a commitment by the United States that they
could count on if attacked; there would be "increased unrest and instability, and
even wider war."

The JCS and McGeorge Bundy had long urged the introduction of U.S. ground
combat forces. McNamara had recently joined them, and Rusk, who almost until
the end had stood by the president in his reluctance to initiate a sustained bombing
program, now provided no such brake. Once it had been decided that jet air power
would be used against the Viet Cong in the South and against North Vietnam, the
foundation had been established for the final great escalation. Much of this aerial
offensive needed to be launched from fields in South Vietnam, which would nat-

urally become targets for the Viet Cong and later Hanoi.[7] It was almost immediately evident that U.S. air power alone could not protect these fields, nor was it often very accurate in operations against the Viet Cong. A laconic report from Cooper to McGeorge Bundy on March 1 vividly illustrated this: "Much activity by U.S. bombers against VC concentrations. Damage (i.e. V.C. casualties) may well be considerable, but reliable readout lacking. The only thing we *know* has happened is that we knocked out an ARVN regimental command post.... Largest chopper operation of the war (about 170) netted nothing."[8]

Airfields and other major U.S. installations, it was clear, could only be secured by ground troops, but it was equally evident that Saigon's disintegrating forces themselves could not effectively protect them. In addition to the concern that many ARVN units were unwilling to court confrontation with Viet Cong forces by carrying out the patrolling necessary to protect American installations, there were now doubts over what at the end of February was termed the lack of "integrity" of some ARVN units. Several of them had participated in demonstrations that were against the United States as well as the Saigon government.[9]

A month before the attack at Pleiku, Westmoreland had advised the president that, if U.S. soldiers alone were to provide "maximum security" to all U.S. personnel and facilities in Vietnam, a total of thirty-four battalions or approximately seventy-five thousand U.S. troops would be required. He pointed out that there were a total of "16 important airfields, 9 communications facilities, one large POL [petroleum, oil, lubricants] storage area, and 289 separate installations where U.S. personnel work or live," and that "any one of these is conceivably vulnerable to VC attack in the form of mortar fire or sabotage." It was from three airfields—Tonsonhut (Saigon), Bien Hoa (near Saigon), and Danang—that most U.S. bombing and napalm attacks against the Viet Cong emanated, and it was natural that these fields would be priority targets. The one at Danang was regarded as by far the most vulnerable.[10]

Thus, even those who opposed the introduction of U.S. ground forces, such as Ambassador Taylor, reluctantly agreed that American soldiers had to augment ARVN units in protecting Danang. Taylor acknowledged this in a cable following a visit to that base just before the sustained bombing campaign got under way:

> Am deeply impressed with the magnitude of the security problem as are
> General Westmoreland and his principal military colleagues. Except for

[7] U.S. planes were also based on carriers of the Seventh Fleet and in Thailand. The B-52s employed against both the North and the Viet Cong in the South flew from Guam until 1967, when airfields able to accommodate them were built in Thailand. The Manila government would not permit B-52s to be based in the Philippines.

[8] As early as February 23, 1965, Rusk called for the immediate stationing of a marine-battalion combat team in Danang, "to be reinforced promptly to a brigade if the security situation calls for it." (Memorandum, "Vietnam.") Cooper quote is from his Memorandum for Bundy, "Vietnam," March 1, 1965, p. 3.

[9] "Integrity" and anti-American demonstrations is from message from CINCPAC to JCS, National Command Center, February 21, 1965.

[10] Westmoreland's assessment is in cable ("For the President") from Taylor to Department of State, January 6, 1965. Westmoreland estimated that to protect any one of the three large jet-capable airfields would require "up to 6 battalions of U.S. ground forces."

chronic shortage of GVN forces in I Corps area, we would be inclined
to urge GVN to allocate several additional battalions to the Danang area.
But we know that such forces could not be made available except at
prohibitive cost to the security of other areas of SVN. For these reasons
we are driven to consider a solution which we have always rejected in the
past, the introduction of US ground combat forces to reinforce the defense of Danang until GVN forces become available for the purpose.

With Taylor's agreement, then, two U.S. marine-corps battalion landing teams (totaling thirty-five hundred men) were brought ashore on March 6, raising the number of U.S. military personnel in the Danang area up to around seventy-three
hundred.[11]

To be effective, the marines who were assigned to help protect the Danang
air base had to patrol out beyond it, at least up to four thousand yards—the range
of the U.S. 81-mm. mortars that the Viet Cong had captured from the ARVN.
Thus, Westmoreland had pointed out that "to keep enemy mortar fire off any one
given point one must secure an area roughly 16 square miles." The sort of active
patrolling required, of course, increased the incidence of combat, leading in turn
to a sharp rise in U.S. casualties. Whole units of American soldiers were now op-
erating in hostile territory—exposed, with their lives hostage to enemy reactions to
their presence. Ultimately this armed the proponents of sustained and increased
military intervention with a more effective weapon than they had ever possessed for
advancing their cause within the U.S. domestic political arena: "defense of the lives
of our boys in Vietnam." As James Thomson later put it, "Once we had all those
men out there to protect, the stakes were no longer primarily that of sustaining the
Saigon government, but rather, our boys out there—a change that gave our military
a much greater say in policy."[12]

As a result of his experience in Vietnam, Taylor possessed a more realistic
basis for assessing the quality of Saigon's armed forces than General Wheeler in
Washington, and he foresaw serious long-term dangers for the United States if large
numbers of American combat forces were introduced. Accordingly, at the beginning of March he reported to the president that, though he accepted the justification for the "important departure from former policy" in the decision to use U.S.
jet aircraft in the South against the Viet Cong and to introduce marine combat units
for the defense of the Danang airfield, he was concerned that the United States "not
rush in and take over the conduct of the war from the Vietnamese," arguing that
"it would be a political and psychological mistake to change our past position that
this is a Vietnamese war in which we are helping in areas where the Vietnamese
cannot help themselves." Taylor's views soon came to be shared in spades by the
CIA's Office of National Estimates. It presciently observed, "There will be constant danger that the war weary people of South Vietnam will let the U.S. assume
an even greater share of the fighting," with the "danger that U.S. troop commit-

---

[11] Taylor quote and personnel total is from his cable to Department of State, February 28, 1965.

[12] Westmoreland quote is in cable ("For the President") from Taylor to Department of State, January
6, 1965. Thomson comment was in discussion with the author, Ithaca, N.Y., November 5, 1979.

ment will lead more South Vietnamese to accept the Communist line that U.S. colonialism is replacing French," and "turn increasing numbers of Vietnamese toward support of the Viet Cong effort to oust the U.S."[13]

Digging in his heels against additional U.S. ground forces, Taylor urged instead that the tempo of bombing the North be increased, "to convince Hanoi authorities they face prospect of progressively severe punishment." He commented, "I fear to date Rolling Thunder in their eyes has been merely a few isolated thunder claps."[14]

Once the Rubicon had been crossed, however, there were swiftly increasing pressures from the JCS and their civilian allies for the dispatch of additional combat elements. After a week in South Vietnam, the army chief of staff, General Harold K. Johnson, recommended to McNamara on March 14 the deployment of a full U.S. division, either to defend the Bien Hoa and Tonsonhut airfields plus some coastal enclaves or to take on the Viet Cong in the highland provinces of Kontum, Pleiku, and Darlac. (Both he and McNamara opted for the latter.) General Johnson also urged the introduction of a four-division force comprised of U.S. and allied SEATO forces to form a counter-infiltration cordon running approximately along the seventeenth parallel, near the demilitarized zone, from the South China Sea to Laos and on to the Mekong River. Taylor promptly parried this recommendation, arguing successfully that judgment on it be reserved.[15]

On March 29, the day Taylor left Saigon for Washington, the Viet Cong exploded a 250-pound bomb outside the Saigon embassy, which killed twenty-two people (two of them American) and injured 186 others (including fifty-two Americans) while providing additional dramatic testimony of the ARVN's inability to protect American installations.[16]

In Washington, Taylor found the JCS pressing for the introduction of two divisions for operations against the Viet Cong, with Westmoreland supporting this and possibly more if bombing the North still proved unsuccessful. The JCS was also proposing the dispatch of one South Korean division for use against the Viet Cong. In discussions with the president on April 1–2, Taylor argued that there was no military necessity for such measures, and that the South Vietnamese might resent being inundated by so many Americans, a concern shared by Prime Minister Quat. Taylor had already found Quat to be sensitive about the proposed introduction of just two marine battalions limited to one small enclave.[17] Three foreign

[13] Taylor quotes are from his Weekly Report to the President, March 2, 1965. CIA quote is from CIA, Office of National Estimates, "Current Trends in Vietnam," Special Memorandum No. 12–65, April 30, 1965.

[14] Cable from Taylor to Secstate, March 8, 1965.

[15] For General Johnson's report, McNamara's concurrence, and preference for second option, see *PP* (Gravel), 3:428–29. For Taylor's response, see Memorandum from McGeorge Bundy, July 24, 1965.

[16] Figures are from CIA, Directorate of Intelligence, "The Situation in South Vietnam (31 March–7 April, 1965)," p. 4. Much smaller figures were released to the press; see *New York Times*, March 30, 31, 1965.

[17] On the two-division request, see *PP* (Gravel), 3:406–7. In this cable to the Department of State of February 28, Taylor stated that in discussions with Quat and top ARVN officers, he and Westmoreland "would emphasize the limited mission of the Marines and their non-involvement in pacification."

divisions, some with "search and destroy" missions, and supporting logistical elements would total around 100,000 and give the war an entirely different character.

McNamara, who had been inclined to favor the three-division proposal, and Rusk then recommended postponing a decision on this until the situation could be reviewed sixty days later. For the present they suggested—and in this compromise Taylor concurred—the United States should send in two additional marine battalions, plus one air squadron and eighteen to twenty thousand U.S. support troops ("to fill out existing units and provide needed logistic personnel"). McGeorge Bundy proposed that U.S. troops in Vietnam be allowed the freedom to engage in combat rather than be confined to static defense. The CIA's John McCone was strongly opposed to Bundy's suggestion and argued against an American ground combat role in the South unless it was accompanied by a much greater weight of air strikes against the North, but his memorandum did not reach the president until well after these crucial discussions—too late to support Taylor or affect the president's decision to approve the McNamara/Rusk and Bundy proposals and what was termed "the present slowly ascending tempo" of Rolling Thunder operations. Indeed, McCone's memorandum was apparently withheld from the president, and the CIA chief was obliged to hand-deliver a copy to him as his last official act before resigning.[18]

The decisions arrived at in these discussions were embodied in an NSC Action Memorandum of April 6, drafted by McGeorge Bundy. He enjoined that the president desired that all these actions he had approved "be taken as rapidly as practicable, but in ways that should minimize any appearance of sudden changes in policy.... The President's desire is that these movements and changes should be understood as being gradual and wholly consistent with existing policy."[19]

Having successfully fended off the three-division proposal, Taylor had gone along with the McNamara/Rusk compromise. But McCone was on his way out and on April 28 was replaced by Admiral William F. Raborn, a CIA director more in tune with Bundy and McNamara, and Ambassador Taylor soon found himself more isolated than before from the center of policymaking. Outflanked by both Westmoreland and the JCS, he stood fast a scant three weeks against the advocates

[18] On three-division proposal and Rusk request for postponement, and on filling out existing units, see Memorandum from McGeorge Bundy, July 24, 1965; NSC Chronology, Departure of Major U.S. forces, July 29, 1965. With respect to the dispatch of the next two marine battalions, see outgoing cable from Department of State (Ball) to Amembassy, April 5, 1965. This message reads, "In discussions with Quat it is considered more desirable to describe the mission of the Marines as engaging initially in counterinsurgency combat operations in the vicinity of the Marine bases (Danang and Phu Bai)." It had, in fact, already been decided that the mission of these marines would not be confined to base protection. For Bundy's proposal on removal of restrictions, see *PP* (Gravel), 3:280; see also the White House Memorandum of April 1, 1965, prepared as a basis for discussion with the president that day, "Key Elements for Discussion, Thursday, April 1, 1965." Memorandum from McCone to Rusk, McNamara, Bundy, and Taylor, April 2, 1965, is in *PP* (Gravel), 3:364–65. In conveying his memorandum to the president, McCone added a covering letter that summarized it and indicated he was aware that his memorandum might never have reached Johnson. (Letter [undated], NSC Vietnam, vol. 32.)

[19] NSC Action Memorandum No. 328, April 6, 1965, in *PP* (*NYT*), pp. 442–43.

of a major deployment of U.S. ground combat forces, now spearheaded by an aggressive Robert McNamara and quietly backed by both McGeorge Bundy and Rusk.

Taylor had left Washington with the understanding—embodied in a National Security Council decision of April 2—that the administration would "experiment with the Marines in a counterinsurgency role before bringing in other U.S. contingents." Apparently, however, Westmoreland and the JCS were able to convince the president that the ARVN was deteriorating too fast to test this. On April 11, Westmoreland urgently revived his request for the dispatch of the 173rd Airborne Brigade. This was promptly supported by CINCPAC and the JCS, recommended by McNamara on April 13, and apparently endorsed by the president that same day.[20]

It is unclear whether Johnson was aware his ambassador had been completely bypassed in this decision. But Taylor certainly knew it, as he informed Rusk the next day, and was clearly resentful. McGeorge Bundy therefore advised the president later on the 14th to restrain McNamara from sending Taylor implementing orders, explaining that this would be "very explosive right now because he will not agree with many of them and he will feel he has not been consulted." Informing the president of a cable in which Taylor "gravely questions the usefulness of immediate additional ground deployments," Bundy reassured Johnson, "I am sure we can turn him around if we give him just a little time to come aboard."[21]

Taylor was also bypassed in the concurrent decision to escalate along another axis—which he referred to in a follow-up cable on April 17 as "what I take to be a new policy of third-country participation in ground combat." In the April 1–2 meetings, it had been agreed that the "possibility" of deploying third-country troops in combat roles (South Korea, Australia, and New Zealand being specifically mentioned) was to be the object of "urgent exploration." That exploration was now proceeding apace, even before Taylor had had a chance to discuss the matter with Quat. Some three months before, Prime Minister Huong and Khanh had agreed to the introduction of two thousand South Korean troops—a battalion of engineers and supporting elements. But five days before the April 1 meeting, Taylor had informed Washington that both Quat and his deputy and minister of defense, General Thieu, believed there was "no present requirement to consider the introduction of third country ground combat forces."[22]

When Taylor received instructions from Rusk on April 15 to secure a request from Quat as soon as possible for the introduction of a South Korean regimental combat team, and was asked by the Pentagon the next day to discuss "several possible uses of U.S. forces beyond the NSC decisions of April 2," the ambassador

---

[20] Quote is in *PP (NYT)*, pp. 403–4; *PP* (Gravel), 3:409. The president's endorsement is to be inferred from cable from the JCS to CINCPAC, April 14, 1965.

[21] On Taylor's being bypassed and his reaction, see Cable from Taylor to State, April 14, 1965. See also *PP* (Gravel), 3:451; *PP (NYT)*, pp. 404, 444. Bundy's advice is in his memorandum to the President of April 14, 1965.

[22] "No present requirement" quote is from cable from Taylor to RUEHCR/SECSTATE, March 26, 1965. Concerning Quat, see also CIA, Monthly Report, "The Situation in South Vietnam," April 2, 1965, p. 17.

rebelled. He replied that he could not present these matters to Quat until he himself was given "clarification of our purposes and objectives" with regard to the introduction of third-country and U.S. combat forces. "Before I can present our case to [the] GVN, I have to know what the case is and why. It is not going to be easy to get concurrence for the large-scale introduction of foreign troops unless the need is clear and explicit." And even so, he warned, Washington's request might initiate "a sharp debate within the GVN."[23]

On April 18, informed of Taylor's views, Johnson directed that all these actions be suspended until after McNamara's scheduled meeting with Westmoreland in Honolulu two days later. Thereafter, the president would review the situation and consult with Taylor. But the reprieve was brief. When Taylor joined McNamara and Westmoreland at Honolulu, he found himself faced by four additional strong advocates of an increased U.S. ground combat role— William Bundy, John McNaughton, Admiral Ulysses G. Sharp (CINCPAC), and General Earle Wheeler (chairman of the JCS). Confronted by this Macedonian phalanx, Taylor capitulated and, as McGeorge Bundy had predicted, now climbed aboard. The unanimous recommendation that McNamara gave to the president on April 21 called for a major escalation. Thirteen U.S. combat battalions, numbering 82,000 men, were to be added to the 33,500 U.S. troops already in Vietnam (this including the four marine battalions stationed at Danang and Chu Lai) along with three South Korean (ROK) and one Australian battalion (totaling 7,250 men).[24]

This was not presented to the president as a prescription for winning the war, but, rather, simply for denying victory to the Viet Cong. The "victory" envisaged for the United States, McNamara explained, was "to break the will of the DRV/VC by depriving them of victory," or, as Taylor had put it, "a demonstration of Communist impotence, which will lead to a political solution." It was agreed that a settlement would come "as much or more from VC failure in the South as from DRV pain in the North," and that it would take "more than six months, perhaps a year or two, to demonstrate VC failure." The participants were also in accord that the existing tempo of air strikes against the North was about right, that this bombing program should continue "at least six months, perhaps a year or more," and that in any case it was "very important that strikes against the North be continued during any talks." The Hanoi–Haiphong–Phuc Yen[25] areas were to be avoided, for all those present appeared to share Taylor's view that it was "important not to 'kill the hostage' by destroying the North Vietnamese assets inside the 'Hanoi do-nut.'" By this Taylor and the others at Honolulu meant that if too much of North Vietnam were destroyed, its leaders, with little left to lose, could not be expected to be

[23] Quotes are from cable from Taylor to Secstate (with copy to the White House for the attention of McGeorge Bundy), April 17, 1965, in both *PP* (*NYT*), pp. 443–46, and *PP* (Gravel), 3:704–5.

[24] For Johnson's postponement of the decision, see cable from McGeorge Bundy to Taylor, April 18, 1965. "Unanimous recommendation" is in Memorandum for the President from Robert S. McNamara, April 21, 1965.

[25] Phuc Yen was the most important MiG air base in the DRV and was located eighteen miles northwest of Hanoi.

influenced by changes in either the bounds or intensity of the bombing. They believed that by sparing the capital and Haiphong (the only major port) the United States could still exert leverage on Hanoi's leaders by threatening to increase the weight and geographic extent of its bombing. If these assets were destroyed, there would be no feasible way of pressuring the DRV's leaders either to limit the flow of arms to the Viet Cong or to induce the Viet Cong to end or at least reduce the level of their insurgency. For most of the president's advisers, it was still an article of faith that Hanoi had this capacity.

It is not clear to what extent Lyndon Johnson had been won over to this view, but he had another reason, more immediate and compelling, for limiting the tempo and geographical extent of the bombing. This was his abiding fear that too rapid an escalation of the bombardment, or one that extended to Hanoi, Haiphong, or the China border areas, might provoke a massive Chinese military response and possibly greater Soviet involvement as well. Though the president's advisers differed as to the point at which they believed the Chinese would intervene, nearly all were convinced that Peking would not passively stand by and see her southern neighbor completely destroyed by American bombing. Some later critics have faulted Johnson for not having "gone for the jugular" and sent American combat troops into the North, but there was scarcely any doubt among his advisers—military or civilian— that, Vietnamese resistance and U.S. casualties aside, such a move might well have led to the introduction of Chinese ground combat forces. Few believed that bombing China would deter such action, and no one wished to risk provoking in Vietnam a repetition of the Chinese role in the Korean War.[26]

Though none of the participants in the April 20 Honolulu meeting expected their measures to lead to any dramatic or immediate improvement in the South, they did believe that the deployment of these additional troops would "bolster the GVN forces while they are building up." What McNamara and his supporters were proposing to Lyndon Johnson, then, was in effect a holding action—a recommendation for a sufficient increment of combat soldiers at least to hold the Viet Cong at bay. That was the minimum, but there was also the hope that with additional external support the Saigon regime might in time become strong enough, and the Viet Cong sufficiently stymied, for the United States to risk negotiations that would preserve the South as a separate, noncommunist state.

For a president whose major preoccupation was a domestic program embodying the revolutionary changes envisaged for his "Great Society," even that minimum objective was sufficient. To secure that, and obviate the loss of prestige and enormous American domestic political backlash he expected would follow a Saigon collapse, Lyndon Johnson evidently did not regard the investment in men and treasure advocated by McNamara and other advisers as excessive. Part of their recommendation he approved on April 21 and the balance on May 15.[27]

[26] See Lyndon Baines Johnson, *The Vantage Point: Perspectives of the Presidency, 1963–1969* (New York: Holt, Rinehart & Winston, 1971), p. 140; William Bundy, Oral History, tape 5, pp. 9, 21–22.

[27] For Johnson's approval of this recommendation, see Memorandum from McGeorge Bundy, July 24, 1965.

The slow pace at which Johnson escalated—still significantly slower than that advocated by the JCS, Westmoreland, and most of his civilian advisers—must in considerable part have reflected his mounting concern that a sharp, clear-cut escalatory move in Vietnam might so rock the boat as to threaten passage of many as-yet-unrealized pieces of Great Society legislation. That program was his highest priority, and with some of the most important bills (including the Voting Rights Act and Medicare) under consideration or soon to be presented, he apparently did not want to risk losing needed support by alarming and antagonizing members of Congress over his actions in Vietnam. He did buy a little time by obfuscating the degree of escalation inherent in implementing McNamara's April 21 recommendations, having the secretary not announce these troop increases publicly until June 16. But by holding back the release of this information, the president laid the foundations for what came to be known as the "credibility gap." ...

By the spring of 1965, Lyndon Johnson had been conditioned by his advisers to assume that pursuit of a negotiated solution was not yet in the national interest. George Ball apart, they continued as vehemently as ever to admonish that such a course was unthinkable until Saigon could bargain politically and militarily from a position of greater strength—sufficient to ensure its survival as a separate, noncommunist state. And for the Johnson administration—like Eisenhower's and Kennedy's—*that* condition remained fundamental and nonnegotiable. Yet for the NLF and Hanoi, the obverse of this remained equally nonnegotiable. For them no solution was conceivable that left their country torn in two as a consequence of the interjection of Western power, with the southern half controlled by a government dependent upon and subserviently aligned with the United States. Negotiations, of course, require compromise arrived at through mutual concessions, but given the incompatibility of fundamental objectives between Saigon and Washington on the one hand, and Hanoi and the NLF on the other, there was little basis for compromise. As Paul Warnke, who was John McNaughton's successor as assistant secretary of defense, later put it, "The intractable fact was that neither Hanoi nor Washington could compromise its position without in effect admitting defeat...." For Hanoi to "compromise," as Washington defined that term, "would be to capitulate and accept the defeat of an idea that had motivated its leadership since World War II. For the United States to 'compromise' and permit the indigenous forces in Vietnam to work their own way would be to condone the demise of the anti-Communist regime we had supported in Saigon for twenty years."[28] The separate southern state that three administrations had been trying to build during the previous decade was still essentially an appendage of the United States. The fragile edifice still lacked a sufficient indigenous foundation to support it. Without massive American economic and military buttresses, the walls would collapse, and U.S. officials knew it. They could not, therefore, envisage a settlement that did not reg-

---

[28] Paul Warnke, "The Search for Peace," in *The Legacy of Vietnam*, ed. Anthony Lake (Council on Foreign Relations–New York University Press, 1976), pp. 318–19. Warnke was general counsel for the Department of Defense, 1966–67, and assistant secretary, 1967–69.

ister the heavy impact of American power, and that sort of outcome neither Hanoi nor the NLF would accept.

The basic incongruity of the American position lay, of course, in the effort to keep a nation divided in two—a nation whose nationalist ferment was as strong as that of any country in the twentieth century. The president and his advisers evidenced precious little empathy for Vietnamese nationalism and never seemed to appreciate its strength and breadth. But their own sense of nationalism—usually defined in terms of American prestige and invincibility—loomed very large in their calculations.

Given the nature and power of Vietnamese nationalism, Dean Rusk's repeated assertions that the American intervention would cease when Hanoi "left its neighbors alone" appears all the more incongruous; for as Warnke observes, "Hanoi regarded the South Vietnamese not as neighbors, but as part of the same family." If there were to have been any progress toward a negotiated solution, the process would have had to provide a significant role for the United States' main adversary, the NLF—whatever its relationship to Hanoi. At this time—before the saturation bombing of American B-52s, U.S. ground and naval artillery, and Phoenix-type assassination teams had destroyed or chewed up a major part of the NLF's infrastructure and combat units—the front-line American adversary in Vietnam was the NLF. The first PAVN units had just arrived in the South and for more than a year were to remain no more than a small fraction of NLF combat strength. Indeed, until at least the end of 1965 the total manpower of PAVN units in the South was less than that of the United States' Korean auxiliaries there, and much less than that deployed by the United States. This must be understood to appreciate Hanoi's approach to negotiations, its leaders insisting that their soldiers had a considerably greater right to be in the southern half of Vietnam than those from two foreign countries. As Warnke observes, "At no point was North Vietnam ever willing to accept the description of its forces as foreign in any part of Vietnam, or to equate its withdrawal with ours."[29]

No political solution could escape providing a place for the NLF. To insist, as did the president's advisers, that to participate politically its adherents would first have to surrender their weapons and submit to the mercy of the well-armed Saigon military was to take up residence with Alice in Wonderland. Yet this was precisely the advice Lyndon Johnson was getting.

Maxwell Taylor later observed: "From 1965 to the end of 1967, there was nothing in the power relationship between the two sides which offered hope of successful negotiations, even if we got them started." Certainly a negotiated settlement that registered the relative political and military power of the contestants would have fallen far short of minimum U.S. objectives. It could not have left all of the South in the hands of those opposed to the NLF, nor barred that area's ultimate reunification with the North. With South Vietnamese leaders acknowledging privately to American officials that their regime could not risk political competition with the NLF, those officials could only hope that in time—after the in-

---

[29] Rusk and Warnke quotes are in *ibid.*, pp. 319, 315.

troduction of sufficient additional U.S. military power—the NLF could be sufficiently weakened to permit this.[30] When this additional American power had weighted the scales sufficiently, then it would be safe to conduct bona-fide negotiations leading to a political settlement. In the meantime, however, Washington would avoid negotiations while hoping to make sufficient gestures in support of them to blunt the efforts of their proponents both in the United States and among allies abroad. And during this period the administration would continue to insist— implicitly or explicitly—upon the same precondition for negotiations that was in fact the nub of its controversy with the NLF and Hanoi—preservation of a separate, anticommunist state in the South. It was some two and a half years later, after the introduction of half a million American troops had shown the unattainability of this objective, before the administration would begin to modify its conditions and its approach to negotiations. . . .

[30] Taylor quote is from "Waging Negotiations—A Vietnam Study," in *Legacy of Vietnam,* ed. Lake, p. 298. For South Vietnamese leaders on the NLF, see CIA, Office of Current Intelligence, "South Vietnamese Government Contacts with the Viet Cong Liberation Front," November 26, 1965.

28

CAREERISM AND EGO INVESTMENT

COMMITTEE OF CONCERNED ASIAN SCHOLARS

In the aftermath of the American invasion of Cambodia in 1970, the Committee of Concerned Asian Scholars, which had been formed in 1968, sought in The

From *The Indochina Story* by the Committee of Concerned Asian Scholars. Copyright © 1970 by the Committee of Concerned Asian Scholars. Reprinted by permission of Bantam Books, a division of BANTAM, DOUBLEDAY DELL PUBLISHING GROUP, INC.

Indochina Story to bring together in one book much of the information and many of the arguments explaining the Vietnam War that heretofore had been scattered through a multitude of books. One set of explanations for American involvement discussed by the committee had to do with patterns of behavior said to belong to the military bureaucracy: institutional momentum, ego investment, military careerism, and military deception.

The Indochina war is in large part a product of sheer institutional momentum. Never in history has such a vast, expensive, and technologically sophisticated governmental apparatus been focused for so long on "success" in one small region abroad. And never in America have the careers of so many public servants been at stake in such an undertaking.

CONFORMITY IN THE CIVILIAN BUREAUCRACY

On the civilian side of the ledger, Vietnam has represented an ongoing "ego investment" in terms of both men and agencies. The State Department, AID, CIA, and other units compete in the field against each other, and also against the military, to produce a non-Communist outcome.

Within the ranks of these agencies, two forms of pressure upon people have long been identifiable. First, there hangs over the heads of Foreign Service officers and others the dark shadow of the "loss of China." From the mid-1950s onward, FSOs were keenly aware of the terrible harm done to their colleagues of the old China service through the investigations and purges of McCarthy, McCarran, and Dulles's security chief, Scott McLeod. One root cause of the China witch-hunt lay in the written and even oral expressions of doubts by officers as to the wisdom of trying to save the Chinese Nationalist government; such doubters later saw their careers ruined or blighted by charges of treason, procommunism, or "softness" on communism. For Vietnam personnel, the bureaucratic lesson of China has been clear and compelling: Keep your doubts to yourself. Such caution was compounded by the excesses of ambassadors in Saigon, Bangkok, and elsewhere who refused to forward reports from those few bold enough to register their doubts. It was also compounded by the "curator mentality" within a service whose promotion system placed a premium on simply staying out of trouble.

A second type of pressure has been the relentless demand for good news from increasingly beleaguered administrators in Washington. Silence about doubts was not enough; what was required from the field, first to Embassy Saigon, then to Washington, was affirmation—positive indicators of success: the strength and numbers of the "strategic hamlet" program (exploded as a myth with the death of Diem), statistics on "pacified" and "secure" villages (exploded as a myth with the Tet offensive), and today optimistic data on the Cambodian adventure and on "Vietnamization."

Such pressures are further intensified by government agencies' demand for Vietnam tours of duty from those who hope to rise within the career ranks. Indochina experience has become a major ingredient in Washington's career development system, a process termed by some "the discipline of disappointment." One significant by-product, of course, is the flight of able men from the career services—and the inability of the services to replenish such lost talent from the younger generation emerging from the colleges.

PERSONAL EGO INVESTMENT

In the field, then, the war has produced severe constraints and muted, distorted reporting among the careerists. But more dangerous is the war's impact back in Washington. Here the phenomenon of ego investment is striking.

At the heart of the matter is the continuity in office of men in the upper echelons who participated in or enlarged upon early Vietnam decisions and who therefore have deep personal stakes in those decisions and the outcome. Such continuity was striking in the 1960s. Among the war's chief civilian architects were Dean Rusk, Walt Rostow, Robert McNamara, McGeorge Bundy, William Bundy, and Alexis Johnson. Of this group, Rusk, Rostow, and William Bundy persisted in one office or another for eight years; and Alexis Johnson, a former ambassador to Thailand, Saigon, and Japan, stays on today as an undersecretary of state and a chief planner of the Cambodian invasion. Such men, during their tenure, rejected innumerable opportunities for an exit from Vietnam. They did so because at moments of decision they simply could not accept the risk of an outcome that was less than "success." Beneath this visible tier of decision makers is also a less visible layer of Indochina careerists in all the agencies, men similarly tied to the mistakes of the past.

As one former White House aide has written:

Men who have participated in a decision develop a stake in that decision. As they participate in further, related decisions, their stake increases. It might have been possible to dissuade a man of strong self-confidence at an early stage of the ladder of decision; but it is infinitely harder at later stages since a change of mind there usually involves implicit or explicit repudiation of a chain of previous decisions. To put it bluntly: at the heart of the Vietnam calamity is a group of able, dedicated men who have been regularly and repeatedly wrong—and whose standing with their contemporaries, and more important, with history, depends, as they see it, on being proven right. These are not men who can be asked to extricate themselves from error.[1]

Little wonder, then, that so many of Vietnam's planners who have left the constraints of government service remain silent even today—Rusk, the two Bundys,

[1] James C. Thomson, Jr., "How Could Vietnam Happen?" *Atlantic Monthly*, April 1968.

McNamara, to name a few; for a repudiation of the enterprise, even now, is an admission of personal failure in the past. Nixon's "silent majority" includes within it a small cheering section of those who still seek personal vindication in the outcome.

MILITARY MOMENTUM

If careerism and ego investment are at work in the civilian end of the Indochina disaster, they are doubly at work and even more significant in the military aspects of our involvement.

From the early 1960s onward, and particularly since the dramatic escalations of 1965, the Vietnam war has served a number of functions for the government's largest and best-financed subdivision, the armed forces. It has provided a unique laboratory and testing ground for an infinite variety of weaponry and tactics; it has provided an arena for interservice competition and therefore growth and development through escalating demands on the federal budget; it has provided that rare and much-desired boon to the peacetime military, a real war and hence a route to rapid rise within the services; and it has kept our military in the national limelight—as "heroic" field commanders (Westmoreland and Abrams), as an entrenched elite with a Washington veto power (the Joint Chiefs), and as soldiers turned policy makers (General Wheeler, at times, and General Maxwell Taylor throughout).

It is no secret that the salesmen of "counterinsurgency" persuaded both Kennedys to press for "covert" ground involvement in Indochina; nor that the salesmen of air power persuaded Lyndon Johnson to bomb North Vietnam; nor even that Nixon's Cambodian lunge, in various forms, has been regularly pressed upon administrations by the Pentagon since the early 1960s. What has been involved in these and other moves is a doctrine or formula in search of proof; and what has happened in each case is a search for further and more elaborate testing once each doctrine or formula fails to achieve its aim. (Once "counterinsurgency" begins to fail, bombing is introduced to force "negotiations"; and as bombing begins to fail, ground forces are brought in massively. What stands waiting offstage, unused but itching for use, is "tactical nukes" and also perhaps not so tactical ones—complete with a full-fledged doctrine to be tested.)

MILITARY CAREERISM

As the war's folly has become more widely understood and accepted, many in the lower ranks of the military have begun to speak out—and, in some cases, to suffer the consequences. But few at the top have lifted the veil on the military ingredient of the Indochina disaster as fully and courageously as the former Marine Corps commandant, General David M. Shoup.[2]

[2] *Atlantic Monthly*, April 1969.

From General Shoup comes a sobering comment on the military's career investment in the Indochina war: "Civilians can scarcely understand or even believe that many ambitious military professionals truly yearn for wars and the opportunities for glory and distinction afforded only in combat. A career of peacetime duty is a dull and frustrating prospect for the normal regular officer to contemplate." Hence the personal as well as institutional involvement of the services in Indochina. And as General Shoup further reports, the institutional aspect is compounded by interservice rivalry: "...in Vietnam during 1965 the four services were racing to build up combat strength in that hapless country. This effort was ostensibly to save South Vietnam from Viet Cong and North Vietnamese aggression. It should also be noted that it was motivated in part by the same old interservice rivalry to demonstrate respective importance and combat effectiveness." As for the bombing of North Vietnam that 1965 produced, Shoup describes it as "one of the most wasteful and expensive hoaxes ever to be put over on the American people.... air power use in general has to a large degree been a contest for the operations planners, 'fine experience' for young pilots, and opportunity for career officers."

The war's "career opportunity" aspect is further spelled out by Lieutenant Colonel Edward L. King, a retired army officer: "Another instrument for enforcing conformity—and getting men to 'voluntarily' serve in Vietnam—is the Army's 'career incentives' policy. Promotion is not possible without a Vietnam tour.... There has therefore been hot competition for combat commands."[3]

MILITARY DECEPTION

On the analysis or reporting of the results of actions undertaken by the various services, General Shoup has some news for the public:

> Each of the services and all of the major commands practice techniques of controlling the news and the release of self-serving propaganda: in "the interests of national defense," to make the service look good, to cover up mistakes, to build up and publicize a distinguished military personality, or to win a round in the continuous gamesmanship of the interservice contest.

Why is the United States fighting in Indochina? In part because several thousand Americans, and especially a large handful in both Washington and Southeast Asia, have their own reasons—their own personal stakes as careerists on the promotion ladder or as upper-echelon leaders answerable to "history"—for supporting the enterprise through thick and thin, however misconceived it may have been, whatever disasters it may produce, until success and vindication are attained. Given such a weight of collective ego investments within the civilian and military bureaucracy, it is hardly surprising that nothing much changes despite new leadership at the top.

[3] *New Republic*, May 30, 1970.

29

THE PENTAGON
PROPAGANDA MACHINE

J. WILLIAM FULBRIGHT

By 1969 Senator Fulbright's analysis of the causes of America's involvement in the Vietnam War had evolved beyond an emphasis on the arrogance of power and missionary idealism to include a wide-ranging criticism of interventionist foreign policies, executive agreements, and military spending rooted in the disproportionate influence wielded by the military establishment on policy and the citizenry. In one Senate speech later expanded into an essay, he warned of the military's public relations activities, the military's attraction to war, and war's encouragement of militarism within the nation.

Although I cannot conceive of a single top-ranking officer in any of the armed services who today would consider an attempt to overturn our constitutional government—in the manner of *Seven Days in May* fiction—militarism as a philosophy poses a distinct threat to our democracy. At the minimum, it represents a dangerously constricted but highly influential point of view when focused on our foreign relations. It is a viewpoint that by its nature takes little account of political and moral complexities, even less of social and economic factors, and almost no account of human and psychological considerations.

Rarely does a general officer invoke the higher loyalty of patriotism—his own concept of it, that is—over loyalty to civilian political authority, as General MacArthur did in his defiance of President Truman.[1] But if, as time goes on, our country continues to be chronically at war, continues to neglect its domestic problems, and continues to have unrest in cities and on campuses, then militarism will surely increase. And even if the military itself does not take over the government directly,

From J. William Fulbright, *The Pentagon Propaganda Machine* (1970; rpt. New York: Vintage Books, 1971), 141–50, 154–56. Reprinted by permission of the author.

[1] *The MacArthur Story*, a film version of the glamorous general's life made by the Office of Information for the Armed Forces, is available to the public in military film libraries.

it could—because of increasing use in domestic crises—come to acquire power comparable to that of the German General Staff in the years before World War I. I hope this never comes to pass. It may not seem likely now, but it is by no means so inconceivable that we need not warn against it and act to prevent it.

I have often warned those students who talk of the need to revise our system by revolution that if such a revolution were to take place, the government that would emerge for our country would not be the one they seek. It would rather be authoritarian and controlled by the very forces who today promote military solutions to foreign policy problems.

The leadership of professional military officer corps stems from a few thousand high-ranking officers of unusual ability and energy that comes of single-mindedness. Marked as men of talents by their rise to the highest ranks through the rigorous competitiveness of the military services, they bring to bear a strength in conviction and a near unanimity of outlook that gives them an influence, in government councils and in Congress, on public policy disproportionate to their numbers. Disciplined and loyal to their respective services, with added prestige derived from heroic combat records, they operate with an efficiency not often found among civilian officials.

The danger to public policy arises from civilian authorities adopting the narrowness of outlook of professional soldiers—an outlook restricted by training and experience to the use of force. As we have developed into a society whose most prominent business is violence, one of the leading professions inevitably is soldiering. Since they are the professionals, and civilian bureaucrats refuse to challenge them, the military have become ardent and effective competitors for power in American society.

The services compete with each other for funds, for the control of weapons systems, and for the privilege of being "first to fight." Constantly improving their techniques for rapid deployment, they not only yearn to try them out but when opportunities arise they press their proposals on civilian authorities. The latter group all too often is tempted by the seemingly quick "surgical" course of action proposed by the military in preference to the long and wearisome methods of diplomacy. For a variety of reasons—from believing it the only course of action to testing equipment and techniques of counterinsurgency, or just to avoid the disgrace of being "left out"—all the military services were enthusiastic about the initial involvement in Vietnam. By now they should have had their fill, but they still push on, trying out new weapons and new strategies—such as "destroying sanctuaries" in Cambodia.

The root cause of militarism is war, and so long as we have the one we will be menaced by the other. The best defense against militarism is peace; the next best thing is the vigorous practice of democracy. The dissent against our government's actions in Southeast Asia, the opposition to the ABM and MIRV, and the increased willingness of many in the Congress to do something about the hitherto sacrosanct military budget are all encouraging signs of democracy being practiced. But there is much in American polity these days that is discouraging.

There seems to be a lack of concern among too many people about the state of the nation, and a too easy acceptance of policies and actions of a kind that a generation ago would have appalled the citizenry. The apparent broad acceptance of the "volunteer army" idea comes to mind—a concept completely at variance with our historic development. Up to now, a blessing of our system has been that those who go into the military service, whether by enlistment or through the draft, could hardly wait to get out.[2] But today, because of the exigencies of the times, there is a chance that we may turn our back on this fundamental principle: a large, standing professional army has no place in this Republic.

Along with promoting militarism as part of our society, the mindless violence of war has eaten away at our moral values as well as our sensitivity. Reporters covering the domestic aspects of the My Lai massacre story in the home area of Lieutenant Robert Calley were surprised to find loud support for the accused—not sympathy, which might be expected, but support. Among these people there seemed to be no recognition of possible wrongdoing or criminal act in the alleged massacre.

Beyond the discouragements—and even the disturbing things such as the Cambodian adventure and our activities in Thailand and Laos—one has to hope, with reason drawn from our history, that the traditional workings of our system and the innate common sense of Americans will prevail. The task certainly is not going to be easy. We have been so stunned, almost desensitized—like Lieutenant Calley's supporters—by what has gone on during the recent past that it is almost possible to turn to total pessimism. History did not prepare the American people for the imperial role in which we find ourselves, and we are paying a moral price for it. From the time of the framing of our Constitution to the two world wars, our experience and values—if not our uniform practice—conditioned us not for the unilateral exercise of power but for the placing of limits upon it. Perhaps it was vanity, but we supposed that we could be an example for the world—an example of rationality and restraint.

Our practice has not lived up to that ideal but, from the earliest days of the Republic, the ideal has retained its hold upon us, and every time we have acted inconsistently with it—not just in Vietnam and Cambodia—a hue and cry of opposition has arisen. When the United States invaded Mexico two former Presidents and a future one—John Quincy Adams, Van Buren, and Lincoln—denounced the war as violating American principles. Adams, the senior of them, is even said to have expressed the hope that General Taylor's officers would resign and his men desert. When the United States fought a war with Spain and then suppressed the patriotic resistance of the Philippines, the ranks of opposition numbered two former Presidents—Harrison and Cleveland—Senators and Congressmen, including the Speaker of the House of Representatives, and such distinguished—and differing—individuals as Andrew Carnegie and Samuel Gompers.

The incongruity between our old values and the new unilateral power we wield has greatly troubled the American people. It has much to do, I suspect, with the current student rebellion. Like a human body reacting against a transplanted organ, our body politic is reacting against the alien values which, in the name of

---

[2] Despite attractive re-enlistment bonuses, the Army's rate of retention in 1969 of men finishing their first term is 14.6 percent for volunteers and 7.4 percent for draftees.

security, have been grafted upon it. We cannot, and dare not, divest ourselves of power, but we have a choice as to how we will use it. We can try to ride out the current convulsion in our society and adapt ourselves to a new role as the world's nuclear vigilante. Or we can try to adapt our power to our traditional values, never allowing it to become more than a means toward domestic societal ends, while seeking every opportunity to discipline it within an international community.

It is not going to help us to reach these ends to have a president fearful that we are going to be "humiliated," nor for him to turn to the military as a prime source of advice on foreign affairs. In the case of Cambodia the President accepted military advice during the decision-making process, apparently in preference to that of the Department of State, thereby turning to an initial military solution rather than a diplomatic or political one. Of course the Senate was not consulted. Once the treaty power of the Senate was regarded as the only constitutional means of making a significant foreign commitment, while executive agreements in foreign affairs were confined to matters of routine. Today the treaty has been reduced to only one of a number of methods of entering binding foreign engagements. In current usage the term "commitment" is used less often to refer to obligations deriving from treaties than to those deriving from executive agreements and even simple, sometimes casual declarations. . . .

The Department of State is not alone among the agencies of government awed as well as outmanned, outmaneuvered, or simply elbowed aside by executive military decision-making. The Defense Department has established a massive bureaucracy, like that at the Department of Commerce, the Atomic Energy Commission, the Department of Health, Education, and Welfare, and all the rest who protect their positions and interests within the mechanism of governmental power and appropriations.

When war was abhorrent to the American people, the military was considered only as a tool to be used if needed. Today, with our chronic state of war, and with peace becoming the unusual, the military has created for itself an image as a comforting thing to have around. In reality, however, it has become a monster bureaucracy that can grind beneath its wheels the other bureaucracies, whatever their prescribed roles in the process of government and their legitimate needs.

One of the arms of the Defense Department monster bureaucracy is the military public relations apparatus that today is selling the Administration's Southeast Asia policy, just as it sold the Vietnam policy of the previous Administration, with increasing emphasis on patriotic militarism and activity directed against its critics. The enthusiasm and dedication of the purveyors of the hard military line are such that their present course could easily be changed so as to direct attention to the removal of those in the Congress who question actions of the executive branch and the growth of military influence.

Considering the normal skepticism of the American citizen, such overt political activity by the military would seem to have small chance of success. But I raise the point, nevertheless; the apparatus exists, and we of the Congress, in another context, have been put on notice that legitimate, and even constitutionally required questioning is viewed by some as interference with executive prerogatives.

It is interesting to compare American government's only *official* propaganda organization, the U.S. Information Agency, with the Defense Department's apparatus. USIA is so circumscribed by Congress that it cannot, with the rarest of exceptions, distribute its materials within this country. Since much USIA output is composed of a filtered view of the United States and its policies, such a prohibition is eminently sensible. But the Defense Department, with more than twice as many people engaged in public relations as USIA has in all of its posts abroad, operates to distribute its propaganda within this country without control other than the executive, and floods the domestic scene with its special, narrow view of the military establishment and its role in the world.

Of course the military needs an information program. But it should be one designed to inform, not promote or possibly deceive. There is no need for production of self-promotional films for public consumption. There is no need for flying private citizens about the country to demonstrate to them our military might. There is no need for sending speakers at taxpayers' expense anywhere from Pensacola, Florida, to Portland, Oregon, to talk to luncheon clubs and veterans organizations. There is no need for setting up expensive and elaborate exhibits at state and county fairs. There is no need for taking VIP's on pleasant cruises to Hawaii abroad aircraft carriers. There is no need for "Red," "White," and "Blue" teams criss-crossing the country, "educating" people about the dangers of communism, the need for patriotism, and the Gross National Product of newly independent lands. There certainly is no need for military production of television shows for domestic, commercial use showing "feature" aspects of the Southeast Asian war....

An observation so widely cited that it is almost an axiom is that no one hates war more than the professional soldier. I think de Tocqueville was closer to the mark when he wrote:

> ...all the ambitious minds in a democratic army ardently long for war, because war makes vacancies [for promotion] available and at last allows violations of the rule of seniority, which is the one privilege natural to a democracy. We thus arrive at the strange conclusion that of all armies those which long for war most ardently are the democratic ones, but that of all peoples those most deeply attached to peace are the democratic nations. And the most extraordinary thing about the whole matter is that it is equality which is responsible for both these contradictory results.[3]

Beyond the ambition of which de Tocqueville wrote, there is even more danger to our democracy from the dehumanizing kind of war we are fighting that produces among the military an insensitivity to life hard for the civilian to comprehend. We have fought many wars before, but none since our Revolution has lasted as long as the present one. Officers and noncoms go back to Southeast Asia for second and third tours of duty, to engage in second and third rounds of killing. Such long

[3] Alexis de Tocqueville, *Democracy in America*, vol. 2 (New York: Harper & Row, 1965), pp. 622–23.

immersion in violence of the kind peculiar to this war cannot but brutalize many of those who go through it.…

Perhaps there is something in the theory advanced by psychologist Erich Fromm that in men there are polar attitudes toward life, "biophilia" (love of life) and "necrophilia" (love of death). Spinoza in his *Ethics,* Fromm says, epitomized the spirit of the biophile: "A freeman thinks of death least of all things and his wisdom is a dedication not of death but of life." The necrophile, on the other hand, has values precisely the reverse, for death, not life, excites and satisfies him. Hitler was a clear case of necrophilia, and Hitler and Stalin with their unlimited capacity and willingness to kill and destroy were loved by the necrophiles.

Fromm goes on to say that the necrophile, by extension in modern society, might be labeled *homo mechanicus* who "has more pride in, and is more fascinated by, devices that can kill millions of people across several thousands of miles in minutes than he is depressed and frightened by the possibility of such mass destruction."[4]…

[4] Erick Fromm, "Creators and Destroyers," *Saturday Review,* January 4, 1964, pp. 22–25.

PART SIX

Pressures and Aims
Politics and Economics

[Johnson's] chief advisers in government believed with him that they would take greater punishment from the right by withdrawing than from the left by pursuing the fight.
—Barbara W. Tuchman, *The March of Folly*, 1984

And so, quite naturally, once again to war . . . to secure the necessary access to the world marketplace.
—William A. Williams, *The Tragedy of American Diplomacy*, 1972

30

FOREIGN POLICY AND ELECTORAL POLITICS

RICHARD J. BARNET

In Roots of War, *Richard J. Barnet's 1972 book about the national security bureaucracy and the Vietnam War, the author described the connections between the bureaucracy, the presidency, Congress, business, and politics. Maintaining that national security managers manipulate international issues to create public moods during presidential election campaigns, he conceded in a chapter on electoral politics that public moods affect the climate in which managers operate.*

Modern American democracy is sustained by two crucial myths. The first is bipartisanship, "Politics stops at the water's edge." In his Farewell Address, George Washington lamented the "baneful effects of the spirits of party" on our foreign relations, although, as Frederick Dutton has pointed out, that very statement was timed to affect the outcome of an election. In the postwar era the "bipartisan foreign policy" worked out by John Foster Dulles, Senator Arthur Vandenberg and the nonpartisan (but largely Republican-voting) national security managers of the Truman Administration, has become, in Kenneth Crawford's words, the "Jehovah of our political tradition." The most casual glance at recent history, however, reveals that some foreign policies are more bipartisan than others. Since the end of the war, some aspect of foreign policy has been injected into every presidential election.

The second myth is that while the handling of the crucial issues of war and peace are entrusted for a period of years to the President and whatever advisers he chooses to help him, the voter has a chance every four years to ratify or to overturn what they have done and even to give some guidance for the future. Thus the President's enormous powers over foreign affairs are subject to a quadrennial check. The President's fear of the voter's displeasure acts as a restraint on the exercise of his lordly discretion. This myth makes it possible to reconcile the sharp increase in presidential prerogatives in foreign relations of recent times and the democratic tradition.

In *Democracy in America* de Tocqueville declared in an often-quoted passage that democracy and effective diplomacy are antithetical:

> As for myself, I do not hesitate to say that it is especially in the conduct of their foreign relations that democracies appear to me decidedly inferior to other governments.... Foreign politics demand scarcely any of those qualities which are peculiar to a democracy; they require, on the contrary, the perfect use of almost all those in which it is deficient.... Democracy can only with great difficulty regulate the details of an important undertaking, persevere in a fixed design, and work out its execution in spite of serious obstacles. It cannot combine its measures with secrecy or await their consequences with patience. These are qualities which more especially belong to an individual or an aristocracy.

The conflict between popular government and aggressive statesmanship, between democracy and empire, is an ancient one. Sometimes, as the historian William A. Williams argues, there is a broad base of support, even some grass-roots initiative, for expansionist policies, as in the agrarian movements of the turn of the century. Sometimes jingoist movements arise, such as the Goldwater-LeMay wing of the "radical right," which press the President toward more adventurous policies than he wishes to undertake. But the historical record shows that the President's view of the national interest typically involves more expense, more taxation, more danger, and more casualties than the public wants to accept. This is surely what Dean Acheson means when he writes that "the limitation imposed by democratic political practices makes it difficult to conduct our foreign affairs in the national interest...." The conflict between democracy and the "national interest" (as revealed to the executive) has been resolved in favor of the latter.

We have noted that a prime consequence of the bureaucratic revolution was the shift of power over national security affairs from Congress to the President. Although the changes in World War II were dramatic, this process had been going on for a long time. According to Woodrow Wilson, the "most striking and momentous consequence" of the Spanish-American War was "the greatly increased power and opportunity for constructive statesmanship given the President by the plunge into international politics and into the administration of distant dependencies...."[1] When foreign affairs play a prominent part in the politics and policy of a nation, Wilson concluded, "its Executive must of necessity be its guide: must utter every initial judgment, take every first step of action, supply the information upon which it is to act, suggest and in large measure control its conduct."

[1] Quoted in Dean Acheson, *A Citizen Looks at Congress* (New York: Harper Bros., 1957), pp. 50–51.

Every postwar President has been a Wilsonian not only in his belief in America's moral duty to bring a reformist vision to the world, but also in his view that the President must have the power to run the crusade his own way. The modern President counts among his major triumphs the preservation of the presidential prerogatives in foreign affairs. In 1951, for example, when the so-called "Great Debate" was taking place in Congress over how many divisions the President had a right to assign permanently to Europe, the White House carried on a high-pitched campaign to prevent the efforts of isolationists led by Taft and Wherry to "tie the President's hands." For Truman the issue at stake was not so much the numbers of troops in Europe but the powers of the Presidency. No modern President wants to be known as the man who weakened the office, and each has endeavored to pass on its awesome powers intact.[2]

Thus the President, being beyond the reach of public opinion for four years in his conduct of foreign affairs, and largely independent of Congress as well, can be influenced only by the quadrennial referendum. Do elections give voters a meaningful choice on foreign policy issues? Are foreign policy issues important in national elections? What guidance do elections give the winning candidate for the exercise of his enormous powers over foreign affairs and how responsive is he to the popular will in foreign policy?

When aspiring candidates consult experts in winning elections, they usually are told that foreign policy issues do not move voters unless they are combined in some fashion with "bread and butter" economic issues. People are interested in the size of the defense budget and whether a new bomber will be built because jobs are at stake. They are interested in tariffs. But only a tiny fraction of the electorate is interested in whether NATO has a "forward defense," whether the United States supports Pakistan or India, whether the United States sends military assistance to Latin American dictators or invites South Africa to participate in NATO maneuvers. On any of these issues the President may receive some unfriendly mail or public criticism from small segments of "elite" opinion, meaning a selected population with some special reason to care deeply about the outcome, but there will be no public mandate. Such matters are not presented as domestic political issues in the context of elections. Indeed, a review of the presidential elections from 1940 to the present reveals that at no time have clear-cut foreign policy alternatives been presented to the electorate by the major parties in such a way as to permit voters to influence future policy. In short, while foreign policy *themes* have played an important role in presidential elections, foreign policy *issues* have been blurred in such a way as to preclude meaningful choice.

In 1940 FDR promised that "your boys are not going to be sent into foreign wars" but he made it clear that the industrial might of America would be dedicated to the defeat of the Axis. Wendell Willkie, the Republican candidate, was also an "internationalist" who, like Roosevelt, believed that it would be necessary to enter

---

[2] This theme runs throughout Truman's memoirs. Lyndon Johnson in his memoirs reveals that shortly after taking office he came to regard the Senate, whose majority leader he was for so many years, as a "threat" to the exercise of presidential power.

the war but hoped that the day could be postponed. The impending war was the primary public concern, but there was no foreign policy issue presented, since both candidates essentially agreed. The real issue was between Roosevelt's experience and the attractions of a fresh face.

In 1944 the war again dominated the election. This time too the choice was a matter of personality and tradition. Should a President attacked by his opponent as a "tired old man" be given a fourth term in the midst of a war in preference to a young man, Thomas E. Dewey, who claimed the ability to pursue the old man's war plans with greater vigor?

In 1948 the election did present the voters with some foreign policy choices on which to express opinion but only because of the presence of the third-party candidate, Henry Wallace. The former Vice-President ran on a platform which condemned the policy of containment, the Truman Doctrine, and rearmament. Because the Wallace movement was infiltrated with Communists and the candidate was successfully tarred as a "dupe," he attracted only about a million votes. The other forty-six million Americans who voted for Dewey or Truman had no foreign policy choices because none were presented. Truman explains in his memoirs:

> One of the things I tried hard to keep out of the campaign was foreign policy. There should be no break in the bipartisan foreign policy of the United States at any time—particularly during a national election. I even asked that a teletype machine be set up on the Dewey train so that the Republican candidate personally could be informed on all the foreign developments as they progressed....[3]

In the midst of the campaign Truman decided to send Chief Justice Fred Vinson as a special emissary to Stalin "to overcome any damage the Wallace campaign may have caused in stirring up the feeling...that the administration was not doing all it could in the interest of peace." But news of the impending mission was leaked to an unfriendly newspaper and Truman, worried about being branded an "appeaser," canceled the mission. Dewey did not attack the main lines of the Truman foreign policy, but he did challenge the sincerity of the Administration's commitment to Israel. He also exploited the issue of Communists in government, but the question whether Truman or Dewey was the more vigilant in rooting Stalinists out of the State Department hardly gave the voters a chance to express their view on what the global role of the United States ought to be.

In 1952 the Communists-in-government issue had become hotter. Richard Nixon had launched his political career on Whittaker Chambers' pumpkin papers and the subsequent conviction of Alger Hiss for lying about them. The hunt for subversives was bipartisan. The Republicans produced the Mundt-Nixon law on controlling subversive activities and Hubert Humphrey proposed outlawing the Communist Party. The Republicans charged the Truman Administration with losing China, inviting the attack in Korea, and pursuing the "negative, defeatist"

[3] Harry Truman, *Memoirs: Vol. 2: Years of Trial and Hope* (New York: New American Library, 1965), p. 2ll.

policy of containment. Foreign policy themes dominated the 1952 election. Eisenhower's greatest appeal beyond his promise to bring a new morality to a Washington of corrupting deep freezes, dubious fur coats, and sleazy "five per-centers," all allegedly the result of twenty years of Democratic rule, was his rep-utation as soldier-statesman. "I will go to Korea," he announced, but like Richard Nixon sixteen years later, he gave no hint of how or on what basis he would settle the Korean War. The only choice on foreign policy offered the voters was a rhe-torical one: "liberation" (of Eastern Europe) versus "containment." Dulles never spelled out how he planned to rescue the "captive peoples" without a world war and when pressed by reporters to explain what he had in mind, the future Secretary made it clear that it wasn't much.

In 1956 Dwight D. Eisenhower could have been re-elected irrespective of platform or opponent. As it happened, two foreign policy crises—the Soviet sup-pression of the freedom fighters of Budapest and the Anglo-French-Israeli invasion of Egypt—at the height of the campaign, probably won Eisenhower extra votes on the "don't change horses in mid-stream" theory. In the campaign Stevenson did differ with the Administration on the matter of nuclear testing and did make use of a somewhat softer rhetoric on foreign policy. But with the exception of the testing issue there was once again little substantive choice for the voter.

The 1960 election campaign was dominated by the atmospherics of foreign policy. John F. Kennedy's major theme, suggested to him by Walt Rostow, was getting the country "moving again." It was clear to anyone listening to Kennedy campaign rhetoric that most of the movement he had in mind was abroad. The great issue, he would repeat throughout the campaign, was America's falling prestige. The Eisenhower Administration, made up of miserly old men, had stinted on the nation's defense and allowed a dangerous "missile gap" to develop. The torch must now be passed to the young and vigorous who would fight the Communists with the courage and subtlety so lacking in the quiet clubhouse atmosphere of the Eisenhower White House. Here was a clear foreign policy difference with the Eisenhower Administration, which maintained (correctly, as it turned out) that there was no missile gap. But the Republican candidate, Richard Nixon, pressed by Nelson Rockefeller, endorsed a military program identical to the one John F. Kennedy asked for and largely obtained once in the White House. On July 23, 1960, Nixon and Rockefeller issued a joint statement proposing "more and improved bombers, airborne alert, speeded production of missiles and Polaris submarines, accelerated dispersal and hardening of bases, full modernization of the equipment of our ground forces, and an intensified program for civil defense."[4]

The second of the famous TV debates between Kennedy and Nixon con-cerned foreign policy. The emphasis was on such emotion-laden issues as whether American prestige was falling or whether Eisenhower should have apologized to Khrushchev for flying a U-2 over his country. Although these issues aroused a certain amount of passion, neither offered the voter a chance to vote on the future. However, two policy alternatives were raised. One was insignificant and the other

[4] Theodore White, *The Making of the President, 1960* (New York: Atheneum, 1961), p. 228.

was a piece of pure theater. The first involved the decision to defend the tiny islands off the Chinese mainland, Quemoy and Matsu, from an attempt by the Chinese Communists to occupy them. (Nixon: Yes; Kennedy: No.) The second concerned an invasion of Cuba. According to Nixon's own account, *Six Crises,* the darkest hour of the 1960 campaign was when he was trapped by circumstances and his opponent into appearing "softer" on Castro than Kennedy. The Democratic candidate, who had been secretly briefed that plans for a covert operation against Castro were under way, argued forcefully that the United States should take strong measures to rid the hemisphere of the Communist "only ninety miles away." Nixon, who was privy to the plans, was forced, in order to protect them, to take a public position that an invasion of Cuba would be illegal and would offend world opinion.

> I was sure then, and I am now, that the position I had to take on Cuba hurt rather than helped me. The average voter is not interested in the technicalities of treaty obligations. He thinks, quite properly, that Castro is a menace, and he favors the candidate who wants to do something about it—something positive and dramatic and forceful—and not one who takes the "statesmanlike" and the "legalistic" view.[5]

The campaign of 1964 was billed by the Goldwater forces as the first in modern times to present the voter with a choice instead of an echo. Goldwater was a religious anticommunist. He believed that freedom, which as an abstract matter he held to be the highest human value, was imperiled by Soviet communism. Goldwater's advisers, including Professor Stefan T. Possoney, William Kintner, Robert Strausz-Hupe, Warren Nutter, David Abshire, and active-duty Air Force Generals such as Dale O. Smith and Brigadier General Robert C. Richardson III instructed him in the virtues of tactical nuclear warfare, the dangers of negotiation, and the plausibility of victory by means of the hydrogen bomb. Goldwater's rhetoric was totally different from Johnson's. It was easy to paint him as "trigger-happy" because he would suggest such things as defoliating jungle trails with nuclear weapons. As an Air Force reserve major general his inclination was to build his campaign around the attacks on Robert McNamara that were then the favorite topics of the day at U.S. officers' clubs around the world. Most of his alternative policies were vague, although the voter instinctively felt that, whatever one could say of him, Goldwater was not a "me-too" candidate. There was indeed a choice. Whenever the choice became explicit, however, as when the Republican candidate suggested that battlefield commanders should have discretion to use nuclear weapons, the public became alarmed. It was all right to be fanatical about Communists, but it was another thing to be cavalier about nuclear weapons when the American people were also under the gun.

Lyndon Johnson successfully exploited Goldwater's Strangelovian image to make himself appear a man of peace by contrast—without sacrificing his reputation for toughness. The irony of the campaign of course was that Johnson adopted the Goldwater policy. Indeed, the contingency planning actually conducted and put

[5] Richard M. Nixon, *Six Crises* (Garden City, N.Y.: Doubleday and Co., 1962), p. 356.

into effect by the Johnson Administration in Vietnam was extraordinarily similar to the following recommendations prepared for Goldwater in early 1964 by one of his top foreign policy advisers. The only difference is that the Goldwater adviser's recommendations were somewhat more modest.[6]

1. An American summons to Hanoi to discontinue the operations against South Vietnam.
2. Demonstrative American overflights for reconnaissance, showing-the-flag purposes, and leaflet missions.
3. Naval patrols in North Vietnam waters, first to show the flag, later to carry out a quarantine and finally, if necessary, to establish a blockade.
4. Aerial harassment of the main supply routes into South Vietnam, including those leading through Laos. This could be undertaken with bombs and land mines plus the landing from the air of demolition squads.
5. Overflight along the Chinese–North Vietnam borders.

During the campaign Goldwater was flooded with such advice from his Air Force friends as the following (from a memorandum of conversation between Air Force General Dale Smith and Robert Richardson): "We must resolve to use nucs as necessary in the Far East, just as in Europe, but this may not be a good campaign line at this time." In 1964 the voters thought they were exercising a choice on the issue of war and peace in Vietnam and were wrong. On the issue of nuclear policy the campaign also presented an important choice, and on this point the voters were not deceived. Lyndon Johnson had come to believe that it was prudent to arrange limited arms control agreements with the Soviets and to exercise some restraint in nuclear matters. But Goldwater, who believed that the most reckless policies actually lessened the risks of war, was a Cold War caricature.

The foreign policy issue of 1968 was of course Vietnam and that issue was decided before the conventions. The McCarthy candidacy had helped to persuade Johnson not to run. The convention split over the Vietnam plank—i.e., whether to have an unconditional bombing halt as an inducement to the enemy to negotiate a settlement. The Johnson forces won at the convention, which was a scene of great frustration, fury, and pitched battles between Mayor Daley's police and antiwar demonstrators. Frederick Dutton gives a good summary of the rest of the campaign:

> Nixon, Humphrey, and Wallace, each in his own way, pledged an end to the war in Southeast Asia and a sweeping reappraisal of America's priorities abroad and at home. Nixon claimed to have a plan (never revealed during the campaign) for an early end to the war. And, by coincidence or otherwise, the incumbent Democrats, after long refusing to de-escalate the Vietnam conflict, suddenly called a bombing halt five days before the election. A close Nixon friend just as quickly got the American-maintained South Vietnamese government to indicate some

---

[6] I am indebted to Karl Hess, former Goldwater adviser, for his information about the Goldwater campaign of 1964.

well-publicized reservations about the move, all on the weekend before
the U.S. balloting.[7]

The "close Nixon friend" was Mrs. Claire Chennault. When I had occasion to talk
to the former Vice-President a few months after the election, he said flatly, "Thieu
and Ky lost me the election."

In the last few days of the 1968 campaign, there were sharp and sudden shifts
of opinion. As Theodore H. White reports in *The Making of the President, 1968,*
"regional poll-masters were finding...a seven-point change in Michigan; a three-
point shift to Humphrey in Ohio was moving that state to the doubtful column....In
California Nixon's ten-point lead of mid-October was melting...."[8] Louis Harris,
whose final poll predicted Humphrey as the winner, attributed the sudden shift to
"the women's vote." The bombing halt "has gotten to them," Harris told White.
The women were for peace. If the election had been held on Saturday or Sunday,
the Nixon campaign leaders believe that they might have lost. But by Tuesday it
was clear that the bombing halt would not lead to a quick end of American battle
casualties.

Thus foreign policy issues are used as campaign vehicles to create political
moods. None of the elections just reviewed, with the exception of 1964, was a referendum, for no clear-cut choices were presented. In 1964, where such a choice was
presented, the Johnson voters ended up with the Goldwater policy on the most
crucial foreign policy issues. Indeed, as the Pentagon papers reveal, Johnson's huge
popular mandate for peace was considered by the national security managers to be
a crucial prerequisite for escalating the war. Had the mandate been less, Johnson
might well have been more cautious.

However, the fact that quadrennial elections do not serve as clear-cut votes on
foreign policy issues does not mean that elections are without influence on the President and the national security managers. On the contrary, elections are kept very
much in mind in the making of policy. Daniel Ellsberg has expressed the view that
the continued escalation in Vietnam despite pessimistic intelligence prognoses was
due primarily to the fear shared by three Presidents that defeat in Vietnam "this
year" would lose an impending election. The memory of the "loss of China" and
the political capital this provided political opponents haunted the Democratic administrations of the 1960's. It was a memory also bound to affect their Republican
successor, for he had made much of the rhetoric of the "China sell-out" in advancing his own career. Having campaigned against Adlai Stevenson by charging
him with membership in "Dean Acheson's College of Cowardly Communist Containment," Nixon was loath to give any opponent the chance to brand him as a man
who accepted defeat.

In the Cuban missile crisis of 1962, to take another example, domestic political considerations were very much in the forefront. In his account, Roger Hilsman,
who was in charge of intelligence in the State Department at the time, concludes

---

[7] Frederick G. Dutton, *Changing Sources of American Power* (New York: McGraw-Hill, 1971), p. 167.

[8] Theodore White, *The Making of the President, 1968* (New York: Atheneum, 1969), p. 446.

that the country may not have been in mortal danger as a result of Khrushchev's placing some missiles in Cuba, "but the Administration certainly was."[9] A Republican Senator, Kenneth Keating, who had received reports from refugees about the Soviet military buildup, began charging the Administration with reckless disregard of the national security. The Administration, which was particularly vulnerable on Cuba, was well aware that the issue could be used to its serious disadvantage in the upcoming Congressional elections. Even though, as Secretary McNamara reported to the "Ex Comm," the group charged with managing the crisis, the missiles in Cuba did not change the military balance, accepting them risked political humiliation. Robert Kennedy, his brother's closest political adviser, told him in the midst of the crisis, "...if you hadn't acted, you would have been impeached."[10] The sensitive manager understands that public outcries and the threat of punishment at the polls do not come from a spontaneous popular reaction to national security decisions but from the political exploitation of these decisions by skillful adversaries—a China Lobby with enough money to haunt every office in Congress, a political opponent with enough demagogic appeal to tag the Administration with the "loss of China," "twenty years of treason," or "bugging out of Vietnam."

The unorganized public mood obviously affects the climate in which the national security managers operate. The conduct of foreign policy has had a different feel since the strong anti-Soviet feelings of the early Cold War years have subsided. Nevertheless, shifts in mood have little impact on specific decisions until voters are politically organized. Relatively small numbers of voters are ever organized for foreign policy issues, for the fundamental fact remains that most people feel incompetent and irrelevant when it comes to foreign affairs. Thus a week after President Kennedy's extraordinary American University speech with its dramatic change in tone of the treatment of U.S.-Soviet relations, the White House received fifty thousand letters, of which 896 had to do with the speech and 28,232 concerned a freight rate bill pending in Congress.

The real influence of the public is exerted through the political coalitions that constitute the major parties. While the public at large has a marginal and unfocused interest in foreign affairs, certain key groups, essential for getting out the vote at election time, do have strong financial or ideological interest in particular foreign policy choices. The dominant majority party during the last forty years has been the Democratic Party, an implausible but remarkably persistent coalition of interests: organized labor, organized ethnic minorities in the cities, New Deal industrialists, the "Deep South," and the Farm Vote. The Democrats cannot win if there are serious defections from this coalition. The Republicans win only if there are.

The organizers of each of these coalitions have had strong commitment to the anticommunist consensus at the heart of American foreign policy. They were able to mobilize opinion and votes for a strong anticommunist and interventionist foreign policy only because such policies served their own parochial interests as they saw them....

---

[9] Roger Hilsman, *To Move a Nation* (New York: Dell Publishing Co., 1967), pp. 196–198.

[10] Robert F. Kennedy, *Thirteen Days* (New York: W. W. Norton, 1969), p. 45.

31

LOBBYISTS FOR DIEM: POLITICS IN THE UNITED STATES AND VIETNAM

GEORGE McTURNAN KAHIN

According to the official U.S. explanation, American military intervention was a response to North Vietnamese aggression against Ngo Dinh Diem's government in South Vietnam. George Kahin has long argued, however, that the war in the south began as an indigenous uprising against Diem's refusal to participate in national unification elections and his authoritarian rule and repressive measures. In Intervention, *his 1986 book on U.S. involvement, Kahin brought new research to bear on the crucial questions of the establishment of the Diem regime, the origins of the NLF, and the causes of the insurrection.*

In the excerpt below, Kahin explains how politics in America and Vietnam helped bring Diem to power. The American Friends of Vietnam, a lobbying group of influential liberals and conservatives, called Diem to the attention of Secretary of State John Foster Dulles in 1953 and then encouraged the Eisenhower administration to back Diem's bid for leadership in South Vietnam after the Geneva Accords of 1954. It was a time when U.S. policymakers were seeking a nationalist, anti-Communist leader to replace the emperor Bao Dai, who had collaborated with the French. They hoped to establish a rival to Ho Chi Minh as claimant to the mantle of Vietnamese nationalism in the southern half of the country. Although U.S. support was qualified until 1955, with the help of the CIA, the State Department, and Vietnamese Catholics, Diem was able to prevail over all his rivals for leadership: candidates backed by the French, factions within the South Vietnamese armed forces, and competing political groups. Among the latter were the Binh Xuyen—a powerful vice league—and the Cao Dai and Hao Ao— both armed religious sects.

From *Intervention: How America Became Involved in Vietnam* by George McT. Kahin. Copyright © 1986 by George McT. Kahin. Reprinted by permission of Alfred A. Knopf, Inc.

The actual transfer of governmental authority by France to Bao Dai was not completed until more than five months after the end of the Geneva Conference.[1] In consolidating the new government in the southern half of Vietnam, Bao Dai proved useful during this transitional period primarily because of his continuing influence with the soldiers and civil servants who had served the French. Bao Dai, however, was certainly not Washington's first choice to lead this government. His undoubtedly sincere efforts to secure independence from France had failed, and many of those South Vietnamese whom the administration hoped to detach from Ho's standard regarded the former emperor as a collaborator with the colonial order. He did not improve this image by remaining in France, from where he conveyed his orders to his subordinates. Nor did he have a large following among the Catholics.

In view of Washington's jaundiced assessment of Bao Dai, and the apparent ineffectiveness of his prime minister, Prince Buu Loc, it is understandable that American officials should have sought an eminent Catholic nationalist, free of any taint of collaboration with the French, to provide more effective anticommunist leadership. And in inducing Bao Dai, apparently without French approval, to appoint Ngo Dinh Diem as his prime minister in mid-May 1954, the Eisenhower administration secured a man with these attributes. Diem was probably in a better position than any other Vietnamese leader to swing the maximum number of Catholics behind the new southern regime. Furthermore, he had given advance assurances that he agreed to the U.S. proposal to take over the training of South Vietnamese armed forces.[2]

Nonetheless, at this stage American officials were by no means euphoric, and still recognized—as they were much less inclined to do a year or two later—his serious limitations. Thus, the U.S. ambassador to Paris cabled Washington on May 24, "On balance we are favorably impressed [by Diem] but only in the realization that we are prepared to accept the seemingly ridiculous prospect that this yogi-like mystic could assume the charge he is apparently about to undertake only because the standard set by his predecessor is so low." Following Diem's arrival in Saigon on June 25, the assessment of the U.S. chargé there was every bit as unenthusiastic:

---

[1] Not until January 1, 1955, was Bao Dai's prime minister, Ngo Dinh Diem, able to proclaim the reality of independence from France, and it was another two months before France transferred control over the Vietnamese component of the French armed forces in Vietnam.

[2] To the French National Assembly, the minister of state for relations with the associated (Indochina) states, Guy La Chambre, explained the choice of Ngo Dinh Diem: "We did not choose Mr. Ngo Dinh Diem. He was already designated when our government came into the act." (*Journal Officiel de la République Française, Débats Parlementaires, Assemblée Nationale*, December 17, 1954, 2nd sess.) See also cable from Dillon to Department of State, May 26, 1954, in *FRUS, 1952–1954*, Indochina, 2:1615. See also S. M. Bao Dai, *Le Dragon d'Annam* (Plon, 1980), p. 328, who acknowledges conversing with Dulles just before appointing Diem, and Chester L. Cooper, *The Lost Crusade: America in Vietnam* (New York: Dodd, Mead, 1970), pp. 127–28, who states that Dulles met with Bao Dai in Paris in the spring of 1954 "in an effort to persuade him to join Diem in Vietnam and help Diem defend the South," but that the emperor declined to go back to a partitioned country. Dulles and Bao Dai agreed, he said, that Bao Dai should "remain in France and return to Vietnam after Diem had won over the country." On the training of South Vietnamese armed forces, see Cable: Dillon to Department of State, May 26, 1954, *FRUS, 1952–1954*, 13:1615. [Ed. note: *FRUS=Foreign Relations of the United States* (Washington, D.C.: GPO, 1969–).]

"Diem is a messiah without a message. His only formulated policy is to ask for immediate American assistance in every form, including refugee relief, training of troops and armed intervention. His only present emotion, other than a lively appreciation of himself, is a blind hatred for the French."[3]

Although some American officials hoped that Diem would emerge as Vietnam's Magsaysay, the only attributes he shared with the Filipino were personal honesty, pecuniary incorruptibility, and a strong anticommunism. A mandarin aristocrat, at once arrogant and reserved and shy, Diem had scant understanding of and little rapport with the peasantry. He felt awkward, and acted so, when prevailed upon to visit rural areas, and his espousal of Catholicism appears to have made no dent in his aloofness from the populace. As Joseph Buttinger, who worked closely with him, has written, "Diem's temperament, social philosophy, and political comportment seemed to preclude all prospects of his ever becoming a popular hero. His stiff demeanor would have doomed any attempt to stir the masses by word or gesture, had he ever been persuaded of the necessity to make himself admired and loved. However, what he wanted was not love but the respect and obedience he considered his due as head of state." Moreover, except in his early years, Diem had actually had very little administrative experience. He had served ably and energetically in the French colonial administration, moving from an initial appointment as district chief in 1921, at the age of twenty, to the position of governor of a small province in 1929. Then, beginning in 1933, he was briefly the young emperor Bao Dai's secretary of the interior in the almost powerless rump Imperial Court at Hué, a position from which he resigned on principle because of French interference with his efforts to introduce reforms, and Bao Dai's unwillingness to give him sufficient backing. But for two decades thereafter he held no administrative post, nor did he show great talent as a political organizer.[4]

Diem stood out in that he had not collaborated with the French. Nevertheless, in the eyes of a significant number of Vietnamese, his nationalist credentials had been tarnished by his willingness to work with Japanese occupation authorities. For a brief period he was their leading candidate for the position of premier in the client Vietnamese government with which they planned to replace the French in March 1945. Only when, at the last minute, the Japanese abandoned their plan for replacing Bao Dai with Prince Cuong De as emperor did Diem lose interest in the premiership.[5] His claim to national leadership was further weakened by his absence

[3] "On balance" quote is from cable from Dillon to Department of State, May 24, 1954, in *FRUS, 1952–1954*, Indochina, 2:1609. "Diem is a messiah" quote is from McClintock to Department of State, July 4, 1954, in *ibid.*, pp. 1783–84.

[4] Buttinger quote is from Joseph Buttinger, *Vietnam: A Dragon Embattled*, vol. 2 (New York: Frederick A. Praeger, 1967), p. 846. For further details of Diem's background, see Bernard Fall, *The Two Vietnams: A Political and Military Analysis* (New York: Frederick A. Praeger, 1967), p. 239; Robert Shaplen, *The Lost Revolution* (Harper and Row, 1965), pp. 107–8.

[5] On Diem and the Japanese, see Masaya Shiraishi, "The Japanese and the Vietnamese 'Nationalists' During World War II," Seminar on the International Relations of Southeast Asia, Cornell University, Ithaca, N.Y., 1979, pp. 19, 20, 23, 27, 30, 36; Ralph B. Smith, "The Japanese Period in Indochina and the Coup of March 9, 1945," *Journal of Southeast Asian Studies*, 9, no. 2 (September 1978): 274, 286, 388. Prince Cuong De had been in exile in Japan since 1906, and Diem clearly held him in higher esteem than Bao Dai. For Diem's relations with the Japanese, see also Buttinger, *Dragon Embattled*, 1:289–90, 602–3.

from the country (he was in Europe and the United States) from August 1950 through the final years of the anti-French struggle.

At least as late as June 1953, Diem appears to have been unknown to Dulles and was unable to get an appointment with him. During that year, however, from a base in the Maryknoll order's headquarters in Lakewood, New Jersey, Diem—encouraged by several American Catholic leaders, the most prominent of whom was Francis Cardinal Spellman—was actively engaged in soliciting American backing. Acknowledging that Ho Chi Minh drew popular support because of his nationalism, he argued that Ho was succeeding primarily because Bao Dai had been so compromised by his association with the French. Only an anticommunist nationalist whose record was free of such collaboration, he argued, could draw this kind of backing away from Ho. (Diem had earlier turned down an offer of a high position in Ho's government, because he regarded the Vietminh as ultimately responsible for the murder of one of his brothers; but Ho's offer itself demonstrated that even he recognized Diem's stature as a nationalist leader.) However dogmatic and narrow in some of his views, Diem appeared completely assured as to his own ability to provide an effective alternative to Ho. He was able to convince a growing number of influential Americans, initially including Congressman Walter Judd and Senators John F. Kennedy and Mike Mansfield—with others such as Hubert Humphrey soon to follow—that he was the man to do this. His campaign to win congressional support was undoubtedly aided by the enthusiastic backing of a remarkably effective lobby of strongly anticommunist, mostly liberal-leaning Americans, which by the fall of 1955 had been organized as the American Friends of Vietnam, and ultimately enlisted these congressmen and a good many others among its members. It is hard to measure how influential Diem's American backers initially were with Dulles and Eisenhower, but as early as February 1954, against the background of Bao Dai's acknowledged incapacity, Under Secretary of State Bedell Smith told an executive session of the Senate Foreign Relations Committee that the administration was thinking of "providing a certain religious leadership."[6]

(The American Friends of Vietnam maintained a vigorous effort to gather U.S. support for Diem until 1961, when most of its members became disillusioned with his leadership, and its activities dwindled until his overthrow. Soon after his death, however, the organization was revived and once more became a significant force for a strongly interventionist policy in Vietnam. Whereas during its early, pro-Diem period the group's activities had been sustained primarily by the generally altruistic zeal and dedication of its members, after its revival it worked in-

---

[6] A Maryknoll priest with service in Vietnam, Thomas O'Melia, attempted unsuccessfully, through Senator James Duff of Pennsylvania, to arrange a meeting for Diem in a letter to Dulles of June 6, 1953. (John Foster Dulles Papers, Princeton University Library, IIa correspondence 1953 [I–K].) Diem acknowledged Ho Chi Minh's stature as a nationalist and expressed the conviction that he could provide an effective alternative to Ho in February 1953, when he visited Cornell University and spent an afternoon discussing his ideas about Vietnam and its future with my seminar. I also had an opportunity to talk with him extensively in private meetings. For accounts of the American Friends of Vietnam, see especially Buttinger, *Dragon Embattled*, 2:927 ff.; Robert Scheer, *How the United States Got Involved in Vietnam* (Center for the Study of Democratic Institutions, 1965), pp. 31–33. Bedell Smith quote is from sess. of February 16, 1954, Senate Foreign Relations Committee, *Executive Sessions*, p. 143.

creasingly closely with the New York public-relations firm representing the Saigon government. By May 1965 the American Friends of Vietnam had developed close though discreet ties with, and a considerable dependence on, the U.S. government, which helped raise private funds for it. Moreover, at least one of the publication ventures planned by the organization's national chairman was undertaken on the initiative of the White House (McGeorge Bundy's aide, Chester Cooper), in conjunction with the Pentagon-supported Historical Evaluation Research Organization, whose executive director, Colonel Trevor N. Dupuy, provided it with an editorial staff and helped arrange for its financing.[7])

Although American officials viewed Diem as the most promising candidate available to head the Saigon government, many were at first circumspect in endorsing him publicly or in offering support. This caution stemmed not only from some lingering doubts as to his qualifications but also from the extremely difficult and precarious political situation he was confronting. The administration's circumspection was clearly reflected in the qualified and conditional offer of support embodied in Eisenhower's letter to Diem of October 1, 1954, written in a hesitant tone and not actually delivered until three weeks later.[8]

Eisenhower made his pledge of aid dependent on Diem's "assurances as to the standards of performance . . . in undertaking needed reforms." American assistance was to be "combined with" Diem's own efforts to "contribute effectively toward an independent Vietnam endowed with a strong government," a government that, Eisenhower hoped, would be "so responsive to the nationalist aspirations of its people" as to attract domestic and international respect. This letter was not the all-out pledge that subsequent American presidents cited to justify their own intervention; it was, however, one of the first in a series of steps by the Eisenhower administration that, starting cautiously, were eventually to constitute a clear, positive, and virtually unqualified commitment to maintain a separate state in the southern half of Vietnam.

But during the first nine months after Geneva, this official circumspection was paralleled by the concurrent pursuit of another option, a second-track, covert policy; and any assessment of the administration's approach must focus heavily on this largely invisible level of policy. As Chester Cooper, then a top CIA official, candidly put it, "The Central Intelligence Agency was given the mission of helping Diem develop a government that would be sufficiently strong and viable to compete with and, if necessary, stand up to the communist regime of Ho Chi Minh in the north." Appointed to head this effort was Colonel Edward Lansdale, whom Dulles reportedly asked to "Do what you did in the Philippines." During Diem's first months in office, Lansdale and a few other American agents provided him with "considerable moral support and

---

[7] On the organization's dependence on the U.S. government, see Memoranda from Chester Cooper for Mr. Valenti, "The American Friends of Vietnam Program," May 5, June 7, 1965. This editorial venture, which sought respectability by attempting to enlist several academic Southeast Asian specialists, ultimately aborted, presumably because the academics approached refused to join despite the offer of a handsome monetary retainer. I have in my possession copies of documents explicitly describing the arrangement between Colonel Dupuy and Wesley Fishel, a key member of the American Friends of Vietnam who was to serve as editor of the journal. See also Cooper's Memorandum, "American Friends," May 5, 1965.

[8] Delivered by Ambassador Donald R. Heath on October 23.

guidance," as well as funds. Lansdale states that on the very day Diem arrived in Saigon he presented him with "notes on how to be a Prime Minister of Vietnam." He and other CIA operatives helped Diem establish dominance over the Vietnamese military forces gradually being turned over by the French, and later gave him critically important assistance in securing the adherence, neutralization, or dispersal of the armed forces of the Cao Dai, Hoa Hao, and Binh Xuyen.[9]

These successes in American covert activity, however, could not have occurred without sufficient displacement of French power. Here the U.S. leverage stemmed primarily from the degree to which both the French forces and their Vietnamese auxiliaries were dependent on American financial support. Since Washington was now substantially reducing its subvention to French troops still in Indochina, and France needed these troops to help contain the mounting nationalist insurrections against French rule in North Africa, their exodus from Vietnam took place more rapidly than either the French or the DRV had expected at the time of the signing of the Geneva Agreements. Moreover, the French desperately needed American support for their current North African policies, and only a few months before, over another issue (Guatemala), Eisenhower had made clear that he was prepared to end American support of the French in North Africa if Paris did not line up with Washington. With France critically dependent on the United States for financial support and for backing in North Africa, Premier Mendès-France was reluctant to risk antagonizing Washington by contesting American policy in Vietnam.[10]

[9] The quote concerning the Central Intelligence Agency is from Cooper, *Lost Crusade*, p. 129. Cooper was to have long experience, in various capacities, in helping shape U.S.-Vietnam policy. See also Edward G. Lansdale, *In the Midst of Wars* (Harper and Row, 1972), ch. 10. Dulles's instructions to Lansdale are from a statement by Lansdale in Michael Charlton and Anthony Moncrief, *Many Reasons Why: The American Involvement in Vietnam* (Hill and Wang, 1978), p. 42. Lansdale's "how to be a Prime Minister" quote is from Charlton and Moncrief, *Many Reasons Why*, p. 55. On helping Diem dominate the military forces see *PP* (Gravel), 1:580. [Ed. note: *PP* (Gravel) = *The Pentagon Papers: The Defense Department History of United States Decisionmaking on Vietnam: The Senator Gravel Edition*, 4 vols. (Beacon Press, 1971).] According to Lansdale, the Binh Xuyen, founded in 1940 as a social club of day laborers and charcoal-makers, had been organized, trained, and armed by the Japanese Kempeitei, who had used them in the 1945 coup against the Vichy French colonial establishment. The French had used them as a militia, assisting their own forces in guarding Saigon and its environs. Lansdale characterized their leader, Bay Vien, as having "developed rapidly into the combination role of the city's Boss Tweed and Al Capone." (*In the Midst of Wars*, p. 153.)

[10] In explaining the U.S. leverage to the French Chamber of Deputies, Guy La Chambre made clear that because of dependency on American funds it was "necessary to determine a policy in common," and that "To find ourselves alone in Indochina meant to cover, with the help of our funds only, the entirety of the expenses of the expeditionary corps and the national armies. We didn't have the means for it yesterday, and we don't have them today." (*Journal Officiel de la République Française, Débats Parlementaires, Assemblée Nationale*, December 17, 1954, 2nd sess.)

On the French need for U.S. support in North Africa, see Memorandum for the Record, Telephone Call from Secretary Dulles to Ambassador Lodge, June 24, 1954; Philippe Devillers and Jean Lacouture, *End of a War: Indochina, 1954* (Frederick A. Praeger, 1969), p. 358. French vulnerability vis-à-vis the United States had already been registered by Prime Minister Mendès-France in his September 5 instructions to the French delegation at the Manila Conference: "It is essential that our policy towards South Vietnam must be worked out in conjunction with the United States. We have a number of points at issue with them in other areas. There must be no additional reasons for a clash over Vietnam." (Devillers and Lacouture, *End of a War*, p. 324; see also *PP* [Gravel], 1:223.)

In the face of this leverage, French efforts to replace Diem with a candidate of their own choosing, Prince Buu Hoi, were doomed to failure, despite the substantial backing he received from General Nguyen Van Hinh (commander in chief of Bao Dai's army), most of his senior officers, and most leaders of the Cao Dai and Hoa Hao. But, though he was anticommunist, Buu Hoi had previously had close contact with Ho Chi Minh's government and favored holding national reunification elections, in the meantime introducing economic, cultural, and postal relations, plus freedom of travel between the North and the South. Even American officials who had grave doubts as to Diem's abilities opposed Buu Hoi's candidacy. Diem was clearly better suited to the administration's objective of preventing possible reunification of the South with a communist North. Thus, in reporting to Paris on November 6 on "the American Government's special addiction to Diem," General Paul Ely referred to him as "the only Vietnamese politician who would absolutely never enter into contact with the Vietminh under any circumstances...." In the face of French efforts to forward Buu Hoi's candidacy, Washington made clear that he, or anyone sharing his views, was unacceptable, and that unless Diem were retained as prime minister, American financial support would be terminated. In concrete terms, this meant ending the salaries of the nascent southern state's army, and most of its civil service. Consequently this effort to displace Diem collapsed.[11] ...

[11] On Buu Hoi, see Buttinger, *Dragon Embattled*, 2:719, 1024, 1099–1100; Cooper, *Lost Crusade*, p. 126; especially Devillers and Lacouture, *End of a War*, pp. 32, 337, 347, 358, 363. Buu Hoi, grandson of the Emperor Minh Mang and Bao Dai's cousin, was a respected cancer specialist with his own laboratory in France. He had earlier been with the Vietminh, and his father had elected to live in the North after the Geneva partition. Ely's report is in Devillers and Lacouture, *End of a War*, p. 363. For Washington's position on Buu Hoi, see *ibid.*, pp. 364-65, n. 5; George Chaffard, *Les Deux Guerres du Vietnam: De Valluy à Westmoreland* (La Table Ronde, 1969), p. 167. See also *PP* (Gravel), 1:221.

32

PAX AMERICANA ECONOMICUS

COMMITTEE OF CONCERNED ASIAN SCHOLARS

The economic dimension of U.S. involvement was one of several perspectives on intervention summarized by the Committee of Concerned Asian Scholars in its book The Indochina Story. *The committee, which included MIT linguist Noam Chomsky, tried to explain how economic imperialism could have led the United States into war in Vietnam even though Vietnam itself was not economically valuable to the United States.*

He who holds or has influence in Vietnam can affect the future of the Philippines and Formosa to the east, Thailand and Burma with their huge rice surpluses to the west, and Malaysia and Indonesia with their rubber, ore and tin to the south. Vietnam thus does not exist in a geographical vacuum—from it large storehouses of wealth and population can be influenced and undermined.
> —Henry Cabot Lodge, *Boston Globe*, February 28, 1965

That empire in Southeast Asia is the last major resource area outside the control of any one of the major powers on the globe....I believe that the condition of the Vietnamese people, and the direction in which their future may be going, are at this stage secondary, not primary.
> —Senator McGee (D.-Wyo.), in the Senate, February 17, 1965

One of Japan's greatest opportunities for increased trade lies in a free and developing Southeast Asia....The great need in one country is for raw materials, in the other for manufactured goods. The two regions complement each other markedly. By strengthening of Vietnam and helping insure the safety of the South Pacific and Southeast Asia, we gradually develop the great trade potential between this region...and highly developed Japan to the benefit of both. In this way freedom in the Western Pacific will be greatly strengthened.

—President Eisenhower, April 4, 1959[1]

There must be a reason for the war in Indochina. Year after year, president after president, the U.S. keeps on fighting, keeps on ignoring chances to withdraw. Blunders, stupidity, inertia, and even saving face can scarcely explain such a costly and consistent policy. Rhetoric to the contrary, important wars are fought for important reasons.

Three government figures, quoted above, suggest a reason for the war. Bluntly, they suggest the U.S. is fighting to defend an economic empire—fighting to control the markets and the resources of a wealthy corner of the globe. In this view, the U.S. is, indeed, fighting to defend freedom: freedom for U.S. economic penetration of Asia.

Claims that U.S. imperialism is involved in Indochina provoke heated controversy. The most common, and most serious, counterargument simply points to the lack of current U.S. economic involvement in the region. U.S. direct private investments in the Far East (excluding India, Japan, and the Philippines) are valued at less than $1 billion, or just over 1 percent of all U.S. direct private foreign investment. All of Southeast Asia, including Indonesia and the Philippines, absorbs about 3 percent of U.S. exports. And many of the "vital" raw materials found in Southeast Asia can be found elsewhere as well. Would sensible imperialists spend over $100 billion and 40,000 soldiers' lives to defend such a small economic stake?

There are two flaws in this demonstration of the economic irrationality of the war. First, it looks only at the current value of Southeast Asia, while the above quotes emphasize the potential future value of the region. Second, and more significant, it assumes too simple a connection between economic interests and military intervention. But this point can be more easily explained after a look at the workings of America's overseas economic involvements.

FOREIGN PROFITS

In 1966 U.S. profits on direct foreign investment totaled $5.1 billion, or 10.4 percent of total corporate profits of $49.3 billion. Of the foreign profits, slightly under half came from Canada, Europe, and Japan; slightly more than half came from the

---

[1] As cited in Harry Magdoff, *The Age of Imperialism* (New York: Monthly Review Press, 1969), p. 53. This section on economic imperialism is indebted to Magdoff's analysis.

third world.[2] However, most U.S. businesses are too small to invest in other countries; the foreign profits are concentrated in the hands of a few giant corporations. Of the 1966 foreign profits which were returned to the U.S. (70 percent of total foreign profits was returned to the U.S.; the remainder was kept in foreign countries), half was received by seventeen companies, all among the forty largest U.S. industrial corporations.[3]

For these companies, which include many of the country's most powerful corporations, foreign profits were very important. For the seventeen companies foreign profits returned to the U.S. were 27.6 percent of total profits, compared to 8.1 percent for the economy as a whole. And some of the seventeen were even more dependent on foreign earnings. Three large oil companies, Standard of New Jersey, Standard of California, and Mobil, reported foreign profits returned to the U.S. were over half of total domestic profits. Although the giant oil companies are notorious for juggling their books, and the exact reported profit figures may be misleading, few people would question that foreign investments are crucial to the oil industry. And the oil companies are not alone. International Telephone and Telegraph and International Business Machines, with half and a third respectively of domestic profits received from abroad, both live up to their names.

FOREIGN INVESTMENT AND UNDERDEVELOPMENT

Giant corporations profit in several ways from their foreign investments. Entering a new country, either with exports or with a local subsidiary, means new and growing markets, and sometimes a chance at gaining a local monopoly. Natural resources are exploited, in mines, oil wells, and plantations, often at amazingly low prices. And foreign labor is available at low wages, with the nuisance of unions eliminated by obliging governments in many countries.

[2] Total profits are from *Economic Report of the President*, 1968, table B–69. Foreign profits are from Walter Lederer and Frederick Cutler, "International Investments of the U.S. in 1966," *Survey of Current Business*, September, 1967. Both foreign and total profit figures are after tax. Under foreign tax credit provisions of U.S. tax laws, most of foreign profits are not taxed by the U.S. For the most recent years for which data are available, 1960–62, foreign tax credits reduce the taxes due on foreign profits by 80 percent (calculated from IRS, *Statistics of Income 1962. Supplemental Report on Foreign Income and Taxes Reported on Corporation Income Tax Returns*, Table 10). Thus on $1000 of profits, the U.S. tax rate was about 50 percent or $500. On foreign profits, foreign tax credits reduced the tax rate by 80 percent or $400 of the $500. Thus the actual U.S. tax paid was around $100 per $1000 of foreign profits. In calculating foreign profits after tax for 1966, the same 80 percent reduction in taxes on foreign profits was assumed to hold.

[3] All data on the seventeen corporations, including data on individual companies in the next paragraph of text, are obtained from IOK forms (Annual Reports Pursuant to Section 13 or 15(d) of the Securities Exchange Act of 1934). The seventeen corporations, in order of foreign profits returned to the U.S., are: Standard Oil of New Jersey; Texaco; Standard Oil of California; Mobil Oil; IBM; Gulf Oil; General Motors; Ford Motors; Eastman Kodak; IT&T; Goodyear; Union Carbide; Procter & Gamble; Continental Oil; National Dairy Products; International Harvester; and RCA. Other corporations among the top forty industrials, known to have significant foreign operations, were not included because foreign profit data are not available. For example, General Electric, Chrysler, and Du Pont each reported foreign sales over 15 percent of total sales, but did not report foreign profits.

But the existence of profits does not prove that foreign investment hurts the country in which it occurs. In fact, foreign investment is often defended as a positive contribution to the development of poor countries. It is said that foreign investment and foreign aid are the only channels through which poor countries can obtain the capital they require for development. This theory of economic development has a grim but allegedly realistic corollary: if political stability is necessary to attract foreign aid and investment, and if military force, perhaps even U.S. military force, is necessary to maintain stability, then...maybe U.S. interventions and military dictatorships are sometimes needed for development.

The defense of foreign investment and aid is false on two grounds. First, very little capital has been transferred from the U.S. to poor countries, either by investment or by aid. Second, even if capital is transferred to poor countries, it is not used to encourage development.

From 1950 to 1965 the flow of direct investment from the U.S. to Europe and Canada totaled $14.9 billion, and income on this capital returned to the U.S. was $11.4 billion, leaving a net outflow from the U.S. of $3.5 billion. For the rest of the world, the corresponding figures were $9.0 billion direct investment outflow, and $25.6 billion income returned to the U.S., a net inflow to the U.S. of $16.6 billion, about a billion dollars a year.[4] U.S. foreign investment, on balance, supplied capital to developed countries, and took capital from underdeveloped countries.

Foreign aid amounts to surprisingly little transfer of capital to poor countries. Nonmilitary aid expenditures by AID and its predecessors, from July 1949 to June 1966, totaled only $11.3 billion, or around two-thirds of the investment inflow of $16.6 billion described above.[5] In the same period, the same agencies spent $12.1 billion on military aid to countries outside Europe. But not nearly all of the $11.3 billion of nonmilitary aid represents net transfer to poor countries. At least $4.8 billion of the total was loaned, not given, to the recipients. Most aid, whether loans or grants, must be spent on purchases from U.S. suppliers, who often sell well above world market prices. Aid purchases must also be shipped on U.S. ships, whose freight charges are far above—sometime double—charges on other countries' ships.[6] President Kennedy described the purposes of these restrictions, if not of the whole nonmilitary aid program, in 1963:

> Too little attention has been paid to the part which an early exposure to American goods, skills, and American ways of doing things can play in forming the tastes and desires of newly emerging countries—or to the fact that, even when our aid ends, the desire and need for our products continue, and trade relations last far beyond the termination of our assistance.[7]

However, the problem would not be solved by more capital flowing through the existing channels. The channels themselves are a part of the problem. Over half

[4] Magdoff, op. cit., p. 198.

[5] *Operations Report, Data as of June 30, 1966* (Agency for International Development), p. 5.

[6] Magdoff, op. cit., pp. 129–36. Magdoff's chap. 4 is an excellent source on the shortcomings of U.S. aid.

[7] Cited in Magdoff, op. cit., p. 133.

of U.S. investment in Latin America, Asia, and Africa is in mining and petroleum.[8] These industries simply exploit the natural resources of the country, creating few jobs and adding little to the country's development. Even in the growing foreign investments in manufacturing in the third world, capital flows primarily into production for useless luxury consumption, rather than for national development. In Karachi, the capital of Pakistan, for example, in 1967 there were only three sources of bottled milk for a city of several million people, while eleven different soft drinks made with imported concentrates could be bought.[9] Other cases may be subtler, but are fundamentally similar. Consider Brazil, one of the supposed success stories of capitalist development in Latin America. Here the major accomplishment of foreign manufacturers has been the creation of an automobile industry, producing 300,000 poorly built cars annually, at prices higher than U.S. car prices. Meanwhile, the vast majority of Brazilians, who cannot afford cars—the farm workers, badly in need of modern equipment; the people of the northeast, dying in 1970 from one of Brazil's periodic droughts; the urban slum dwellers, living in shantytowns—are all untouched by the progress of industry.

Foreign investors did not create all the inequalities of Brazil or Pakistan. But in these countries, as in others, foreign manufacturers reinforce an unequal society, and profit from it in the only way they can, through producing useless luxury consumption items. Any capital invested in this kind of manufacturing simply creates another vested interest in the status quo, without contributing anything to development.

In summary, it is hard to believe foreign aid and investment help poor countries. Taking out more capital than it puts in, going into extractive industries and luxury production, foreign investments are profitable almost exclusively for the foreign investor. More than half of foreign aid is military aid; the small amounts of nonmilitary aid are encumbered with restrictions that benefit American exporters rather than the aid recipients.

PROFITS AND FOREIGN POLICY

American military intervention abroad is nothing new. It has occurred almost continuously since World War II, and its origins can be traced back much further.[10] In Greece in 1947–1948, Iran in 1953, Guatemala in 1954, the Dominican Republic in 1965, and many other cases, American troops, "advisers," or the CIA have helped to overthrow governments suspected of communism. On countless other occasions, local armed forces trained and equipped by the U.S. have done the same job.[11] The war in Indochina is not unusual because the U.S. is intervening; it is merely unusual because the U.S. is losing.

[8] Lederer and Cutler, op. cit.

[9] Magdoff, op. cit., p. 126.

[10] For example see William A. Williams, *The Tragedy of American Diplomacy* (New York: Delta, 1962).

[11] In addition to Magdoff, op. cit., and Williams, op. cit., see Carl Oglesby and Richard Shaull, *Containment and Change* (New York: Macmillan, 1967); and David Horowitz, ed., *Containment and Revolution* (Boston: Beacon, 1967).

From the point of view of most Americans, U.S. military interventions abroad seem like unfortunate, irrational blunders. But multinational corporations with large foreign investments have sound financial reasons for wanting the free world kept "free." From their point of view, U.S. interventions are quite rational. American interventions are almost always against governments which threaten to curtail foreign business operations; the regimes created by interventions, whatever else they do, are careful to preserve freedom for business.

This is not to imply that foreign policy decisions are made in corporate boardrooms. Obviously the world is more complex than that. The anti-Communist ideology which shapes U.S. foreign policy has deep roots in American history. Still, whatever its origins, whatever its supposed virtues in the minds of its supporters, American anti-Communist foreign policy brings only the draft and high taxes to most American families, military dictatorship and economic exploitation to the third world, and huge profits to a few large corporations. It is the effects of American foreign policy that matter, and in its effects, if not in its motivations, it is a foreign policy well suited to the interests of major corporations.

An interventionist, anti-Communist foreign policy requires a large military machine. U.S. military spending is currently about $80 billion a year, enough to absorb almost all personal income tax payments (which totaled $90.5 billion in 1969). About half of military spending, or $36.9 billion in fiscal 1969, goes to defense contractors. Like foreign profits, defense contracts are concentrated in the hands of a few large corporations: two-thirds of all Pentagon contracts go to the hundred largest contractors.[12] To a great extent, these are the same companies that benefit from foreign investment. In 1968, twenty of the twenty-five largest industrial corporations were among the hundred largest defense contractors.[13] Cost overruns and padded profits on defense work are well known, but there are no figures for total profits on military contracts.

So, from the corporate point of view, defense of the free world and foreign profits is itself a profitable activity. The two sources of profit—foreign investment and military contracts—combine to create a powerful corporate interest in maintaining an interventionist, anti-Communist foreign policy.

THE THREAT OF REVOLUTION

Revolutions have always been a threat to America's "free world" empire. Since World War II, three successful revolutions (in China, Cuba, and Vietnam) have closed their doors to foreign capital, and reoriented their economies toward the needs of the masses. In Cuba, illiteracy has been virtually eliminated, and each year Cuban medical schools graduate three times as many doctors per capita as do medical schools in the United States. In China, the threat of starvation has been overcome for the first time in history, and impressive beginnings of industrialization

[12] Calculated from Defense Department figures in *Congressional Record*, May 1, 1970.

[13] R. F. Kaufman, "We Must Guard Against Unwarranted Influence by the Military-Industrial Complex," *New York Times Magazine*, June 22, 1969.

have been forged. In Vietnam, before the escalation of the war, land reform was carried out by the NLF in the South, and schools and hospitals were built in every province of the North.

These revolutions and their accomplishments inspire revolutionaries elsewhere, creating an ever-present threat to free world stability. Preventing the spread of revolution has therefore become a major goal of U.S. foreign policy. Throughout the 1950s Latin American countries were forgotten neighbors—until the Cuban revolution prompted the Alliance for Progress, a hastily-constructed "alternative" to further revolutions. In addition to its more dramatic military interventions, the U.S. has aid programs, CIA agents, and military advisers at work throughout Latin America, making sure it doesn't happen again.[14]

A revolution anywhere is seen as a setback to U.S. foreign policy, even in an area with no major U.S. economic interests—even in Indochina. Successful revolution in Indochina not only deprives the U.S. of any potential profits in the area, but also in the corporate view, sets a "bad example" for more immediately valuable countries. If a peasant revolution can drive out the U.S. in Southeast Asia, what will stop the guerrillas in the Middle East, Brazil, Guatemala...?

IMPERIALISM AND THE WAR

By now the relevance of economic imperialism to the war in Indochina should be clear. It is true that the current value of Indochina to U.S. business interests is virtually nil. But, as mentioned above, there are two reasons why this does not prove the war is irrational from the corporate point of view. First, the potential value of the region is believed to be great; second, defense of the "free world" empire requires the suppression of revolution everywhere, not just in the more valuable regions. Both of these reasons can be illustrated in the recent history of Southeast Asia.

In the early days of the war, before the Tet offensive of 1968, many U.S. businessmen thought the war would soon be over, and began planning postwar investments in Vietnam. As Henry M. Sperry, vice-president of the First National City Bank of New York, saw it in 1965:

> We believe that we're going to win this war. Afterwards you'll have a major job of reconstruction on your hands. That will take financing and financing means banks.... It would be illogical to permit the English and French to monopolize the banking business because South Vietnam's economy is becoming more and more United States oriented.[15]

Thoughts about possible postwar reconstruction in Vietnam, however, were just a part of the broader consequences of the war. For as a Chase Manhattan Bank vice-president explained in 1965:

[14] See, for instance, John Gerassi, *The Great Fear in Latin America* (New York: Collier Books, 1963).
[15] Cited in Peter Wiley, "Vietnam and the Pacific Rim Strategy," *Leviathan*, June 1969; also in Magdoff, op. cit., p. 68. Original source is *New York Times*, December 9, 1965.

In the past, foreign investors have been somewhat wary of the over-all political prospect for the [Southeast Asia] region. I must say, though, that the U.S. actions in Vietnam this year—which have demonstrated that the U.S. will continue to give effective protection to the free nations of the region—have considerably reassured both Asian and Western investors. In fact, I see some reason to hope that the same sort of economic growth may take place in the free economies of Asia that took place in Europe after the Truman Doctrine and after NATO provided a protective shield. The same thing also took place in Japan after the U.S. intervention in Korea removed investor doubts.[16]

American business, however, was by no means united on its long-range interests in Southeast Asia, or on its relation to the conflict in Vietnam. But until the Tet offensive, opposition was relatively muted. Thereafter enthusiasm for America's military involvement was confined predominantly to defense contractors, while the increasingly obvious costs of failure and impact of the war on the overall economy made the search for "disengagement" more pronounced among business leaders. Nevertheless, the economic reasons that formed the backdrop to political miscalculation remain.

[16] Magdoff, op. cit., p. 176.

33

THE DRIVE FOR A GLOBAL POLITICAL ECONOMY

GABRIEL KOLKO

In Anatomy of a War *historian Gabriel Kolko deployed several theories to explain American involvement, including the mind-set of containment, the search for new*

From *Anatomy of a War: Vietnam, the United States, and the Modern Historical Experience* by Gabriel Kolko. Copyright © 1985 by Gabriel Kolko. Reprinted by permission of Pantheon Books, a Division of Random House Inc.

military strategies, and the workings of the national security bureaucracy. Paralleling an argument stressed by realist critics, he also claims that U.S. government goals in Vietnam were beyond its needs and means to accomplish. Kolko, however, concentrated on trying to show that American concern about falling dominoes was not so much the accidental product of complex interactions between individuals and groups as it was the intellectual rationalization of policymakers' deep commitment to global, capitalist, economic hegemony—the worldwide regulation of investments, raw materials, and markets. In this respect, Vietnam was not unique. At first, in the 1940s and 1950s, U.S. leaders saw the revolution in Vietnam as a direct challenge to their search for an integrated capitalist world order. As the commitment grew by the 1960s, Vietnam increasingly became a symbolic testing ground of American credibility.

The Vietnam War was the United States' longest and most divisive war of the post-1945 epoch, and in many regards its most important conflict in the twentieth century. Obviously, the Vietnamese Communist Party's resiliency made Vietnam distinctive after 1946, but that the United States should have become embroiled with such formidable adversaries was a natural outcome of the logic and objectives of its role in the modern era. In retrospect, it is apparent that there existed two immovable forces, one of which had no conceivable option but to pursue the policy it had embarked on, and that it was far more likely for America to follow in the footsteps of the French than to learn something from their defeat. How and why it made that momentous decision and what it perceived itself to be doing reveals much about our times and the social and political framework in which contemporary history is made. For Vietnam was ultimately the major episode in a larger process of intervention which preceded and transcended it. All of the frustrations and dilemmas which emerged in Vietnam existed for Washington before 1960, and they persist to this day. The only thing that made the Vietnam War unique for the United States was that it lost completely.

The hallmark of American foreign policy after 1945 was the universality of its intense commitment to create an integrated, essentially capitalist world framework out of the chaos of World War Two and the remnants of the colonial systems. The United States was the major inheritor of the mantle of imperialism in modern history, acting not out of a desire to defend the nation against some tangible threat to its physical welfare but because it sought to create a controllable, responsive order elsewhere, one that would permit the political destinies of distant places to evolve in a manner beneficial to American goals and interests far surpassing the immediate needs of its domestic society. The regulation of the world was at once the luxury and the necessity it believed its power afforded, and even if its might both produced and promised far greater prosperity if successful, its inevitable costs were justified, as all earlier imperialist powers had also done, as a fulfillment of an international responsibility and mission.

This task in fact far transcended that of dealing with the USSR, which had not produced the world upheaval but was itself an outcome of the first stage of the protracted crises of the European and colonial system that had begun in 1914, even though the United States always held Moscow culpable to a critical extent for the many obstacles it was to confront. The history of the postwar era is essentially one of the monumental American attempts—and failures—to weave together such a global order and of the essentially vast autonomous social forces and destabilizing dynamics emerging throughout the world to confound its ambitions.

Such ambitions immediately brought the United States face to face with what to this day remains its primary problem: the conflict between its inordinate desires and its finite resources, and the definition of realistic priorities. Although it took years for the limits on American power to become clear to its leaders, most of whom only partly perceived it, it has been this problem of coherent priorities, and of the means to implement them, rather than the ultimate abstract goals themselves that have divided America's leaders and set the context for debates over policy. What was most important for much of the post-1945 era was the overweening belief on the part of American leaders that regulating all the world's political and economic problems was not only desirable but also possible, given skill and power. They would not and could not concede that the economic, political, and social dynamics of a great part of the world exceeded the capacities of any one or even a group of nations to control. At stake were the large and growing strategic and economic interests in those unstable nations experiencing the greatest changes.

The interaction between a complex world, the constraints on U.S. power, and Washington's perceptions, including its illusions and ignorance, is the subject matter for most of the history of contemporary American foreign policy. The "accidental" nature of that policy after 1946 was a consequence of the intrinsic dilemmas of this ambition rather than its cause. To articulate its priorities was quite simple. Europe was, and still is, at the top of the list of America's formally defined economic, strategic, and political interests. The dilemma of priorities was that none precluded others wholly, so that America's leaders never excluded intervention in any major part of the world. In the last analysis, it was the sheer extent of its objectives, and the inevitable crises and issues which emerged when the process of intervention began, that imposed on the United States the loss of mastery over its own priorities and actions.

By the late 1940s the United States had begun to confront the basic dilemmas it was to encounter for the remainder of the century. The formulation of priorities was an integral part of its reasoning, and so was resistance to communism in whatever form it might appear anywhere in the world. Its own interests had been fully articulated, and these found expression in statements of objectives as well as in the creation of international political, military, and economic organizations and alliances the United States effectively dominated, with American-led "internationalism" becoming one of the hallmarks of its postwar efforts.

Describing the various U.S. decision makers' motives and goals is a necessary but inherently frustrating effort because American capitalism's relative ideological underdevelopment produces nuances and contradictions among men of power which often become translated into the tensions and even ambivalences of American diplomacy. But the complex problem of explaining the causes of U.S. foreign policy can never obviate a description of the real forces and considerations which lead to certain actions and to an optimizing of specific, tangible interests rather than of others. Complexity in serious causal explanations has existed since time immemorial and is intrinsic to the analytic process, yet the importance many care to assign to caprice and accident itself looks frivolous on closer examination of the historical facts and political options. There are, ultimately, main trends and forces, and these must be respected regardless of coincidental related factors.

Prevention of the expansion of communism, the "containment" doctrine, became formally enshrined no later than 1947, and in 1950 the "rollback" of communism was secretly adhered to in the famous National Security Council 68 policy. In 1947 the so-called domino theory first emerged in the form of the Truman Doctrine on Greece. Were Greece to fall, Secretary of State George C. Marshall argued in February of that year, Turkey might follow and "Soviet domination might thus extend over the entire Middle East and Asia."[1] Later that year the same logic required the reconstruction of West Germany, lest its weakness create a vacuum of power into which communism could enter and thereby spread throughout Europe. An area was, by this calculation, no stronger than its weakest link, and the domino mode of analysis, involving interconnections and linkages in estimating the effects of major political upheavals, well before Indochina was becoming the first and probably the most durable of conventional U.S. doctrines on the process of change and power in the modern world.

Such perceptions led irresistibly to the official decision in mid-1949, when the Communists triumphed in China, to draw a line against any new communist states in Asia, even though Washington was then preoccupied with European problems. But in Indochina the interaction of European with Asian affairs was always important to American leaders, for France's growing absorption with Indochina was causing it to veto West German rearmament, and the more quickly France won and brought it troops back home to balance projected German power, the sooner it could be brought into existence. No less crucial was the future position of Japan in Asia and in the world economy should it lose access to Southeast Asian raw materials and markets.

In a word, intervening in Vietnam never generated original international political dilemmas and issues for the United States. America's leaders clarified their ideas about dominoes, the credibility of their power, or the raw-materials system in the world long before their action on Indochina had more than a routine significance. It was precisely because of the repeated definitions of containment, dominoes, intervention, and linkages of seemingly discrete foreign policy questions elsewhere in the world that the United States made the irreversible decision to see the war in Vietnam through to the end. Even many of the purely military dilemmas that were to emerge in Vietnam had been raised earlier in Korea. Until well into the 1960s Vietnam was but one of many nations the United States was both involved in and committed to retaining in friendly hands, and from 1953 through 1962 it

[1] Joyce and Gabriel Kolko, *The Limits of Power: The World and United States Foreign Policy, 1945–54*, (New York, 1972), 340. Both in this volume and in my *Main Currents in Modern American History* (New York, 1984), chaps. 6 and 10, I have developed and documented many of the ideas presented here.

provided more military and economic aid to Turkey, South Korea, and Taiwan, about as much to Pakistan, and only somewhat less to Greece and Spain. Given its resources and goals, America was deeply involved throughout the world as a matter of routine. This fact encouraged a new intervention to the extent that it succeeded in maintaining client regimes but could also be a restraint once the demands of one nation became so great as to threaten the United States' position elsewhere.

SOUTHEAST ASIA AND THE DOMINOES

The domino theory was to be evoked initially more than any other justification in the Southeast Asian context, and the concept embodied both strategic and economic components which American leaders never separated. "The fall of Indochina would undoubtedly lead to the fall of the other mainland states of Southeast Asia," the Joint Chiefs of Staff argued in April 1950, and with it Russia would control "Asia's war potential...affecting the balance of power." Not only "major sources of certain strategic materials" would be lost, but also communications routes.[2] The State Department maintained a similar line at this time, writing off Thailand and Burma should Indochina fall. Well before the Korean conflict this became the United States' official doctrine, and the war there strengthened this commitment.

The loss of Indochina, Washington formally articulated in June 1952, "would have critical psychological, political and economic consequences....the loss of any single country would probably lead to relatively swift submission to or an alignment with communism by the remaining countries of this group. Furthermore, an alignment with communism of the rest of Southeast Asia and India, and in the longer term, of the Middle East (with the probable exceptions of at least Pakistan and Turkey) would in all probability progressively follow. Such widespread alignment would endanger the stability and security of Europe." It would "render the U.S. position in the Pacific offshore island chain precarious and would seriously jeopardize fundamental U.S. security interests in the Far East." The "principal world source of natural rubber and tin, and a producer of petroleum and other strategically important commodities" would be lost in Malaya and Indonesia. The rice exports of Burma and Thailand would be taken from Malaya, Ceylon, Japan, and India. Eventually, there would be "such economic and political pressures in Japan as to make it extremely difficult to prevent Japan's eventual accommodation to communism."[3] This was the perfect integration of all the elements of the domino theory, involving raw materials, military bases, and the commitment of the United States to protect its many spheres of influence. In principle, even while helping the French to fight for the larger cause which America saw as its own, Washington's leaders prepared for greater intervention when it became necessary to prop up the leading domino—Indochina.

There were neither private nor public illusions regarding the stakes and goals for American power. Early in 1953 the National Security Council reiterated, "The

[2] *PP*, I, 187, 364.

[3] *PP*, I, 83–84. See also ibid., 375–90; NSC paper 48/4, May 4, 1951, DDRS 77:41C.

Western countries and Japan need increased supplies of raw materials and food-stuffs and growing markets for their industrial production. Their balance of pay-ments difficulties are in considerable part the result of the failure of production of raw materials and foodstuffs in non-dollar areas to increase as rapidly as industrial production."[4] "Why is the United States spending hundreds of millions of dollars supporting the forces of the French Union in the fight against communism?" Vice-President Richard Nixon explained publicly in December 1953. "If Indo-china falls, Thailand is put in an almost impossible position. The same is true of Malaya with its rubber and tin. The same is true of Indonesia. If this whole part of Southeast Asia goes under Communist domination or Communist influence, Japan, who trades and must trade with this area in order to exist, must inevitably be oriented towards the Communist regime."[5] Both naturally and logically, references to tin, rubber, rice, copra, iron ore, tungsten, and oil were integral to American policy consider-ations from the inception. As long as he was President, Eisenhower never forgot his country's dependence on the importation of raw materials and the need to control their sources. When he first made public the "falling domino" analogy, in April 1954, he also discussed the dangers of losing the region's tin, tungsten, and rubber and the risk of Japan's being forced into dependence on communist nations for its industrial life—with all that implied. Always implicit in the doctrine was the as-sumption that the economic riches of the neighbors of the first domino, whether Greece or Indochina, were essential, and when the United States first intervened in those hapless and relatively poor nations, it kept the surrounding region foremost in its calculations. This willingness to accept the immense overhead charges of re-gional domination was constantly in the minds of the men who made the decisions to intervene.[6]

The problem with the domino theory was, of course, its intrinsic conflict with the desire to impose priorities on U.S. commitments, resources, and actions. If a chain is no stronger than its weakest link, then that link has to be protected even though its very fragility might make the undertaking that much more difficult. But so long as the United States had no realistic sense of the constraints on its power, it was ready to take greater risks. The complex interaction of America's vast goals, its perception of the nature of its power, the domino vision of challenges, and the more modest notions implicit in the concept of priorities began in 1953 to merge in what became the start of the permanent debate and crisis in American strategic and diplomatic doctrine.

THE SEARCH FOR A COHERENT STRATEGY

Washington had by 1947 become wholly convinced that the Soviet Union was in some crucial manner guiding many of the political and social upheavals in the world that were in fact the outcome of poverty, colonialism, and oligarchies, and that it

[4] NSC paper 141, Jan. 16, 1953, 18, DDRS 77:44B.

[5] Kolko, *Limits of Power*, 685.

[6] Ibid., 684–86; State Dept. memo, July 10, 1953, DDRS 78:278B, 11.

was, thereby, seriously subverting the United States' attainment of its political and economic objectives of a reformed, American-led capitalist world order. Toward the end of the Korean War, the incipient conflicts built into such a definition of the world were paralleled and aggravated by a crisis in U.S. military technology and doctrine. These two threads inevitably intertwined late in 1953 in the "New Look" debate and in the beginnings of a perpetual search for a global strategy that could everywhere synthesize America's objectives and resources.

The Korean War tested the U.S. military's overwhelming superiority of firepower and technology, along with its capacity to sustain the economic and political costs of protracted war. Given the inconclusive end of the war along the thirty-eighth parallel after three years of combat, and given the total failure of Washington's September 1950 goal of reuniting the country by force of arms, the war had fully revealed the limits of American power. The domestic political controversy it created was less decisive, but it, too, disclosed the formidable political liabilities that such dismal struggles brought to the party in power. And in fiscal 1953, with military spending at 13.8 percent of the gross national product—three times the 1950 proportion—inflation and budget deficits exposed the constraints on American economic resources. In a word, the United States had undertaken a massive effort and achieved only inconclusive results; this reality raised the issue of the credibility of its power. No less important was the fact that it had become bogged down in Asia at the very moment its main priorities and attention were focused on Europe and the Middle East. To resolve these dilemmas became an obsession in Washington, one that affected every area of the world and influenced the U.S. strategy debate for the remainder of the century.

The effort to define a "New Look" for American foreign policy, culminating in Dulles's famous January 12, 1954, speech, was stillborn, for the Soviet test of a hydrogen bomb in August 1953 decisively broke the U.S. monopoly of strategic nuclear weapons. Land war, Dulles declared, could be fought with the forces of America's allies but the United States itself would rely on its "massive retaliatory power...by means and at places of our choosing." It was the only "modern way of getting maximum protection at bearable cost," for limited conventional war in Korea had involved potentially unlimited costs.[7] The dark intimation that America might destroy Peking or Moscow because of events in some distant place was the beginning of a search for a new strategy, but the internal contradictions of that view were immediately criticized in Washington. That quest did not preclude relatively minimal responses to what seemed to be small challenges, and even as the weight of military spending on the national economy was reduced substantially over the remainder of the decade and as strategic weapons became more prominent, the White House increased its reliance on covert warfare waged by the CIA—the success of which in Iran and Guatemala greatly encouraged this relatively low-cost, often inconspicuous form of intervention. For whatever the theory, in practice the United States continued to be deeply involved in very different political contexts in every corner of the globe. Throughout the 1950s Washington never husbanded finite

[7] Kolko, *Limits of Power*, 699.

resources rationally to attain its primary goals, because, while it could reduce the role of military spending in the economy, it was unwilling and unable to scale down its far more decisive political definitions of the scope and location of American interests in the world.

To a remarkable extent, America's leaders perceived the nature of the contradiction but never ceased to believe that they could find a solution. The intense defense debates of the middle and late 1950s, which made the reputations of numerous articulate and immensely self-confident military intellectuals like Henry Kissinger, Maxwell Taylor, and W. W. Rostow, inconclusively contradicted and neutralized each other. But what was constant in all such theories was the need to be active rather than passive in responding to new problems and challenges, for American power both to appear and to be credible, and to seek to control and direct, rather than be subject to the dictates of, highly fluid outside forces and events. To develop a sense of mastery was the objective, but the fact that the technologies and strategies for attaining it were constantly being debated produced a perpetual dilemma.

It was in this larger context of a search for a decisive global strategy and doctrine throughout the 1950s that the emerging Vietnam issue was linked to so many other international questions. Washington always saw the challenge of Indochina as just one part of a much greater problem it confronted throughout the world: the efficacy of limited war, the danger of dominoes, the credibility of American power, the role of France in Europe, and much else. Vietnam became the conjunction of the postwar crisis of U.S. imperialism at a crucial stage of America's much greater effort to resolve its own doubts about its capacity to protect the larger international socioeconomic environment in which its interests could survive and prosper. By 1960 every preceding event required that the credibility of U.S. power be tested soon, lest all of the failures and dilemmas since 1946 undermine the very foundations of the system it was seeking to construct throughout the world. It was mainly chance that designated Vietnam as the primary arena of trial, but it was virtually preordained that America would try somewhere to attain successes—not simply one but many—to reverse the deepening pattern of postwar history....

It was for the United States in 1961 to resolve whether there would be war or peace in Vietnam. It alone could aspire to reverse the social and political forces irresistibly making the southern half of the country again an integral part of one Vietnam. Washington's definition of its national interests would determine its responses to the political imbroglios of the RVN and South Vietnam's social dynamics. Arms and war would serve, as always, as a final means of attaining what politics and the remnants of a colonial order could not.

WASHINGTON DEFINES THE STAKES IN VIETNAM

The credibility of American power since 1945 touches the overarching issue of the relationship of America's resources to its problems, interests, and goals. Above all, it raises the question of its confidence in itself and its capacity to attain its ends. The goals and interests of U.S. foreign policy are sometimes defined in connection with the problem of credibility but often also quite autonomously of it. Precisely because objectives often transcend the instruments for achieving them and because they are ultimately the result of interests, the gap between desire and reality creates an impasse in Washington's policies. The American obsession with the successful application of power—"credibility"—is the inevitable overhead charge of its foreign policy after 1945 with its ambition to integrate a U.S.-led international political and economic order.

By 1960 the issue of U.S. potency possessed Washington. Each new challenge or sense of failure, whether the space race or a local upheaval, intensified its frustration. The fluidity of the world order, with its constant and diverse changes, guaranteed a steady succession of trials. And with each new advance in U.S. instruments for imposing its military or organizational hegemony, there was a desire to prove their efficacy in reality. It was this autonomous logic of arms and power that always threatened to transcend the narrower economic and geopolitical aims of imperialism.

Because they assumed that the employment of power was a matter less of principle than of tactics and priorities, even when they disagreed about the choice of Vietnam as a testing ground for the United States' counterrevolutionary role, key figures in American foreign relations never doubted that the global goals of the foreign policy were attainable with proper management of resources and that the means were both appropriate and sufficient. This deep consensus on the utilization of American power was the legacy of the entire post-1945 U.S. ambition and interaction with an unsettled, changing world. Because of it, American power and prestige were deeply invested in Vietnam before anyone raised pragmatic doubts about this application of its strength.

Vietnam was a conjunction not merely because the domino theory made every nation the key to a region, which in turn had varying but always significant implications for the U.S. position in the entire world, or even because by 1960 the debate over local and strategic war had reached a shrill pitch, which colored the 1960 presidential campaign. The domino and credibility theories began to merge into a unified conception, credibility growing weightier over time. More crucial in 1960–62 was the specific impact of the Cuban revolution on Washington's self-confidence. The failure of the Bay of Pigs invasion in April 1961 was a humiliating reverse for the counterinsurgency and local-war concepts just then coming into great vogue. The Berlin confrontation of the spring of 1961 also goaded the United States to seek to exhibit its power elsewhere.

The year 1961 was thus one in which the accumulated postwar frustrations in regulating the affairs of so many little states outside Vietnam galvanized America's leaders to take yet stronger action in Indochina. Laos was an especially pernicious problem; it consumed a vast amount of the Kennedy administration's time during its first several months in office. The United States' ability to keep the Pathet Lao out of power became a test of U.S. influence, motivated by fear of the domino effect of a Laotian coalition government on the stability of the RVN. The Kennedy administration saw Laos as "a symbolic test of strengths between the major powers of the West and the Communist bloc" and perceived U.S. weakness there as requiring stronger policies in South Vietnam to counterbalance its impact on the region and the world.[8] The day after the Bay of Pigs, it created a special task force on Vietnam with the mandate "to grasp the new concepts, the new tools" of counterinsurgency, that might defeat "subversion" everywhere in the world.[9] Vietnam was becoming a test case in counterinsurgency, and with an eye to Laos, Cuba, and the entire world, the administration was to begin a long series of escalations, each raising the ante to establish credibility.

This perception of Vietnam from 1961 onward gave it a symbolic global significance that far outweighed the specific U.S. interests there, but behind this notion there nonetheless existed more tangible goals, which varied somewhat in importance but always remained a part of a justification of the effort. Raw materials, though less publicly cited than earlier, were still prominent in the decision makers' vision. This included the preservation of existing markets. The retention of South Vietnam was invariably linked to U.S. relations with other nations in the region, particularly with Indonesia, where Washington considered Sukarno the most important threat to its interests.

Credibility rose in importance with the successive failures of each escalation of advisers and resources in Vietnam, reaching 11,000 by the end of 1962 and 23,000 two years later. The domino and the global contexts were incorporated into all justifications of the war. The concepts finally merged late in 1964, when General Maxwell Taylor, a leading limited-war theorist and the ambassador to Saigon, argued typically, "If we leave Vietnam with our tail between our legs, the consequences of this defeat in the rest of Asia, Africa, and Latin America would be disastrous."[10]

As Washington's commitment grew, both the credibility and the domino concepts became more refined and comprehensive. Washington generally regarded the open Sino-Soviet split after 1962 as a direct threat, seeing a seemingly unrestrained China as much more hostile and in favor of wars of national liberation against the American "paper tiger" throughout the world. By 1963 the Kennedy administration had come increasingly to believe that resisting the Revolution in South Vietnam was also a matter of U.S.-Chinese relations. As John T. McNaughton stated the dominant idea in March 1965, the United States' war aims were "70%—To avoid a humiliating US defeat (to our reputation as a guarantor)" and "20%—To keep SVN (and then adjacent) territory from Chinese hands."[11] The containment of China, presumably now the dominant influence in the villages in the south, was treated in a comprehensive March 1964 National Security Council articulation of war aims, which linked the domino theory with credibility to define the war in the south "as

[8] *PP*, II, 33. See also ibid., 22, 48–49.

[9] Ibid., 34.

[10] Ibid., 336. See also ibid., 174–75, 663–65, 817; III, 51, 500; NSC report, n.d. [1962], 10, DDRS 80:281A; Guy J. Pauker, "Indonesia's Grand Design...," RM-4080, May 1964, RC, iv–vi, DDRS 75:60A; State Dept. mss, n.d. [early 1964], 20, DDRS 79:90B.

[11] *PP*, III, 695. See also ibid., 592; Gerald Segal, *The Great Power Triangle* (London, 1982), chaps. 2–3.

a test case of U.S. capacity to help a nation to meet the Communist 'war of liberation.'"[12]

By increasingly making credibility the overarching consideration in the escalation of the war, America's leaders positioned Vietnam in the world power balance and postwar history, touching the efficacy of its traditional counterrevolutionary policies, and in this manner its symbolic role enormously enlarged the stakes involved there. All the important leaders supported this logic until its deficiencies appeared after the damage had been done. In a certain way this definition was rational. The loss of U.S. mastery in the Third World was a reality, but the changes occurring in the world were not the consequences of U.S. passivity. Rather, they resulted from the normal transformations of all societies, a fact that brings the Left to the fore repeatedly as an integral element of modern history. Weapons might in some places abort this process temporarily; the cost to America was variable. Essential to the counterrevolutionary role is the selection of a war at the right time and at the right place. The dilemma of credibility is that even the slightest error in the application of power must lead to the utilization of yet more force, or else the price to America's reputation mounts. As a basis of foreign policy, it is the highest-risk game any nation can play. If there is no valid sense of the constraints of social reality, then credibility leads to escalation, humiliation, or both. For while the United States could measure its resources and interests clearly, it could not fathom their relevance to the more crucial social, human, and military conditions which existed. Colossal self-confidence made it appear virtually certain that its power could compensate for any surprises.

Given the dilemmas of the United States since 1949, with its growing sense of impotence and frustrations over the course of events in the world, it was not in the least accidental that a foreign policy based both on symbolism and on interest merged at some point to plague the nation. The challenges in Vietnam at the start were no more problematical than those in many other nations, and American interventions elsewhere had often succeeded. The process of reasoning during 1961–64 was not, therefore, unique to Vietnam but merely a legacy of post-1945 U.S. foreign policy. Had the United States avoided Indochina entirely, it would eventually have become involved elsewhere in much the same way, for two decades later it was to confront its Central American problems with virtually identical reasoning and responses.

---

[12] *PP*, III, 51. See also ibid., 153, 598–99, 622–23, 683.

The following code abbreviations are used in the notes:

DDRS—Declassified Documents Reference System (Carrollton Press). In most cases, only the author, nature of the document, date, and exact microfiche citation are given, but not the title of the document.
NSC—U.S. National Security Council 1964–68 files on Vietnam (University Publications of America microfilm edition). Author, nature of document, and date only. The collection is chronological.
PP—The Senator Gravel Edition, *The Pentagon Papers: The Defense Department History of United States Decisionmaking on Vietnam*, 4 vols. (Boston: Beacon Press, 1971).
RC—Rand Corporation, Santa Monica, California.

34

NEOCOLONIAL AGGRESSION

NGUYEN KHAC VIEN AND VO NGUYEN GIAP

During the time of direct U.S. support of the French in the early 1950s, Ho Chi Minh and other Vietnamese Communists interpreted American policy as an example of U.S. capitalist aggression working through a less powerful French colonialism. During the Diem period and afterward, their explanation emphasized the neocolonial purposes and methods of U.S. policy; that is, having reached a new stage of neo-colonial development, American imperialism sought to achieve global economic and strategic objectives in Vietnam by crushing the Vietnamese revolution in the south through covert action, new methods of "special warfare," and indirect, repressive rule carried out by a client regime. In the first excerpt, historian Nguyen Khac Vien traces the history of U.S. expansionism across North America, into Latin America, and finally into Asia, and he identifies the origins of indirect imperial administration—the key element of neocolonialism—in American policies after the Spanish-American War. On the causes of U.S. intervention, he ascribes primary importance to America's anti-Communist, counterrevolutionary goals in Vietnam and the third world during the post–World War II period and secondary importance to direct U.S. economic aims in Vietnam. In the second excerpt, General Vo Nguyen Giap explains the nature of the war of liberation in the south after the American escalations of 1965.

A SHORT HISTORY OF U.S. NEO-COLONIALISM

NGUYEN KHAC VIEN

Any capitalist economy reaching a certain stage of development is inevitably impelled to reach out of the national frontiers, into the industrially less developed

From Nguyen Khac Vien, "A Short History of U.S. Neo-colonialism," *Glimpses of U.S. Neo-colonialism,* Vol. I: *Neo-colonialism and Global Strategy, Vietnamese Studies,* no. 26 (Hanoi: Foreign Languages Publishing House, 1970), 15–28; and Vo Nguyen Giap, "The Liberation War in South Vietnam: Its Essential Characteristics," *South Vietnam, 1954–1965: Articles and Documents, Vietnamese Studies,* no. 8 (Hanoi: N.p., 1966), 5–11.

countries, for new markets, raw materials, cheap labour and profitable investment of capital. This colonial expansion takes on most varied forms, for numerous factors interfere and give colonialism its very diverse looks. Of prime importance is the balance of forces between the colonial power and the colonized peoples, between the different imperialisms that confront each other on the same territory; in our times, the existence of socialist countries considerably affects the colonial policy of the imperialist powers. The present epoch is profoundly different from the 19th century as regards the balance of forces in the international arena, and the classical methods of colonialism are no longer possible. On the other hand, neo-colonialism is part of a policy of world counterrevolution, which has become a vital necessity for the imperialist powers. Colonial policy is subject to the needs of world strategy. Colonial exploitation, the prime and often sole objective in the last century, can in some places, be momentarily relegated to the second rank for the benefit of this strategy.

The above considerations enable us to bring out the characteristics of US colonial policy at different times; conversely, a short historical outline will shed light on the various factors that give this colonialism its present features.

I. Control over the American Continent

The American nation was born of a fierce struggle against British colonialism. Moreover, during a long period, US capitalism concentrated its efforts on the exploitation of the immense resources of an almost unoccupied national territory. The extermination of Indians, the slave exploitation of Negroes were phenomena of "internal colonization." Those facts have supplied some people with the argument that, contrary to European capitalist powers, the USA had no colonial ambitions, at least for a long period of its history.

But historical reality is quite the opposite. As early as the beginning of the 19th century, while "internal colonization" was far from being completed, US capitalism already looked beyond the national frontiers, especially having an eye to its neighbours of Central America and further to those of South America.

The American continent was then shaken by a fierce struggle of the people against Spanish and Portuguese colonialism; this struggle, however, did not result in total independence, for the landed oligarchy which had come to power in the various Latin American countries, incapable of building truly independent nations, rapidly established relations of close dependence with the European powers, in particular with Great Britain.

Thus, right at the start, US colonialism met with two powerful adversaries: the people in revolt against Spanish and Portuguese colonialism, and a redoubtable rival, British imperialism. US colonial expansion had to take on indirect forms, other than outright conquest.

In 1823, under the signboard of pan-Americanism, President Monroe proclaimed his famous "doctrine," interdicting all direct intervention by European powers on the American continent. In fact, the formula "America for the Americans" covered a policy which was to take shape rapidly and prompt the great Latin American patriot Simon Bolivar to utter these bitter words: "The United States seems to be destined by Providence to overwhelm America with misery in the name of liberty." (December, 17, 1830). The American continent was to become gradually an exclusive preserve for Yankee capitalism.

In 1831, US Marines landed on the Falkland Islands and as early as 1834 the USA intervened in Mexican affairs; a series of plots and intrigues which led in 1845 to a war against Mexico, half of whose national territory, about two million square kilometres, was seized by its powerful neighbour. Other American States, Colombia, Nicaragua, Uruguay, the Dominican Republic, Cuba, made acquaintance with US interventionist policy one after another, during the 19th century.

By the end of that century, US capitalism had strengthened its economic power and become more and more enterprising. Senator Beveridge openly stated:

American factories are making more than the American people can use. American soil is producing more than they can consume. Fate has written our policy for us; the trade of the world must and shall be ours. And we shall get it as our mother England has told us how. We will establish trading posts throughout the world as distributing points for American products. We will cover the ocean with our merchant marine. We will build a navy to the measure of our greatness. Great colonies, governing themselves, flying our flags and trading with us will grow about our posts of trade. Our institutions will follow our trade on the wings of our commerce. And American law, American order, American civilisation and the American flag will plant themselves on the shores hitherto bloody and benighted, by those agencies of God henceforth made beautiful and bright.

The year 1898, during which Senator Beveridge, a spokesman of the business circles, made that profession of faith, was that of the Spanish-American war. The scenario is well known: the US cruiser Maine exploded in a mysterious way in the port of Havana, and Washington made this a pretext to declare war on Spain, a war which enabled it to seize not only Cuba, the scene of the explosion, but also Puerto Rico and the Philippines. US troops occupied Cuba till 1901. Then they withdrew, but only after having imposed a pro-US government, tied to Washington by the Platt amendment,[1] subjoined to the Cuban constitution, which permitted US troops to intervene whenever the need arose. US troops continued to occupy the Guantanamo base; the Cuban economy was completely dependent on the USA. One can understand why, in "independent" Cuba, the US ambassador was generally acknowledged to be the most important man in the country.

Thus, as early as the 19th century, US imperialism already worked out a formula of colonialism rather different from methods adopted by European countries in Africa or Asia. US control was disguised behind the screen of a native government, which was politically, economically and militarily in complete dependence. This indirect administration has become one of the main characteristics of neocolonialism.

---

[1] Platt, who had proposed this amendment, was a US Senator.

The first years of the 20th century were marked, during the presidency of Theodore Roosevelt, by numerous financial and military interventions in the Dominican Republic, Nicaragua, Honduras and Venezuela. In 1903, with the assistance of US troops, a new republic, that of Panama, was created, cut off from Colombia, which had to surrender its sovereignty over this zone where the interoceanic canal passes, henceforth put at the disposal of the USA.

Theodore Roosevelt openly proclaimed the right of the USA to intervene militarily in Latin America, and it was he who first used the now classical phrases of "big-stick policy" and "international gendarme." This big-stick policy materialized in numerous military actions against Cuba in 1906 and 1912, against the Dominican Republic in 1907, against Nicaragua in 1909, against Mexico in 1913 and 1914. All those brutal interventions were justified by Theodore Roosevelt by "the permanent injustice or impotence which results from a general loosening of the rules of civilized society, which finally requires the intervention of a civilized nation" (retranslated from the French—Tr.). General MacArthur (father of the MacArthur who made the Korean War), when he was governor of the Philippines, declared: "We implant in the East the idea of freedom. Wherever the American flag goes, this idea propagates. Implantation of freedom, not money, is what we seek" (retranslated from the French—Tr.). Senator Beveridge was still more lyrical: "God has not during a thousand years prepared the Teutonic and English-speaking peoples for only vain and lazy self-admiration. He has made us the master organizers of the world so that we could establish order where chaos reigns. He has made us able to govern so that we could administer barbaric and senile peoples. Without such a force, this world would fall back into barbarity and darkness. Of all the races, He has appointed the American people as the nation of His choice eventually to lead the first generation of the world" (retranslated from the French—Tr.).

General Smedley Butler, commander of the Marine Corps, put it more bluntly in his memoirs written after his retirement:

> I spent 35 years 5 months in the active service as a member of this country's most agile force, the Marine Corps. I helped make Mexico, especially Tampico, safe for the oil interests in 1914. I helped make Haiti and Cuba a decent place for the National City Bank to collect revenue in. I helped purify Nicaragua for the Banking House of Brown Brothers in 1909 to 1912. I brought light to the Dominican Republic for American sugar interests in 1916.

President Taft, succeeding Theodore Roosevelt, declared that he wanted to replace bombs by the dollar, to substitute dollar diplomacy for that of the stick. In fact, Taft and Roosevelt made lavish use of both. One can say that from Monroe to Theodore Roosevelt and Taft, US colonialism, with regard to the American continent, had gained long experience in combining the action of the Marines with that of the dollar; it even worked out a "doctrine" to justify its actions.

However, a latecomer in the colonial competition, US capitalism still played second fiddle to British imperialism, up to the First World War. In 1913, US investments in Latin America amounted to 1,242 million dollars as against nearly 5,000 million for the British.

The First World War (1914–1918), having caused the European imperialisms to lose their pre-eminence, compelled them to yield ground, especially in Latin America, to the benefit of US imperialism. In 1929, US investments, which had increased rapidly since 1918, almost equalled those of Great Britain, which had hardly advanced (5,587 million dollars against 5,889 million).

The long crisis of 1929 which lasted until 1938, up to the eve of the Second World War, and the rise of Hitlerite and Mussolinian fascisms, quite active in Latin America, considerably limited Yankee expansion. Franklin D. Roosevelt, on becoming President of the USA, was obliged to proclaim a "good-neighbour policy." That did not prevent Washington from imposing economic sanctions against the Mexican government for nationalizing its oil industries, and demanding from Mexico large reparations for US companies. Neither did F. D. Roosevelt hesitate to make use of local dictators as instruments of Washington's policy.

It is safe to say that until the Second World War, US colonial expansion had been directed solely at the American continent. Attempts at penetration into Asia had run into resistance by Asian peoples and active competition by European, then Japanese, imperialisms. Let us point out that while Washington had proposed the formula "America for the Americans" for the American continent, in China it proposed a policy of "open door" and not "China for the Chinese."

Latin America gradually became the "backyard" of the USA, supplying it with oil, minerals, tropical goods necessary for US industries and the maintenance of US living standards. Through financial, political and military means, Washington managed to put under its control the local bourgeoisies and landed oligarchies. The defence of the interests of US companies and the maintenance of backward socio-economic structures are closely interconnected and are ensured by a militarist caste trained, formed and supported by Washington.

This collusion between US imperialism and the local reactionary forces and the impotence of the local bourgeoisie to promote real independence and real economic development have led Latin America to that state of external dependence, misery, and glaring social injustice described by observers of all tendencies.

II. Neo-colonialism and Global Strategy

The end of the Second World War was marked by sweeping changes in the international arena. The German, Italian and Japanese fascist regimes collapsed, the British, French and Dutch imperialisms were considerably weakened. With its resources undamaged by war, with its economic power stimulated by war and a scientific and technological revolution of wide scope, with the monopoly of atomic weapons and the possession of considerable stores of conventional weapons, the USA became the undisputed leader of the capitalist world. US troops occupied South Korea, Japan, were stationed in Western Europe as far as Berlin. Scores of countries in the world were bound to Washington by loans, grants, subsidies in food and arms. US imports and exports exceeded by far those of pre-war years, and investments abroad increased rapidly. Here are some figures:

	Exports (in million dollars)	Imports	Investments Abroad
1939–1940	3,177	3,192	10,746
1945	16,273	10,232	16,818
1960–61	20,962	14,713	71,497

The dollar had become the dominating currency, serving as standard currency in international transactions. The USA drained raw materials from the five continents, exported its goods to every part of the world. Let us also mention the fact that the war had enabled it to settle the very serious question of unemployment (9 million unemployed people in 1939).

To assume leadership of the capitalist world, the USA possesses industrial, agricultural and scientific power that surpasses by far the means of any other imperialist countries at any time. This economic power, in a capitalist regime, has a double consequence:

• it exacerbates the needs in raw materials and markets and strongly impels the investment of capital abroad;
• it provides US imperialism with tremendous and multiform means of domination, incomparably superior to those of European powers.

The era of isolationism had utterly ended; pretensions to world hegemony asserted themselves. Some authors tried to minimize the needs in raw materials and in foreign markets and the necessity to invest capital abroad, by arguing that US industry could easily find substitutes for any raw materials and has an enormous home market. We shall not go into the details of those economic considerations.... Let us point out simply that in his inaugural speech on January 20, 1953, President Eisenhower laid particular emphasis on this problem of raw materials coming from other countries, just as Nelson Rockefeller did in his report to the President in 1951.[2] Worldwide colonial expansion had become an imperative necessity from the economic point of view.

An extra-economic factor was to come to the fore, however, after 1945, for having become the ringleader of the capitalist world, the USA had to face a problem which did not confront the imperialist powers in the 19th century. It had to assume colonial responsibilities in a world where revolution had made decisive headway. The Soviet Union had clearly displayed its vitality by defeating Hitlerite fascism; new socialist States were coming into being, while the colonized peoples began to rise up in an irresistible movement. Even the rear areas of the major capitalist countries were no longer safe because the workers' and people's movement for better

---

[2] See Claude Julien, *L'Empire americain* (Paris: B. Grasset, 1968). For American attempts at self-justification see the No. 4, 1969 issue of the French review *Esprit*. Let us recall that in 1953, to justify American aid to the French in IndoChina, Eisenhower spoke of the necessity for the USA to get control of the sources of raw materials in South-East Asia.

living conditions, for democracy and peace, had influenced broad strata of the population. The very survival of the capitalist system was at stake. The crucial question for the USA henceforward was how to get rid of this world revolution, how to face this surging tide, how to "stem" it, to "contain" it, to destroy its main bastions, to nip in the bud the nascent movements, to drain the already formed abscesses.

In short, economic expansion and counter-revolution, both worldwide, are two closely inter-connected policies. Thus, at the end of the Second World War, the USA found itself in a situation which could be characterized as follows:

- It possessed obvious, even absolute, material and technical superiority over all other countries.
- It was politically on the defensive, having to fight the forces of social progress, of national liberation and of peace in the world. This was really a rearguard action.

US policy vis-à-vis the industrially under-developed countries of Asia, Africa, and Latin America was thus determined in terms of its global strategy, which was itself defined mainly by Washington's policy vis-à-vis the bastion of world revolution, the socialist camp. One can say that, broadly speaking, US neo-colonial policy has taken two different directions, each prevailing in a different period.

Immediately after the end of the Second World War, US leaders geared their action towards a direct offensive against the Soviet Union. They believed they could easily attack the Soviet Union which had suffered tremendous destruction by the war, and which did not possess the atomic weapon as yet. In 1945, the political future of the East European countries was still unsettled. A US–Western European coalition would command overwhelming material and technical superiority over the Soviet Union.[3]

One of the post-war primary tasks was to restore and strengthen the economic and military potential of the Western allies so as to integrate them into an anti-Soviet coalition later on. The other major preoccupation of the US was to "stop" the Soviet Union on its eastern frontiers by a counter-revolutionary China under the dictatorship of Chiang Kai-shek; the occupation of Japan and Korea had already given US troops access to the Asian continent.

Under those circumstances, the under-developed countries interested Washington only in so far as they could serve as military bases against the Soviet Union, in so far as they had common frontiers with the socialist countries. Economic preoccupations were only of secondary importance, relegated to the background by strategic considerations. At the time, India was of less interest than Turkey, Greece, Iran.[4] In the Middle East, oil and strategic interests coincided; but

[3] To give an idea of this material superiority and hence of US aggressiveness, let us recall simply that in 1945 US steel output was more than four times that of the Soviet Union; a US–Western Europe–Japan coalition would result in an output eight times that of the Soviet Union.

[4] Turkey, Greece, Taiwan, South Korea, South Viet Nam, with a total population of 75 million, received from 1946 to 1961 8,700 million dollars of economic aid, 7,900 million of military aid, i.e. a far higher amount than that received by India with a population of 450 million.

the whole of Africa, and South-East Asia, with their vast riches, still remained, if not outside, at least in the background of US preoccupations. For the reasoning of Washington strategists was simple: if the Soviet Union fell, the USA would pick all those countries like so many ripe fruit.

In the ideological field, anti-Communism, outright anti-Communism and anti-Sovietism, served to justify all measures taken in the world arena as well as at home. John Foster Dulles called all neutralism immoral, and a witch-hunt started in the USA culminated in McCarthyism.

THE LIBERATION WAR IN SOUTH VIETNAM: ITS ESSENTIAL CHARACTERISTICS

VO NGUYEN GIAP

I. Strength and Weakness of the Enemy

The present war of national liberation in South Vietnam is directed against the neo-colonialism of the US imperialists and their lackeys, an extremely reactionary and wicked enemy who is materially and technically strong but morally and politically very weak.

In the previous resistance war of national salvation, the revolution in South Vietnam as in the rest of our country was directed against the French colonialists and their lackeys assisted by the U.S. interventionists. After peace had been restored in Indochina, U.S. imperialism kicked out defeated French colonialism and set up in South Vietnam the pro-U.S. Ngo Dinh Diem regime. Unlike old-type French colonialism, U.S. imperialism did not build up an administrative machine and bring in an expeditionary corps but nevertheless its control over the South Vietnam regime was complete.

Neo-colonialism is a product of imperialism in the present period. Faced with the powerful influence of the socialist system and the upsurge of the national liberation movement in Asia, Africa and Latin America, the imperialists can no longer use old methods to impose their rule on their colonies; the local reactionary forces, especially the comprador bourgeoisie and the feudal landlord class feel great fears for their interests and privileges. Neo-colonialism is the result of the collusion and compromise between the foreign imperialists on the one hand and the local comprador bourgeoisie and feudal landlord class on the other, with a view to maintaining colonial rule under new forms and with new methods, and repressing the revolutionary movement of the mass of the people.

The aims of imperialism remain fundamentally the same: enslavement of the weaker nations, grasping of markets and raw materials, ruthless oppression and exploitation of the subjugated peoples. Its principal method remains violence under various forms. It differs from old-type colonialism in only one aspect: while old-type colonialism directly takes in hand the enslavement of the peoples and uses violence through an administration under its direct control and an army of aggression under its direct command, neo-colonialism carries out enslavement and uses violence in an indirect and more sophisticated manner through a puppet administration and a puppet army camouflaged with the labels of "independence and democracy," and a policy of "aid" or "alliance" in every field. Neo-colonialism, more wily and more dangerous, uses every possible means to conceal its aggressive nature, to blur the contradictions between the enslaved nations and the foreign rulers, thereby paralyzing the peoples's vigilance and will to wage a revolutionary struggle.

U.S. neo-colonialism has its own specific characteristics. When U.S. capitalism reached the stage of imperialism, the western great powers had already divided among themselves almost all of the important markets in the world. At the end of World War II, when the other imperialist powers had been weakened, the United States became the most powerful and the richest imperialist power. Meanwhile, the world situation was no longer the same: the balance of forces between imperialist and the camp of peace, national independence, democracy and socialism had fundamentally changed; imperialist no longer rules over the world, nor does it play a decisive role in the development of the world situation. In the new historical conditions, U.S. imperialism, which has a long tradition of expansion through trade, different from the classical policy of aggression through missionaries and gunboats, is all the more compelled to follow the path of neo-colonialism. The countries under its domination enjoy nominal political independence, but in fact are dependent on the United States in the economic, financial, national defence and foreign relations fields.

At the end of World War II, U.S. imperialism already cast covetous eyes on Vietnam and the other Indochinese countries. In the early fifties, as the situation of the French colonialists was becoming more and more desperate, the U.S. imperialists gradually increased their "aid" and intervention in the Indochina dirty war. When the war ended with the defeat of the French expeditionary corps, they thought that the opportunity had come for them to take the place of the French colonialists. The images of former colonial rule—perfidious and cruel governor-generals and high commissioners, ferocious expeditionary corps—now belonged to the past. The U.S. imperialists could not, even if they wanted to do it, restore to life the decaying corpse of old colonialism. In 1954, when the defeat of the French colonialists was imminent, the U.S. imperialists envisaged the use of "national forces," made up of reactionary forces in the country, in an attempt to give more "dynamism" to the war. And they began to prepare their "special war" against the South Vietnamese people.

U.S. neo-colonialism uses its lackeys in South Vietnam as its main tool to carry out its policy of aggression. Neo-colonialism derives its strength on the one hand from the economic and military potential of the metropolitan country, and on the other hand, from the social, economic and political bases of the native reactionary forces. In the South of our country, the puppet regime was set up by the U.S. imperialists at a moment when our people had just won a brilliant victory against imperialism. That is why since it came into being, it has never shown any vitality, and has borne the seeds of internal contradictions, crisis and war. Its social bases are extremely weak. The feudal landlord class and the comprador bourgeoisie, which had never been very strong under French rule, had become even weaker and more divided in the course of the Revolution and the Resistance. After peace was restored, they became still more divided, as a result of U.S.-French contradictions. These reactionary classes have long since shown themselves to be traitors to their fatherland, and are hated and opposed by the people. The defeat of the French expeditionary corps was a severe blow to their morale.

Under those circumstances, U.S. imperialism used every possible means to set up a relatively stable administration, camouflaged with the labels of "independence" and "democracy," in an attempt to rally the reactionary forces and at the same time win over and deceive other strata of the population. With this aim in view, they staged the farce of founding the "Republic of Vietnam" in order to perpetuate the partition of our country. Their puppets, claiming to have reconquered "independence" from the French colonialists, proclaimed a "constitution" with provisions on "freedom" and "democracy," and put forth slogans of anticommunism, ordered an "agrarian reform" and noisily publicized a programme for the "elimination of vices" and the "protection of good traditions," etc.

However, the puppet regime could not remain in power if they did not cling to their masters and obey the latter's orders. Outwardly, the "Republic of Vietnam" has all the usual government organs of internal and external affairs, defence, economy and culture, but all these organs, from the central to the local level, are controlled by U.S. "advisers." The latter, who enjoy diplomatic privileges, are not under the jurisdiction of the puppet administration, whose civil and penal codes cannot be applied to them. They are directly under the U.S. ambassador's control. It is U.S. imperialism which determines the fundamental line and policies of the South Vietnam regime. Ngo Dinh Diem, fostered by U.S. imperialism, was "pulled out of Dulles' sleeve" after Dien Bien Phu. The Diem regime, far from springing, as it claimed, from a movement of "national revolution," was only the result of the replacement of French masters by U.S. masters.

Faced with a popular revolutionary upsurge, the puppet regime soon took the road of fascism, and frantically pursued a policy of militarization and war preparation. To gain a reason for existence, it had to bluntly oppose the Geneva Agreements and the deepest aspirations of our people, namely peace, independence, democracy and national reunification. It trampled on the people's most elementary rights and resorted to a most barbarous policy of terror and repression. For these reasons, despite the labels of "independence and democracy" and certain reforms of a demagogic character, the popular masses immediately saw behind the puppet regime the hideous face of U.S. imperialism, that self-styled international gendarme, and that of the inveterate traitor Ngo Dinh Diem. And resolutely the masses rose up against them.

The U.S. imperialists also hurriedly built up and trained an army of mercenaries to be used as a tool for the repression of the revolutionary movement, carrying out their perfidious policy of pitting Asians against Asians, Vietnamese against Vietnamese.

With this army of native mercenaries dubbed "national army," the imperialists hope to camouflage their aggression and save American lives. U.S. experts have calculated that expenses for an Asian mercenary soldier are twenty-four times less than those required for an American soldier.

The South Vietnam "national army" is staffed by puppet officers from the rank of general downwards, but this is coupled with a system of military "advisers" controlling the puppet national defence ministry and extending down to battalion and company level, in the militia as well as the regular forces. U.S. advisers in the puppet army supervise organization, equipment, training and operations. The U.S. imperialists try to camouflage under the labels of "mutual assistance" and "self-defence" the participation of their troops in fighting. With a view to turning South Vietnam into a U.S. military base, they have put under their effective control a large number of strategic points, all the main airfields and military ports.

Economic "aid" is used by the imperialists as a principal means to control South Vietnam's economy. This "aid" is essentially a way of exporting surplus goods and capital to serve their policy of expansion and war preparation. Three-fourths of the amount of yearly "aid" derives from the sale of imported goods. The U.S. aid organs completely ignore both the requests of the puppet regime and the needs of the country, and dump into the South Vietnam market surplus farm products, luxury goods and also consumer goods that could have been produced locally. Furthermore this aid clearly has a military character. It turns South Vietnam's economy into a war economy, $8/10$ of the money being used to cover the military expenses of the puppet regime. This "aid" makes this regime totally dependent on the U.S. imperialists.

At first, the U.S. imperialists, thinking that they could rapidly consolidate the puppet regime and stabilize the political and economic situation in South Vietnam, had prepared the ground for the signing of unequal treaties to open the way to a large-scale penetration of U.S. finance capital. But the situation did not develop as they had expected, and so the money they invested in South Vietnam was insignificant, representing hardly two per cent of the total investments in various branches of the economy. In general, U.S. money was invested in joint enterprises, in a very wily economic penetration. Although present conditions are not favourable to the development of the U.S. sector in the South Vietnam economy, U.S. "aid" and the creation of counterpart funds have ensured to U.S.O.M. (United States Operations Mission) complete control over the budget, finances and foreign trade, in fact over the whole economic structure of South Vietnam.

For many years now, the puppet administration and army have been maintained in existence only thanks to U.S. aid. They relentlessly pursue a policy of violence and war in order to repress the patriotic movement, while granting many privileges to a handful of traitors. The social basis of this regime is made up of the most reactionary elements in the comprador bourgeoisie and the feudal landlord class....

PART SEVEN

Ways of Living
Cultural Misunderstanding
and Conflict

cul · ture (kul' ch̯ər), n....Sociol., the sum total of ways of living built up by a group of human beings and transmitted from one generation to another....
—*The Random House College Dictionary,* 1982

Men make their own history, but they do not make it just as they please; they do not make it under circumstances chosen by themselves, but under circumstances directly encountered, given, and transmitted from the past.
—Karl Marx, *The Eighteenth Brumaire of Louis Bonaparte,* 1852

We were not insane. We were not ignorant. We knew what we were doing, I mean we were crazy, but it's built into the culture. It's like institutionalized insanity.
—Private First Class Reginald Edwards, *Bloods,* 1984

35

CULTURE OF THE EARTH

FRANCES FITZGERALD

Drawing on her own experience as a journalist in Vietnam as well as on the work of French, Vietnamese, and American scholars, Frances FitzGerald attempted an ambitious study of American involvement in the war in the context of Vietnamese history and culture. Published in book form in 1972, the fruits of her effort, Fire in the Lake, *won the Pulitzer Prize, the National Book Award, and the Bancroft Prize for History. Some critics, however, thought her account of Vietnamese culture was flawed, and, in the heated atmosphere of the debate over the war, they also took exception to her sympathetic understanding of the Vietnamese and the National Liberation Front (NLF). Nonetheless, the focus she put on cultural context and on the political, social, and economic effects of the war on the Vietnamese has had a profound influence on subsequent authors, who now not only pay more attention to cultural factors in explaining the war but who still accept her essential insight—that of misunderstanding and conflict between Vietnamese and American cultures as a cause of why Americans intervened and of how they fought the war. In her 1976 biography of Lyndon Johnson, for example, political scientist Doris Kearns wrote:*

Johnson assumed that in war, as in the Senate, everyone knew the rules of the game, what kind of agreement would be reasonable, and that eventually an agreement would be reached. The need for continuing relationships required at least this much. But this assumption closed his mind to the argument Frances FitzGerald and others have since made: that the Vietnamese people were interested in unanimity, not pluralism. Their culture embodied the moral principles of Confucius; they believed in the possibility—indeed, the necessity—of finding the one true way of life. Politics was not a matter of negotiable opinion, a realm unto itself; in Vietnam, morality, politics, and society were inextricably joined. The war was a revolutionary war, which promised to affect not only the political system but the entire structure of Vietnamese society—its ethos, its customs, its religious expression. These cultural differences, profound as they were, seemed to be unknown not only to Lyndon Johnson but to all his top advisers.*

In the following excerpt from Fire in the Lake, *FitzGerald describes some of the differences between American and Vietnamese cultural perspectives, discusses the importance of the village in Vietnamese life, and explains how the political appeal of the NLF to the peasantry bridged the gap between a traditional culture of the earth and the demands of modernization. Elsewhere in the book, she argues that Americans' failure to understand the politics of the NLF helped lead them into the tragedy of the Vietnam War.*

Somewhere, buried in the files of the television networks, lies a series of pictures, ranging over a decade, that chronicles the diplomatic history of the United States and the Republic of Vietnam. Somewhere there is a picture of President Eisenhower with Ngo Dinh Diem, a picture of Secretary McNamara with General Nguyen Khanh, one of President Johnson with Nguyen Cao Ky and another of President Nixon with President Thieu. The pictures are unexceptional. The obligatory photographs taken on such ceremonial occasions, they show men in gray business suits (one is in military fatigues) shaking hands or standing side-by-side on a podium. These pictures, along with the news commentaries, "President Nixon today reaffirmed his support for the Thieu regime," or "Hanoi refused to consider the American proposal," made up much of what Americans knew about the relationship between the two countries. But the pictures and news reports were to a great extent deceptions, for they did not show the disproportion between the two powers. One of the gray-suited figures, after all, represented the greatest power in the history of the world, a nation that could, if its rulers so desired, blow up the world, feed the earth's population, or explore the galaxy. The second figure in the pictures represented a small number of people in a country of peasants largely sustained by a technology centuries old. The meeting between the two was the meeting of two different dimensions, two different epochs of history. An imagined picture of a tributary chieftain coming to the Chinese court represents the relationship of the United States to the Republic of Vietnam better than the photographs from life. It represents what the physical and mental architecture of the twentieth century so often obscures.

At the beginning of their terms in office President Kennedy and President Johnson, perhaps, took full cognizance of the disproportion between the two countries, for they claimed, at least in the beginning, that the Vietnam War would require only patience from the United States. According to U.S. military intelligence, the enemy in the south consisted of little more than bands of guerrillas with hardly a truck in which to carry their borrowed weapons. The North Vietnamese possessed anti-aircraft guns and a steady supply of small munitions, but the United States could, so the officials promised, end their resistance with a few months of intensive

*Doris Kearns, *Lyndon Johnson and the American Dream* (New York: Harper & Row, 1976), 265–66.

bombing. In 1963 and 1965 few Americans imagined that a commitment to war in Vietnam would finally cost the United States billions of dollars, the production of its finest research and development laboratories, and fifty-five thousand American lives. They did not imagine that the Vietnam War would prove more politically divisive than any foreign war in the nation's history.

In one sense Presidents Kennedy and Johnson had seen the disproportion between the United States and Vietnam, but in another they did not see it at all. By intervening in the Vietnamese struggle the United States was attempting to fit its global strategies into a world of hillocks and hamlets, to reduce its majestic concerns for the containment of Communism and the security of the Free World to a dimension where governments rose and fell as a result of arguments between two colonels' wives. In going to Vietnam the United States was entering a country where the victory of one of the great world ideologies occasionally depended on the price of tea in a certain village or the outcome of a football game. For the Americans in Vietnam it would be difficult to make this leap of perspective, difficult to understand that while they saw themselves as building world order, many Vietnamese saw them merely as the producers of garbage from which they could build houses. The effort of translation was too great.

The televised pictures of the two chiefs of state were deceptive in quite another way: only one of the two nations saw them. Because of communications, the war was absurd for the civilians of both countries—but absurd in different ways. To one people the war would appear each day, compressed between advertisements and confined to a small space in the living room; the explosion of bombs and the cries of the wounded would become the background accompaniment to dinner. For the other people the war would come one day out of a clear blue sky. In a few minutes it would be over: the bombs, released by an invisible pilot with incomprehensible intentions, would leave only the debris and the dead behind. Which people was the best equipped to fight the war?

The disparity between the two countries only began with the matter of scale. They seemed, of course, to have come from the same country, those two figures in their identical business suits with their identical pronouncements. "The South Vietnamese people will never surrender to Communist tyranny," "We are fighting for the great cause of freedom," "We dedicate ourselves to the abolition of poverty, ignorance, and disease and to the work of the social revolution." In this case the deception served the purposes of state. The Chinese emperor could never have claimed that in backing one nomad chieftain against another he was defending the representative of Chinese civilization. But the American officials in supporting the Saigon government insisted that they were defending "freedom and democracy" in Asia. They left the GIs to discover that the Vietnamese did not fit into their experience of either "Communists" or "democrats."

Under different circumstances this invincible ignorance might not have affected the outcome of the war. The fiction that the United States was defending "freedom and democracy" might have continued to exist in a sphere undisturbed by reality, a sphere frequented only by those who needed moral justification for the pursuit of what the U.S. government saw as its strategic interests. Certain "tough-minded" analysts and officials in any case ignored the moral argument. As far as they were concerned, the United States was not interested in the form of the Vietnamese government—indeed, it was not interested in the Vietnamese at all. Its concerns were for "containing the expansion of the Communist bloc" and preventing future "wars of national liberation" around the world. But by denying the moral argument in favor of power politics and "rational" calculations of United States interests, these analysts were, as it happened, overlooking the very heart of the matter, the issue on which success depended.

The United States came to Vietnam at a critical juncture of Vietnamese history—a period of metamorphosis more profound than any the Vietnamese had ever experienced. In 1954 the Vietnamese were gaining their independence after seventy years of French colonial rule. They were engaged in a struggle to create a nation and to adapt a largely traditional society to the modern world. By backing one contender—by actually creating that contender—the United States was not just fighting a border war or intervening, as Imperial China so often did, in a power struggle between two similar contenders, two dynasties. It was entering into a moral and ideological struggle over the form of the state and the goals of the society. Its success with its chosen contender would depend not merely on U.S. military power but on the resources of both the United States and the Saigon government to solve Vietnamese domestic problems in a manner acceptable to the Vietnamese. But what indeed were Vietnamese problems, and did they even exist in the terms in which Americans conceived them? The unknowns made the whole enterprise, from the most rational and tough-minded point of view, risky in the extreme.

In going into Vietnam the United States was not only transporting itself into a different epoch of history; it was entering a world qualitatively different from its own. Culturally as geographically Vietnam lies half a world away from the United States. Many Americans in Vietnam learned to speak Vietnamese, but the language gave no more than a hint of the basic intellectual grammar that lay beneath. In a sense there was no more correspondence between the two worlds than that between the atmosphere of the earth and that of the sea. There was no direct translation between them in the simple equations of x is y and a means b. To find the common ground that existed between them, both Americans and Vietnamese would have to re-create the whole world of the other, the whole intellectual landscape. The effort of comprehension would be only the first step, for it would reveal the deeper issues of the encounter. It would force both nations to consider again the question of morality, to consider which of their values belong only to themselves or only to a certain stage of development. It would, perhaps, allow them to see that the process of change in the life of a society is a delicate and mysterious affair, and that the introduction of the foreign and the new can have vast and unpredictable consequences. It might in the end force both peoples to look back upon their own society, for it is contrast that is the essence of vision.

The American intellectual landscape is, of course, largely an inheritance from Europe, that of the Vietnamese a legacy from China, but in their own independent development the two nations have in many respects moved even further apart from each other. As late as the end of the nineteenth century Americans had before them a seemingly unlimited physical space—a view of mountains, deserts, and prairies into which a man might move (or imagine moving) to escape the old society and create a new world for himself. The impulse to escape, the drive to conquest and expansion, was never contradicted in America as it was in Europe by physical boundaries or by the persistence of strong traditions. The nation itself seemed to be less of a vessel than a movement. The closing of the frontier did not mean the end to expansion, but rather the beginning of it in a new form. The development of industry permitted the creation of new resources, new markets, new power over the world that had brought it into being. Americans ignore history, for to them everything has always seemed new under the sun. The national myth is that of creativity and progress, of a steady climbing upward into power and prosperity, both for the individual and for the country as a whole. Americans see history as a straight line and themselves standing at the cutting edge of it as representatives for all mankind. They believe in the future as if it were a religion; they believe that there is nothing they cannot accomplish, that solutions wait somewhere for all problems, like brides. Different though they were, both John Kennedy and Lyndon Johnson accepted and participated in this national myth. In part perhaps by virtue of their own success, they were optimists who looked upon their country as willing and able to right its own wrongs and to succor the rest of the world. They believed in the power of science, the power of the will, and the virtues of competition. Many Americans now question their confidence; still, the optimism of the nation is so great that even the question appears as a novelty and a challenge.

In their sense of time and space, the Vietnamese and the Americans stand in the relationship of a reversed mirror image, for the very notion of competition, invention, and change is an extremely new one for most Vietnamese. Until the French conquest of Vietnam in the nineteenth century, the Vietnamese practiced the same general technology for a thousand years. Their method of rice culture was far superior to any other in Southeast Asia; still it confined them to the river-fed lowlands between the Annamite cordillera and the sea. Hemmed in by China to the north and the Hindu kingdom of Champa to the south, the Vietnamese lived for the bulk of their history within the closed circle of the Red River Delta. They conquered Champa and moved south down the narrow littoral, but they might by American or Chinese standards have been standing still, for it took them five centuries to conquer a strip of land the length of Florida. The Vietnamese pride themselves less on their conquests than on their ability to resist and to survive. Living under the great wing of China, they bought their independence and maintained it only at a high price of blood. Throughout their history they have had to acknowledge the preponderance of the great Middle Kingdom both as the power and as the hub of culture. The Vietnamese knew their place in the world and guarded it jealously.

For traditional Vietnamese the sense of limitation and enclosure was as much a part of individual life as of the life of the nation. In what is today northern and central Vietnam the single form of Vietnamese settlement duplicated the closed circle of the nation. Hidden from sight behind their high hedges of bamboos, the villages stood like nuclei within their surrounding circle of rice fields. Within the villages as within the nation the amount of arable land was absolutely inelastic. The population of the village remained stable, and so to accumulate wealth meant to deprive the rest of the community of land, to fatten while one's neighbor starved. Vietnam is no longer a closed economic system, but the idea remains with the Vietnamese that great wealth is antisocial, not a sign of success but a sign of selfishness.

With a stable technology and a limited amount of land the traditional Vietnamese lived by constant repetition, by the sowing and reaping of rice and by the perpetuation of customary law. The Vietnamese worshiped their ancestors as the source of their lives, their fortunes, and their civilization. In the rites of ancestor worship the child imitated the gestures of his grandfather so that when he became the grandfather, he could repeat them exactly to his grandchildren. In this passage of time that had no history the death of a man marked no final end. Buried in the rice fields that sustained his family, the father would live on in the bodies of his children and grandchildren. As time wrapped around itself, the generations to côme would regard him as the source of their present lives and the arbiter of their fate. In this continuum of the family "private property" did not really exist, for the father was less of an owner than a trustee of the land to be passed on to his children. To the Vietnamese the land itself was the sacred, constant element: the people flowed over the land like water, maintaining and fructifying it for the generations to come.

Late in the war—about 1968—a Vietnamese soldier came with his unit to evacuate the people of a starving village in Quang Nam province so that the area might be turned into a "free fire zone." While the villagers were boarding the great American helicopters, one old man ran away from the soldiers shouting that he would never leave his home. The soldiers followed the old man and found him hiding in a tunnel beside a small garden planted with a few pitiful stunted shrubs. When they tried to persuade him to go with the others, he refused, saying, "I have to stay behind to look after this piece of garden. Of all the property handed down to me by my ancestors, only this garden now remains. I have to guard it for my grandson." Seeing the soldiers look askance, the old man admitted that his grandson had been conscripted and that he had not heard from him in two years. He paused, searching for an explanation, and then said, "If I leave, the graves of my ancestors, too, will become forest. How can I have the heart to leave?"

The soldiers turned away from the old man and departed, for they understood that for him to leave the land would be to acknowledge the final death of the family— a death without immortality. By deciding to stay he was deciding to sacrifice his life in postponement of that end. When the soldiers returned to the village fourteen months later, they found that an artillery shell had closed the entrance to the tunnel, making it a grave for the old man.[1]

Many American officials understood that the land and the graves of the ancestors were important to the Vietnamese. Had they understood exactly why, they might not have looked upon the wholesale creation of refugees as a "rational" method

[1] Viet Hoai, "The Old Man in the Free Fire Zone," in *Between Two Fires: The Unheard Voices of Vietnam*, ed. Ly Qui Chung (New York: Praeger, 1970), pp. 102–105.

of defeating Communism. For the traditional villager, who spent his life immobile, bound to the rice land of his ancestors, the world was a very small place. It was in fact the village or *xa*, a word that in its original Chinese roots signified "the place where people come together to worship the spirits." In this definition of society the character "earth" took precedence, for, as the source of life, the earth was the basis for the social contract between the members of the family and the members of the village. Americans live in a society of replaceable parts—in theory anyone can become President or sanitary inspector—but the Vietnamese lived in a society of particular people, all of whom knew each other by their place in the landscape. "Citizenship" in a Vietnamese village was personal and untransferable. In the past, few Vietnamese ever left their village in times of peace, for to do so was to leave society itself—all human attachments, all absolute rights and duties. When the soldiers of the nineteenth-century Vietnamese emperors came to the court of Hue, they prayed to the spirits of the Perfume River, "We are lost here [*depaysée*] and everything is unknown to us. We prostrate ourselves before you [in the hope that] you will lead us to the good and drive the evil away from us."[2] The soldiers were "lost" in more than a geographical sense, for without their land and their place in the village, they were without a social identity. To drive the twentieth-century villager off his land was in the same way to drive him off the edges of his old life and to expose him directly to the political movement that could best provide him with a new identity....

The Americans began by underestimating the Vietnamese guerrillas, but in the end they made them larger than life. During the invasion of Cambodia in 1970, American officials spoke of plans to capture the enemy's command headquarters for the south as if there existed a reverse Pentagon in the jungle complete with Marine guards, generals, and green baize tables. In fact the American generals knew there was no such thing, but in the press and the mind of the public the image kept returning. After all those years of fighting, the NLF and the North Vietnamese had taken on a superhuman dimension. Paradoxically, the exaggeration diminished them, for in the dimension of mythology all things are fabulous and unaccountable. By turning their enemy into a mirror image of themselves, the Americans obscured the nature of the Vietnamese accomplishment.

The National Liberation Front, after all, began in a world where men walked behind wooden plows and threshed the rice by beating it with wooden flails. The NLF recruits were largely illiterate or semiliterate, men who spent their life working on one hectare of paddy land, hoping only that one day they might afford a bullock. The NLF taught these men to operate radio sets, to manufacture explosives, to differentiate one type of American bomber from another. It taught them to build small factories, hospitals, and logistical systems that ran the length and breadth of the country without touching a road. With these men the Front cadres shot down helicopters, designed gas masks against American chemicals, and invented small-unit tactics that would add chapters to the history of the art. With them the NLF built a government and an army out of the disoriented and intractable society of South Vietnam.

---

[2] Léopold Cadière, *Croyances et pratiques religieuses des viêtnamiens* (Saigon: École Française d'Extrême Orient, 1955–58), vol. 2, p. 308.

This change, that in most countries takes several generations to perform, the NLF telescoped into five years. The movement was founded in 1960. By the spring of 1965, when the American regular troops entered the war, the Liberation Front had seriously damaged the Saigon government's armed forces and isolated its city outposts from the countryside. With an army of southerners and a supply of weapons largely obtained from their enemy, the NLF was on the point of defeating a state the United States had provided with hundreds of millions of dollars' worth of military assistance, artillery, bombers, and some seventeen thousand American advisers. Five years is a short period in which to make a revolution, but it is a long one in which to fight a major war. Over the next half-decade the NLF with the help of North Vietnamese forces stood up to an American army of over half a million men armed with the most sophisticated array of weaponry the world has ever seen. In 1971 the Liberation forces remained undefeated, and the Front was still the most important political force in the south.

Over the years of war American officials spoke of the NLF as if it were an illustration of some larger principle, some larger menace to the security of the United States. To Walt Rostow the National Liberation Front was but one instance of the "disease of Communism" that affected developing countries around the world. To Robert McNamara it was a test case for the "new" Communist strategy of promoting "wars of national liberation" around the world. To many American military men it was but an example of the threat that guerrillas in general provided to the established governments of the earth. By this attempt at generalization, duplicated in other terms by many Americans on the left, the officials reduced the NLF to the status of a symbol and, again, obscured its achievement.

For the Vietnamese revolution in the south was in many ways unique. If it belonged to a category, then that category was extremely small. Since the period of international turmoil following the Second World War there were only two successful Communist insurgency movements, one in Cuba, the other in Vietnam. In Bolivia Che Guevara brought all his theory and practical experience to bear on the miserable, exploited hinterlands, only to find the Bolivian peasants as unreceptive as stones. In Southeast Asia the Communist movements had an almost complete record of failure. In Burma, the Philippines, and Malaya, they did not succeed in gaining support from the majority of the population. In Indonesia the Party relied upon the magical figure of Sukarno and did not take the necessary steps to seize and hold power.[3] Then, too, since the Second World War only two countries have won their independence after a protracted war with a European power: Algeria and Vietnam. In many respects the Vietnamese war of the 1960's was unprecedented in the history of revolutionary and independence wars. The Chinese Communists and the Viet Minh had, after all, secure base areas within their own country and a relatively weak enemy on their soil. At their greatest strength, the French forces in Vietnam numbered only seventy thousand. The United States by contrast gave the best of its armed forces and two billion dollars a month to the Vietnam War. At one

---

[3] The Communist insurgencies in Cambodia and Laos have always been inextricably bound up with that in Vietnam.

point General Vo Nguyen Giap himself admitted that until the war for the south he knew nothing about "people's war."

During the course of the war Americans wrote a great deal about the military strategy of the NLF and relatively little about its politics. The reason is simple. Most research on Vietnam was official research, and the official American line was that the guerrilla war involved no internal political issues, but that it was merely part of the attempt of the North Vietnamese to conquer the south. As *The Pentagon Papers* showed, many American officials did not believe this line themselves, but it provided them with a convenient method of avoiding crucial and potentially damaging questions, such as what the political problems of South Vietnam were, and how it was that from the same population base the NLF managed to create an organization so much superior to that of the GVN. The result was that even those Americans responsible for the conduct of the war knew relatively little about their enemy, for within the NLF politics was all: it was at the same time the foundation of military strategy and its goal. For the NLF military victories were not only less important than political victories, but strictly meaningless considered in isolation from them. Those few American officials who studied the NLF saw the political focus, but did not understand its significance. Had they understood it, they might have warned that it would be better to send the Saigon regime's army to fight without weapons than to send it to fight without a political strategy, as was the case.

For a non-Vietnamese to write a full account of the NLF is finally an impossible undertaking. It is not that the evidence is lacking. On the contrary. By 1967 the U.S. government possessed more information on the NLF than on any other political phenomenon in Asia. The American mission in Vietnam collected not only "captured documents"—a vast array of reports, orders, laundry lists, tax receipts, soldiers' journals, promotion forms, and propaganda leaflets—but thousands of interviews with defectors and prisoner interrogations that described everything from the movement of battalions to the sensibilities of the individual soldier. By 1970 the collection must have filled entire buildings and, like a section of Borges's Library of Babylon, contained (buried and irretrievable) every written statement the NLF ever made about itself. From this information it is possible to reconstruct the entire scheme of NLF operations and even to some extent the lives of its cadres. The political strategies are clear enough—the NLF itself proclaimed them. But still the task of description remains difficult, for no American can follow the NLF cadres into the world in which they live to see the point where these strategies touch upon the life of the Vietnamese villager. Hypotheses can be made, theories abstracted, but the very essence of the revolution will remain foreign and intractable.

POLITICS OF THE EARTH

The American soldiers in Vietnam discovered their own ignorance in an immediate way. The NLF guerrillas chose the night and the jungles to fight in, similarly, and they chose to work with that part of the population which was the most obscure to the Americans and to the Saigon government officials. For the Americans to discern the enemy within the world of the Vietnamese village was to attempt to make out figures within a landscape indefinite and vague—underwater, as it were. Landing from helicopters in a village controlled by the NLF, the soldiers would at first see nothing, having no criteria with which to judge what they saw. As they searched the village, they would find only old men, women, and children, a collection of wooden tools whose purpose they did not know, altars with scrolls in Chinese characters, paths that led nowhere: an economy, a geography, an architecture totally alien to them. Searching for booby traps and enemy supplies, they would find only the matting over a root cellar and the great stone jars of rice. Clumsy as astronauts, they would bend under the eaves of the huts, knock over the cooking pots, and poke about at the smooth earth floor with their bayonets. How should they know whether the great stone jars held a year's supply of rice for the family or a week's supply for a company of troops? With experience they would come to adopt a bearing quite foreign to them. They would dig in the root cellars, peer in the wells, and trace the faint paths out of the village—to search the village as the soldiers of the warlords had searched them centuries ago. Only then would they find the entrance to the tunnels, to the enemy's first line of defense.

To the American commanders who listened each day to the statistics on "tunnels destroyed" and "caches of rice found," it must have appeared that in Vietnam the whole surface of the earth rested like a thin crust over a vast system of tunnels and underground rooms. The villages of both the "government" and "Viet Cong" zones were pitted with holes, trenches, and bunkers where the people slept at night in fear of the bombing. In the "Viet Cong" zones the holes were simply deeper, the tunnels longer—some of them running for kilometers out of a village to debouch in another village or a secret place in the jungle. Carved just to the size of a Vietnamese body, they were too small for an American to enter and too long to follow and destroy in total. Only when directed by a prisoner or informer could the Americans dig down to discover the underground storerooms.

Within these storerooms lay the whole industry of the guerrilla: sacks of rice, bolts of black cloth, salt fish and fish sauce, small machines made of scrap metal and bound up in sacking. Brown as the earth itself, the cache would look as much like a part of the earth as if it had originated there—the bulbous root of which the palm-leaf huts of the village were the external stem and foliage. And yet, once they were unwrapped, named, and counted, the stores would turn out to be surprisingly sophisticated, including, perhaps, a land mine made with high explosives, a small printing press with leaflets and textbook materials, surgical instruments, Chinese herbal medicines, and the latest antibiotics from Saigon. The industry clearly came from a civilization far more technically advanced than that which had made the external world of thatched huts, straw mats, and wooden plows. And yet there was an intimate relation between the two, for the anonymous artisans of the storerooms had used the materials of the village not only as camouflage but as an integral part of their technology.

In raiding the NLF villages, the American soldiers had actually walked over the political and economic design of the Vietnamese revolution. They had looked at it, but they could not see it, for it was doubly invisible: invisible within the ground and then again invisible within their own perspective as Americans. The revolution could only be seen against the background of the traditional village and in the perspective of Vietnamese history.

In the old ideographic language of Vietnam, the word *xa*, which Westerners translate as "village" or "village community," had as its roots the Chinese characters signifying "land," "people," and "sacred." These three ideas were joined inseparably, for the Vietnamese religion rested at every point on the particular social and economic system of the village. Confucian philosophy taught that the sacred bond of the society lay with the mandarin-genie, the representative of the emperor. But the villagers knew that it lay with the spirits of the particular earth of their village. They believed that if a man moved off his land and out of the gates of the village, he left his soul behind him, buried in the earth with the bones of his ancestors. The belief was no mere superstition, but a reflection of the fact that the land formed a complete picture of the village: all of a man's social and economic relationships appeared there in visual terms, as if inscribed on a map. If a man left his land, he left his own "face," the social position on which his "personality" depended.

In the nineteenth century the French came, and with their abstraction of money they took away men's souls—men's "faces"—and put them in banks.[4] They destituted the villages, and though they thought to develop the economy and to put the landless to work for wages in their factories and plantations, their efforts made no impression upon the villagers. What assets the French actually contributed to the country in the form of capital and industrial plants were quite as invisible to the villages as the villagers' souls were to the French. At a certain point, therefore, the villagers went into revolt.

Ngo Dinh Diem and his American advisers, however, did not, or could not, learn from the French example. Following the same centralized strategy for modernization, they continued to develop the cities, the army, and the bureaucracy, while leaving the villages to rot. As it merely permitted a few more rural people to come into the modern sector in search of their souls, this new national development constituted little more than a refugee program. For those peasants with enough money and initiative to leave their doomed villages it meant a final, traumatic break with their past. For the nation as a whole it meant the gradual division of the South Vietnamese into two distinct classes or cultures.

Of necessity, the guerrillas began their program of development from the opposite direction. Rather than build an elaborate superstructure of factories and banks (for which they did not have the capital), they built from the base of the country up, beginning among the ruins of the villages and with the dispossessed masses of people. Because the landlords and the soldiers with their foreign airplanes owned the surface of the earth, the guerrillas went underground in both the literal and the metaphorical sense. Settling down among people who lived, like an Orwellian

---

[4] John T. McAlister, Jr., and Paul Mus, *The Vietnamese and Their Revolution* (New York: Harper & Row, 1970), p. 90.

proletariat, outside the sphere of modern technology, they dug tunnels beneath the villages, giving the people a new defensive distance from the powers which reigned outside the village. The earth itself became their protection—the Confucian "face" which the village had lost when, for the last time, its hedges had been torn down. From an economic point of view, their struggle against the Diem regime with its American finances was just as much of an anticolonial war as that fought by the Viet Minh against the French—the difference being that now other Vietnamese had taken up the colonial role.

As an archaeologist might conclude from examination of the NLF's goods and tools, the guerrillas were attempting not to restore the old village but rather to make some connection between the world of the village and that of the cities. The land mine was in itself the synthesis. Made of high explosives and scrap metal—the waste of foreign cities—it could be manufactured by an artisan with the simplest of skills. A technically comprehensible object, it could be used for the absolutely comprehensible purpose of blowing the enemy soldiers off the face of the village earth. Having themselves manufactured a land mine, the villagers had a new source of power—an inner life to their community. In burying it—a machine—into the earth, they infused a new meaning into the old image of their society. The Diem regime had shown a few of them a way out of the village. The NLF had shown all of them a way back in, to remake the village with the techniques of the outside world. "Socialism"—*xa hoi*, as the Viet Minh and the NLF translated it—indicated to the Vietnamese peasantry that the revolution would entail no traumatic break with the past, no abandonment of the village earth and the ancestors. Instead of a leap into the terrifying unknown, it would be a fulfillment of the local village traditions that the foreigners had attempted to destroy.[5]

[5] Ibid., p. 117.

36

AMERICAN EXCEPTIONALISM

LOREN BARITZ

In Backfire: A History of How American Culture Led Us into Vietnam and Made Us Fight the Way We Did, *historian Loren Baritz drew on Frances Fitz-Gerald's ideas as other authors had, though he located cultural misunderstanding mainly in the myopia of American culture.*

> America was involved in Vietnam for thirty years, but never understood the Vietnamese. We were frustrated by the incomprehensible behavior of our Vietnamese enemies and bewildered by the inexplicable behavior of our Vietnamese friends. For us, this corner of Asia was inscrutable. These Asians successfully masked their intentions in smiles, formal courtesies, and exotic rituals. The organic nature of Vietnamese society, the significance of village life, the meaning of ancestors, the relationship of the family to the state, the subordinate role of the individual, and the eternal quest for universal agreement, not consensus or majorities, were easily lost on the Americans.... Our difficulties were not with the strangeness of the land or the inscrutability of its people.... The problem was us, not them.... There was something about the condition of being an American that prevented us from understanding the "little people in black pajamas" who beat the strongest military force in the world.*

One aspect of "the condition of being American" was the myth of American exceptionalism, which was rooted in the Puritan settlers' original belief in colonial America as the "city on a hill." When this notion became intertwined through the course of U.S. history with other elements of American culture—Protestant nationalism, the missionary spirit, isolation and ignorance of others, the American obsession with mental concepts, racism, imperial ambition and power, the influence of individuals

*Loren Baritz, Backfire: A History of How American Culture Led Us into Vietnam and Made Us Fight the Way We Did (New York: Morrow, 1985), 19–20, 22.

*like Woodrow Wilson, and a sense of military omnipotence—it carried the potential
for leading Americans into war. Senator Fulbright and other authors had also
discussed some of these ideas, but in* Backfire *Baritz self-consciously tried to place
them all into the interconnected context of American history and culture.*

... Americans were ignorant about the Vietnamese not because we were stupid, but
because we believe certain things about ourselves. Those things necessarily distorted our vision and confused our minds in ways that made learning extraordinarily difficult. To understand our failure we must think about what it means to be
an American.

The necessary text for understanding the condition of being an American is
a single sentence written by Herman Melville in his novel *White Jacket:* "And we
Americans are the peculiar, chosen people—the Israel of our time; we bear the ark
of the liberties of the world."[1] This was not the last time this idea was expressed
by Americans. It was at the center of thought of the men who brought us the Vietnam
War. It was at the center of the most characteristic American myth.

This oldest and most important myth about America has an unusually specific
origin. More than 350 years ago, while in mid-passage between England and the
American wilderness, John Winthrop told the band of Puritans he was leading to
a new and dangerous life that they were engaged in a voyage that God Himself not
only approved, but in which He participated. The precise way that Brother Winthrop
expressed himself echoes throughout the history of American life. He explained to
his fellow travelers, "We shall find that the God of Israel is among us, when ten of
us shall be able to resist a thousand of our enemies, when he shall make us a praise
and glory, that men shall say of succeeding plantations [settlements]: the Lord make
it like that of New England: for we must Consider that we shall be as a City upon
a Hill, the eyes of all people are upon us."[2] The myth of America as a city on a hill
implies that America is a moral example to the rest of the world, a world that will
presumably keep its attention riveted on us. It means that we are a Chosen People,
each of whom, because of God's favor and presence, can smite one hundred of our
heathen enemies hip and thigh.

The society Winthrop meant to establish in New England would do God's
work, insofar as sinners could. America would become God's country. The Puritans
would have understood this to mean that they were creating a nation of, by, and for
the Lord. About two centuries later, the pioneers and farmers who followed the
Puritans translated God's country from civilization to the grandeur and nobility of
nature, to virgin land, to the purple mountains' majesty. Relocating the country of
God from civilization to nature was significant in many ways, but the conclusion
that this New World is specially favored by the Lord not only endured but spread.

In countless ways Americans know in their gut—the only place myths can
live—that we have been Chosen to lead the world in public morality and to instruct

[1] Herman Melville, *White Jacket* (London: Oxford University Press, 1924), p. 189.

[2] John Winthrop, *Papers*, A. B. Forbes, ed. (Boston: Massachusetts Historical Society, 1931), Vol. II,
p. 295.

it in political virtue. We believe that our own domestic goodness results in strength adequate to destroy our opponents who, by definition, are enemies of virtue, freedom, and God. Over and over, the founding Puritans described their new settlement as a beacon in the darkness, a light whose radiance could keep Christian voyagers from crashing on the rocks, a light that could brighten the world. In his inaugural address John Kennedy said, "The energy, the faith, the devotion which we bring to this endeavor [defending freedom] will light our country and all who serve it—and the glow from that fire can truly light the world."[3] The city on a hill grew from its first tiny society to encompass the entire nation. As we will see, that is one of the reasons why we compelled ourselves to intervene in Vietnam.

An important part of the myth of America as the city on a hill has been lost as American power increased. John Winthrop intended that his tiny settlement should be only an example of rectitude to the cosmos. It could not have occurred to him that his small and weak band of saints should charge about the world to impose the One Right Way on others who were either too wicked, too stupid, or even too oppressed to follow his example. Because they also had domestic distractions, the early American Puritans could not even consider foreign adventures. In almost no time they had their hands full with a variety of local malefactors: Indians, witches, and, worst of all, shrewd Yankees who were more interested in catching fish than in catching the spirit of the Lord. Nathaniel Hawthorne, brooding about these Puritans, wrote that civilization begins by building a jail and a graveyard, but he was only two-thirds right. Within only two generations, the New England saints discovered that there was a brothel in Boston, the hub of the new and correct Christian order.

The New World settlement was puny, but the great ocean was a defensive moat that virtually prohibited an onslaught by foreign predators. The new Americans could therefore go about perfecting their society without distracting anxiety about alien and corrupting intrusions from Europe. This relative powerlessness coupled with defensive security meant that the city on a hill enjoyed a favorable "peculiar situation." It was peculiarly blessed because the decadent world could not come here, and we did not have to go there. The rest of the world, but especially Europe, with its frippery, pomp, and Catholicism, was thought to be morally leprous. This is what George Washington had in mind when he asked a series of rhetorical questions in his farewell address in 1796:

> Why forego the advantages of so peculiar a situation? Why quit our own
> to stand upon foreign ground? Why, by interweaving our destiny with
> that of any part of Europe, entangle our peace and prosperity in the toils
> of European ambition, rivalship, interest, humor, of caprice?[4]

This is also what Thomas Jefferson told his countrymen when he was inaugurated five years later. This enlightened and skeptical philosopher-President an-

---

[3] John F. Kennedy, *Public Papers of the Presidents*, Jan. 20, 1961 (Washington, D.C.: G.P.O., 1962), p. 3.

[4] Worthington Chauncey Ford, ed., *The Writings of George Washington* (New York: Putnam's Sons, 1889–93), Vol. XIII, p. 317.

nounced that this was a "chosen country" which had been "kindly separated by nature and a wide ocean from the exterminating havoc of one quarter of the globe." He said that the young nation could exult in its many blessings if it would only keep clear of foreign evil. His prescription was that America should have "entangling alliances with none."[5]

One final example of the unaggressive, unimperial interpretation of the myth is essential. The entire Adams family had a special affinity for old Winthrop. Perhaps it was that they grew up on the soil in which he was buried. On the Fourth of July, in 1821, John Quincy Adams gave a speech that captured every nuance of the already ancient myth. His speech could have been the text for the Vietnam War critics. He said that America's heart and prayers would always be extended to any free and independent part of the world. "But she goes not abroad in search of monsters to destroy." America, he said, hoped that freedom and independence would spread across the face of the earth. "She will recommend the general cause by the countenance of her voice, and by the benignant sympathy of her example." He said that the new nation understood that it should not actively intervene abroad even if such an adventure would be on the side of freedom because "she would involve herself beyond the power of extrication." It just might be possible for America to try to impose freedom elsewhere, to assist in the liberation of others. "She might," he said, "become the dictatress of the world. She would no longer be the ruler of her own spirit."[6]

In 1966, this speech was quoted by George F. Kennan, the thoughtful analyst of Soviet foreign affairs, to the Senate Foreign Relations Committee which was conducting hearings on the Vietnam War. Perhaps not knowing the myth, Mr. Kennan said that he was not sure what Mr. Adams had in mind when he spoke almost a century and a half earlier. But whatever it was, Mr. Kennan told the senators who were then worrying about Vietnam, "He spoke very directly and very pertinently to us here today."[7]

The myth of the city on a hill became the foundation for the ritualistic thinking of later generations of Americans. This myth helped to establish nationalistic orthodoxy in America. It began to set an American dogma, to fix the limits of thought for Americans about themselves and about the rest of the world, and offered a choice about the appropriate relationship between us and them.

The benevolence of our national motives, the absence of material gain in what we seek, the dedication to principle, and our inpenetrable ignorance were all related to the original myth of America. It is temptingly easy to dismiss this as some quaint idea that perhaps once had some significance, but lost it in this more sophisticated, tough-minded, modern America. Arthur Schlesinger, Jr., a close aide to President Kennedy, thought otherwise. He was concerned about President Johnson's vastly ambitious plans to create a "Great Society for Asia." Whatever the President meant, according to Professor Schlesinger, such an idea

[5] Saul Padover, ed., *The Complete Jefferson* (New York: Irvington Publishers, 1943), pp. 385–86.
[6] *The Vietnam Hearings* (New York: Random House, 1966), p. 115.
[7] *Ibid.*

...demands the confrontation of an issue deep in the historical consciousness of the United States: whether this country is a chosen people, uniquely righteous and wise, with a moral mission to all mankind.... The ultimate choice is between messianism and maturity.[8]

The city myth should have collapsed during the war. The war should have taught us that we could not continue to play the role of moral adviser and moral enforcer to the world. After the shock of the assassinations, after the shock of Tet, after President Johnson gave up the presidency, after the riots, demonstrations, burned neighborhoods, and the rebellion of the young, it should have been difficult to sustain John Winthrop's optimism. It was not difficult for Robert Kennedy who, after Senator Eugene McCarthy had demonstrated LBJ's vulnerability in New Hampshire, finally announced that he would run for the presidency himself. The language he used in his announcement speech proved that the myth was as alive and as virulent as it had ever been: "At stake," Senator Kennedy said, "is not simply the leadership of our party, and even our own country, it is our right to the moral leadership of this planet."[9] Members of his staff were horrified that he could use such language because they correctly believed that it reflected just the mind-set that had propelled us into Vietnam in the first place. He ignored their protests. This myth could survive in even the toughest of the contemporary, sophisticated, hard-driving politicians. Of course, he may have used this language only to persuade his listeners, to convince the gullible. But, even so, it showed that he believed that the myth was what they wanted to hear. In either case, the city on a hill continued to work its way.

In some ways American nationalism resembles that of other countries. Between God's Country and Holy Russia there is not much of a choice. Between ideas of moral superiority and racial superiority there is even less of a choice, since one invariably leads to the other. The Middle Kingdom of China, the Sacred Islands of Japan, the Holy Islamic Republic of Iran, all rest in some sense on being Chosen. Israel also knows about this. More secular bases for self-congratulation are nearly ubiquitous: the glory of France, dominion of Britain, power and racial purity of the Third Reich, the satisfaction of thinking of oneself as the "cradle of civilization," as claimed by Egypt, Syria, Greece, and virtually every other ancient country on the face of the earth, along with the *Pax Romana*. *Pro patria mori*, the willingness to die for one's uniquely favored country, has no national boundary. The longer such a list grows the more trivial it is. National myths become important to the rest of the world only when they are coupled to national power sufficient to impose one nation's will on another. The old Puritans were only interesting, not important, because they were so weak.

A whisper runs throughout our history that the people of the world really want to be like us, regardless of what they or their political leaders say. The evidence that this is true is very powerful. Immigration to this country was the largest

---

[8] Arthur M. Schlesinger, Jr., *The Bitter Heritage* (Boston: Houghton Mifflin Co., 1967), p. 79.

[9] David Halberstam, *The Best and the Brightest* (New York: Random House, 1972), p. 41.

movement of people ever. Our entire history is the history of a magnet. However, the slave runners were obliged to use a whip instead of a lure, and so the record is far from consistent. But, since the Civil War, the overwhelming majority of new immigrants came voluntarily. Many were forced to leave their old countries, but almost all chose to come here rather than to go elsewhere. We refused to admit additional millions who wanted to become Americans. For most of this century our standard of living was the world's highest, and Americans ate better, had more leisure, and suffered less political or religious oppression. The Statue of Liberty meant what it said. Its torch lights the way to a better life. Who could deny it?

In fact, almost anyone could. For all the accomplishments of the American nation, its promises so far outstrip its reality as to leave its many victims gasping in disbelief at the betrayal of their dreams. This culture detests poverty and fears the poor. The ladder of economic mobility is a conceit of the many who have climbed it and a reproach to the many who cannot get on it. To defend themselves against their new country, many of the immigrants maintained their own cultures, their own ways of speaking and of doing things, instead of integrating into what Americans in the mainstream of American life call the mainstream of American life.

Everyone naturally prefers their own language, diet, and funeral customs. The ancient Greeks defined a barbarian as one who did not speak Greek. The classical Chinese defined the civilized man as one who spoke Chinese and used chopsticks. Much of the rest of the world would surely like to be richer and more powerful. But an unknown number would not exchange the familiarity of their local horizon, ritual comforts of the family graveyard, or their daily competence for greater material strength. We all prefer who we are and what we know, sometimes at the expense of the chance to make it big. It is an old story to almost everyone, except that American nationalism in its purest form thinks of the world as populated by frustrated or potential Americans. This is unique among the world's nationalisms. Thus, we believe that we can know others reasonably easily because of our assumption that they want to become us.

The great ocean that defended us throughout our history also kept us from knowing others. The less one knows of the world, the more appalling the local customs of others may seem. The other side of that is also true: The less one knows of the world, the more one's own little daily rituals seem to have been decreed either by God or nature. People in other countries have different domestic customs. This may make them seem colorful, and for the most strident nationalists, even stupid or disgusting. For some of us it is hard to imagine that there are people for whom the day of rest, the day when the stores and banks are closed, is Friday, and for others it is Saturday. For some people, belching during a meal is a compliment to the chef. Some people wear white to funerals.

The cultural arrogance that comes from cultural isolation is not, of course, an American monopoly. Many South Vietnamese considered Americans as barbarians. For example, Bruce Lawlor, a CIA case officer in Vietnam during the war, said,

they thought we were animals. A lot of little things that we took for granted offended them fiercely, such as putting your hand on a head.

Sitting with your feet crossed, with your foot facing another person, is a high insult.[10]

We seem to think that people who have such strange ideas do not really mean them. We seem to believe that they do such things out of ignorance or poverty. They cannot help it. If they could, they would become more like us. It is apparently beyond reason to believe that anyone would follow these exotic customs for deep cultural reasons, as deep as the reasons that compel us to shake hands instead of bowing.

This way of thinking about the world has a name—solipsism—and means that someone believes that he is the world. In the foreign affairs of the nation, solipsistic thinking—they are us—has been dangerous. The advantage of imposing the imperial American self on the rest of humanity is that it serves as a justification of ignorance.

Solipsism supports American optimism. Because they are thought really to be us, we think that we know what we are doing, know what makes them tick, and know what we can do that will work. In Southeast Asia this optimism proved to be brutal in the sense that American power was believed sufficient to compensate for our ignorance, to make the detailed particularities of Vietnam's otherness beside the point. This combination of solipsism and optimism finally revealed its enabling ignorance. Because we were ignorant, we could proceed. It is a reasonably good guess that had we somehow repressed our solipsism; had we as a result learned something of both North and South Vietnam, we would not have intervened quite so smugly. Our ignorance, in short, permitted us to trust our guns in the first place and to fail in our stated national objectives in the last place.

The myth of the city on a hill combined with solipsism in the assumptions about Vietnam made by the American war planners. In other words, we assumed that we had a superior moral claim to be in Vietnam, and because, despite their quite queer ways of doing things, the Vietnamese shared our values, they would applaud our intentions and embrace our physical presence. Thus, Vice-President Humphrey later acknowledged that all along we had been ignorant of Vietnam. He said that "to LBJ, the Mekong and the Pedernales were not that far apart."[11] Our claim to virtue was based on the often announced purity of our intentions. It was said, perhaps thousands of times, that all we wanted was freedom for other people, not land, not resources, and not domination.

Because we believed that our intentions were virtuous, we could learn nothing from the French experience in Vietnam. After all, they had fought only to maintain their Southeast Asian colonies and as imperialists deserved to lose. We assumed that this was why so mighty a European power lost the important battle of Dien Bien Phu to General Giap's ragged army. America's moral authority was so clear to us that we assumed that it also had to be clear to the Vietnamese. This self-righteousness was the clincher in the debate to intensify the conflict in Vietnam, according to

---

[10] Interview in Al Santoli, *Everything We Had* (New York: Ballantine, 1981), p. 172.

[11] Hubert Humphrey, "Building on the Past," in Anthony Lake, ed., *The Legacy of Vietnam* (New York: New York University Press, 1976), p. 358.

George W. Ball, an undersecretary of state for Presidents Kennedy and Johnson. Washington's war planners, Mr. Ball said in 1973, had been captives of their own myths.[12] Another State Department official also hoped, after the fact, that Americans "will be knocked out of our grandiosity...[and] will see the self-righteous, illusory quality of that vision of ourselves offered by the high Washington official who said that while other nations have 'interests' the United States has 'a sense of responsibility.'"[13] Our power, according to this mentality, gives us responsibility, even though we may be reluctant to bear the burden. Other peoples' greed or self-ishness gives them interests, even though they may not be strong enough to grab all they want.

Our grandiosity will, however, not be diminished so easily. At least since World War II, America's foreign affairs have been the affairs of Pygmalion. We fall in love with what we create. We create a vision of the world made in what we think is our own image. We are proud of what we create because we are certain that our intentions are pure, our motives good, and our behavior virtuous. We know these things to be true because we believe that we are unique among the nations of the world in our collective idealism.

There are many authors of this myth of American idealism, but the supreme American political idealist of our century was Woodrow Wilson. He had grown up in the South during the Civil War, the son of a Presbyterian minister from whom he learned the meaning of Christian duty, charity, and discipline. He was some-times criticized for being a cold fish. Mr. Wilson built his career as a professor of government, president of Princeton University, and President of the United States on his quite remarkable talents as a writer and a speaker.

A man of peace, it was his misfortune to lead the United States into World War I. He had a vision of how the world should organize itself after the killing stopped, and a vision of open diplomacy that would not be dictated by bullies, with interests and without responsibility, behind closed doors. He supported national self-determination in place of domination by more powerful nations. His central vision was of an international forum, the League of Nations, where debate would replace carnage. In 1919, the terms of the peace were to be negotiated in a con-ference of the victorious nations to be held at the Versailles Palace. Despite warn-ings that he should stay away from Paris, President Wilson sailed to the Old World to cleanse it of the murderous decadence that had kept it, and the world, in flames for so long.

It is clear that President Wilson was a resident of the city on a hill. As he expressed it: "America was born a Christian nation; America was born to exemplify that devotion to the elements of righteousness which are derived from the revela-tions of Holy Scripture."[14] But as Commander in Chief he wanted actually to con-vert the heathen Europeans, not merely to provide them with America's healing

---

[12] George W. Ball, "Have We Learned or Only Failed?" *The New York Times Magazine*, April 1, 1973, p. 13.

[13] Walter H. Capps, *The Unfinished War* (Boston: Beacon Press, 1982), pp. 70–71.

[14] Woodrow Wilson, *Public Papers* (New York: Harper and Bros., 1925–1927), Vol. II, p. 302.

example. His Presbyterian zeal easily enough became enmeshed in his nationalistic fervor, and he sailed to the cynical Old World to extirpate its sinning ways in the names of God and America.

He was welcomed in Europe as no mortal had ever been received before or since. In France, England, and Italy, millions of people cheered his triumphal march, lighted candles in his name, and brightened the streets of a continent with flowers to show his way. He was the incarnation of the best hopes of a wounded world, and the bright young men who were assembling in Paris to begin the work of making a permanent peace were ecstatic under the President's guiding light. He was the prophet who had foreseen that this war would be the war to end war. John Maynard Keynes, the English economist, was there, and he expressed the excited hopes of the world: "With what curiosity, anxiety, and hope we sought a glimpse of the features and bearing of the man of destiny who, coming from the West, was to bring healing to the wounds of the ancient parent of his civilization and lay for us the foundations of the future."[15]

Thinking about the role he had assigned himself to play in the Hall of Mirrors at Versailles, the President explained his larger vision to his secretary: "Well...this trip will either be the greatest success or the supremest tragedy in all history; but I believe in a Divine Providence. If I did not have faith I should go crazy." He believed that his inspiration would overcome, no matter what. "No body of men, however they concert their power or their influence, can defeat this great world enterprise, which after all is the enterprise of Divine mercy, peace, and good will."[16] Clemenceau, representing France, who was called "the tiger," was rarely without his skullcap and suede gloves, and wore, as one observer said, "the half-smile of an irritated, sceptical and neurasthenic gorilla."[17] This tiger-gorilla complained that President Wilson thought he was the messiah returned. The stage was set.

When the President arrived, Paris was overflowing with the men who were there to plan the peace. The Big Five—France, Great Britain, Italy, Japan, and the United States—were joined by representatives of virtually every state, minority, and tribe of Eurasia. None of the weak representatives were seriously consulted about anything. The salesmen peddling rugs, oil wells, and assorted blueprints for Utopia, along with the pimps and prostitutes, scurried around the edges of the picturesque throngs in Paris, doing their business with bits of every European language. To round out the fantastic scene, Germany and the other Central Powers, as well as the new Soviets, were not there. But a young man later called Ho Chi Minh was, and he actually rented a formal morning suit to look his western best for a meeting with Woodrow Wilson that would not be granted. He had wanted to make a case for an independent Vietnam. Later in his life he changed into shorts and sandals as he abandoned the role of supplicant to the deaf.

The tragedy was that Mr. Wilson failed in Paris. He tried to persuade politicians who responded only to power. The President had the power to force com-

[15] J. M. Keynes, *The Economic Consequences of the Peace* (New York: Cambridge University Press, 1920) pp. 38–39.

[16] Sigmund Freud and William C. Bullitt, *Thomas Woodrow Wilson* (Boston: Houghton Mifflin Co., 1967), p. 204.

[17] Harold G. Nicolson, *Peacemaking, 1919* (Boston: Constable, 1933), p. 256.

pliance with his vision, but he was unwilling to use it. It would have been inconsistent with the purity of his motives and the humility of his Christian mission. He traded away much of what he believed to win acceptance of the League of Nations. Along with millions, Mr. Keynes was devastated. He discovered that the President "had no plan, no scheme, no constructive ideas whatever for clothing with the flesh of life the commandments he had thundered from the White House." But, Keynes went on, "he could have preached a sermon on any one of them or have addressed a stately prayer to the Almighty for their fulfillment; but he could not frame their concrete application to the actual state of Europe."[18] A brokenhearted attaché of the American peace commission wrote a letter of resignation to the President: "I am sorry that you did not fight our fight to the finish and that you had so little faith in the millions of men, like myself, in every nation who had faith in you."[19] Nonetheless, when President Wilson returned to America he was sufficiently satisfied with his accomplishment to announce, "At last the world knows America as the savior of the world!"[20]

The League was described in a letter which Sigmund Freud wrote to Albert Einstein in 1932, just before Hitler was elected to power in Germany: It was, he wrote, "an attempt to base upon an appeal to certain idealistic attitudes of mind the authority which otherwise rests on the possession of power."[21] Freud was allergic to American idealism. For example, he explained that all of our dreams are motivated by pure egotism, and told this story: "One of my English friends put forward this proposition at a scientific meeting in America, whereupon a lady who was present remarked that that might be the case in Austria, but she could maintain for herself and for her friends that *they* were altruistic even in their dreams."[22]

President Wilson's idealism, read in the context of Vietnam, shows the consequences of American goodness. "When men take up arms," he said, "to set other men free, there is something sacred and holy in the warfare. I will not cry 'peace' as long as there is sin and wrong in the world."[23] Now the Christian soldiers could march onward, armed with M-16s and napalm, to free the world of evil. Dr. Kissinger understood that "our entry into the [Vietnam] war had been the product not of a militarist psychosis but of a naive idealism that wanted to set right all the world's ills and believed American good will supplied its own efficacy."[24]

President Wilson's failure shook the world's confidence in America's capacity to rejuvenate Europe, that "old bitch gone in the teeth."[25] That bitch, however,

[18] Keynes, *Economic Consequences,* pp. 42–43.

[19] Freud and Bullitt, *Wilson,* p. 272.

[20] *Ibid.,* p. 287.

[21] Sigmund Freud, "The Disillusionment of War," in Philip Rieff, ed., *Character and Culture* (New York: Collier Books, 1963), p. 140.

[22] *Ibid.,* p. 119.

[23] Garry Wills, *Nixon Agonistes* (New York: Mentor, 1971), p. 439.

[24] Henry Kissinger, *White House Years* (Boston: Little, Brown, 1979), p. 230.

[25] Ezra Pound, "Hugh Selwyn Mauberley," in F. J. Hoffman, *The Twenties* (New York: Free Press, 1965), p. 438.

was soon enough to go into heat and produce a new generation of beasts to savage the world. In the process, America did not lose its own confidence in its intrinsic goodness and benignity. Its moral revulsion led it to withdraw from the sordid affairs of the world in the 1930s. Since Pearl Harbor, however, it has felt obliged to drive "sin and wrong" off the face of the planet.

Although the nationalists of the world all share a peoples' pride in who they are, a loyalty to place and language and culture, there are delicate but important differences. Because of its Puritan roots, it is not surprising that America's nationalism is more Protestant than that of other countries. It is more missionary in its impulses, more evangelical. It typically seeks to correct the way other people think rather than to establish its own physical dominion over them. It is, as it were, more committed to the Word, as befits serious Protestants, than other nationalisms.

One of the peculiarities of American Protestant nationalism, especially in its most aggressive mood, is its passion about ideas. What we want is to convert others to the truth as we understand it. We went to war in Vietnam in the name of ideas, of principles, of abstractions. Thus, President Johnson said in his inaugural, "We aspire to nothing that belongs to others."[26] And added in his important address at John Hopkins in April 1965: "Because we fight for values and we fight for principles, rather than territory or colonies, our patience and our determination are unending."[27] This is what we mean when we think of ourselves as idealists, magnanimous and moral. It is what cold warriors mean when they say over and over that we are engaged with the Soviet Union "in a competition of ideas."

This is the Protestant face of diplomacy and war. It is Protestant in its commitment to the Word, the Book, instead of to what the founding Protestants believed was the impious Catholic emphasis on persons, the person of the Pope, or the superstitions about the person of the Virgin. When they abolished Christmas and Easter, these radical Puritans showed that they were even suspicious about worshipers of the person of Jesus. America's political founding fathers rebelled against the person of the king and replaced him with written ideas and codes. The Word shall make you free. It is no wonder that America has the world's oldest written Constitution. When America attacks, it does so to protect an abstract principle. This may make it a little less concerned with the welfare of the individuals we are trying to help than with the abstractions that we believe justify war.

Graham Greene, in *The Quiet American*, fully understood this American obsession with the mind, not so much ours as others. Greene's central character, Pyle, an American in Vietnam in the middle fifties, had a "young and unused face," and "with his gangly legs and his crew-cut and his wide campus gaze he seemed incapable of harm." Pyle's head was filled with theories about the Far East. He wanted more than anything else to help the Vietnamese, not as individual people, but as a nation. Pyle could not regard them as people. Greene's narrator could, and he responded, for instance, to the Vietnamese women dressed in their *ao dais:*

[26] Lyndon B. Johnson, *Public Papers of the Presidents*, Jan. 20, 1965 (Washington, D.C.: G.P.O., 1966), p. 73.

[27] *Ibid.*, April 7, 1965, p. 172.

Up the street came the lovely flat figures—the white silk trousers, the long tight jackets in pink and mauve patterns slit up the thigh: I watched them with the nostalgia I knew I would feel when I left these regions for ever. "They are lovely, aren't they?" I said over my beer, and Pyle cast them a cursory glance as they went on up the rue Castinat. "Oh, sure," he said indifferently: he was a serious type.

The narrator wondered why he liked "to tease the innocent," like Pyle. The young man had only just arrived in this complex and ancient place:

Perhaps only ten days ago he had been walking back across the Common in Boston, his arms full of the books he had been reading in advance on the Far East and the problems of China. He didn't even hear what I said: he was absorbed already in the dilemmas of Democracy and the responsibilities of the West: he was determined... to do good, not to any individual person but to a country, a continent, a world. Well, he was in his element now with the whole universe to improve.

Young, dedicated Pyle, and others like him, could not see the wounds on a dead body. What they responded to was a representative of an idea, "a Red menace, a soldier of democracy." The innocence of these defenders of the true faith made them "like a dumb leper who has lost his bell, wandering the world, meaning no harm." The innocent Americans could, with the best intentions, infect the world.... Pyle inevitably caused havoc at every turn.[28]

In an astonishing literary exchange during a hearing before the House of Representatives Select Committee on Intelligence in 1975, Congressman William Lehman of Florida asked William Colby, the head of the CIA, if he had read *The Quiet American*. Congressman Lehman was concerned about whether Americans could ever have understood Vietnamese culture: "I am just concerned about how we can possibly prevent the kinds of miscalculations, the misconceptualizing or lack of understanding of what is going on—the basic limitations of someone like this fellow Pyle... who is dealing from one culture into another culture without knowing what the hell he was doing." Mr. Colby acknowledged the difficulties in understanding another culture, but insisted that "the professional intelligence service," not "amateurs," had the best chance of success. Mr. Lehman was not convinced, because of the CIA's Vietnam record, and because he thought that we were "going to have to intuitively assess things—which is sometimes better than what the professionals can do."[29]

Some of the war's generals understood America's cultural rigidity, along with the military price that would ultimately be paid, as they said after, not during, the American war in Vietnam. In 1974, retired Brigadier General Douglas Kinnard mailed a questionnaire to 173 army generals who had served in Vietnam. Some of them commented about the problem of American ignorance. "We erroneously tried

---

[28] Graham Greene, *The Quiet American* (London: Heinemann, 1955), pp. 11, 12, 27, 34, 101.

[29] U.S. House of Representatives, Select Committee on Intelligence, *Hearings*, 94th Cong., 1st sess., Nov. 4, 6, Dec. 2–17, 1975, part 5, pp. 1706–7.

to impose the American system on a people who didn't want it, couldn't handle it and may lose because they tried it." Another said that "as in all our foreign wars, we never really established rapport." That was because of "our overinflated hypnosis with the myth of the American way." A third, using the same hindsight, said that "we never took into account the cultural differences." Another general officer reported that the South Vietnamese army never made any substantial progress because, he said, "most of us did not want to associate with them."[30]

How was it possible for the Vietnamese to fail to realize that the ideas of Democracy and God are more important than life? American nationalism, especially when its fist clenched, went forward not to pillage, but to instruct. That is what missionaries do. And, therefore, we did not need to bother about learning who it was we were saving. We knew, as both JFK and LBJ told us, that the South Vietnamese were uneducated and poor. We believed that this made them susceptible to bad ideas. To stiffen their resistance we undertook a program of "nation-building" that would provide a "stable" government in the South, provide more and better education for the children, and improve the economy. To protect them from their lunatic northern brothers, we would make them a new country. We would invent South Vietnam. They would be delighted, we assumed, because we believed their old country was a mess and was responsible for the ignorance, disease, and illiteracy. They must have hated it all along.

Tangled up in old myths, fearful of speaking plain English on the subject, the political conscience of many Americans must be troubled. There is bad faith in accepting the city myth of American uniqueness as if the myth can be freed from its integral Protestantism, almost always of a fundamentalist flavor. Conservatives have less need to launder the myth of its religion. Because liberals require a secular version of nationalism, and if they need or want to retain some sense of the unique republic, they are required to rest their case on a secular basis. Wilsonian idealism was the answer in the 1960s, as liberals argued that America was the only society capable of creating social justice and genuine democracy at home and abroad. These ideals merged with the cold war and persuaded the best of American liberals to bring us Vietnam.

In America, as elsewhere, elected officials are especially susceptible to the fundamental myths of nationalism because they must embody them to get elected and act on them to govern. The vision of the world that suffused Mr. Wilson's Fourteen Points and League of Nations was also the vision of John Kennedy and his circle. They were pained by the knowledge that a people anywhere in the world struggled toward freedom but was frustrated by the imposition of force. So it was that John F. Kennedy's inspired inaugural address carried the burden of Woodrow Wilson's idealism, and also carried the deadly implication that America was again ready for war in the name of goodness.

[30] Douglas Kinnard, *The War Managers* (Hanover, N.H.: University Press of New England, 1977), p. 92.

President Kennedy's language must be understood in the light of what was just around the corner in Vietnam. He announced to the world, "We shall pay any price, bear any burden, meet any hardship, support any friend, oppose any foe to assure the survival and the success of liberty." He said that it was the rare destiny of his generation to defend freedom when it was at its greatest risk. "I do not shrink from this responsibility—I welcome it."[31]

The difference between the two sons of the Commonwealth of Massachusetts, John Quincy Adams and John Fitzgerald Kennedy, was the difference between good wishes and war, but also the difference between a tiny and isolated America and the world's most powerful nation. Presidents Wilson and Kennedy both fairly represented American liberalism at its most restless and energetic. This was a liberalism that wanted, as President Wilson put it, to make the world safe for democracy, or as President Kennedy said, to defend "those human rights to which this nation has always been committed, and to which we are committed today at home and around the world." JFK described this as "God's work."[32]

An important part of the reason we marched into Vietnam with our eyes fixed was liberalism's irrepressible need to be helpful to those less fortunate. But the decency of the impulse, as was the case with President Wilson, cannot hide the bloody eagerness to kill in the name of virtue. In 1981, James C. Thomson, an aide in the State Department and a member of the National Security Council under President Johnson, finally concluded that our Vietnamese intervention had been motivated by a national missionary impulse, a "need to do good to others." In a phrase that cannot be improved, he and others called this "sentimental imperialism."[33] The purity of intention and the horror of result is unfortunately the liberal's continuing burden.

American conservatives had it easier, largely because they believed in the actuality of evil. In his first public statement, President Eisenhower informed the American public, "The forces of good and evil are massed and armed and opposed as rarely before in history." For him the world struggle was not merely between conflicting ideologies. "Freedom is pitted against slavery; lightness against the dark."[34]

Conservatives in America are closer than liberals to the myth of the city on a hill because they are not embarrassed by public professions of religion. They are therefore somewhat less likely to ascribe American values and behavior to other cultures. This is so because of the conservatives' conviction that America is so much better—more moral, godly, wise, and especially rich—than other nations that they could not possibly resemble us. Thus, President Eisenhower announced that one of America's fixed principles was the refusal to "use our strength to try to impress upon another people our own cherished political and economic institutions."[35] The idea of uniqueness means, after all, that we are alone in the world.

[31] *Public Papers of the Presidents*, Jan. 20, 1961, pp. 1–3.

[32] *Ibid.*

[33] Fox Butterfield, "Vietnam Is Not Over," *The New York Times*, Feb. 11, 1983, p. A14.

[34] Dwight D. Eisenhower, *Public Papers of the Presidents*, Jan. 20, 1953 (Washington, D.C.: G.P.O., 1960), p. 4.

[35] *Ibid.*, p. 5.

Conservatives shared with liberals the conviction that America could act, and in Vietnam did act, with absolute altruism, as they believed only America could. Thinking of this war, President Nixon, another restless descendent of Mr. Wilson, declared that "never in history have men fought for less selfish motives—not for conquest, not for glory, but only for the right of a people far away to choose the kind of government they want."[36] This was especially attractive because in this case the kind of government presumably sought by this faraway people was opposed to Communism, our own enemy. It was therefore an integral part of the universal struggle between freedom and slavery, lightness and dark. As a result it was relatively easy for conservatives to think of Vietnam as a laboratory to test ways to block the spreading stain of political atheism.

Power is sometimes a problem for liberals and a solution for conservatives. When Senator Goldwater rattled America's many sabers in his presidential campaign of 1964, and when General Curtis LeMay wanted to bomb North Vietnam "back to the stone age,"[37] they both made liberals cringe, partly from embarrassment, and partly because the liberals were appalled at the apparent cruelty. In the 1950s, Dr. Kissinger cleverly argued that the liberal embarrassment over power made its use, when necessary, even worse than it had to be. "Our feeling of guilt with respect to power," he wrote, "has caused us to transform all wars into crusades, and then to apply our power in the most absolute ways."[38] Later, when he ran America's foreign policy, his own unambivalent endorsement of the use in Vietnam of enormous power inevitably raised the question of whether bloody crusades are caused only by the squeamishness of liberals or also by the callousness of conservatives.

Implicit in John Winthrop's formulation of the city myth was the idea that the new Americans could, because of their godliness, vanquish their numerically superior enemies. The idea that warriors, because of their virtue, could beat stronger opponents, is very ancient. Pericles spoke of it in his funeral oration to the Athenians. The Christian crusaders counted on it. *Jihad*, Islam's conception of a holy war, is based on it. The Samurai believed it. So did the Nazis.

In time, the history of America proved to Americans that we were militarily invincible. The Vietnam War Presidents naturally cringed at the thought that they could be the first to lose a war. After all, we had already beaten Indians, French, British (twice), Mexicans, Spaniards, Germans (twice), Italians, Japanese, Koreans, and Chinese. Until World War II, the nation necessarily had to rely on the presumed virtue, not the power, of American soldiers to carry the day, and the war. This was also the case in the South during our Civil War.

Starting in the eighteenth century, the nation of farmers began to industrialize. As the outcome of the war increasingly came to depend on the ability to inject

---

[36] Richard Nixon, *Public Papers of the Presidents*, April 7, 1971 (Washington, D.C.: G.P.O., 1972), p. 525.

[37] Halberstam, *Best and Brightest*, p. 462.

[38] Henry A. Kissinger, *Nuclear Weapons and Foreign Policy* (New York: W. W. Norton & Co., 1957), p. 427.

various forms of flying hardware into the enemy's body, victory increasingly depended on technology. The acceleration of industrialization in the late nineteenth century inevitably quickened the pace of technological evolution. By then no other power could match the Americans' ability to get organized, to commit resources to development, and to invent the gadgets that efficiently produced money in the marketplace, and, when necessary, death on the battlefield. The idea of Yankee ingenuity, American know-how, stretches back beyond the nineteenth century. Our admiration for the tinkerer whose new widget forms the basis of new industry is nowhere better shown than in our national reverence of Thomas Edison.

Joining the American sense of its moral superiority with its technological superiority was a marriage made in heaven, at least for American nationalists. We told ourselves that each advantage explained the other, that the success of our standard of living was a result of our virtue, and our virtue was a result of our wealth. Our riches, our technology, provided the strength that had earlier been missing, that once had forced us to rely only on our virtue. Now, as Hiroshima demonstrated conclusively, we could think of ourselves not only as morally superior, but as the most powerful nation in history. The inevitable offspring of this marriage of an idea with a weapon was the conviction that the United States could not be beaten in war—not by any nation, and not by any combination of nations. For that moment we thought that we could fight where, when, and how we wished, without risking failure. For that moment we thought we could impose our will on the recalcitrant of the earth.

A great many Americans, in the period just before the war in Vietnam got hot, shared a circular belief that for most was probably not very well formed: America's technological supremacy was a symptom of its uniqueness, and technology made the nation militarily invincible. In 1983, the playwright Arthur Miller said, "I'm an American. I believe in technology. Until the mid-60s I never believed we could lose because we had technology."[39]

The memory of World War II concluding in a mushroom cloud was relatively fresh throughout the 1950s. It was unthinkable that America's military could ever fail to establish its supremacy on the battlefield, that the industrial, scientific, and technological strength of the nation would ever be insufficient for the purposes of war. It was almost as if Americans were technology. The American love affair with the automobile was at its most passionate in the 1950s, our well-equipped armies stopped the Chinese in Korea, for a moment our nuclear supremacy was taken for granted, and affluence for many white Americans seemed to be settling in as a way of life.

It is, of course, unfortunate that the forces of evil may be as strong as the forces of virtue. The Soviet Union exploded its first atomic bomb way ahead of what Americans thought was a likely schedule. This technology is not like others because even a weak bomb is devastating. Even if our bombs are better than theirs, they can still do us in. America's freedom of action after 1949 was not complete. President

[39] "Lessons from a War," speech at conference *Vietnam Reconsidered*, University of Southern California, Feb. 9, 1983.

Eisenhower and John Foster Dulles, the Secretary of State, threatened "massive retaliation" against the Soviet Union if it stepped over the line. They knew, and we knew, that this threat was not entirely real, and that it freed the Soviets to engage in peripheral adventures because they correctly believed that we would not destroy the world over Korea, Berlin, Hungary, or Czechoslovakia.

Our policy had to become more flexible. We had to invent a theory that would allow us to fight on the edges without nuclear technology. This theory is called "limited war." Its premise is that we and the Soviets can wage little wars, and that each side will refrain from provoking the other to unlock the nuclear armory.

Ike threatened the Chinese, who at the time did not have the bomb, with nuclear war in Korea. JFK similarly threatened the Soviets, who had nuclear capability, over Cuba. But, although some military men thought about using nuclear weapons in Vietnam, the fundamental assumption of that war was to keep it limited, not to force either the Soviets or the Chinese, who now had their own sloppy bombs, to enter the war. Thus, we could impose our will on the recalcitrant of the earth if they did not have their own nuclear weapons, and if they could not compel the Soviets or the Chinese to force us to quit.

In Vietnam we had to find a technology to win without broadening the war. The nuclear stalemate reemphasized our need to find a more limited ground, to find, so to speak, a way to fight a domesticated war. We had to find a technology that would prevail locally, but not explode internationally. No assignment is too tough for the technological mentality. In fact, it was made to order for the technicians who were coming into their own throughout all of American life. This war gave them the opportunity to show what they could do. This was to be history's most technologically sophisticated war, most carefully analyzed and managed, using all of the latest wonders of managerial procedures and systems. It was made to order for bureaucracy.

James C. Thomson, who served both JFK and LBJ as an East Asia specialist, understood how the myths converged. He wrote of *"the rise of a new breed of American ideologues who see Vietnam as the ultimate test of their doctrine."* These new men were the new missionaries and had a trinitarian faith: in military power, technological superiority, and our altruistic idealism. They believed that the reality of American culture "provides us with the opportunity and obligation to ease the nations of the earth toward modernization and stability: toward a full-fledged *Pax Americana Technocratica."*[40] For these parishioners in the church of the machine, Vietnam was the ideal laboratory.

[40] James C. Thomson, Jr., "How Could Vietnam Happen?" *The Atlantic*, April 1968, p. 53.

37

TECHNOWAR

JAMES WILLIAM GIBSON

In The Perfect War, *historian James William Gibson, like Baritz, expressed the belief that in order to understand American policy toward Vietnam, it was necessary to peer beyond personalities and institutions to uncover their cultural, historical, and conceptual underpinnings. In his words: "Societies go to war, not disembodied foreign policies. After one has found the Light at the End of the Tunnel, the question becomes, What does one see?" In his own search for the Vietnam war, Gibson, like Baritz, found that by the 1960s a new breed of American technocrats had come to regard Vietnam as a test of their doctrine. Putting less emphasis than Baritz on the historic missionary spirit, Gibson traced the roots of the new technocracy in the socioeconomic transformations that occurred within the United States during and after World War II, wherein politics, science, technology, and economics were united in a new way—one geared toward production for war. This in turn gave rise to military and civilian war managers, who possessed culturally based, historically evolved, self-contained, and self-interested conceptions of nature, policy, strategy, and the foreign enemy. Their Vietnam War represented "the perfect functioning of this closed, self-referential universe," and "technowar"—an expression of modern American culture—was the mode of warfare by which they waged it.*

...The search for war begins in this country, at a time when defeat anywhere appeared *unthinkable*—the end of World War II. The United States emerged from that war as the only true victor, by far the greatest power in world history. Although the other Allies also won, their victories were much different. Great Britain's industrial strength was damaged and its empire was in disarray. France had been defeated and occupied by Nazi Germany. Much French industry had either been bombed by Britain and the United States or looted by Germany. The Soviet Union "won," but over twenty million of its people were killed and millions more wounded.

Many of its cities and large areas of countryside were nothing but ruins. China "won," but despite American funding, the warlord Chiang Kai-shek and his subordinate warlords lost to the peasant Communist revolution led by Mao Tse-tung. Even before Chiang Kai-shek's defeat, post–World War II China was largely a wasteland, suffering from famine and civil war. In other words, the United States won World War II and everyone else lost.

It is important to comprehend the changes that occurred *within* the United States that made its success overseas possible. Before World War II, both the world economy and the American economy had been in severe crisis. Unemployment was extremely high. Many factories and other businesses closed; those that remained open had underutilized production capabilities. Compared to 1986, the economy was decentralized. Even as late as 1940, some 175,000 companies produced 70 percent of all manufactured goods, while the hundred largest companies produced 30 percent.

Relationships between the economy and the state changed during the Depression. The United States had long practiced "free-market" capitalism. Franklin Roosevelt and the Democratic-controlled Congress attempted to regulate capitalism in their "New Deal" program. Some endeavors, such as the minimum wage, Social Security, and laws making it easier for labor unions to organize, had impact and became enduring features of advanced capitalism. Federal efforts to organize the economy, however, did not succeed. The Supreme Court declared the National Recovery Act to be unconstitutional; the Court in effect ruled that state powers to regulate and organize the economy were limited. In any case, the New Deal did not succeed in its economic revitalization program. Unemployment levels in 1940 were close to what they had been in 1932, when Roosevelt was first elected.

Then came Pearl Harbor and the Second World War. Phenomenal changes occurred within a few short years. By 1944, the hundred largest manufacturing firms produced 70 percent of the nation's manufactured goods, while all the rest produced only 30 percent.[1] Economic mobilization for war necessitated radical state intervention in the economy. State war-managers favored awarding huge contracts to the largest industrial firms. These administrators thought that only the largest firms had truly "scientific" production lines and that only the largest firms had managerial expertise to produce huge quantities of goods. By the end of the war leading manufacturers had received billions of dollars from the state. Contracts were awarded on a "cost-plus" basis, meaning that the state financed machinery and other production facilities, as well as the costs of labor, and beyond that guaranteed specific profit rates. The federal government thus violated the customary operations of the "free market" and created a state-organized and -financed, highly centralized form of capitalism in which a few firms dominated the economy. The gross national product increased from $91 billion in 1939 to $166 billion in 1945. Such tremendous economic expansion was unprecedented in world history.

Science had always been involved in the production process; you can't produce steel without detailed knowledge of physics, chemistry, metallurgy, and so

[1] John Morton Blum, *V Was for Victory: Politics and American Culture during World War II* (New York: Harcourt Brace Jovanovich, 1976), p. 123.

forth. But in some ways, during the prewar period, science was not fully integrated into the economy. During World War II, however, thousands of scientists were hired by the government and large corporations. As Gerald Piel, a former editor of *Scientific American*, says, "The universities transformed themselves into vast weapons laboratories. Theoretical physicists became engineers, and engineers forced solutions at the frontiers of knowledge."[2] Science was enlisted in the economic production process and military destruction process to an unprecedented degree.

So-called managerial science also was incorporated into the war effort. The original master of "scientific management," Frederick Taylor, had won many adherents among businessmen in the 1920s and 1930s, especially among larger industrial firms confronted by massive unionization. For workers, scientific management meant progressive dissolution of their control over work processes.[3] By the 1940s, management had become a more esoteric discipline. For example, during World War II, Professor Robert McNamara of the Harvard University Business School developed statistical techniques of systems analysis for the War Department as management tools in controlling large organizations. McNamara became famous for organizing flight patterns of bombers and fighters in the air war against Germany. After the war, in the 1950s, he served as general manager and vice president of Ford Motor Company. In 1960, President Kennedy chose him as secretary of defense. Advanced "scientific" methods thus took root in both government and business.

This radical shift from a capitalist economy organized around small to medium-sized firms to an advanced capitalist economy organized around relatively few firms with high-technology production thus occurred through federal government intervention and was directed toward war production. Politics, economics, and science were now united in a new way. Just as the state changed capitalism and changed the practice of science, so too did the now vastly expanded economy and scientific apparatus change the nature and practice of politics, particularly the conduct of foreign policy. As the possessor of an advanced technological system of war production, the United States began to view political relationships with other countries in terms of concepts that have their origin in physical science, economics, and management. A deeply mechanistic world view emerged among the political and economic elite and their intellectual advisers.

The writings of Dr. Henry Kissinger provide a good introduction to modern power and knowledge relationships as they shaped American foreign policy in the post–World War II era. Kissinger was national security adviser to President Richard Nixon from 1969 through 1972 and was later secretary of state under Nixon and then Gerald Ford from 1973 to 1976. Before his ascension to formal political power, he was an important adviser to Nelson Rockefeller and a key intellectual in the foreign-policy establishment. His books and essays were held in great esteem.

Kissinger writes that since 1945, American foreign policy has been based "on the assumption that *technology plus managerial skills* gave us the ability to reshape

---

[2] Ibid., pp. 144–145.

[3] For an analysis of "scientific management" and the rationalization of production in the United States see Harry Braverman, *Labor and Monopoly Capital* (New York: Monthly Review Press, 1976).

the international system and to bring domestic transformations in 'emerging countries.'"[4] He indicates that there are virtually no limits to this technical intervention in the world: "A scientific revolution has, for all practical purposes, removed technical limits from the exercise of power in foreign policy."[5] Power thus becomes measured solely in technical terms: political power becomes physically embedded in the United States' large, efficient economy, its war production system capable of creating advanced war machines, and its economic-managerial science for administering these production systems. By this standard the United States has virtually unlimited power to control the world.

Moreover, since these physical means of power were created in large part through science, the United States also maintains a highly privileged position of *knowledge*. The United States knows more about "reality" itself, reality being defined in terms of physical science. Power and knowledge thus go together. Knowing "reality" is also "hard work." The West, in Kissinger's view, had been committed to this hard epistemological work since Sir Isaac Newton first formulated his laws of physics. Although Kissinger never speaks of "virtues" in connection with the hard work of the West, such connotations are implicit in his writings—Max Weber's *Protestant Ethic and the Spirit of Capitalism* is tacitly enlisted in his program.[6] Power, knowledge, and virtue all accrue to the United States. Its foreign-policy endeavors are thus blessed. From this perspective Kissinger discusses the differences between the Third World and the West. Ultimately, he claims that the West knows reality and the underdeveloped countries live only in their own delusions:

> As for the difference in philosophical perspective, it may reflect the divergence of the two lines of thought which since the Renaissance have distinguished the West from the part of the world now called underdeveloped (with Russia occupying an intermediate position). The West is deeply committed to the notion that the real world is external to the observer, that knowledge consists of recording and classifying data—the more accurately the better. Cultures which have escaped the early impact of Newtonian thinking have retained the essentially pre-Newtonian view that the real world is almost entirely internal to the observer.
>
> Although this attitude was a liability for centuries—because it prevented the development of the technology and consumer goods which the West enjoyed—it offers great flexibility with respect to the contemporary revolutionary turmoil. It enables the societies which do not share our cultural mode to alter reality by influencing the perspective of the observer—a process which we are largely unprepared to handle or even perceive. And this can be accomplished under contemporary conditions without sacrificing technological progress. Technology comes as a gift; acquiring it in its advanced form does not presuppose the philosophical

---

[4] Henry A. Kissinger, *American Foreign Policy*, expanded edition (New York: W. W. Norton, 1974), p. 57.

[5] Ibid., p. 54.

[6] Max Weber, *The Protestant Ethic and the Spirit of Capitalism*, translated by Talcott Parsons (New York: Charles Scribner, 1958).

commitment that discovering it imposed on the West. Empirical reality
has a much different significance for many of the new countries because
in a certain sense they never went through the process of discovering it
(with Russia again occupying an intermediate position).[7]

By this theory, American intervention in the Third World not only brings
technology and consumer goods into play but also brings *reality* to the Third World.
In claiming the West's radical monopoly on knowing reality, the Third World becomes *unreal*. Those who live there and have retained "the essentially pre-Newtonian
view that the real world is almost entirely internal to the observer" are therefore
totally unlike the West and its leading country. Those who are totally unlike us and
live in their own delusions are conceptualized as foreign Others. The foreign Other
can be known only within the conceptual framework of technological development
and production systems. For instance, the Other may have bicycles. Bicycles can
be readily comprehended by the West as a form of "underdeveloped" transporta-
tion, as opposed to the trucks and automobiles found in the "developed" West.
Bicycles are "less" than cars by definition. In this sense the Other can be known.
Insofar as he is like us he is far down on the scale of power and knowledge; insofar
as he is not like us, he remains the foreign Other living his self-delusions in an
unreal land.

Who defeated the most powerful nation in world history? Who defeated several hundred thousand troops equipped with the most advanced weaponry that the
most technologically sophisticated nation had to offer? Who defeated a war budget
more than one trillion dollars? For the most part, peasants of underdeveloped agricultural economies defeated the United States. The insurgents of what was called
"South Vietnam" were peasants. What was called "North Vietnam" was also a
relatively primitive, agricultural economy with little industrial base.

How could a nation of peasants with bicycles defeat the United States? By
Kissinger's theory such a defeat is *unthinkable*. Kissinger's claim to a monopoly of
true knowledge for the West turns into its opposite. Classifying nations and peoples
purely on the basis of their possession, or lack, of technologically advanced production and warfare systems leads only to radical reduction of what can be considered as valid knowledge about the world. The regime of power and knowledge
thus creates a world that is "almost entirely internal to the observer." Kissinger
writes that "the West is deeply committed to the notion that the real world is external to the observer, that knowledge consists of recording and classifying data—
the more accurately the better." He calls this the "Newtonian" view of the world,
after the eighteenth-century theoretical physicist Sir Isaac Newton.

However, Newtonian mechanics is a theory about nature. It says nothing about
society, about human social relationships. Newtonian mechanics says nothing about
societies where millions of peasants are dominated by a few hundred landlords; it says
nothing about countries where the population may be yellow or brown or black in skin

---

[7] Kissinger, *American Foreign Policy*, pp. 48–49.

color, but their rulers have white skins and come from distant lands. It says nothing about social conflict, about social relationships of domination and subordination; and in particular, Newtonian mechanics says nothing about social revolution.

Instead, the deeply mechanistic view of the world can see bicycles of the Third World only as compared to the cars of the West. Bicycles cannot "beat" cars and trucks and planes and railroads. But in 1954, the Vietnamese beat the French in a battle at Dien Bien Phu. Thousands of peasants cut trails through jungles and across mountains; thousands more dug tunnels close to French fortifications; thousands more walked alongside bicycles loaded with supplies for the Vietminh army. Social relationships between the Vietminh soldiers and the peasantry were such that thousands of peasants could be mobilized for the war effort. Social relationships that are rendered invisible by the modern regime of power and knowledge can defeat a system of power that conceives the world only in terms of technological-production systems. At the time, the French were amazed at their loss. The Americans were similarly amazed years later. They did not learn from the French because they thought that the French simply did not have enough tools of war; the United States had many more.

What is at issue concerns conceptually mapping "nature" onto society, of rendering the social world invisible. This false scientific project has historical precedent in the theory of capitalism, the famous naturelike "laws of supply and demand" that govern the market. Adam Smith, eighteenth-century author of *The Wealth of Nations,* is usually awarded credit for positing capitalism as economic nature, the true discovery of the actual order of things, the social organization that imitates nature best. Viewing capitalism as nature, this theory of immutable laws of supply and demand, was later criticized by Karl Marx.

Marx contended that the production process constituted a social relationship between those who owned the means of production (the capitalist) and those who were employed by capitalists as laborers (the working class). The working class collectively produced all wealth, but received only a fraction back as wages; the rest went to capitalists. Capitalism was based on a specific kind of class domination, not a "natural" order. However, structural relationships of class domination are rendered invisible by the phenomenal form of capitalist production, the commodity. Everything *appears* as a commodity to be bought and sold, even the workers. A loaf of bread appears as an object to be eaten, which is sold in a store for a price. No relationships of class structure are written on the package cover. "The commodity is a mysterious thing," wrote Marx. "In it definite social relationships among men assume the fantastic form of relationships among things." Marx called this project of mapping nature onto society "commodity fetishism."[8]

Ironically, Marx thought that the phenomenal force of commodity fetishism would be attenuated when *science* became a *"direct force of production,* integral to the operation of all basic industry."[9] Science to Marx represented the collective knowl-

---

[8] Karl Marx, *Capital: A Critique of Political Economy,* vol. 1: *The Process of Capitalist Production,* edited by Frederick Engels (New York: International Publishers, 1967), p. 72.

[9] Karl Marx, *Grundrisse: Foundations of the Critique of Political Economy,* translated by Martin Nicholaus (Middlesex, England: Penguin Books in association with *New Left Review,* 1973), p. 706.

edge of society. Although individual bits of knowledge could be privately owned—as in patents—basic scientific advancement resulted from social "poolings" of thousands of individual efforts to know the world. Thus, when science became a "direct force of production, integral to the operation of all basic industry," the relationship of knowledge to the production process would make the social character of production more evident.

Men and women would more readily see that since knowledge was a collective product of the human species, then the goods produced by privately owned industry (using scientific knowledge in the production process) rightfully belonged to society as a whole, not only to the capitalist class. People would see both the moral right and logical necessity for collective ownership and control of the society. Because people would be organizing economic activity together, the goods produced would not appear as independent entities obeying naturelike laws of supply and demand. Collective social organization and decision-making about social development and resource allocation replaces the market. No longer do "definite social relationships among men assume the fantastic form of relationships among things." With the transition to socialism, commodity fetishism and other forms of falsely mapping a model of nature onto society would end. Scientific rationalization of capitalist production was thus a crucial stage in Marx's theory of the transition from capitalism toward socialism.

This prediction for radical social change in advanced capitalist countries did not come true. Instead, a new kind of fetishism came into existence in the post–World War II period. The scientific rationalization and expansion of the production process occurred during wartime; it was directed by the state toward the *production of war*. The largest industrial firms became quantum levels larger, and their owners and top executives entered into new relationships with the government. Privately owned production facilities still dominated the economy, but these firms were state financed to a considerable degree and their products were used by the state to wage war and conduct foreign policy. C. Wright Mills called this new social organization rule by "the power elite."[10] Seymour Melman has used the term "the permanent war-economy."[11] Both men have written works of great merit, but neither fully conveys the transformations of power and knowledge that mark American foreign policy since World War II.

Whereas Marx saw the locus of fetishism and naturalization as structurally situated in the system of commodity production, this new fetishism involved rationalized capitalist production as it was organized for war production. Political and social power became conceptualized and practiced solely in terms of how societies ranked in their ability to produce high-technology warfare. To those in command of the system, the world's international political and economic relationships appeared as a series of technical or physical problems to be solved by the correct, scientifically determined administration of force: how much war production or threat

[10] C. Wright Mills, *The Power Elite* (New York: Oxford University Press, 1956).

[11] Seymour Melman, *The Permanent War Economy: American Capitalism in Decline* (New York: Simon and Schuster, 1974).

of war production was necessary to achieve American policy objectives in other nations.

This new fetishism is thus a kind of social physics, a metaphorical transposition of Sir Isaac Newton's world of physical forces and mechanical interactions onto the social world. War-production systems become the units of this social physics. To appropriate Marx's phrasing, in this new fetishism definite social relationships among men assume the fantastic form of relationships among high-technology production systems for producing warfare. And when relationships appear as warfare systems, then social relationships disappear from view just as they do with the system of simple commodity production. For example, how can complex social revolutions be understood by war-managers, when for them the highest form of political power is an atomic bomb that could literally vaporize the revolution? At best, war-managers can only translate social revolution into their own fetishized, technical categories of control and production. How many weapons does the revolution have? What is its structure of command, control, and communication? How do enemy war-managers instrumentally manipulate their people? In this way, Kissinger's claim that the West in general and the United States in particular have an epistemological monopoly on "the notion that the real world is external to the observer" turns back on itself. The question must be asked, who is the foreign Other for whom "the real world is almost entirely internal to the observer"?

The Other is the man mesmerized by his own system of production, his own system for the production of destruction, his own "technology plus managerial skills," which creates the possibility of bringing "domestic transformations in 'emerging countries.'" The Other is the man who writes, "A scientific revolution has, for all practical purposes, removed technical limits from the exercise of power in foreign policy." The history of modern foreign policy is the history of this power and knowledge regime. It is the history of a system totally enclosed upon itself, the history of a regime whose basic assumptions of knowledge are never questioned by those in power. At the same time, these men legitimate their decisions and subsequent actions in terms of a radical monopoly of knowledge: they have a scientific right to intervene in the Third World.

Kissinger is but one man. He has been cited both because of his position and fame and because his writings are so clearly concerned with the questions at hand. Still, he is not solely responsible for the modern regime of power and knowledge. To the contrary, the basic assumptions about power and knowledge articulated by Kissinger were shared by thousands of academics and policymakers. Much of the literature on international relations and development or "modernization" of the Third World shares these same mechanistic assumptions. Fetishism is not an individual problem; it is a characteristic of particular social structures and how those social structures are conceived by members of the society.

In the 1950s, there was one contradiction in the regime of power and knowledge that worried political elites and defense intellectuals. The problem had to do with using the atomic bomb, especially the difficult situation created when both the United States and the Soviet Union had the bomb. Using the atomic bomb became more dangerous to the United States, because the Soviet Union could retaliate in kind. In this event, the vast systems of production on both sides would be destroyed. During the 1950s, this projected scenario was called mutually assured destruction. The scenario placed limits on American ability to intervene militarily in the world. Much effort was expended in attempting to solve this contradiction of virtually limitless technical power that now seemed highly limited.

The most renowned scholar who helped solve this problem was, again, Dr. Henry Kissinger. His book on the subject was entitled *Nuclear Weapons and Foreign Policy* (1957). Kissinger was opposed to all-out nuclear war because such war destroyed the American advantage: "We have seen . . . that the power of modern weapons reduces the importance of our industrial potential in an all-out war because each side can destroy the industrial plant of its opponent with its forces-in-being at the very outset. With modern weapons [atomic weapons], industrial potential can be significant only in a war in which it is not itself the target."[12] From the necessity to preserve American industrial potential, Kissinger derives a strategic doctrine in which this potential can be best used. By virtue of its technological production system, the United States can achieve its foreign-policy objectives by *limited wars* fought as *wars of attrition:*

> As a result, limited war has become the form of conflict which enables us to derive the greatest strategic advantage from our industrial potential. It is the best means for achieving a continuous drain of our opponent's resources without exhausting both sides. The prerequisites for deriving a strategic advantage from industrial potential is a weapons system sufficiently complex to require a substantial production effort, but not so destructive as to deprive the victor of any effective margin of superiority. Thus the argument that limited war may turn into a contest of attrition is in fact an argument in favor of a strategy of limited war. A war of attrition is the one war the Soviet bloc could not win.[13]

Kissinger even said that the purpose of limited war was to demonstrate the capacity for destruction by our advanced war-production system, not literally to destroy an enemy: "Strategic doctrine must never lose sight that its purpose is to affect the will of the enemy, not to destroy him, and that we can be limited only by presenting the enemy with an unfavorable calculus of risks."[14] In another formulation of the same theoretical point, Kissinger wrote: "In a limited war the problem is to apply graduated amounts of destruction for limited objectives and also to permit the necessary breathing spaces for political contacts."[15]

All that remained necessary was to reorganize the American military so that it could fight limited wars of attrition. Kissinger gave great priority to preparing the military for this new kind of warfare: "One of the most urgent tasks of American

[12] Henry A. Kissinger, *Nuclear Weapons and Foreign Policy*, published for the Council on Foreign Relations (New York: Harper and Brothers, 1957), p. 155.

[13] Ibid., p. 155.

[14] Ibid., p. 226.

[15] Ibid., pp. 156–157.

military policy is to create a military capability which can redress the balance in limited wars and which can translate our technological advantage into local superiority."[16]

For the army these were golden words. When preparing for nuclear war during the 1950s, the air force had received most of the money allocated to the Department of Defense; the navy came second and the army got what was left. Prospects for a new mission involving a capital-intensive, technologically sophisticated army were exciting! Now the army, too, could speed up its transformation in organization and doctrine to fit smoothly into modern warfare. This transition had started in the Second World War with Chief of Staff George C. Marshall's decision to adopt the corporate model of organization as a means of managing military logistics. Corporatization of the military continued in the fifties. Close association with business and science in preparing new weapons systems accentuated the trend.

However, the full implications of this transformation go far beyond matters of management and weaponry considered as just *parts* of the American military. The same "fetishism" of technological production systems found in foreign policy similarly occurs within the military. The *social relationships* within the military disappear and all that remain are technological-production systems and ways of managing them. In the early 1950s, Morris Janowitz, a military sociologist, detected conflict between the traditional idea of the officer corps as being composed of "heroic" combat leaders or "gladiators," and the emerging career path of the "military manager."[17] Combat leaders inspire troops to fight in dangerous battle; social relationships of loyalty from top to bottom and bottom to top are crucial. Managers allocate resources. As two other military sociologists, Richard Gabriel and Paul Savage, say, "no one expects anyone to die for IBM or General Motors."[18]

Second, in a world where only technology and production count, the enemy begins to be seen *only* in those terms. The bicycle example in Vietnam was no joke. Limited war fought as a war of attrition means that only information about technological-production systems will count as valid knowledge about the enemy. For the military as well as civilian policymakers, the enemy becomes a mirror image of ourselves, only "less" so. Military strategy becomes a one-factor question about technical forces; success or failure is measured quantitatively. Machine-system meets machine-system and the largest, fastest, most technologically advanced system will win. Any other outcome becomes *unthinkable*. Such is the logic of *Technowar*.

The search for war now leads to the enemy. The enemy, of course, is communism. Although it is self-evident that Communist countries, particularly the Soviet Union, have been the enemy of American foreign policy in the post–World War II era, this same self-evidence tends to obscure just *how* this Communist enemy is conceptualized. Much debate could well ensue: the merits of "private property" capitalism versus "state-planning" of the economy; "representative democracy"

[16] Ibid., pp. 154–155.

[17] Morris Janowitz, *The Professional Soldier: A Social and Political Portrait* (Glencoe, Ill.: Free Press, 1960).

[18] Richard A. Gabriel and Paul L. Savage, *Crisis in Command* (New York: Hill and Wang, 1978), p. 20.

versus "democratic centralism" in the Communist party; a privately owned "free press" versus a state-owned and state-censored press. All of these issues are worthy of great scrutiny, research, and debate. Only one subject will be considered here, though, and that is the question of Communist "expansion."

By the end of World War II, the Soviet Union's army occupied Eastern Europe. In most countries except Yugoslavia and Czechoslovakia, the preexisting *internal* Communist movements were relatively weak. The invading Red Army with its accompanying Communist party political officers proceeded to establish a series of "puppet" or "satellite" governments, all under relatively firm control by the Soviet Union. In Yugoslavia, a large Communist movement, led by Marshal Tito, had fought a guerrilla war against the Nazis and had much popular support. Yugoslavia consequently did not become a "puppet" regime of the Soviet Union. Czechoslovakia did not retain its independence.

The original American concept of Communist expansion comes from Soviet occupation and control of Eastern Europe. Expansion meant "foreign" Communists occupying a country and ruling it without any consent of the native population. This original concept of Communist expansion thus had great historical truth. But historical truth is sometimes detached from its historical context. Communism as the ultimate foreign Other had a theoretical position already prepared for it by the capitalist West.

Capitalists, both the old variant called "laissez-faire" and the new capitalist order coming into existence during the war, understood themselves as being modeled on *nature*. If capitalism was nature, then communism by definition had to be *antinature*. By logical extension, if capitalism represented the natural economic structure of all nations, then by definition a Communist movement could only be *foreign;* it had to come from the *outside* because nature itself occupied the *inside*. In this way the historical truth of the Soviet conquest of Eastern Europe moved into a theoretical position of communism as the inevitable foreign Other.

This fetishized concept of communism as foreign Other, antinature itself, did not permit the United States to comprehend the Chinese revolution in 1949. Parts of China had long been occupied by the capitalist West. Its sovereignty as a nation had been diminished by imperialist conquest. Where the West did not rule, feudal landlord-warlords governed. The United States had special "trade agreements" with China, and sent troops and gunboats to maintain its economic position. Communist-led peasant revolution began in the 1920s in this milieu. Peasants wanted land for themselves and sovereignty from foreign governments.

Japan displaced Western powers in 1939 when it invaded China; the country now became subject to Japanese imperialism. When the United States entered World War II, it supported those Chinese political factions that had benefited from previous business arrangements with the West. These forces, led by Chiang Kai-shek, were known in the United States as the *Nationalist Chinese*. The very semantic construction of the phrase meant that the Communists were "unnational," and therefore "foreign," not a real Chinese movement by any means. Consequently, the internal social dynamics of the Chinese revolution disappeared. When the Communist-led peasant revolution won in 1949, it appeared to the United States not as an internal social revolution, but as another instance of external Communist expansion ultimately controlled by the Soviet Union. Ironically, the Chinese Communist party had long been in severe conflict with the Soviet Union. Joseph Stalin had not supported the revolution during the war because it conflicted with his own policy of a "united front" with the West against fascism! Some members of the United States State Department knew about the internal dynamics of the Chinese revolution, but they were purged during the 1950s because they were held responsible for the "loss of China" to communism.

In 1950, war began in Korea. The country had been provisionally divided into a Communist northern region and a right-wing military regime in the south. After a long period of military probes by both sides along the provisional boundary, North Korea invaded South Korea. The Korean War will not be explored in depth here; it is sufficient to say that the Korean War consolidated the notion that all Communist movements inevitably come from outside a country's borders and are ultimately controlled by Moscow. Subsequently the United States began massive funding to the French to help them retain their colony, Vietnam, against internal national and social revolution led by Communists. When the French were defeated in 1954, the United States announced a doctrine which would make Vietnam contested grounds for decades.

The domino theory has been much discussed, but rarely scrutinized. "Domino" is a metaphor, but the *nature* of that metaphor has not been seen. On April 7, 1954, the original dominoes—the nations of Southeast Asia—stood up to be counted. President Dwight D. Eisenhower said: "You have a row of dominoes set up, and you knock over the first one, and what will happen to the last one is the certainty that it will go over very quickly, so you could have the beginning of a disintegration that would have the most profound influences."[19]

The falling dominoes were soon joined by a *popping cork*. On April 26, Eisenhower said that Indochina resembled "a sort of cork in the bottle, the bottle being the great area that includes Indonesia, Burma, Thailand, all the surrounding areas of Asia." Secretary of State Dulles added his verse a few days later in an address to a Senate and House Committee: "If Indochina should be lost, there would be a *chain reaction* throughout the Far East and Southeast Asia."[20]

"Falling dominoes," "cork in the bottle," "chain reaction"—what theory is being proposed here? According to one radical historian, Gabriel Kolko, the domino theory constitutes a theory of modern history: "Translated into concrete terms, the domino theory was a counterrevolutionary doctrine which defined modern history as a movement of Third World and dependent nations—those with strategic value to the United States or its capitalist associates—away from colonialism or capitalism and toward national revolution and forms of socialism."[21]

---

[19] Quoted by F. M. Kail, *What Washington Said: Administration Rhetoric and the Vietnam War, 1949–1969* (New York: Harper and Row, 1973), p. 66.

[20] Ibid., p. 85.

[21] Gabriel Kolko, "The American Goals in Vietnam," in *The Pentagon Papers: Critical Essays*, edited by Noam Chomsky and Howard Zinn, vol. 5 of *The Pentagon Papers: The Senator Gravel Edition* (Boston: Beacon Press, 1972), p. 1.

The failure of Kolko's analysis concerns *translation*. He has translated the domino theory into the Marxist theory of society, a theory in which concreteness, history, national revolution, and forms of socialism—emphasis on the plurality—exist as elements of a conceptual framework for understanding the social world. However, in the domino theory, none of these concepts exists: the domino theory effectively abolishes the possibility of history, national revolution, and forms of socialism. The conceptual order it elaborates is entirely different.

"Falling dominoes," "cork in the bottle," "chain reaction"—these terms find their theoretical reference not in the social world of history, where men live and die, but in the lifeless world of Newtonian mechanics. The foreign Other, Communist antinature, invades and destroys the natural order of Vietnam (capitalism). If Vietnam "falls" to communism, then the rest of Asia will surely follow, each fall from grace faster than its predecessor—an inevitable, inexorable mechanical process. Countries no longer have real histories, cultures, and social structures. The names of Asian countries become just that—names marking undifferentiated objects. And these names are inscribed upon a vast ledger, debit or credit, Communist or anti-Communist.

It is now time to name this ledger, to tie together constituent elements of the domino theory and other ideas that conceptualize the social world in terms of nature. The universe of post–World War II American foreign policy will be called *mechanistic anticommunism*. The demonic machine that lives outside of the natural capitalist order is the *foreign Other*. *Technowar* or the *production model of war* designates the military mode of strategy and organization in which war is conceptualized and organized as a high-technology, capital-intensive production process. The military and civilian executives who command the foreign policy and military apparatus are *war-managers*. History for them becomes a series of static points, each point measuring the balance of technological forces between the United States and the foreign Other. Some countries belong on the "credit" or capitalist side of the ledger; other countries belong to the "debit" or socialist side of the ledger. And still other countries, particularly Third World countries, become abstract sites for confrontation. No movement of a Third World country into the "debit" column is ever permanent: the ledger can be transformed by the introduction of more forces. To the war-managers, the policy of mechanistic anticommunism and Technowar against the foreign Other will ultimately produce victory. Since the United States has the most technologically advanced economy and warfare production system, then defeat by a nationalist social revolution in a peasant society becomes *unthinkable*.

There were no "mistakes" made during the Vietnam War. Nor was there a failure of will; the "self-imposed restraints" were only on official paper, not in Technowar practice. Instead, the Vietnam War should be understood in terms of the deep structural logic of how it was conceptualized and fought by American war-managers. Vietnam represents the perfect functioning of this closed, self-referential universe. Vietnam was *The Perfect War*.

38

THE COMBATIVE
STRUCTURE OF THE
ENGLISH LANGUAGE

JOHN M. DEL VECCHIO

*A character in combat correspondent John M. Del Vecchio's novel of Vietnam
fighting,* The Thirteenth Valley, *Rufus Brooks was a well-educated, contemplative,
black first lieutenant of the U.S. Army 101st Airborne Division (Airmobile). In 1970
he commanded a company of infantry fighting the People's Army of Vietnam, or, as
American grunts called it, the NVA, the North Vietnamese Army. In a letter to his
wife, Brooks explained why he would begin to keep a notebook of his thoughts about
war.*

...Lila, I want to tell you something I found tonight. In a discussion with
several of my men, I should call them my friends, I could feel the old Rufus
return. We were discussing the war and racial conflict—they bicker as if
they are trying to place blame on someone other than themselves or their
particular ancestors—when it came to me...[*sic*] a semantic determinant
theory of war. I can feel it, see it, hear it. It may be the most significant
lesson that I or anyone may learn from Vietnam.

I must analyze this, concentrate upon this, answer this. What causes
war? The situation here is perfect for study. I've brought with me all my
knowledge of philosophy. It is dusty and tarnished but it is here, in me.
And here are all the elements of war about me. Here are all the major races
of mankind, representatives from every socio-economic group, from every
government-politico force, all clashing. And the language groups: English,
French, Vietnamese, Chinese, American technologese, Spanish. Here a
democracy upholds a dictatorship in the name of freedom while a dictatorial
governing group infiltrates five percent of its nation's population to a

different country [*sic*] in the name of nationalism. The answer to the question must be here, waiting to be discovered.*

Later, in the midst of campaigning in the rain forest of the Khe Ta Laou river valley of the Annamite Mountains between Hue and Khe Sanh, Brooks wrote his thoughts about the causes of war into his notebook. Viewing Western culture from the vantage point of linguistics, he focused on the polarized and lineal structure of the English language, which, he argued, accentuated competitive behavior. This was perhaps the ultimate abstraction: all the politics, social relationships, technology, and economics of culture were the offspring of ideas, which, rooted in language, preceded behavior. War was semantical, the product of patterns of thought determined by the competitive structure of speech.

AN INQUIRY INTO PERSONAL, RACIAL AND INTERNATIONAL CONFLICT— RUFUS BROOKS—AUGUST 1970

We think ourselves into war. The antecedents are in our minds.

Conflict, major conflict, does not just happen. It evolves. It may explode over a particular incident but the tension evolves leading gradually to the incident and the explosion. The elements of any conflict, whether it be between individuals or between nations, must form, grow, approach, collide and ignite. Let us here explore the causes and dynamics of conflict and of ultimate conflict—*War.*

Our world is coming apart and it is imperative that we go one step farther and develop a new perspective about, and response to, conflict. Conflicts are actions. Conflict is active disagreement, in its final stage violent disagreement, fights, riots, wars. Here we must set a premise—action, all human action, is preceded by thought. The argument can then be drawn, if thought precedes action then thought precedes conflict. Let us explore the thoughts, and the origins and dynamics of those thoughts, which lead to conflict.

Exploration One The roots of conflict and the expansion and escalation to violence grow from our competitive instincts and are accentuated by our language patterns. When we get into a conflict-compete situation we accentuate the differences in order to strengthen our position. Why? Is this innate in man or is it a part of our *mythos,* a culturally transferred response handed down from generation to generation? Is the mechanism for transfer language? Written and spoken? What elements in human languages cause us to think ourselves into war? What causes us to perceive a given situation as a conflict situation? What forms our character? What passes xenophobic responses?

Language Thought structured by language. And whose language? English. The white man's language.

*John Del Vecchio, *The Thirteenth Valley* (New York: Bantam, 1982), pp. 115–16.

Language is a verbal network developed over eons. Written language developed from concrete pictographs to lineal abstract ideography. In language, words, as symbols of reality, are connected one to the next to develop thoughts and concepts. Words evoke other words at a measurable frequency. Given a specific word the word which follows it has a pre-determined tendency to be another specific word. In linguistics this is known as a frequency response. This word to word response frequency is the structure of our language. It has been, to a great extent, formalized. Nouns as subjects of sentences are followed by verbs as predicates. Infants are taught the language of their fathers and later pass the same language to their sons. This is the mechanism for the transfer of acceptable behavior and knowledge from generation to generation. This vast body of a society's knowledge and responses is its *mythos*. The mechanism for socializing an infant to his culture has a specific though complex structure and that structure controls a human being's potential thoughts. That learned structure determines how a human perceives the world about him. It controls his actions.

The verbal network of western cultures (White) to which we (Black Americans) find ourselves prescribing, accepting, assimilating, has and is proliferating from its western base (America & Western Europe) and has encompassed nearly the entire globe with the possible exceptions of the Asian countries which still maintain pictographic languages. Western verbal structure interprets inter-peoples' differences as problems. This, Western Culture teaches, leads to the need for a solution. In Western Cultures solutions may be forced upon situations. This is confrontation and conflict, and this, we are taught, leads to a higher level structure.

This network is built on a view of reality as thesis-antithesis clash resulting in synthesis—a network which forces polarization of entities, which forces, by definition, the entities to contrast, which leads to verbalization of threats, military threats, which heightens our insecurity and raises our defensiveness, which makes us ever more threatening to others and causes them to raise their defensiveness, which leads finally to warfare.

White America would do well to study Eastern thought where synthesis is perceived as the undesirable limiting of natural circles, a thought pattern where every thesis must have an antithesis for it to exist and in which the elimination of either eliminates both. It is a matter of attempting to describe hot while denying the existence of cold. They are not simply opposites. They are varying quantities of one quality and to wipe out one means not to raise by synthesis both to a higher level but to destroy the entity, the quality, itself.

Perhaps we should look to see where language has come from, what road it has traveled to arrive at its present structure. Formal language, like history, is created, established and passed on by the victorious. The winners throughout history are the ones who have passed on language forms and frequencies, patterns which structure our perceptions and thoughts. The way the defeated thought, the structure of their speech and the frequency of their words, has been lost with their military losses. Perhaps it would be more accurate to say the structure of their thought has been repressed with their losses. Victors are allowed to speak, to write, and to publish.

In English-speaking cultures we have a language tradition in which people voice their exposure and contact with other cultures in xenophobic patterns. We are not taught to rejoice in meeting strangers. We are taught to beware, to be fearful. This language also provides a set of cognitive models and expectations which guide our cultural response to publicly articulated threats, threats often posed by politicians with self-serving motives, politicians threatening us with the supremacy or domination of us by another nation. A man says, "Do you want your children to live under the domination of Red Russia?" One must answer, "No." The "No" is built into our language system. The question is a yes or no question. You're going out of the system if you say anything else. If you say something else you're a radical. Then the Man says, "If South Vietnam falls, it will topple all the staggering unstable dominos we support. If they fall your children will be in forced labor camps and communal farms with Red Guards. Do you want that?" Our response is built into our language structure. The politicians and the news media are very aware of the predetermined patterns (though for different reasons—one for direct control, one for sales, equals $ equals a power of sorts).

I am proposing we break that conformity with a re-thinking, a total restructuring of our semantic network in a manner that the popular rhetoric of inter-peoples differences and tensions reconstructs the experience of those tensions and then directs our responses into alternate manners of eliminating tension. No more rhetorical questions. No more 'Yes-No' questions. Only questions which recreate reality, not lies, and ask us to answer in manners as complex as the reality.

Perhaps part of the problem is that words are only lineal. Western languages have lineal structure. Reality is not lineal. Therefore, words are inadequate to describe reality. According to Cherry visual imagery and spatial relationships are controlled by the right hemisphere of the brain while language is an exclusive property of the left hemisphere. Is it possible Western and Eastern cultures differ so greatly in perspective because the Chinese language is pictorial, is a non-lineal language in which symbols are built to portray reality instead of strung together to describe reality? Is it possible the inscrutableness of the Chinese is due to Western language-thought being founded in the left hemisphere and Eastern language-thought being founded in the right? Neurologically the right hemisphere (again according to Cherry) is the location of what we call the subconscious and also dream and spatial relationships. It is difficult for a man to communicate between his own conscious and subconscious. It must be near impossible for understanding to pass between Western and Eastern minds because it must be like one man's conscious attempting to communicate with another man's subconscious.

Western language tradition analyzes phenomena by breaking them down into components, into separately strung together parts. Preceding parts are considered to cause following parts. Everything is broken into cause-effect dichotomies. Is it possible our political tradition of left-right dichotomy is caused by our language tradition and that by using this descriptive model we structure our perception of reality and affect our reality by forcing it to polarize? (Ref. El Paso.)

Our perception of our political world role is affected by our language tradition. If our language-determined role model is skewed toward dichotomy, toward perceiving and establishing opposing parts, is that not the same as saying, the model causes tension? Our response to tension is also predetermined in our political rhetoric. Our language and thought patterns cause us to react to insecurities both aggressively and defensively. Our actions then cause others to react to us defensively and aggressively. The severity of conflict is heightened. This psychotic behavior propels us into divorce courts, into race riots and into war. Internationally this behavior is military threats and arms escalation. Why do we believe these will lessen tension? They increase it. Is it any wonder that the Soviet Union (its leaders also under the Western language tradition) maintains that if America builds a Safeguard system to protect its Minuteman ICBM force from destruction by Soviet SS-9 missiles, then they, the Soviets, must build a system that will destroy Safeguard. If they do not, the argument goes, they will be unprepared to deter an American assault. Then America says if we do not build a Safeguard system the Soviets may make a first strike against us and with it wipe out our ability to strike back. That will heighten their desire to strike. Each side says it desires to make nuclear war so devastating it will be unthinkable. No one would start such a war. America says do it by limiting your defensives. Russia says do it by expanding your offensive. Either way all the people die. It is a paradox—the more insecure we feel the more defensive we become. The more defensive we become the more we force those about us to be defensive. We thus increase the tension in an unintentional psychotic spiraling manner because of our inability to respond in any other way. Things often are not what they seem. (Minh.)

Exploration Two: Politicians, Political Rhetoric—How the System Works From the perception of the world in thesis-antithesis terms, more simply an us-vs-them mentality, rises the politician. In America, the pattern of government separated into branches with checks and balances is both an expression of conflict mentality and a cause of future conflict (institutionalizes the pattern—Egan). The political party system is an expression of the same thing. The politician is the tie between the two. It is he who elevates difference, purposefully creating conflict whether conflict exists or not.

It happens this way. A man saying he is the representative of many men about him declares his ideology and he declares his policy and he says his are the best for everyone. In order to defend his stand he must note the differences between him and others. In so doing he establishes conflict where only differences before existed. (There is nothing intrinsically wrong or conflicting about differences.) The man's philosophy is self-serving to both him and the men supporting him. It must be. Politicians are a psychotic form unto themselves. They must gain power to serve. They live on power, by power, for power. They greedily accept it but it must be 'sold' to the masses. An effective 'sales tool' is fear, fear of differences the politician has just established and will now focus on selectively and accentuate. The policy becomes In The National Interest, or Manifest Destiny, or The Red Menace. The differences become conflicts, the conflicts are accentuated, the response to the heightened conflict is defensive and self-righteous. The interest of one man for the benefit of a select group of men has come to be the party or the nation's policy. The party or the nation becomes aggressively defensive and forces the group who has become the 'bad guys' or the 'political opposition' into a defensive posture. The mutual perception of each other's aggressive/defensive posture, the fear for one's own security, results in a crystallization of differences, the establishment of obstacles to creative thought and finally to actions to eliminate the threat.

It begins with a dichotomy structure of rationality in our language, spreads to polarization of opinions with ever increasing tension. What we lack is a structure to drain off the tension. A country prepares for war and war is very unreal to those who prepare for it and who have never fought. Politicians make it noble to do your best for the men there. For the soldier it becomes his 'Duty' or his 'Mission.' (Ref. Pop. R.) The men are often confused.

I enjoy some of the word games we play at war. Pacification. Vietnamization. Mechanical Ambush. Do I enjoy these because they stimulate me? Do I seek stimulation thusly? (Ref. Cherry.) Those are the little word games the military machine has come up with. Perhaps there are others which are so buried in our language tradition we never notice them. Some are big ones. By recognizing just what language is, we immediately recognize some of the more poorly camouflaged, some of the poor substitutes for reality. These are the words and phrases with extended connotations and denotations politicians and other leaders love to use. *Beware:* Servant-of-the-people; communist takeover; human rights; civil rights; self-determination; freedom. If someone threatens you with one of these or promises you one of these, beware. Beware. Governments do not give freedoms anymore than they give taxes. Governments are in the business of restricting human action from unlimited freedom to parameters the people will find acceptable.

The People That's a good one. Who are the people? Why is it that whoever uses that phrase is referring to himself and the people he wants to control?

Let us develop a new mode of thinking which is more closely tied to reality than our present mode. A mode where every man is independent because his language allows him alternatives. This new way to think, to speak, will, should, allow greater freedom to participate in our culture's therapy. Beware: political rhetoric is self-serving and self-limiting. In many instances it is, at best, irrelevant. The outcome of inter-peoples contacts often depends on factors totally detached from spoken words.

Using this matter of thinking in ref. to international conflict gives the individual person, the man-in-the-street, a new freedom to participate in the flow of history, in the direction of his nation's policies, in the humanity of mankind. He need not have one voice with the president and only be able to express opposition in the form of a vote, one vote every forty-eight months. We can learn to become more independent of external pressures from politicians telling us that X people is trying to destroy us, from business trying to tell us we are not whole without their product, from race leaders telling us that every man from that other race is prejudiced against us and thus we best defend ourselves.

A common adverse effect of every organized system of thought, religious or governmental, is the encouragement of dependence. Governments make us feel that international and indeed even interpersonal relationships are beyond our comprehension and ability. Correct relations can be achieved only through the augmentation of their system powered by our supportive backing. People today consider it impossible not to leave international affairs to the government. They consider it normal for the government to establish goals and quotas for racial and sexual harmony, equal-opportunity reinforcement. We have become victims of the establishment even as we have become part of it.

People who understand that conflict in interpersonal relations is a normal event, that it tends to come and go in cycles, that they are capable of dealing with others themselves without a rigid set of regulations directing them, these people will not wind up as victims, as automatons of the machine. They will not become dependent upon external sources for their security therefore they will not become defensive, then aggressively defensive forcing others into aggressive-defensive postures simply because X leader from Y country or B leader from C race says their security is threatened—says that because he needs that to keep him in power. People who understand will not become dependent on external sources for their security because they will be confident of their own competence to interrelate, to relate with all people of the world. They may consult professionals for information and advice when a problem seems beyond their own competence but they will accept responsibility for the routine management of their own relationships and extend them as far as they may go.

Exploration Three: Thoughts of Friends

EL PASO: With the exception of oil, world primary commodity prices dropped in relationship to the price of manufactured goods during the past several decades. The United States is partly to blame. During the 1950s the US produced vast quantities of inexpensive, exportable rice through a farm subsidy program. This resulted in an oversupply on the world market and it destroyed the export market for Vietnam and it caused increased poverty in this land. (Incredible, how we are all tied together.) The industrialized West controls the price of manufactured goods because it alone is capable of producing such goods and it has the ability and wealth to control the price of raw materials. Poverty, need, causes conflict.

EGAN: There are two ways to solve the problem of poverty and wealth between the haves and the have-nots. One, the poor can increase their wealth through increased production so that simply there is more wealth and everybody lives better and has a better standard of living; or two, wealth can be redistributed so the rich don't have so much and the poor don't have so little. Here the amount of wealth stays the same.

The first view is capitalistic, the second communistic or socialistic. Now, I ask you, under what systems in the world do we see people having the best standard of living? (Note rhetorical Q? Eg asks.) Empirically, is there any doubt?

DOC: The wars of the 20th century may be due to population pressures caused by longer life expectancy. In Vietnam, the introduction of Western medical practices caused the population to increase from sixteen million in 1900 to twenty-eight million in 1950. A 56% increase. Doc says he is not sure of his figures but that is what they tell new medics in San Antonio.

FO: If you think our society is sick maybe it's because we are catering to the illness instead of promoting good health.

CAHALAN: Critics and English teachers tend to see all stories as conflicts between antagonists and protagonists. In reality your best stories are written with the characters being people doing things people do. In good literature each character has good and bad qualities which interact with the good and bad qualities of the other characters. They intertwine, not oppose. That's how it should be. That's how life is.

JAX: All wars are expressions by suppressed people of their desires to rule themselves.

CHERRY: Maslow once said, "If the only tool you have is a hammer, you tend to see every problem as a nail." If you're a soldier, I guess you tend to see every problem as a target.

BROWN: Sports are war. You'd kill a man to beat him on a basketball court if it were for the NCAA championship. Man, I love the game. I love the competition. But, we got to realize it's part of our society which helps a crazy man like Nixon control the people.

MINH: Nothing happens by itself. Everything is unity. Though you may seem isolated from the rest of the world, everything you do is interconnected with the universe. You are not here alone.

The state does not exist apart from the individuals who comprise its citizenry.

There is no such thing as inconsistency. Inconsistencies are a product of a static view of life. (To me this rings true. I have heard and expressed these views before myself, in a slightly different slant. Minh, sometimes I think you are inside my head.) Life is a balance. For everything we acquire, we lose something. To dam a river to generate electrical power you must be willing to accept the loss of the river. You say love is inconsistent with hate. I say they are one. To eliminate hate is also to destroy love. (Perhaps he means to destroy the capacity to hate is also to destroy the capacity to love.) Perhaps that may be taken some steps further. I do not know. Is peace a quality of war? Can one be eliminated without eliminating both?

Exploration Four: Personal Conflict—Marriage Conflict at all levels follows a pattern. At all levels it has seeds, it grows, evolves and finally explodes or perhaps the final level is, it dies. We liked each other, respected each other and perhaps loved each other. Or perhaps we only loved the image we each held of the other. Did our learned language control our perception of each other? Were our ideals of marriage and mates limited, controlled by that language? Were our responses within that marriage, our responses to each other, pre-established by language and thus predestined for conflict? I believe our respect for each other forbade us from stepping over pre-determined bounds and the limiting of our responses to each other destroyed us. These limits, these restrictions were both qualitative and quantitative. They confined our acceptable behavior to a mass-produced, language-induced, artificial rut. If we could graph emotions, ours would have been flat lines with no peaks of elation nor dips to despair. We became excessive only in our limitations and our boundaries were closing on the center. The limits on our emotions because a progressively steeper descent, a self-enhancing restrictiveness ever concentrating until we had no acceptable responses left and had to explode. The more thwarted I, and now I realize, she, became, the more we allowed ourselves to die. Suffocation was evident in physical and sexual as well as psychological and social events in our lives. We had locked ourselves together in a decaying relationship. All this I believe was due to our accepting pre-established frequency responses in our language and they controlled our thoughts. Hawaii was an effect. It began like a movie script— every word and motion perfectly culturally acceptable, perfectly played. Oh, how well we knew our roles without even realizing we were playing them. The perception of differences we did not know how to accept led to irritation we could not diffuse. The irritation led us to entrench, to build false securities, to build walls. We sought and built separate support systems and we prepared for war. The walls heightened our fears and insecurities. We passed from defensive to offensive. We exploded. Perhaps divorce is the death of conflict.

Exploration Five: The American Ideal in Vietnam We came not to conquer. We came to help. We came to insure security and independence. We came to end conflict. We said and we showed that we would selflessly lay down our lives to end this conflict. And yet our altruism has corrupted itself until we can only be satisfied with annihilation. We define everything about us in terms of conflict. As long as there are two sides there will be conflict and we have said we will not tolerate conflict. We will stamp it out. It is the same as sentencing Vietnam to total destruction and annihilation. Perhaps they do not need us. Perhaps without us they will annihilate themselves for they too are determined to end the conflict....

Glossary of Abbreviations

AID Agency for International Development

ARVN Army of the Republic of Vietnam

CIA Central Intelligence Agency

CINCPAC Commander in Chief, Pacific

DIA Defense Intelligence Agency

DPM Draft presidential memorandum

DRV Democratic Republic of Vietnam (see NVN)

GVN Government of Vietnam. The designation used by the United States to describe the government of the Republic of Vietnam (RVN)

JCS Joint Chiefs of Staff

LOC Lines of communication

MAAG Military Assistance Advisory Group

MACV Military Assistance Command, Vietnam

NIE National Intelligence Estimate

NLF National Liberation Front (see VC)

NSC National Security Council

NVA North Vietnam Army. The U.S. designation for the People's Army of Vietnam (PAVN)

NVN North Vietnam. The U.S. designation for the Democratic Republic of Vietnam (DRV)

PAVN People's Army of Vietnam; the army of the Democratic Republic of Vietnam (DRV); see NVA

PLAF People's Liberation Armed Forces; the army of the National Liberation Front (NLF); see VC

POL Petroleum, oil, lubricants

ROK Republic of Korea, also known as South Korea

RVN Republic of Vietnam (see SVN)

SAM Surface-to-air missile

SEATO Southeast Asia Treaty Organization

SNIE Special National Intelligence Estimate

SVN South Vietnam. The U.S. designation for the Republic of Vietnam (RVN)

USIB United States Intelligence Board

VC Vietcong. Contraction of *Viet-nam Cong-san* (Vietnamese Communist). Pejorative U.S. and RVN designation for the National Liberation Front and the PLAF

Vietminh Contraction of *Viet Nam Doc Lap Dong Minh* (Vietnam Independence League)